Programming in C++

M.T. SOMASHEKARA
Department of Computer Science and Applications
Bangalore University
Bangalore

PHI Learning Private Limited
New Delhi-110001
2009

Rs. 425.00

PROGRAMMING IN C++
M.T. Somashekara

ISBN-978-81-203-3288-1

The export rights of this book are vested solely with the publisher.

Third Printing ... ... **July, 2009**

Published by Asoke K. Ghosh, PHI Learning Private Limited, M-97, Connaught Circus, New Delhi-110001 and Printed by Rajkamal Electric Press, Plot No. 2, Phase IV, HSIDC, Kundli-131028, Sonepat, Haryana.

To

My Parents

Contents

Preface

C++ is a modern high-level programming language. It is often referred to as superset of C language since it provides all the features of C along with its own. The popularity of the language is attributed to its object oriented programming (OOP) features, which include data encapsulation, polymorphism and inheritance. It is these features which made the line of demarcation between the problem space and the programming environment thinner. The OOP's features provide the programmers the ability to create their own data types, the ability to implement many programming tasks through a common interface, the ability to enhance the hierarchical growth of a program and to reuse the existing code. The book covers all these at considerable depth by illustrating each concept through well planned programs. The book is designed in such a way that the readers need not know C language as a prerequisite. It covers both structured programming concept (modular programming) and object oriented programming concept.

The whole book is organized in well-planned 21 chapters. First few chapters introduce the fundamentals of C++. Chapter 1 is meant for evincing interest about C++ language in the minds of the readers by discussing the need for the language and enumerating its salient features. Here, general structure of C++ programs and steps involved in executing them are also discussed. Chapter 2 deals with the preliminaries of the language like character set, keywords, identifiers, different types of constants, variables and data types. Chapter 3 covers the wide variety of operators which are available in C++. Each category of the operators is illustrated by means of a separate program. Topics like operator precedence, associativity and type conversion are discussed in detail. Chapter 4 explains decision-making and branching statements in C++. It shows how conditional execution of statements is implemented with the use of **if** statement and its variations, and **switch** statement. Chapter 5 introduces looping statements in C++. A number of problems which needed repeated execution of statements are programmed here. Chapter 6 reviews modular programming in C++ through functions. Classifications of functions are discussed in detail. The concept of recursion is introduced and a number of programs are included to demonstrate the concept of functions. The concepts like function overloading, inline functions, functions with default arguments, reference variables, passing arguments by reference, return by reference and different storage classes of variables are discussed. Chapter 7 introduces the concept of arrays. Here, the need for arrays, dimensionality of arrays, declaration and processing of arrays of different dimensions are discussed in depth. The concept of C-style strings are dealt in Chapter 8. Here, various string manipulations, built-in functions to perform the manipulations, the working of the built-in functions (by simulating them) are discussed. Chapter 9 is meant for dealing with the concept of structures, which enables C++ programmers to group the data items, which may be of different types logically. Structures in combination with arrays, functions, strings are described.

Other concepts like union, bit-fields, enumerated data type, typedef are duly discussed. Chapter 10 deals with the concept of pointers. The advantages offered by pointers are mentioned in the beginning of the chapter to highlight the significance of the concept. Declaration of pointer variables, pointer operators, pointer arithmetic are illustrated. The concept of pointers is then discussed in combination with arrays, strings, functions and structures. The concept of dynamic memory allocation is discussed at the end of the chapter, one of the major advantages offered by pointers. Chapter 11 throws light on preprocessor directives, another distinctive feature of C++ language. Here, topics like macros, file inclusion and conditional compilation are reviewed. Chapter 12 discusses the concept of classes and objects, the fundamental aspect of.OOPs. It also throws light on the concepts static members, friend functions and friend classes, const member functions, pointer and nesting of member functions. Chapter 13 presents the roles of constructors and destructors in classes. Different types of constructors like default constructor, copy constructor, parameterized constructor and dynamic constructor are also discussed. Chapter 14 explores operator overloading, which enables the operators to be used with objects in much the same way as they are used with built-in type variables, in detail. Conversion from basic type to derived type and vice-versa is also discussed. Chapter 15 describes the concept of inheritance, one of the most important striking features of OOPs, in depth. Different types of inheritance are discussed to substantiate the fact that inheritance concept enhances reusability of existing code. The constructors and destructors in the inheritance hierarchy are discussed. The concepts like virtual functions, pure virtual functions, runtime polymorphism, private inheritance, protected inheritance are discussed. Chapter 16 deals with I/O operations in C++. It explains the built-in classes supporting I/O operations. It also deals with formatting of outputs with the help of the I/O built-in class functions and flags. Formatting of outputs through manipulators and user-defined manipulators are also discussed. Chapter 17 covers file management in C++. Various operations over files like opening, closing, writing, appending, updating, etc. are discussed at length. The file oriented built-in classes, random accessing of files, differences between text files and binary files are also discussed. Chapter 18 deals with string handling in C++ through **string** class objects. Different member functions of the class are explained, and different operators overloaded in the class are also dealt with. Chapter 19 discusses exception handling. The mechanism of notifying exceptions and handling them so that the underlying program is not abruptly terminated is discussed. Chapter 20 introduces the concept of templates, which offer a way for generic programming. Chapter 21 discusses the advanced topics in C++ like new data types, new-style casts, new-style headers, new keywords for operators, the explicit keyword, the mutable keyword, namespaces, run time type information (RTTI) and smart pointers, etc.

All the chapters are followed by relevant review questions and the chapters involving programs are provided with programming exercises in addition to review questions. The book is targetted to the students of computer science and management courses both at undergraduate level and the postgraduate level, which offer C++ language as part of their syllabi.

Constructive criticism and suggestions are welcome. Your valuable suggestions will go a long way in further improvement of the book.

M.T. SOMASHEKARA

Acknowledgements

I wish to extend my sincere thanks to one of my dearest friends, Mr. K. Shylesh, without whose encouragement and support, this book would not have been a reality. He is the one who reviewed all the chapters during the course of the preparation of the manuscript for the book and gave valuable and meaningful suggestions. My special thanks are due to Prof. Pradeep G. Siddeshwar, The Chairman, Department of Computer Science and Applications, Bangalore University, Bangalore. My sincere thanks are also due to the Principal and the Management of St. Joseph's College, Bangalore. The suggestions and encouragement given by Mr. K.S. Manjunatha, Department of Computer Science, Maharani's College, Bangalore, Mr. B.L. Muralidhara and Mr. M. Hanumanthappa both of Department of Computer Science and Applications, Bangalore University, Mr. Doreswamy, Department of Computer Science, Mangalore University, Mangalore, Mr. M.N. Ravishankar, Department of Computer Science, Field Marshal Kariyappa College, Madikeri, Mr. Shivananda Siddramappa, Department of Computer Science, Government First Grade College, Bidar, Mr. Chinnaswamy, Department of Computer Science, Bharathi College, Bharatinagar, Dr. Jeena Narayan Singh, Technical Director, Department of MCA, Al-Ameen College, Bangalore, are gratefully acknowledged.

I am grateful to the publisher Prentice-Hall of India, and their editorial and production teams for the processing of the manuscript and bringing it out in the present form.

I would also place on record the support and encouragement of all my beloved family members.

M.T. SOMASHEKARA

Chapter 1

Overview of C++ Language

1.1 INTRODUCTION

A programming language is a means of communication between a programmer and a computer. In the era of high-level languages, many programming languages have been developed such as BASIC, Pascal, Fortran, COBOL and C. Invention of new programming language is normally driven by two factors: (a) Changing programming environment (b) New programming methodology. The C++ language is not an exception.

The earlier languages supported procedural programming technique. In the case of this technique, the programming solution to a problem is realized by means of a series of instructions or commands. When the number of instructions increased and when some sets of instructions are required to be repeated, the program itself is divided into a number of subprograms. In languages BASIC and Fortran they are called **subroutines**; In Pascal they are called **functions** or **procedures** and in C they are called **functions**. The basic idea behind the procedural programming methodology is dividing a program into a number of smaller, easily manageable subprograms and integrate them later to achieve the given task. The procedural programming paradigm is thus action centric since we think programming solution to a problem in terms of statements in the programs. The following limitations of this technique came to light when the program size grew:

Data undervalued: In procedural languages, more emphasis is on statements or functions. Data are not given prominence that they deserve. This fact gives rise to the following problems. Many procedural languages support global and local variables. Global variables are those which can be accessed by all functions and local variables are declared within functions and they are accessible to only those functions in which they are declared. The relationship among local variables, global variables and functions is shown in Fig. 1.1. Local variables have limited use. Since we may require to use data in more than one function, the variables are declared as global. These are the variables which are vulnerable to corruption inadvertently leading to dangerous consequences. It is very difficult to keep track of which function has changed the values of which variables. Another problem with this approach is that if we need to add any new data to the program, all the functions which access the data should be modified. This may provide room for errors to creep in.

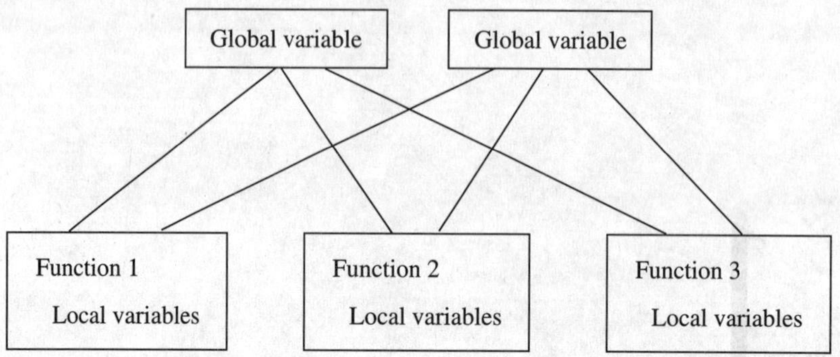

Fig. 1.1 Relationship among local variables, global variables and functions.

Relationship to the real world: There is considerable gap between problem space and solution space in procedural oriented software systems. This is once again attributed to the action centric nature of these languages.

These limitations are eliminated with the introduction of object oriented programming technique. This programming paradigm is data centric. This technique advocates bundling both data and the functions, which operate on them together through *classes*. Quests began to develop programming languages, which support object oriented programming. In 1980's at AT & T Bell laboratory, Bjarne Stroustroup designed the C++ language to support the object oriented paradigm while retaining all the features of C. So C++ supports both procedural programming and object oriented programming. In fact he derived C++ from C by retaining almost all the constructs in C even in C++ also. For this reason, C++ is referred to as the superset of C. All the programs written in C (Except those which use keywords of C++ as identifiers) can be complied by C++ compilers and run. But the converse is not true.

1.2 SALIENT FEATURES OF C++ LANGUAGE

The C++ language in addition to being procedural oriented (having been inherited from the C language), shares the following features:

Data encapsulation: The bundling of both data and functions into a single entity (class) is called **data encapsulation**. Data encapsulation is the most important feature of any object oriented language. The data can not be accessed any other function other than those bundled with them. Any manipulation over the data should be performed only through the functions that are bundled in the class. Thus, the functions provide an interface to the outside world to access the data. The phenomenon of denying permission to access the data to outside functions is known as **data hiding** or **information hiding**. The concept of classes enables us to create our own data types also. The data types thus created are called **Abstract Data Types (ADT)** since they provide mechanism for data abstraction wherein the internal details of the operations, the data are subjected to, are hidden from the external world.

Inheritance: Once a class is designed, the facilities provided by the class can be readily used in other classes, which require the same functionality as that of the class and in addition to their own. The classes thus defined are said to have been derived from the class. The concept of inheritance, by enabling us to reuse the existing code (already tested to perfection), it facilitates even the hierarchical growth of a program.

Polymorphism: The term polymorphism means one in many forms. This is another important feature of C++. A single operation defined can mean different behaviours with different types of data, we come across the terms function overloading, operator overloading later which exhibit polymorphism. We even come across terms like dynamic binding, runtime polymorphism etc.

These three features are the guiding principles of object oriented programming. The term *object oriented* means that we organize software as a collection of discrete objects that incorporate both data structure and behaviour. This is in contrast to conventional programming in which data structure and behaviour are only loosely connected. We start our discussion with the procedural features and then march towards the object oriented features of the language.

1.3 THE STRUCTURE OF A C++ PROGRAM

```
documentation
include files
classes declaration and Definition
macros definition
global Variables Declaration

int main(void)
{
   Local Variables

   Statements

   return 0;
}
```

Documentation consists of comment lines, which indicate program title, author name and other relevant details related to the program. Appropriate and meaningful comment lines can be embedded anywhere in the body of a program, not necessarily in the beginning itself. Judicious usage of comments while coding is a good programming practice since it increases the degree of readability and understandability of programs and helps during maintenance stage of larger programs. In C++, any segment of text preceded by // is taken as a comment. The compiler just ignores the comments.

EXAMPLE

// Program to find the area of a circle

Here, the piece of text *Program to find the area of a circle* is considered as a comment by the C++ compiler and it is ignored by it during compilation.

Include files is to specify the files, the contents of which are to be included as part of the program. C++ compilers are provided with what is called a **standard library**, which consists of definitions of a large number of commonly used built-in functions. Since these functions are readily available, we do not need to write them if we want to use the functions. Our programs can simply utilize them. In order to use them, we need to include some files as part of our program. These files are generally called **header files** since they are included in the beginning of the program itself. Examples of header files include iostream.h, iomanip.h and string.h.

The preprocessor directive `#include` is used for this purpose.

EXAMPLE

```
#include <iostream.h>
```

In response to the above directive, the contents of the file iostream.h are added to the source program by the preprocessor. Note that the file iostream.h is surrounded by pointed brackets. This is to indicate the compiler to search for the file in the include directory.

Classes declaration and definition is to declare and define the classes that are used by the program. Since C++ is a language of classes, we define classes in almost all the programs.

Macros definition is to assign symbolic names to constants and define macros. The preprocessor directive `#define` is used for the purpose.

EXAMPLE

```
#define PI 3.14
```

assigns the symbolic name `PI` to the constant value 3.14.

Global variables are those, which are required to be accessed by all the functions defined after their declaration. So, the variables declared before the main() can be accessed by all the functions, which follow their declaration.

All the above parts are optional, they can be used only when they are required. They can appear in any order. Then comes the function main(). Every C++ program will have one main(). This is where the execution of a program starts from and ends with. Opening brace { of the main() marks the physical beginning of a program and the closing brace } marks the physical end of the program. The statements enclosed within the opening brace and the closing brace form the body of the main(). It consists of two parts: (a) Local variables declaration, where all the variables, which are accessed only by the main() are declared and (b) Statements, which include the executable statements. The executable statements can be calls to different functions also.

After the closing brace of the main(), user-defined functions, if any, can be defined. The word int before the main() indicates that the main() returns an int value to its caller, the underlying operating system and the word void within the parentheses indicate that the main() does not require any inputs from the calling program.

A C++ program in its simplest form appears as follows:

```
#include <iostream.h>
int main(void)
{
    statements

    return 0;
}
```

The inclusion of the header file iostream.h is mandatory to use the input and the output facility. There should be at least one statement in the body of the main().

1.4 SAMPLE C++ PROGRAMS

Program 1.1

```
#include <iostream.h>

int main(void)
{
    cout << "Data Encapsulation\n";
    cout << "Inheritance\n";
    cout << "Polymorphism";

    return 0;
}
```

The program is to display the strings data encapsulation, inheritance and polymorphism on the screen.

Program 1.2

```
// To find the area of a triangle

#include <iostream.h>

int main(void)
{
    int base, height;
    float area;


    cout << "Enter base \n";
    cin >> base;
    cout << "Enter height \n";
    cin >> height;

    area = 0.5 * base * height;

    cout << "Area =" << area;

    return 0;
}
```

The program is to accept the values of base and height of a triangle and calculate its area and display it.

1.5 THE INPUT AND OUTPUT STATEMENTS (CIN AND COUT)

1.5.1 The cin Statement

The **cin** is the input statement. The syntax of the statement is as follows:

cin >> variable;

The statement is used to accept the value of the variable. The symbol >> is called the **insertion operator**.

EXAMPLE

```
int b;
```

The statement `cin >> b;` accepts a value to the variable **b**.

If we have more than one variable, the values can be accepted with the single cin statement preceding each variable by the insertion operator.

The statement `cin >> a >> b;` accepts the values of the variables **a** and **b**.

1.5.2 The cout Statement

The **cout** statement is used for displaying the outputs. The syntax of its usage is as follows:

```
cout << variable;
```

The symbol << is called the **extraction operator**. The syntax is to display the value of the variable.

EXAMPLE

```
int a = 10;
cout << a;
```

Displays the value of the variable **a**.

```
cout << "a =" << a;
```

Displays the output as `a = 10`. Note that the string `"a="` displayed before the value of the variable **a** is displayed.

1.6 EXECUTION OF A C++ PROGRAM

Following are the four general steps involved in the execution of a program written in the C++ irrespective of the operating system being used:

1. Creating the source program. Creation of the source program is done with the help of a text editor. A text editor enables us to create a new text file, modify the contents of an existing file, etc. The source program is typed into a file, say, demo.cpp. Note that the C++ program files end with the extension .cpp.

2. Compiling the source program. Once the source program is ready in a text file, next, the file is submitted to the C++ compiler. The C++ compiler processes the source program and if the program is syntactically correct, produces the object code.

3. Linking the program with the user-defined functions and the functions in the standard library. Once the object code of the program is obtained after successful compilation, the linker links the object code with the functions in the standard library referred to by the program. After successful linking, the linker will then produce the final executable code.

4. Executing the program to get the expected outputs. The executable code produced by the linker is then run.

1.6.1 Under MS-DOS Environment

The following sequence of commands is used to create and execute a C++ program in MS-DOS environment.

At the command prompt

1. Creating the source program.

```
edit demo.cpp
```

The utility program edit has been used to create the source file demo.cpp.

2. Compiling the source program.

```
bc demo.cpp
```

bc is the Borland C++ compiler. On successful compilation, it produces the object program file demo.obj.

3. Linking the program with the functions in the standard library.

```
Link demo.obj
```

4. Executing the program to get the expected outputs.

```
demo
```

Turbo C++/ Borland C++ Integrated Development Environment

(The sequence of commands)

1. To create a source file

Select file option
    Select new option
        Type the program code in the edit window
            Press F2 to Save the file

2. To compile the program

Select compile option
    Click on compile menu item

Or

Press Alt + F9 (+ indicates that both Alt and F9 keys should be pressed simultaneously)

3. To run the program

Select Run option or press Ctrl + F9

4. To see the result

Press Alt + F5

1.6.2 Under Unix AT & T Environment

The following sequence of commands are used to create and execute a C++ program in Unix environment. The source file names end with the extension .C. Note that C is in upper case.

1. Creating the source program.

```
ed demo.C
```

or

```
vi demo.C
```

`ed` and `vi` are the editor programs in the Unix environment.

2. Compiling and linking.

```
CC demo.C
```

In Unix environment, both compiling and linking take place together and on success, they produce the executable object code stored in the file **a.out.**

3. Executing the program to get the expected outputs.

```
a.out
```

The final executable code can be collected by a file other than the default file **a.out**. The general syntax of this variation is as follows:

```
CC -o objectfile sourcefile
```

where `sourcefile` is the file containing the C++ program code and `objectfile` is the file which collects the final executable code.

```
CC -o demo.out demo.c
```

Here, the final executable object code is stored in the file `demo.out`. It can be run by just specifying it at the shell prompt as:

```
$ demo.out
```

We can even combine several source files and produce a single executable object code if needed. The general syntax of the compilation command for combining *n* source files is as follows:

```
CC filename1.C filename2.C ......filenamen.C
```

EXAMPLE: To combine three source files `demo1.C,` `demo2.C` and `demo3.C` and produce a single executable object file, the command is:

```
CC demo1.C demo2.C demo3.C
```

After successful compilation and linking, the final executable object code is collected by the default file `a.out`. It can be run by typing it at the shell prompt.

The command `CC -o demo.out demo1.C demo2.C demo3.C` on successful compilation and linking produces the executable code stores it in the file `demo.out`.

1.7 ERRORS

Programming without errors is quite a difficult task. We do come across different types of errors while executing program. Following is the classification of errors depending on the order of timing they crop up:

- Compile-time errors

- Linker errors
- Runtime errors
- Logical errors

All these errors should be dealt with. Only then do we get the expected behaviour and get the expected results from the program.

The **compile-time errors** occur if the programs do not conform to the grammatical rules of the language being used. Thus, the compile-time errors are also called **syntactical errors**. They are caught during compilation itself. We correct the syntactical errors and recompile the programs until the compiler is satisfied with the syntactical correctness of the programs and produces the equivalent object code.

The **linker errors** occur during the linking process when the external symbols referred to by the program are not resolved. For example, if we call a function which is not defined, the linker figures out and reports the appropriate error. The linker errors (if any) occur after the successful compilation of the program.

The **runtime errors** occur while a program is being run and hence the name. They occur due to both program internal factors and external factors. Examples of runtime errors due to internal factors include "division by zero", "array subscript out of bounds". Examples of runtime errors due to external factors include "running out of memory", "Printer out of paper", etc. We need to exercise extra care to handle these errors. We should identify the potential segment of code where these errors are anticipated and take corrective steps when they occur thereby avoiding abnormal termination of a program. The runtime errors (if any) occur after the successful compilation and successful linking of the program.

The **logical errors** occur if the solution procedure for the given problem itself is wrong. In this case, the outputs produced by the programs would be incorrect. Correcting the solution procedure itself by better understanding of the problem eliminates these errors. The logical errors (if any) are to be figured out by ourselves by verifying the outputs that are produced by the program.

REVIEW QUESTIONS

1.1 What are the limitations of the procedural programming technique higher level languages?

1.2 What are the salient features of C++ language?

1.3 Explain the structure of a C++ program.

1.4 What are local variables?

1.5 What are global variables?

1.6 How do we define a constant?

1.7 What are the steps involved in executing a C++ program?

1.8 How do you compile multiple source programs in the Unix environment?

1.9 What are the different types of errors?

1.10 What are syntactical errors? Give examples.

1.11 What are linker errors? Give examples.

1.12 What are runtime errors? Give examples.

1.13 When do we get logical errors?

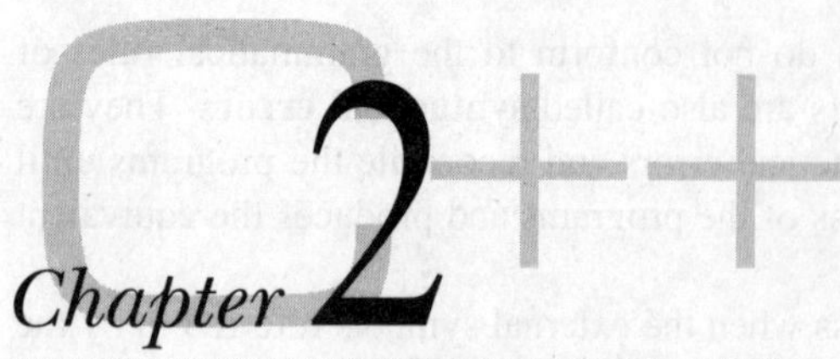

C++ Language Preliminaries

2.1 INTRODUCTION

Each language will have its own set of permissible characters. The characters form the most basic building blocks of the language. Using only these characters, the language constructs are formed. For instance, if we consider our natural language, English, it consists of 52 (26 lower case 26 upper case) permissible symbols . English words are constructed using appropriate combination of only these characters. So the 52 characters form the *character set* of English. Character set of a language is also called its *alphabet*.

Computer programming languages are not exceptions in this regard. They will also have their own set of permissible characters which are used to form their program elements. So is C++. The character set of C++ includes:

Letters of English alphabet (Both upper case and lower case):

A…….Z a……z

All symbols of the decimal number system:

0…….9

Special symbols:

. Dot
, Comma
; Semicolon
: Colon
? Question mark
‘ Single quote
“ Double quote
! Exclamation symbol
| Vertical bar
& Ampersand symbol
^ Caret
* Asterisk
– Minus sign
+ Plus sign
< Opening pointed bracket
> Closing pointed bracket
(Opening parenthesis
) Closing parenthesis

/	Right slash	[	Opening square bracket
\	Back slash	]	Closing square bracket
~	Tilde symbol	{	Opening brace
_	Underscore	}	Closing brace
$	Dollar sign	#	Number sign
%	Percent symbol	=	Equal symbol

The class of characters, which are not printed, but instead, cause some action are commonly referred to as the **control characters** or **white spaces**. They are represented by a backslash followed by another character. Following are the control characters:

Backspace	\b
Horizontal tab	\t
Vertical tab	\v
Carriage return	\r
New line	\n
Form feed	\f
Alert character	\a

A combination of characters from the alphabet of C++ is called a **C++ word**.

2.2 KEYWORDS AND IDENTIFIERS

Keywords are those words of C++ which have predefined meaning assigned by the C++ language. They form a part of the database required by the C++ compiler itself. They should not be used for any other purpose other than the purpose for which they are meant. The keywords are also called **reserved words**. Following are the keywords supported by C++:

Auto	asm	bool	break	case	catch
char	class	const	const_cast	continue	default
delete	do	double	dynamic_cast	else	enum
explicit	extern	Float	for	friend	goto
if	inline	int	long	mutable	namespace
new	operator	private	protected	public	register
reinterpret_cast	return	short	signed	sizeof	static
struct	static_cast	switch	template	this	throw
try	typedef	typeid	union	unsigned	using
void	volatile	virtual	while		

An **identifier** is one which is used to designate program elements like variables, constants, array names, function names, etc. There are a couple of rules governing the construction of valid identifiers. They are:

1. An identifier can have maximum 31 characters. The permissible characters in an identifier include letters, digits and an optional underscore symbol.
2. It should start with a letter.
3. Special characters other than underscore are not permitted.
5. It should not be a keyword.

Example of valid identifiers:

Number
A1
A_1
A1b

Invalid identifiers: Reason

1a	starts with a digit
a 1	space in between is not allowed
a,b	, is not allowed

2.3 CONSTANTS

The value of a constant does not change during the execution of the program enclosing it. A constant also gets stored in a memory location but the address of the location is not accessible to the programmer. Depending on the types of data they represent, constants are broadly classified into three classes.

2.3.1 Numeric Constants

Numeric constants, as the name itself reveals, are those which consist of numerals, an optional sign and an optional period . They are further classified into two types:

Integer constants: Integer constants are whole numbers (i.e., without fractional part). These are further classified into three types depending on the number systems they belong to. They are:

(i) Decimal integer constants. A decimal integer constant is characterized by the following properties:

(a) It is a sequence of one or more digits [0…9, the symbols of decimal number system]
(b) It may have an optional + or – sign. In the absence of sign, the constant is assumed to be positive.
(c) It should not have a period as part of it.
(d) Commas and blank spaces are not permitted.

Valid decimal integer constants

345
–987

Invalid decimal integer constants

3.45	Decimal point is not permissible.
3,34	Commas are not permitted.

(ii) Octal integer constants. An octal integer constant is characterized by the following properties:

(a) It is a sequence of one or more digits [0…7, symbols of octal number system]
(b) It may have an optional + or – sign. In the absence of sign, the constant is assumed to be positive.
(c) It should start with the digit 0.

(d) It should not have a period as part of it.
(e) Commas and blank spaces are not permitted.

Valid octal integer constants

0345
–054
+023

Invalid octal integer constants

03.45	Decimal point is not permissible.
03,34	Commas are not permitted.
x45	x is not a permissible symbol.
678	8 is not a permissible symbol.

(iii) Hexadecimal integer constants. An hexadecimal integer constant is characterized by the following properties:

(a) It is a sequence of one or more symbols [0…9, A...Z, a...z, the symbols of hexadecimal number system]
(b) It may have an optional + or – sign. In the absence of sign, the constant is assumed to be positive.
(c) It should start with the symbols 0X or 0x.
(d) It should not have a period as part of it.
(e) Commas and blank spaces are not permitted.

Valid hexadecimal integer constants

0x345
–0x987
0x34A
0XA23

Invalid hexadecimal integer constants

0X3.45	Decimal point is not permissible.
0X3,34	Commas are not permitted.

2.3.2 Real Constants

The real constants, also known as **floating point constants**, are written in two forms:

Fractional notation: The real constants in fractional form are characterized by the following characteristics:

(a) They must have at least one digit and a decimal point.
(b) An optional sign (+ or –) can precede a real constant. In the absence of any sign, the real constant is assumed to be positive.
(c) Commas or blank spaces are not permitted as part of a real constant.

Valid real constants.

345.67
–987.87

Invalid real constants.

3 45	Blank spaces are not permitted.
3,34	Commas are not permitted.
123	Decimal point missing.

Exponential notation: The exponential form offers a convenient way for writing very large and small real constants. For example, 23000000.00, which can be written as 23 * 10^8, is written as **0.23E8** or **0.23e8** in exponential form.

0.000000123, which can be written as 0.123 * 10^{-6}, is written as **0.123E-6** or **0.123e-6** in exponential form. The letter E or e stands for exponential form.

A real constant expressed in exponential form has two parts: (a) Mantissa (b) Exponent. Mantissa is the part of the real constant to the left of E or e, and the exponent of a real constant is to the right of E or e. Mantissa and exponent of the above two numbers are:

Mantissa	Exponent	Mantissa	Exponent
0.23	E 8	0.123	E –6

In the above examples, 0.23 and 0.123 are the mantissa parts of the first and second numbers respectively, and 8 and –6 are the exponent parts of the first and second number respectively.

The real constants in exponential form are characterized by the following characteristics:

(a) The mantissa must have at least one digit.
(b) The mantissa is followed by the letter E or e and the exponent.
(c) The exponent must have at least one digit and must be an integer.
(d) A sign for the exponent is optional.

Valid real constants in exponential form.

1E3
12e-5
0.12E5

Invalid real constants in exponential form.

12E	No digit specified for exponent
12e3.4	Exponent should not be a fraction
12,3e4	Commas are not allowed
234 * e9	* not allowed

2.3.3 Character Constants

Character constants, as the name itself indicates, are those which consist of one or more characters of the alphabet of C++. Depending on the number of characters present, character constants are further classified into two types:

Single character constant: A single character constant consists of only one character and it is enclosed within a pair of single quotes. For example,

'a' is a single character constant.
'9' is a single character constant.

String constant: A string constant consists of one or more characters and it is enclosed within a pair of double quotes. For example,

"abc" is a string constant.
"12bn" is a string constant.

Note that "123" and "1" are also string constants.

2.4 VARIABLES

A **variable** is a named memory location, the value of which can change during the execution of the program containing it. The name of a variable should be a valid C++ identifier. In addition to the rules for forming identifiers, the general convention followed while naming variables is that the name selected for a variable reflect the purpose of the variable. However, this is not the compiler requirement but only to increase the readability of the variables.

In C++, variables can be declared anywhere in a program but before their usage. The syntax of declaring a variable is as follows:

```
data-type variable;
```

Note that the declaration ends with a semicolon.

EXAMPLE

```
int a;
```

To declare more than one variable of same type, the variables are separated by commas as shown hereinafter:

```
data-type variable1, variable2, variable3,...,variablen;
```

EXAMPLE

```
int a, b, c;
```

2.5 DATA TYPES

Data types refer to the classes of data that can be manipulated by C++ programs. The three fundamental data types supported by C++ are character, integer, real type.

char: All single characters used in programs belong to character type. The keyword `char` is used to denote character type. The size of a variable of `char` type is one byte. The range of values that can be stored in a variable of char type is –128 to 127, that is, (-2^7 to 2^7-1). When a character is assigned to a variable of type char, what is stored in the variable is the ASCII value of the character.

```
char c;
```

variable **c** is declared to be a variable of type `char`.
`c = 'a';` assigns the character 'a' to the variable **c**.

unsigned char: The `unsigned char` is a variation of `char` type. The size of a variable of `unsigned char` type is also one byte. As the name itself indicates, the range of values that can be stored in a variable of type `unsigned char` is 0 to 255 (0 to 2^8-1).

int: All numeric data items with no fractional part belong to integer type. The keyword `int` is used to represent integer type. Normally, the size of a variable of type `int` is the word size of the computer system being used. We will consider a 16-bit machine. In the case of 16-bit machines, it is 2 bytes. The range of values that can be stored in an `int` variable is –32768 to 32767 (i.e., -2^{15} to $2^{15}-1$).

A variable of `int` type provides three more modifiers: `unsigned int`, `short int`, `long int`. These variations are to have control over the range of values which can be stored.

unsigned int. The size of a variable of `unsigned int` is also 2 bytes (16-bit machine) . It can store only positive range of values. The range of values that can be stored in a variable of `unsigned int` is 0 to 65535 (0 to $2^{16}-1$).

```
unsigned int ui;
```

Variable `ui` is declared to be a variable of `unsigned int` type.

short int. The size of a variable of `short int` is also 2 bytes. It is similar to `int` type in the case of 16-bit machines.

```
short int s;
```

Variable `s` is declared to be a variable of `short int` type.

long int. The size of a variable of `long int` type is 4 bytes. The range of values that can be stored in a variable of this type is –2147483648 to 2147483647. Note that there is a substantial increase in the range of values.

```
long int l;
```

Varibale `l` is declared to be a variable of `long int` type.

The combinations `unsigned short int` and `unsigned long int` are also permissible. In 16 bit machines, the `unsigned short int` is similar to `unsigned int`. But the range of values that can be stored in a variable of `unsigned long int` is 0 to $2^{32}-1$.

In all of the modifiers of `int` type, the keyword `int` is optional and can be skipped while declaring variables of their type.

EXAMPLE

```
unsigned ui;
short s;
long l;
unsigned short us;
unsigned long ul;
```

are all valid declarations.

float: All numeric data items with fractional part belong to real type. The keyword `float` is used to declare variables of real type. A variable of `float` type requires 4 bytes and the range of values that can be stored in it is 3.4e – 38 to 3.4e + 38. It stores floating point numbers with 6 digits of precision. The floating point numbers stored in a float variables are called **single-precision numbers**.

```
float f;
```

Variable **`f`** is declared to be a variable of **`float`** type.

Modifiers of **float** type include `long float (double)` and `long double`. The modifiers facilitate storage of higher range of floating point numbers and they provide increased accuracy.

double. A variable of `double` type requires 8 bytes of memory space and the range of values that can be stored in it is 1.7e – 308 to 1.7e + 308. It stores floating point numbers with 14 digits of precision. The degree of accuracy provided by `double` type is more than that provided by `float` type.

```
double d;
```

Variable **d** is declared to be a variable of `double` type.

long double. A variable of `long double` type requires 10 bytes of memory space and the range of values that can be stored in it is 3.4e – 4932 to 1.1e + 4932. It stores floating point numbers with more than 14 digits of precision. The degree of accuracy provided by long `double` type is even more than that provided by `double` type.

```
long double f2;
```

Variable **f2** is declared to be a variable of long double type.

z: The void data type is used in two situations: (a) To explicitly declare functions which do not return any value (b) To create generic pointers. The usage of the data type becomes clear when we learn the concept of functions and pointers, which are covered later.

REVIEW QUESTIONS

2.1 What do you mean by the alphabet of a language?

2.2 What is a C ++ word?

2.3 What is a keyword?

2.4 Mention any five keywords of C++.

2.5 What is an identifier? Mention the rules to be followed while forming identifiers.

2.6 Identify whether the following are valid or invalid identifiers:

(a) a1 (b) a b (c) rollno (d) _count (e) ISPRIME

2.7 Define a constant. Give an account of classifications of constants.

2.8 What are the rules for integer constants?

2.9 What are the rules for real constants?

2.10 Differentiate between a single character constant and a string constant.

2.11 What is a variable? Write the syntax of declaration of variables.

2.12 C++ is rich in data types. Justify.

2.13 What are the modifiers of `int` data type and mention their significance.

2.14 What are the modifiers of `float` type and mention their significance.

2.15 What is the range of values which can be stored in a variable of type `int`.

2.16 What is the size of a variable of type `double`?

2.17 What is the number of digits of precision provided in the case of `float` type.

Chapter 3

Operators and Expressions

3.1 INTRODUCTION

An operator is a symbol, which instructs the computer to perform the specified manipulation over some data. The rich set of operators available in C++ (and C) enable us to write efficient and concise programs and this fact serves to set C++ apart from any other programming languages.

Depending on the type of operations they perform, they are classified into the following types:

- Assignment operator
  =
- Arithmetic operators
  +, –, *, /, %, unary +, unary –
- Relational operators
  <, <=, >, >=, ==, !=
- Logical operators
  [&&, ||, !
- Increment/Decrement operators
  ++, – –
- Shorthand arithmetic assignment operators
  +=, –=, *=, /=, %=
- Conditional operator
  ?:
- Bitwise operators
  &, |, ^, <<, >>
- sizeof() operator
- Comma operator
  ,

Operators can not be used in isolation. They have to be used in combination with either variables or constants or with combination of variables and constants. When used in combination, they are said to form what are called **expressions**. An expression in C++ is thus a combination of variables or constants and operators conforming to the syntax rules of the language. The variables or constants used with an operator are the ones, which are subjected to the operation specified by the operator, and hence they are called **operands** for the operator. Depending on the operators used, the expressions are further classified into *arithmetic expressions*, *relational expressions*, *logical expressions* and so on.

Even operators are also classified into three types depending on the number of operands used: (a) Unary operators, (b) Binary operators and (c) Ternary operators. A unary operator is one which is defined over a single operand. A binary operator is one which is defined over two operands. A ternary operator is one which is defined over three operands.

3.2 ASSIGNMENT OPERATOR [=]

The single equal symbol (=) is referred to as the assignment operator. It is used to assign the value of an expression to a variable. The statement used for this purpose is called the **assignment statement**. The general form of an assignment statement is as follows:

```
Variable = Expression;
```

The expression can be a constant, variable or any valid C++ expression.

EXAMPLES

(a)
```
int a;
a = 10;
```

The variable **a** is assigned the value 10.

(b)
```
int a, b =10;
a = b;
```

The variable **a** is assigned the value of **b**.

(c)
```
int a =5, b =10, c;
c = a + b;
```

Here, the value of the expression **a + b**, which is 15, is assigned to the variable **c**.

Program 3.1 To illustrate Assignment Operators [=]

```
#include <iostream.h>
int main(void)
{
    int a, b, c;

    a = 10;
    cout << "a = "<< a << endl;
    b = a; /* Value of a is assigned to b */
    cout << "b = " << b << endl;
    c = a + b; /* Value of the expression a + b is assigned to c */
    cout << "c = " << c << endl;

    return 0;
}
```

Input-Output:

```
a = 10
b = 10
c = 20
```

3.3 ARITHMETIC OPERATORS [UNARY +, UNARY –, +, –, *, /, %]

The arithmetic operators are used to perform arithmetic operations like addition, subtraction, multiplication, etc. over numeric values by constructing arithmetic expressions. An arithmetic expression is one which comprises arithmetic operators and variables or constants. Here variables and constants are called **operands**. The operators unary + and unary – are defined over a single operand and hence the name unary operators. Their usage is of the form `+operand` and `-operand` respectively. The unary + has no effect on the value of `operand`. But unary – changes the sign of the `operand`.

EXAMPLE

`a = 10;`

`+a, -a` are the valid arithmetic expressions.

`+a` evaluates to 10 only, the value of a.

`-a` evaluates to –10.

The remaining +, –, *, / and % are binary arithmetic operators since they are defined over two operands. Note that + and – play dual roles.

A simple arithmetic expression with binary arithmetic operators is of the form:

```
operand1 operator operand2
```

where `operator` is any binary arithmetic operator, `operand1` and `operand2` can both be variables or constants or a combination of variable and constant.

EXAMPLE

```
a + b
a - 7
4 * 9
a/4
b % 3
```

are all valid arithmetic expressions.

If a and b are two operands, then

`a + b` is a simple arithmetic expression and it evaluates to the sum of `a` and `b`. The assignment statement `s = a + b` on its execution assigns the sum of `a` and `b` to the variable **s**.

`a - b` is a simple arithmetic expression and it evaluates to the difference between `a` and `b`. The assignment statement `d = a - b` on its execution assigns the difference between `a` and `b` to the variable **d**.

`a * b` is a simple arithmetic expression and it evaluates to the product of `a` and `b`. The assignment statement `p = a + b` on its execution assigns the product of `a` and `b` to the variable **p**.

`a/b` is a simple arithmetic expression and it evaluates to the quotient after division of `a` by `b`. The assignment statement `q = a/b` on its execution assigns the quotient after division of `a` by `b` to the variable **q**.

`a % b` is a simple arithmetic expression and it evaluates to the remainder after division of `a` by `b`. The assignment statement `r = a% b` on its execution assigns the remainder after division of `a` by `b` to the variable **s**. The operator `%` is defined over integers only. Detail of the arithmetic operators are given in Table 3.1.

Table 3.1 Arithmetic Operators

Operator	*Meaning*	*Example*	*Value*
+	Addition	4 + 5	9
-	Subtraction	4 - 5	-1
*	Multiplication	4 * 5	20
/	Division	4 / 5	0
%	Remainder	4 / 5	4

Program 3.2 To Illustrate Arithmetic Operators [+, –, *, /, %]

```
#include <iostream.h>
int main(void)
{
   int a, b, sum, diff, product, rem, quotient;
   cout << "Enter two numbers" << endl;
   cin >> a >> b;
   sum = a + b;
   diff = a - b;
   product = a * b;
   quotient = a / b;
   rem = a % b;

   cout << "a = " << a << "b = " << b << endl;
   cout << "Sum = " << sum << endl;
   cout << "Difference = " << diff << endl;
   cout << "Product = " << product << endl;
   cout << "Quotient = " << quotient << endl;
   cout << "Remainder = " << rem << endl;
   return 0;
}
```

Input-Output:

```
Enter two numbers
4
5

a = 4   b = 5
Sum = 9
Difference = -1
Product = 20
Quotient = 0
Remainder = 4
```

Explanation

In the above program, all the assignment statements are of the form:

Result = operand1 arithmetic-operator operand2;. In each of the assignments, the expression on the right-hand side of the assignment operator gets evaluated and the result of the expression is assigned to the variable on the left-hand side of the assignment operator. The values of the collecting variables are displayed.

3.3.1 Types of Arithmetic Expressions

Depending on the type of operands used, arithmetic expressions are further classified as:

Integer mode expressions: If all the operands of an expression are integers (char, unsigned char, int, short, long, unsigned int), the expression is called an **integer mode expression**. The resultant value of an integer mode expression is always an integer.

EXAMPLE

`4 + 5` is an integer mode expression
`= 9` is an integer

Real mode expressions: If all the operands used in an expression are real values (float, double, double) then it is called a **real mode expression**. The resultant value of a real mode expression is always value of float type.

EXAMPLE

`5.4 + 4.0` is a real mode expression
`= 9.4` is a value of float type

Mixed mode expressions: If some operands are of integer type and some are of float type in an expression then it is called a **mixed mode expression**. The resultant value of a mixed mode expression will always be of float type.

EXAMPLE

`5.4 + 4` is a mixed mode expression

3.3.2 Precedence of Arithmetic Operators and Associativity

In reality, an arithmetic expression can even have more than one arithmetic operator wherein each operator is surrounded by two operands (Except unary operators).

EXAMPLE

```
int a = 4, b = 5, c = 6;
a + b * c
```

The above expression has two operators + and *. While evaluating the expression, if we consider part of the expression consisting of + first; and * next, the value obtained would be `9 * 6 = 54`. On the other hand, if we take * first and + next, the value of the expression turns out to be `4 + 30 = 34`. As observed, there are two possible outcomes. This is ambiguous. This problem is eliminated by associating relative precedence to the operators. **Operator precedence** determines the order of evaluation of an arithmetic expression and ensures that the expression produces only one value. Following is the precedence level and associativity of arithmetic operators.

Precedence level	*Operators*	*Associativity*
I	Unary +, Unary –	Right to left
II	*, /, %	Left to right
III	+, –	Left to right

According to the operator precedence rules, the value of the above expression `a + b * c` would be `4 + 30 = 34`. Since `b` and `c` are multiplied first and then the product and `a` are summed.

If an arithmetic expression has more than one operator, which are at the same level, then the order of evaluation is determined by a rule called **associativity**. In the case of arithmetic operators, they will be evaluated from left to right.

EXAMPLE

```
int a = 4, b = 12, c = 6, d=7;
a + b / c * d
```

In the above expression, since both / and * are present, which are at the same level, first / gets evaluated and then evaluation of * follows. After these, + gets evaluated. As a result of this, the value of the expression turns out to be:

```
 4 + 12 / 6 * 7
= 4 + 2 * 7
= 4 + 14
= 18
```

However, we can override the default order of evaluation of an expression by using the pairs of parenthesis. In this case, the subexpressions enclosed within the parenthesis is given top priority while evaluating.

EXAMPLE

```
int a = 4, b = 5, c = 6;
(a + b) * c
```

Here, even though * is at higher level than +, `a` and `b` are added first. `c` is then multiplied with the sum. The result of the expression would thus be:

```
 (4 + 5) * 6
= 9 * 6
= 54
```

Program 3.3 To Illustrate Operator Precedence in Arithmetic Operators [unary +, unary –, +, –, *, / and %]

```
#include <iostream.h>

int main(void)
{
    int a = 4, b = 6, c = 3, d, e, f, g;

    cout << " a=" << a << " b = " << b << " c = " << c << endl;
```

```
    d = -a + b * c;
    e = (a + b) * c;
    f = a * b / c;
    g = a * (b / c);

    cout << "\n -a + b * c = " << d << endl;
    cout << "(a + b) * c = " << e << endl;
    cout << "a * b / c = " << f << endl;
    cout << "a * (b / c) = " << g << endl;

    return 0;
}
```

Input-Output:

```
a = 4   b = 6    c = 3

-a + b * c = 14
(a + b) * c = 30
a * b / c = 8
a * (b / c) = 8
```

Explanation

In Program 3.3, the evaluation of the statement `d = -a + b * c;` proceeds as follows:

`d = -4 + 6 * 3`	The value of `a`, i.e., 4 gets negated since the operator unary – enjoys the highest priority.
`= -4 + 18`	The values of `b` and `c`, `6` and `3` respectively are multiplied since the arithmetic operator * is at the next higher level
`= 14`	The intermediate results are added and the sum is then assigned to the variable `d`.

The evaluation of the statement `e = (a + b) * c;` proceeds as follows:

`e= (a + b) * c`	
`= (4 + 6) * 3`	
`= 10 * 3`	The sub-expression `(4 + 6)` gets evaluated first since it is enclosed within a pair of parentheses.
`e = 30`	`10` and `3` are then multiplied to produce `30` which is then assigned to the variable `e`.

Note that in the above expression, even though the multiplication operator * is at a higher precedence level than that of the addition operator +, addition is performed first. This is because of the fact that the subexpression `4 + 6` is enclosed within a pair of parentheses.

The evaluation of the statement `f = a * b / c;` proceeds as follows:

`f = a * b / c;`	
`= 4 * 6 / 3`	
`= 24 / 3`	The subexpression `4 * 6` gets evaluated first to produce `24` since both * and /are at the same precedence level and the associativity of the operators is from left to right.
`f = 8`	`24` is divided by `3` to produce `8`, which is then assigned to the variable `f`.

Note that in the above expression, even though the multiplication operator * is at a higher precedence level than that of the addition operator +, addition is performed first. This is because of the fact that the

subexpression `4 + 6` is enclosed within a pair of parentheses. The usage of the set of parentheses has thus overridden the precedence rule.
The evaluation of the statement `g = a * (b / c);` proceeds as follows:

```
g = a * (b / c);
  = 4 * (6 / 3)
  = 4 * 2
g = 8
```

`= 4 * 2` — The subexpression `6/3` gets evaluated first to produce 2 since the subexpression is enclosed within a pair of parentheses .

`g = 8` — 4 and 2 are multiplied to produce `8`, which is then assigned to the variable `g`.

Note that in the above expression, even though the multiplication operator * and the division operator / are at the same level and their associativity is from left to right, the subexpression `6/3` is evaluated first. This is because of the fact that the subexpression is enclosed within a pair of parentheses. The usage of the set of parentheses has thus overridden the associativity rule.

3.4 RELATIONAL OPERATORS [<, <=, >, >=, ==, !=]

The relational operators are used to construct relational expressions, which are used to compare two quantities. A relational expression is of the form **`operand1 operator operand2`**, where `operator` is any relational operator, `operand1` and `operand2` are variables or constants or a combination of both, which are being compared. The value of a relational expression in C++ is `one` or `zero`. One indicates that the condition is true and `zero` indicates that the condition is false. A relational expression is also called a **conditional expression** or a **Boolean expression**.

EXAMPLE

```
a < b, a > 10, 5 == 10
```

are all valid relational expressions.

Relational expressions are excessively used as parts of decision making and branching statements, and looping statements. We will see this later. The details of the relational operators are given in Table 3.2.

Table 3.2 Relational Operators

Operator	*Meaning*	*Example*	*Value*
<	Less than	4 < 5	1
<=	Less than or equal to	4 <= 5	1
>	Greater than	4 > 5	0
>=	Greater than or equal to	4 >= 5	0
==	Equal to	4 == 5	0
!=	Not equal to	4 != 5	1

Program 3.4 To Illustrate Relational Operators [<, <=, >, >=, ==, !=]

```
#include <iostream.h>

int main(void)
{
    int a, b, c, d, e, f, g, h;
```

```
    cout << "Enter two numbers" <<endl;
    cin >> a >> b;
    cout << "a = " << a << " b = " << b << endl;

    c = a < b;
    d = a <= b;
    e = a > b;
    f = a <= b;
    g = a == b;
    h = a != b;

    cout<< " a < b = "<< c<< endl;
    cout<< " a <= b = " << d << endl;
    cout << " a > b = " << e << endl;
    cout << " a >= b = " << f << endl;
    cout << " a == b = " << g << endl;
    cout << " a != b = " << h << endl;

    return 0;
}
```

Input-Output:

```
Enter two numbers
5
6

a = 5  b = 6

a < b = 1
a <= b = 1
a > b = 0
a >= b = 1
a == b = 0
a != b = 1
```

Explanation

In Program 3.4, all the assignment statements are of the form `Result = operand1 relational-operator operand2;`. In each of the statements, the expression on the right hand side of the assignment operator gets evaluated and the result of the expression, which is either one (true) or zero (false) is assigned to the variable on the left hand side of the assignment operator.

3.4.1 Precedence Levels and Associativity within Relational Operators

Precedence level	*Operators*	*Associativity*
I	<, <=, >, >=	Left to right
II	==, !=	Left to right

3.5 LOGICAL OPERATORS [&&, | |, !]

These logical operators are used to construct compound conditional expressions. The operators && and || are used to combine two conditional expressions and ! is used to negate a conditional expression.

Logical AND (&&): The general form of a compound conditional expression constructed using && is:

```
c1 && c2
```

where `c1` and `c2` are conditional expressions.
The working of `&&` is depicted in Table 3.3:

Table 3.3 Logical AND (&&) Operator

c1	c2	c1 && c2
T	T	T
T	F	F
F	–	F

First c1 is checked. If c1 is true then c2 is checked. If c2 is also true, c1& &c2 evaluates to true. If c2 is false then c1& &c2 evaluates to false (c2 is checked only when c1 is true). If c1 itself is false, irrespective of whether c2 is true or false (indicated by – for c2), c1& &c2 evaluates to false.

Note: The resultant condition (c1& &c2) is true only when both the conditions c1 and c2 are true. Otherwise it will be false.

Logical OR (||): The general form of a compound conditional expression constructed using || is:

```
c1 || c2
```

where `c1` and `c2` are conditional expressions.
The working of || is depicted in Table 3.4.

Table 3.4 Logical OR (||) Operator

c1	c2	c1 || c2
T	–	T
F	T	T
F	F	F

First c1 is checked. If c1 is true, irrespective of whether c2 is true or false (indicated by – for c2), c1 || c2 evaluates to true. If c1 is false, c2 is checked. If c2 is true c1 || c2 evaluates to true. On the other hand, if c2 is false, c1 || c2 evaluates to false. c2 is checked only when c1 is false.
Note: The resultant condition (c1 || c2) is false, only when both the conditions c1 and c2 are false. Otherwise it will be true.

Logical NOT (!): The general form of a compound conditional expression using ! is as follows:

!c

where c is a test-expression. The working of ! operator is shown in Table 3.5.

Table 3.5 Logical Not (!) Operator

c1	!c1
T	F
F	T

Here c1 is simply negated.
In all these cases, c1 and c2 can by themselves be compound conditional expressions.

Knowledge of the working of these operators is essential while constructing compound conditional expressions to suit our requirement.

Program 3.5 To Illustrate Logical Operators [&&, ||, !]

```
#include <iostream.h>

int main(void)
{
   int a = 5, b = 6, c = 7, d;

   cout << "a = " << a<< " b = "<< b << " c = " << c << endl;
   cout << "\n Working of Logical &&" << endl;

   d = (a < b) && (b < c);
   cout << " (a < b) && (b < c) = " << d << endl;

   d = (a < b)&& (b > c);
   cout << " (a < b) && (b > c) = " << d << endl;

   d = (a > b)&& (b < c);
   cout << " (a > b) && (b < c) = " << d << endl;

   d =(a > b)&& (b > c);
   cout << " (a > b) && (b > c) = " << d << endl;

   cout << "\n Working of Logical ||" << endl;

   d = (a < b)|| (b < c);
   cout << " (a < b) || (b < c) = " << d << endl;

   d = (a < b)|| (b > c);
   cout << " (a < b) || (b > c) = " << d << endl;

   d = (a > b)|| (b < c);
   cout << " (a > b) || (b < c) = " << d << endl;

   d = (a > b)|| (b > c);
   cout << " (a > b) || (b > c) = " << d << endl;

   cout << "\n Working of Logical NOT !" << endl;
   d = !(a < b);
   cout << "!(a < b) = " << d;
```

```
    d = !(a > b);
    cout << "!(a > b) = " << d;
    return 0;
}
```

Input-Output:

```
a = 5 b = 6 c = 7

Working of Logical &&
 (a < b) && (b < c) = 1
 (a < b) && (b > c) = 0
 (a > b) && (b < c) = 0
 (a > b) && (b > c) = 0

Working of Logical ||
 (a < b) || (b < c) = 1
 (a < b) || (b > c) = 1
 (a > b) || (b < c) = 1
 (a > b) || (b > c) = 0

Working of Logical NOT !
!(a < b) = 0!(a > b) = 1
```

Explanation

The program serves the purpose of illustrating the working of all the logical operators. Note that for both logical OR (||) and the logical AND (&&), all the four possible combinations of two conditions have been tested and the values of the resultant expressions are displayed. This reinforces the behaviour of the operators. Similarly, the working of the logical NOT (!) is also demonstrated.

3.5.1 Precedence Levels within Logical Operators

The precedence levels and associativity among the logical operators are given in Table 3.6.

Table 13.6

Precedence levels	*Operators*	*Associativity*
I	!	Right to left
II	&&	Left to right
III	||	Left to right

3.6 SHORTHAND ARITHMETIC ASSIGNMENT OPERATORS [+=,-=,*=,/=,%=]

Suppose **a** is a variable with the value 10. If its value is to be incremented by, say, 5. With the available knowledge of arithmetic expressions and assignment statement, we would use `a = a + 5`. This assignment statement can now be written as `a += 5;` which produces the same effect as the assignment statement `a = a + 5`. Note that the variable **a** needs to be used only once.

Similarly,

`a = a - 5` can be written as `a -= 5,`
`a = a * 5` can be written as `a *= 5`
`a = a / 5` can be written as `a /= 5`
`a = a % 5` can be written as `a %= 5`

As the name itself indicates, these operators enable us to perform both arithmetic and assignment operations. The syntax of using these operators is as follows.

```
operand1 operator operand2;
```

where `operator` is any shorthand arithmetic assignment operator. Here `operand1` should be a variable with an initial value and `operand2` can be a variable, a constant or an arithmetic expression. The details of the shorthand arithmetic assignment operators is given in Table 3.7.

EXAMPLE

```
a += 10;
a += b;
a += (b + c);
```

Table 3.7 Shorthand Arithmetic Assignment Operators $a = 4$

Operator	*Example*	*New value of a*
+=	a += 5	a = 9
-=	a -= 5	a = -1
*=	a *= 5	a = 20
/=	a /= 5	a = 0
%=	a %= 5	a = 4

Program 3.6 To Illustrate Shorthand Arithmetic Assignment Operators [+=, –=, *=, /=, %=]

```
#include <iostream.h>
#include <iomanip.h>

int main(void)
{
    int a, b, c, d, e;

    a = b = c = d = e = 10;
    cout << "a = " << a << " b = " << b << " c = " << c
         << " d = " << d << " e = " << e << endl;

    a += 5;
    b -= 5;
    c *= 5;
    d /= 5;
    e %= 5;
    cout << "after a += 5; a = " << a << endl;
    cout << "after b -= 5; b = " << b << endl;
    cout << "after c *= 5; c = " << c << endl;
```

```
    cout<< "after d /= 5; d = " << d << endl;
    cout << "after e %= 5; e = " << e << endl;

    return 0;
}
```

Input-Output:

```
a = 10 b = 10 c = 10 d = 10 e = 10

after a += 5; a = 15
after b -= 5; b = 5
after c *= 5; c = 50
after d /= 5; d = 2
after e %= 5; e = 0
```

Explanation

In Program 3.6, all the variables **a**, **b**, **c**, **d** and **e** are assigned the value 10 using the statement `a = b = c = d = e = 10;`. This statement is perfectly valid in C++. Here the value `10` is assigned to the variable **e**. The value of the variable **e** is assigned to the variable **d**. The value of the variable **d** is then assigned to **c**. Likewise, the variable **b** will get the value of **c** and the variable **a** will get the value of **b**. As a result, all the five variables will get the same value `10`.

When the statement `a += 5` gets executed, `5` gets added to the variable **a** and the value of **a** now becomes `15`. Similarly, the other statements involving the shorthand arithmetic assignment operators change the value of the variable to the left of the operators appropriately.

3.7 INCREMENT/DECREMENT OPERATORS [++, --]

Increment operator ++ is to increment the value of a variable by one and the decrement operator -- is to decrement the value of a variable by one. The syntax of using ++ and – is as follows:

`operand++;`	Here, ++ is said to have been suffixed to the operand.
`++operand;`	Here, ++ is said to have been prefixed to the operand.
`operand--;`	Here, -- is said to have been suffixed to the operand.
`--operand;`	Here, -- is said to have been prefixed to the operand.

Suppose **a** is a variable with an initial value, say, 10. If we have to increment it by one, we will normally be inclined to use the assignment statement `a = a + 1`. Using increment operator ++ , the assignment can now be written as:

```
a++;
```

There is no difference between suffixing and prefixing ++ if `a++` and `++a` are used as independent statements as:

```
a++;
++a;
```

Both have the effect of increasing the value of **a** by 1.

But, if they are used as part of an expression, the timing of incrementation will be different. For instance,

```
b = a++;
```

Here, ++ has been suffixed to the variable **a**. As a result, the value of **a** is assigned to **b** and then **a** gets incremented, that is, assignment precedes incrementation. Now, consider the statement :

```
b = ++a;
```

Here, ++ has been prefixed to the variable **a**. As a result, **a** gets incremented first and then it is assigned to the variable **a**, that is, incrementation precedes assignment.

Similar arguments hold good with respect to decrement operator -- also. The working of Increment and decrement operators is shown in Table 3.8.

Table 3.8 Increment/Decrement Operators a = 6

Operator	*Example*	*New value of a*
++	a++	a = 7
	++a	a = 7
--	a--	a = 5
	--a	a = 5

Program 3.7 To Illustrate Increment Operators and Decrement Operators [++, --]

```
#include <iostream.h>
int main(void)
{
    int a = 10, b;

    cout << "a = " << a << endl;
    a++;
    cout << "After a++; a = " << a << endl;
    ++a;
    cout << "After ++a; a = " << a << endl;
    b = a++;
    cout << "After b = a++;" << " b = " << b << " a = " << a << endl;
    b= ++a;
    cout << "After b = ++a;" << " b = " << b << " a = " << a << endl;
    a--;
    cout << "After a--;" << "a = " << a << endl;
    --a;
    cout << "After --a;" << "a = " << a << endl;
    b = a--;
    cout << "After b = a--;" << " b = " << b << " a = " << a << endl;
    b = --a;
    cout << "After b = --a;" << " b = "<< b << " a = "<< a << endl;

    return 0;
}
```

Input-Output:

```
a = 10

After a++; a = 11
After ++a; a = 12
```

```
After b = a++; b = 12 a = 13
After b = ++a; b = 14 a = 14
After a--; a = 13
After --a; a = 12
After b = a--; b = 12 a = 11
After b = --a; b = 10 a = 10
```

3.8 CONDITIONAL OPERATOR [?:]

The conditional operator, denoted by the symbol **?:**, is an unusual operator provided by C++. It helps in two-way decision making. The general form of its usage is as follows:

```
(Expression1) ? (Expression2): (Expression3);
```

`Expression1` is evaluated. If it is true `Expression2` becomes the value otherwise `expression3` becomes the value. Since three expressions are involved, the operator is called **ternary operator**.

Program 3.8 To Illustrate Conditional Operator [?:]

```
#include <iostream.h>

int main(void)
{
    int a, b, c;

    cout << "Enter two numbers" << endl;
    cin >> a >> b;
    cout << "a = " << a << "b = " << b << endl;
    c = (a > b) ? a : b;
    cout << "Largest = " << c;

    return 0;
}
```

Input-Output:

```
Enter two numbers
6
8

a = 6  b = 8
Largest = 8
```

Explanation

In Program 3.8, the two-way decision making ability of the conditional operator is used to find out the largest of two numbers collected by the variables **a** and **b**. In the statement `c = (a > b > ? a : b;`, If the expression `a > b` evaluates to true, **a** is assigned to the variable **c**. Otherwise **b** is assigned to the variable **c**. So the variable **c** would collect the largest of the values in **a** and **b**.

3.9 THE SIZEOF( ) OPERATOR

The `sizeof()` operator is used to find the size of a variable or the size of a data type in terms of the number of bytes. The syntax of its usage is as follows:

```
sizeof(data-type)
or
sizeof(variable)
```

EXAMPLE

The `sizeof(float)` evaluates to the value four, the number of bytes required by float type variables.

```
double d;
```

The `sizeof(d)` evaluates to the value eight, the number of bytes required by the variable d, which is of double type.

Normally, `sizeof()` is used to find the size of user-defined data type.

Program 3.9 To Illustrate the Sizeof( ) Operator

```
#include <iostream.h>

int main(void)
{
    cout << "No. of Bytes occupied by:" << endl;
    cout << " char = " << sizeof(char) << endl;
    cout << "unsigned char = " << sizeof(unsigned char) << endl;
    cout << "int = " << sizeof(int) << endl;
    cout << "short int = " << sizeof(short int) << endl;
    cout << "long int = " << sizeof(long int) << endl;
    cout << "unsigned int = " << sizeof(unsigned int) << endl;
    cout << "float = " << sizeof(float) << endl;
    cout << "double = " << sizeof(double) << endl;
    cout << "long double = " << sizeof(long double) << endl;
    return 0;
}
```

Input-Output:

```
No. of Bytes occupied by:

char          = 1
unsigned char = 1
int           = 2
short int     = 2
long int      = 4
unsigned int  = 2
float         = 4
double        = 8
long double   = 10
```

3.10 THE COMMA OPERATOR [,]

The comma operator is basically used to link two related expressions. The general form of its usage in its simplest form is as follows:

```
e1, e2
```

where `e1` and `e2` are two related expressions. The expressions are evaluated from left to right, Initially `e1` is evaluated and then `e2` is evaluated. The value of the comma separated expression is the value of the right most expression, `e2` in this case, i.e., the value of the subexpression `e2` becomes the value of the whole expression `e1, e2`.

EXAMPLE

```
a = 4, b = a + 2
```

Here initially 4 is assigned to the variable **a** then the variable **b** is assigned `a + 2` i.e., `4 + 2 = 6` and `6` becomes the value of the whole expression.

If the comma separated expressions appear on the right hand side of an assignment statement, the collecting variable collects the value of the right most expression in the list of expressions.

```
a = (b = 3, c = 4 + b)
```

Here firstly, **b** is assigned 3. The value of **b** is then used to get the value of `c = 4 + 3 = 7`. The value of the right most expression, which is 7, is then assigned to the variable **a**.

Similarly, the following three related expressions separated by comma operators interchange the values of **a** and **b**,

```
a = a + b, b = a - b, a = a - b
```

Program 3.10 To Illustrate Comma Operator

```
#include <iostream.h>

int main(void)
{
    int a, b, c;
    int x = 2, y = 4, t;

    a = (b = 3, c = b + 2);
    cout << "a = " << a << "\n";

    t = x, x = y, y = t;
    cout << "x = " << x << "y = " << y;

    return 0;
}
```

Input-Output:

```
a = 5
x = 4 y = 2
```

Explanation

The expression `a = (b = 3, c = b + 2);` is evaluated as follows:

The sub-expression enclosed within the parentheses gets evaluated first. The comma separated expressions within the parentheses are evaluated from left to right. As a result, **b** is assigned 3 and then the variable **c** is assigned the sum of `b` and `2`, which is `5`. We know that the value of the right most expression in the list of comma separated expressions becomes the value of the whole expression and it is assigned to the variable **a**.

The next set of statements swap the values of **x** and **y**. Since they are related to each other during the swapping process, they are separated by commas.

3.11 BITWISE OPERATORS [&, |, ^, ~, <<, >>]

The availability of bitwise operators is another distinctive feature of the C++ language. As the name itself indicates, these operators enable us to perform manipulations over data at bit level. The ability provided by the bitwise operators to deal with data items at bit level will in turn help us to perform low level functions. These operators will work on only integers. The Table 3.9 given below shows the operators, which come under this category.

Table 3.9

Operator symbol	*Name of the operator*
&	Bitwise AND
|	Bitwise OR
^	Bitwise exclusive OR
~	Bitwise complement
<<	Bitwise left shift
>>	Bitwise right shift

Bitwise AND (&), bitwise OR (|) , bitwise exclusive OR (^), bitwise left shift (<<) and bitwise right shift (>>) are binary operators. Whereas bitwise complement (~) is unary operator.

Bitwise AND (&): The general syntax of the usage of the bitwise AND operator is as follows:

```
op1 & op2,
```

where `op1` and `op2` are integer expressions. The value of the expression would also be an integer. If the corresponding bits of `op1` and `op2` are both 1's then the bit in the corresponding position of the result would be 1, otherwise, it would be 0.

Bit1	*Bit2*	*Bit1 & Bit2*
0	0	0
0	1	0
1	0	0
1	1	1

EXAMPLE

```
int a = 4, b = 5;
```

Binary equivalent of `a`	0000 0000 0000 0100
Binary equivalent of `b`	0000 0000 0000 0101
`a & b`	0000 0000 0000 0100

Bitwise OR (|) : The general syntax of the usage of the bitwise OR operator is as follows:

```
op1 | op2,
```

where `op1` and `op2` are integer expressions. The value of the expression would also be an integer. If the corresponding bits of `op1` and `op2` are both 0's then the bit in the corresponding position of the result would be 0, otherwise, it would be `1`.

Bit1	*Bit2*	*Bit1 | Bit2*
0	0	0
0	1	1
1	0	1
1	1	1

EXAMPLE

```
int a = 4, b = 5;
```

Binary equivalent of `a`	0000 0000 0000 0100
Binary equivalent of `b`	0000 0000 0000 0101
`a	b`	0000 0000 0000 0101

The bitwise OR operator is used to set some specific bits On without affecting the other bits in the value.

Consider the bit-pattern 1000 0100 0000 0010. To turn only the third bit On without affecting other bits in the value, the value is bitwise ORed with the bit-pattern 0000 0000 0000 0100, i.e.,

0000 0000 0000 0010
0000 0000 0000 0100
0000 0000 0000 0110

Decimal equivalents of the above bit-patterns

2
4
6

Bitwise exclusive OR (^) : The general syntax of the usage of the bitwise exclusive OR operator is as follows:

```
op1 ^ op2,
```

where `op1` and `op2` are integer expressions. The value of the expression would also be an integer. If any one of the bits of `op1` and `op2` is 1 then the bit in the corresponding position of the result would be 1, otherwise, it would be 0.

Bit1	*Bit2*	*Bit1 ^ Bit2*
0	0	0
0	1	1
1	0	1
1	1	0

EXAMPLE

```
int a = 4, b = 5;
```

Binary equivalent of `a`	0000 0000 0000 0100
Binary equivalent of `b`	0000 0000 0000 0101
`a ^ b`	0000 0000 0000 0001

The bitwise exclusive OR operator is used to toggle bits.

Bitwise left shift (<<) : The bitwise left shift operator is used to shift the given number of bits of an integer towards left. The vacant positions on the right of the integer would be filled with zeros. The general syntax of its usage is as follows:

```
Operand << n
```

where `n` is the number of bits of `operand` to be shifted towards left.

EXAMPLE

```
int a = 5;
```

Binary equivalent of `a`	0000 0000 0000 0101
`a << 4`	0000 0000 0101 0000

Note: Shifting an unsigned integer to left by *n* bits has the effect of multiplying the integer by 2 to the power of *n*.

Bitwise right shift (>>): The bitwise right shift operator is used to shift the given number of bits of an integer towards right. The vacant positions on the left of the integer would be filled with zeros. The general syntax of its usage is as follows:

```
operand >> n
```

where `n` is the number of bits of `operand` to be shifted towards right.

EXAMPLE

```
int a = 5;
```

Binary equivalent of `a`	0000 0000 0000 0101
`a >> 2`	0000 0000 0000 0001

Note: Shifting an unsigned integer to right by *n* bits has the effect of dividing the integer by 2 to the power of *n*.

Bitwise complement (~): The bitwise complement operator is used to invert the bits of an integer, that is, it replaces all ones by zeros and all zeros by ones of an integer.

EXAMPLE

```
int a = 4;
```

Binary equivalent of a   0000 0000 0000 0100

~a   1111 1111 1111 1011

The bitwise complement operator ~ is used to find out the 1's complement of a number.

Program 3.11 To Illustrate Bitwise Operators [&, |, ^, ~, <<, >>]

```
#include <iostream.h>

void show_bits(int);

int main(void)
{
    int x, y, n, x_or_y, x_and_y, x_exor_y, x_lshift, x_rshift;

    cout << "Enter x and y\n";
    cin >> x >> y;
    cout << "x= "; show_bits(x);
    cout << "y = "; show_bits(y);

    x_or_y = x | y;
    cout << "x_or_y = "; show_bits(x_or_y);

    x_and_y = x & y;
    cout << "x_and_y = "; show_bits(x_and_y);

    x_exor_y = x ^ y;
    cout << "x_exor_y = "; show_bits(x_exor_y);

    cout << "Enter the no of bits to be shifted by \n";
    cin >> n;
    x_lshift = x << n;
    cout << "x_lshift = ";  show_bits(x_lshift);

    x_rshift = x >> n;
    cout << "x_rshift = "; show_bits(x_rshift);

    return 0;
}

void show_bits(int n)
{
    int i, mask, result;

    for(i = 15; i >= 0; i--)
    {
        mask = 1 << i;  /* Application of << operator */
        result = mask & n; /* Application of & operator */
        if (result != 0 )
                cout << "1";
        else
                cout << "0";
    }
    cout << "\n";
}
```

Input-Output:

```
Enter x and y
4
5

x         = 0000000000000100
y         = 0000000000000101
x_or_y    = 0000000000000101
x_and_y   = 0000000000000100
x_exor_y  = 0000000000000001

Enter the no of bits to be shifted by
2

x_lshift = 0000000000010000
x_rshift = 0000000000000001
```

Explanation

`x` and `y` are declared to be variables of `int` type. The values of these variables are subjected to the bitwise operations discussed earlier and hence they become the operands for the bitwise operators. The resultant value of each expression (constructed out of `x`, `y` and a bitwise operator) is assigned to a different variable. It is important to note that the operands `x` and `y`, and the resultant values of the bitwise operations are displayed in bit-patterns (in terms of 1's and 0's). This is to enhance better understanding of the working of the bitwise operations.

The user-defined function `show_bits()` accomplishes the task of displaying an integer value in bit-pattern, the width of the pattern is 16 bits, which is the number of bits in the size of an integer in C++. Let us now understand how this function works. The function takes an integer value *n* as its input. It employs left-shift and bitwise AND operators to accomplish the assigned task.

The following segment in the function is responsible for the said task:

```
for(i = 15; i >= 0; i--)
{
    mask = 1 << i;              /* Application of left-shift operator */
    result = n & mask;          /* Application of bitwise AND operator */
    if (result != 0 )
        cout << "1";
    else
        cout << "0";
}
```

In the **for**-loop, the loop variable `i` ranges from 15 to zero downwards. Initially, `i` takes the value 15 and the loop is entered. Inside the loop, as a result of the execution of the statement `mask = 1 << i` , the integer constant 1 (Binary equivalent 0000000000000001) is subjected to left-shift operation by 15 bits. As a result, the variable `mask` will collect the binary equivalent 1000000000000000. Note that the most significant bit in mask is 1. The value of mask is then bitwise ANDed with `n` in the statement `result = n & mask`, the result of the bitwise AND operation is assigned to the variable `result`. The value of result would be non-zero if *n* also has 1 in its most significant position of its bit-pattern. Otherwise it would be zero. The following segment:

```
if (result != 0 )
        cout << "1";
else
        cout << "0";
```

displays the numerical digit 1 if `result` is non-zero, otherwise it displays the numerical digit 0.

In the next iteration, the variable `i`, takes 14, the procedure repeats displaying the numerical digit 1 if the bit in the fourteenth position in n is 1. Otherwise displaying the numerical digit 0. This continues till the least significant bit of n is considered.

3.11.1 Application of Bitwise Operators

Turning bits off: The bitwise AND (&) operator is used to turn specific bits of a value `Off` without affecting the other bits. Consider an integer **a**. In order to turn the *n*th bit in it Off, the integer has to be bitwise ANDed with another integer whose *n*th bit is 0 and all the other bits are 1's.

EXAMPLE

Suppose the value in **a** is 5. The bit-pattern in 16-bits width is 0000 0000 0000 0101. To turn Off the third bit of the number, it has to be bitwise ANDed with another integer, which has 0 in the third bit position and all the other bit positions have 1's, i.e., 1111 1111 1111 1011. The number which has this kind of bit-pattern is ~4 (complement of 4). So, the following statement accomplishes the task of setting the third bit of the value in **a** off.

```
a = a & ~4;
```

```
  0000 0000 0000 0101
& 1111 1111 1111 1011
  -------------------
  0000 0000 0000 0001
```

Turning bits On: The bitwise OR (||) operator is used to turn On specific bits of a value without affecting the other bits. Consider an integer **a**. In order to turn the *n*th bit in it On, the integer has to be bitwise ORed with another integer whose *n*th bit is 1 and all the other bits are 0's.

EXAMPLE

Let the value of **a** be 5. The bit-pattern in 16-bits width is 0000 0000 0000 0101. To turn On the second bit of the number without affecting the other bits in it, it has to be bitwise ORed with another integer, which has 1 in the second bit position and all the other bit positions have 0's. The integer number which has this kind of bit-pattern is 2 (bit-pattern of 2 = 0000 0000 0000 0010). So, the following statement accomplishes the job of setting the second bit on:

```
a = a|2;
```

```
  0000 0000 0000 0101
| 0000 0000 0000 0010
  -------------------
  0000 0000 0000 0111
```

Toggling bits: The bitwise exclusive OR (^) operator is used to toggle bits in a value. Consider an integer **a**. In order to toggle the *n*th bit in it, the integer has to be bitwise exclusive ORed with another integer whose *n*th bit is 1 and all the other bits are 0's.

EXAMPLE

Let the value of **a** be 5. The bit-pattern in 16-bits width is 0000 0000 0000 0101. To toggle the second bit of the number without affecting the other bits in it, it has to be bitwise exclusive ORed with another integer, which has 1 in the second bit position and all the other bit positions have 0's. The integer number which has this kind of bit-pattern is 2 (Bit-pattern of 2 = 0000 0000 0000 0010). So, the following statement accomplishes the job of setting the second bit on:

```
a = a ^ 2;
```

```
  0000 0000 0000 0101
^ 0000 0000 0000 0010
  0000 0000 0000 0111
```

To check whether a bit is On or Off: Suppose **a** is an integer. To check whether the *n*th bit of **a** is On or Off, we take another integer, say, b, which has 1 in its *n*th bit position and all the other bits are 0's and we bitwise AND **a** with **b**. If the result of the operation is **b** itself then we can say that the *n*th bit in **a** is On. Otherwise, it is Off.

Precisely, the *n*th bit in **a** is On if the expression ((a & b) == b) evaluates to true. Otherwise, it is Off.

EXAMPLE

The following segment of code checks whether the least significant bit in **a** is On or Off.

```
if (( a & 1) == 1)
    cout << ("The least significant bit is on";
else
    cout << "The least significant bit is off";
```

3.12 OTHER SPECIAL OPERATORS

Table 3.10 contains the special operators supported by C++ and their purposes:

Table 3.10

Operator	*Purpose*
::	Scope resolution operator
::*	Pointer to member decelerator
->*	Pointer to member operator
.*	Pointer to member operator
new	Memory allocation operator
delete	Memory deallocation operator
endl	Line feed operator
setw	Field width operator

These operators will be discussed later at the appropriate places.

3.13 TYPE CONVERSION

We are now aware of the fact that C++ is rich in data types. It allows an expression to have data items of different types. It is quite interesting to understand how an expression gets evaluated and what the type of the expression would be.

Conversion takes place at two instances:

(a) At the time of evaluation of an expression. Whenever an expression has two data items which are of different types. Lower type gets converted into higher type. The result of the expression will be in higher type mode.

(b) At the time of assignment of the value of an expression or source variable to a target variable. The value of the expression on the right hand side of an assignment statement gets converted into the type of the variable collecting it.

The hierarchy of data types in the increasing order is:

`char` - the lowest data type
`short`
`int`
`unsigned`
`long`
`float`
`double`
`long double` - the highest data type

EXAMPLE

```
int a = 10;
float f = 3.4;
```

Let us consider the expression `a + f`. The variable **a** is of `int` type and `f` is of `float` type. Since `float` is the dominating type. The value of `a` gets converted into `float` type first and then the summation proceeds. The sum also turns out to be of `float` type.

`a + f`

`= 10 + 3.4`

`= 10.0 + 3.4`   `10` gets converted into 10.0

`= 13.4`

Now, consider the assignment statement `a1 = a + f;` where **`a1`** is a variable of `int` type. The Right hand side of the assignment statement gets evaluated to `13.4`. But the variable `a1` on the Left hand side collects only `13` since it is a variable of `int` type.

```
a1 = a + f
a1 = 13.4
a1 = 13
```

If the collecting variable **`a1`** were of **`float`** type, it would have collected the exact result.

Under some circumstances, automatic type conversion does not work out for us. For instance, consider the arithmetic expression `5/2`. In C++, the value of this expression would be 2. Since both 5 and 2 are integers, the result of the expression would also be of `int` type. This is according to the rules of automatic type conversion. But the exact result of this expression is 2.5. How do we get it? *Type casting* or *forcible conversion* is the answer to this.

Forcible conversion or type casting: The general form of casting a value is as follows:

`(type-name) Expression`

The type-name is any data type supported by C++ or any user-defined type and expression may be a single variable, constant or an expression itself. By using the type-name, we are forcibly converting the type of the expression to type-name specified.

EXAMPLE

`(float) 5/2`	will now evaluate to 2.5 as follows:
`= 5.0 / 2`	The operator float forcibly converts 5 to 5.0
`= 5.0/2.0`	Now, automatic conversion takes over. The denominator 2 also gets converted to 2.0
`= 2.5`	The result of the expression 5.0/2.0 would then be a float value 2.5.

Program 3.12 To Illustrate Automatic Conversion and Forcible Conversion

```
#include <iostream.h>

int main(void)
{
    int i = 10, j;
    float f = 8.5, g;

    j = f;
    cout << "j = " << j << endl;

    g = i;
    cout << "g = " << g << endl;

    j = 5 / 2;
    cout << "j = 5 / 2 = " << j << endl;

    j = 5.0 / 2;
    cout << "j = 5.0 / 2 = " << j << endl;

    g = 5 / 2;
    cout << "g = 5 / 2 = " << g << endl;

    g = 5.0 / 2;
    cout << "g = 5.0 / 2 = " << g << endl;
    g = (float)5/2;
    cout << "(float)5 / 2 = " << g << endl;
    return 0;
}
```

Input-Output:

```
j = 8
g = 10
j= 5 / 2 = 2
j = 5.0 / 2 = 2
g = 5 / 2 = 2
g = 5.0 / 2 = 2.5
(float)5 / 2 = 2.5
```

Explanation

In the assignment statement `i1 = f;` the source variable **`f`** is of type `float` and the target variable **`i1`** is of `int` type so, the variable **`i1`** would collect only the integral part of **`f`**.

In the assignment statement `f1 = i;` the source variable **`i`** is of `int` type and the target variable **`f1`** is of `float` type so, the variable **`f1`** would collect the value of **`i`** with fractions.

Upon execution of the statement `i1 = 5 / 2;`, the variable **i1** would collect only 2 since both 5 and 2, the operands to / operator are integers. Upon execution of the statement `i1 = 5.0/2`, even though the RHS of the statement produces exact result of division 2.5, the variable **`i1`** being of `integer` type could collect only 2. As a result of the execution of the statement `f = 5/2`, the variable is assigned 2.0. But upon execution of the statements `f = 5.0/2` and `f = (float) 5/2`, the variable **`f`** could collect the exact result of division of 5 by 2.

In general, the following rules apply in sequence during the automatic conversion:

Operands of type `char` or `short int` type are by default converted into `int` type.

In an expression having two data items of different types

- If one of the operands is of `long double` type, the other will also be converted to `long double`. The result of the expression is of type `long double`.
- Otherwise, if one of the operands is of `double` type, the other will also be converted to `double`. The result of the expression is of type `double`.
- Otherwise, if one of the operands is of `float` type, the other will also be converted to `float`. The result of the expression is of type `float`.
- Otherwise, if one of the operands is of `unsigned long int` type, the other will also be converted to `unsigned long int`. The result of the expression is of type `unsigned long int`.
- Otherwise, if one of the operands is of `unsigned int` type and the other is of type `long int` then, there are two cases:
  (a) If `unsigned int` can be converted into `long int`, the `unsigned int` is converted into `long int` and the result will also be of `long int` type.
  (b) Otherwise, both are converted into `unsigned long int` and the result will also be of `unsigned long int`.
- Otherwise, if one of the operands is of `long int` type, the other will also be converted to `long int`. The result of the expression is of type `long int`.
- Otherwise, if one of the operands is of `unsigned int` type, the other will also be converted to `unsigned int`. The result of the expression is of type `unsigned int`.

3.14 PRECEDENCE LEVELS AND ASSOCIATIVITY AMONG ALL THE OPERATORS

Precedence	*Operators*	*Associativity*
1.	::	Left to right
2.	-> . () [] postfix ++ postfix --	Left to right
3.	Prefix ++ prefix -- ~ ! unary + unary – Unary * unary & (type) sizeof new delete	Right to left
4.	->* .*	Left to right
5.	* / %	Left to right
6.	+ –	Left to right
7.	<< >>	Left to right
8.	< <= > >=	Left to right
9.	== !=	Left to right
10.	&	Left to right
11.	^	Left to right
12.	|	Left to right
13.	&&	Left to right
14.	||	Left to right
15.	?:	Left to right
16.	= += –= *= /= %= <<= >>= &= ^= |=	Right to left
17.	, comma	Left to right

REVIEW QUESTIONS

3.1 What is an operator?

3.2 C++ is rich in operators. Justify.

3.3 What is an arithmetic expression? Mention different types of arithmetic expressions.

3.4 What do you mean by the terms precedence and associativity?

3.5 Give an account of precedence and associativity of arithmetic operators.

3.6 Why do we use relational operators? List out them in C++.

3.7 What is a relational expression? Give an example.

3.8 Give an account of precedence and associativity of relational operators.

3.9 What is the significance of logical operators? List out logical operators in C++.

3.10 Explain the working of logical && operator.

3.11 Explain the working of logical || operator.

3.12 What is the use of logical ! operator?

3.13 Give an account of precedence and associativity of logical operators.

3.14 Differentiate between prefixing and suffixing ++ to a variable.

3.15 Give an account of shorthand arithmetic assignment operators.

3.16 Why do we use conditional operator? Why is it called a ternary operator?

3.17 Write the output of the following programs:

(a)
```
int main(void)
{
    int a = 4, b = 6, c = 7, d;

    d = a + b * c;
    cout << d;

    return 0;
}
```

(b)
```
int main(void)
{
    int a = 4, b = 5, c = 7, d;

    d = (a - b) / c;
    cout << d;

    return 0;
}
```

(c)
```
int main(void)
{
    int a = 4, b = 5, c;
```

```
    c = a < b + 10;
    cout << c;

    return 0;
}
```

(d)
```
int main(void)
{
    int a;

    a = 4 > 5 && 5 > 3;
    cout << a;

    return 0;
}
```

(e)
```
int main(void)
{
    int a = 10, b = 6, c;

    c = a++ + b;
    cout << c;
    c = ++a + b;
    cout << c;

    return 0;
}
```

(f)
```
int main(void)
{
    int a = 10, b = 6, c;

    c = a++ + b + a++;
    cout << c;
    c = ++ a + b ++a;
    cout << a;

    return 0;
}
```

(g)
```
int main(void)
{
    int a = 5;

    cout << a++ << a++ << a++;
    cout << a << a++ << ++a;

    return 0;
}
```

(h)
```
int main(void)
{
    int a = 5;
    cout << ++a << ++a << ++a;

    return 0;
}
```

PROGRAMMING EXERCISES

P3.1 Write a program to accept no. of seconds and display its equivalent no. of hours, no. of minutes and no. of seconds. (**Hint:** Use / and % operators.)

P3.2 Write a program to find the area and circumference of a circle, given its radius r.

Area = $3.14 * r^2$ Circumference = $2 * 3.14 * r$

P3.3 Write a program to accept the length and the breadth of a rectangle and display its area and perimeter. The area is given by the product of the length and the breadth, the perimeter is twice the sum of the length and the breadth.

P3.4 If a and b are two numbers, find out the values of $(a + b)^2$ and $a^2 + b^2 + 2ab$.

P3.5 If a and b are two numbers, find out the values of $(a - b)^2$ and $a^2 + b^2 - 2ab$.

P3.6 Write a program to find the value of s, the distance travelled by an object.

$s = u * t + 0.5 * a * t^2$

where u is the initial velocity, t is the time taken and a is the acceleration.

P3.7 Write a program to find the value of v, the final velocity.

$v^2 = u^2 - 2 * a * s$

P3.8 Write a program to calculate net salary of an employee given his basic pay.

Allowances

DA	45%
HRA	14%
CCA	10%

Deductions

PF	12%
LIC	15%

All the allowances are based on basic pay.

Gross salary = Basic pay + Allowances

Net salary = Gross salary – Deductions

P3.9 Write a program to find the largest of three numbers using conditional operator.

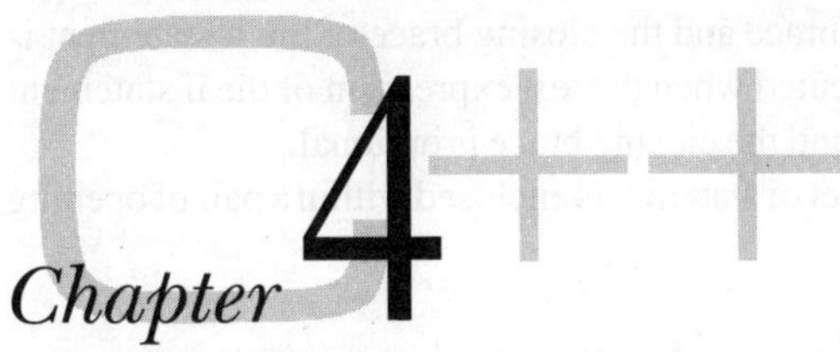

Chapter 4

Selection

4.1 INTRODUCTION

The common thing shared by all the programs written so far is that in each of the programs, all the statements from the first statement till the last statement get executed without fail in a serial manner. That is, one after the other. This kind of execution of statements in a program is called **sequential execution**.

As we proceed towards the real programming world, we do realize that the circumstances which can not be implemented using only **sequential execution** are in plenty. These programming circumstances require selecting some statements for execution if some condition is satisfied; skipping the block of statements if the condition is not satisfied. Thereby resulting in a change in the order of execution of statements. To be precise, selection of some statements for execution depends on whether a condition is true or false. This kind of execution of statements is called conditional execution or selection.

For instance, suppose we have to write a program to find whether a number *n* is divisible by 5 or not. The program written for this purpose will have the statement `r = n % 5`. We know that % is to get the remainder after division of one number by another. Here, the value of *r* determines whether *n* is evenly divisible by 5 or not. The program should thus check the value of *r*. If it finds that *r* takes 0, it should display that *n* is divisible by 5. If *r* takes a non-zero value, the program should display that the number is not divisible by 5. As seen, there is decision-making involved in the program.

C++ provides built-in decision-making structures to implement conditional execution in the form of `if statement and its variations`, `switch` statement and conditional operator. Let us now try to follow the syntax of each of these and illustrate each of these with example programs.

4.2 THE SIMPLE-IF STATEMENT

The syntax of **`if`** statement in its simplest form is as follows:

```
if (test-expression)
{
   statements;
}
```

This is known as **simple-if** statement. The test-expression can be a relational expression, a logical expression or any other expression which evaluates to a non-zero (true) value or zero (false). The statements enclosed within the braces get executed when the test-expression evaluates to true. Otherwise they will simply be skipped. The control gets transferred to the statement after the closing brace of the `if`-statement.

The set of statements enclosed within the opening brace and the closing brace of the if statement is called the **if-block**. If only one statement is to be executed when the test expression of the if statement evaluates to true, enclosing it within the opening brace and the closing brace is optional.

A single statement is called a **simple statement**. A set of statements enclosed within a pair of opening and closing braces is called a **compound statement**.

EXAMPLE 1

```
if (a == b)
    cout << " a and b are equal";
```

If the values of the variables **a** and **b** are same then only the cout statement gets executed. Otherwise, it is skipped.

EXAMPLE 2

```
if ((a > b) && (a > c))
    cout << "a is the largest":
```

If the value of the variable **a** is greater than the values of both **b** and **c** then only the cout gets executed. Otherwise, the statement is skipped.

EXAMPLE 3

```
if (n % 2)
    cout <<"n is odd";
```

If the value of the variable n is not divisible by 2, i.e., if the remainder after division of n by two is one, then only the cout statement gets executed. Otherwise, the cout statement gets executed.

EXAMPLE 4

```
if ( a > b)
{
    t = a;
    a = b;
    b = t;
}
```

If the value of **a** is greater than the value of **b** then only the statements within the pair of braces get executed. Otherwise, the statements are skipped.

To find whether a number is even or odd:

Input: A number, *n*

Output: Whether *n* is even or odd.

if *n* is divisible by 2, it is even. If *n* is not divisible by 2, it is odd.

Program 4.1 To Find Whether a Number is Even or Odd

```
#include <iostream.h>

int main(void)
{
   int number, rem;

   cout << "Enter a number" << endl;
   cin >> number;

   rem = number % 2;
   if (rem == 0)
      cout << number << "is even" << endl;

   if (rem != 0)
      cout << number << "is odd" << endl;
   return 0;
}
```

Input-Output:

```
Enter a number
5
5 is odd
```

Explanation

number and **rem** are declared to be variables of `int` type. **number** is to collect a number (input). **rem** is to collect the remainder after division of **number** by 2.

If the relational expression (**rem** = 0) evaluates to true, which means **number** is evenly divisible by 2 then we display that **number** is even. If the relational expression (**rem** != 0) evaluates to true, which means **number** is not evenly divisible by 2 then we display that **number** is odd.

To find the largest of three numbers:

`Input:` Three numbers *a, b c*
`Output:` The largest of *a, b* and *c*

Program 4.2 To Find the Largest of Three Numbers

```
#include <iostream.h>

int main(void)
{
   int a, b, c, largest;

   cout << "Enter three numbers" << endl;
   cin >> a >> b >> c;

// Finding the largest begins

   largest = a;

   if (b > largest)
      largest = b;
```

```
    if (c > largest)
        largest = c;

// Finding the largest ends

    cout << "a = " << a << "b = " << b << "c = " << c << endl;
    cout << "Largest = " << largest;
    return 0;
}
```

Input-Output:

```
Enter three numbers
5
7
8

a = 5 b = 7 c = 8
Largest = 8
```

Explanation

a, **b**, **c**, and **largest** are declared to be variables of `int` type. The variables **a**, **b** and **c** are to collect three numbers (inputs). The variable **largest** is to collect the largest of the three numbers (output).

We accept the values of three numbers into the variables **a**, **b** and **c**. In the process of finding out the largest of **a**, **b** and **c**, we start with the assumption that **a** is the largest and assign it to the variable **largest**. We then check if **b** is greater than **largest**. If it is, we assign **b** to **largest**. We then check if **c** is greater than **largest**. If it is, we assign **c** to **largest**. Eventually **largest** collects the largest of **a**, **b** and **c**.

Variations of if-statement: It is obvious that the `simple-if` statement would not suffice to implement selection which involve complex conditions. In such situations, the following variations of the if-statement can be used:

1. The if-else statement
2. The nested if-else statement
3. The else-if ladder

We will now discuss the syntax and illustrate each of these variations by means of suitable programming examples.

4.3 THE IF-ELSE STATEMENT

The syntax of the if-else statement is as follows:

```
if (test-expression)
{
    statements-1;
}
else
{
    statements-2;
}
```

If test-expression evaluates to true, `statements-1` will be executed, and `statements-2` will be skipped. On the other hand, if it evaluates to false, `statements-2` will get executed, `statements-1` will be skipped. Thus, `if-else` structure acts as a selector of one block of statements out of two blocks.

The set of statements enclosed within the braces following `if` is called `if-block` and the set of statements enclosed within the braces following `else` is called `else-block`.

EXAMPLE 1

```
if(a > b )
    cout << "a is larger than b";
else
    cout << "a is not larger than b";
```

If *a* is greater than *b* then the message "*a* is larger than *b*" will be displayed, otherwise the message "*a* is not larger than *b*" will be displayed.

EXAMPLE 2

```
if (n % 2)
    cout << "n is odd";
else
    cout << "n is even";
```

Here if *n*% 2 evaluates to true "*n* is odd" is displayed. Otherwise "*n* is even" is displayed.

Program 4.3 To Illustrate if-else Statement

```
#include <iostream.h>

int main(void)
{
    int number, rem;

    cout << "Enter a number" << endl;
    cin >> number;

    rem = number % 2;
    if (rem == 0)
        cout << number << "is even";
    else
        cout << number << "is odd";
    return 0;
}
```

Input-Output:

```
Enter a number
4

4 is even
```

Explanation

In Program 4.3, **number** and **rem** are declared to be variables of `int` type. The variable **number** is to collect a number (input); **rem** is to collect the remainder after division of **number** by 2. The value of **rem** determines whether **number** is even or odd. If (`rem == 0`) evaluates to true then **number** is displayed as even. Otherwise (else part of if) **number** is displayed as odd.

Finding whether a year is a leap year or not: A leap year is one which has 366 days in it. In the month of February of the year, the no. of days would be 29. We say that a year is a leap year if it is evenly divisible by 400 or if it is evenly divisible by 4 but not by 100.

Program 4.4 To Find Whether a Year is a Leap Year or Not

```
#include <iostream.h>

int main(void)
{
    int year, r4, r100, r400;

    cout << "Enter a year" << endl;
    cin >> year;

    r4 = year % 4;
    r100 = year % 100;
    r400 = year % 400;

    if (( r4 == 0) && (r100 != 0) || (r400 == 0))
        cout << year << "is a leap year";
    else
        cout << year << "is not a leap year";
    return 0;
}
```

Input-Output:

First Run:

```
Enter a year
1998
1998 is not a leap year
```

Second Run:

```
Enter a year
1900
1900 is not a leap year
```

Third Run:

```
Enter a year
2000
2000 is a leap year
```

Explanation

year, r4, r100 and **r400** are declared to be variables of `int` type. The variable **year** is to collect year number (input); **r4, r100** and **r400** are to collect the remainders after division of **year** by 4, 100 and 400 respectively.

After accepting year number into the variable **year**, the variables **r4, r100** and **r400** are assigned the remainders after division of **year** by 4 , 100 and 400 respectively. If **year** is divisible by 4 but not by 100 or divisible by 400 alone , the year is displayed as leap year. Otherwise it is displayed as not leap year.

4.4 THE NESTED IF-ELSE STATEMENT

We now know that if execution of a block of statements is conditional, we can use one `if` statement. What if the conditional execution of the block of statements is itself conditional. Here, we need to enclose one `if` statement within another `if` statement. On the similar lines, we can even enclose on `if-else` within another `if-else`. If one `if-else` is enclosed within another `if-else`, the resulting structure is called `nested if-else`. The syntax of nested if-else is as follows:

```
if (test-expression1)
{
    if (test-expression2)
    {
        statements-1;
    }
    else
    {
        statements-2;
    }
}
else
{
    statements-3;
}
```

Here, one `if-else` is enclosed within another `if-else`. The if structure, which encloses another is called **`outer-if`**. The if structure, which is enclosed within another is called **`inner-if`**.

Statements-1, statements-2 and statements-3 are three blocks of statements. Selection of one of these blocks of statements for execution proceeds as follows.

First, test-expression 1 is checked. If it evaluates to true, test-expression 2 is checked. If test-expression 2 also evaluates to true then `statements-1` would get executed. If test-expression 2 evaluates to false then else-block of the inner-if , `statements-2` would get executed. If test-expression 1 itself evaluates to false then the else-block of the outer-if, `statements-3` would get executed. Thus, this variation acts as a selector of one out of three blocks of statements.

EXAMPLE 1

```
if ( a >= b)
    if (a > b)
        cout << "a is larger than b";
    else
        cout << "a and b are equal";
else
    cout << "a is less than b";
```

The segment finds out the relationship between the values *a* and *b*.

Program 4.5 To Illustrate Nested If Statement

```
#include <iostream.h>

int main(void)
{
    int number;
    cout << "Enter a number" << endl;
    cin >> number;
    if (number <= 0)
        if (number < 0)
            cout << number << "is negative";
        else
            cout << "Zero";
    else
        cout << number << "is positive";
    return 0;
}
```

Input-Output:

First Run:

```
Enter a number
5
5 is positive
```

Second Run:

```
-9
-9 is negative
```

Explanation

The variable **number** is declared to be of `int` type. It is to collect a number (input). We accept a number into the variable **number**. We then use `nested-if-else` to find whether **number** is positive, negative or zero. If the test expression in the `outer-if`, **(number <= 0)** evaluates to true then the test expression in the `inner-if`, **(number < 0)** is checked; if **(number < 0)** also evaluates to true then **number** is displayed as negative. If **(number < 0)** evaluates to false then **number** is displayed as zero. If the test expression of the `outer-if`, **(number <= 0)** itself evaluates to false, the inner-if condition is not checked at all; **number** is displayed as positive.

Program 4.6 To Illustrate Nested If Statement

```
#include <iostream.h>

int main(void)
{
    int a, b, c, largest;

    cout << "Enter three numbers" << endl;
    cin >> a >> b >> c;
```

```
   if (a > b)
   {
      if (a > c)
         largest = a;
      else
         largest = c;
   }
   else
   {
      if (b > c)
         largest = b;
      else
         largest = c;
   }
   cout << "a = " << a << "b = " << b<< "c = " << c << endl;
   cout << "Largest = " << largest;
   return 0;
}
```

Input-Output:

```
Enter three numbers
3
4
5

a = 3b = 4c = 5
Largest = 5
```

4.5 THE ELSE-IF LADDER

The else-if ladder helps select one out of many alternative blocks of statements for execution depending on the mutually exclusive conditions. The syntax of the else-if ladder is as follows:

```
if (test-expression1)
{
   statements-1;
}
else if (test-expression2)
{
   statements-2;
}
else if (test-expression3)
{
   statements-3;
}
:

else if (test-expression-n)
{
   statements-n;
}
```

```
else
                              {
    statements;
                              }
```

Here test-expression 1, test-expression 2….test-expression-*n* are mutually exclusive. That is, only one test-expression of all will be true. There are $n + 1$ blocks of statements.

Initially, test-expression 1 is checked. If it is true, the block of statements `statements-1` would get executed; all the other blocks of statements would be skipped. If test-expression1 is false, test-expression 2 is checked. If it is true, the block of statements `statements-2` would get executed; all the other statements would be skipped. If test-expression 2 is false, test-expression 3 is checked. If it is true, `statements-3` would get executed; all the other statements would be skipped. This continues. In general, *i*th test-expression is checked only when first *i*-1 test-expressions evaluate to false. If none of the expressions is found to be true, the last block of statements would get executed. Thus, `else-if` ladder acts as a selector of one out of $n + 1$ blocks of statements.

Program 4.7 To Find Whether a Number is +ve, –ve or Zero

```
#include <iostream.h>

int main(void)
{
    int number;

    cout << "Enter a number" << endl;
    cin >> number;

/* Finding whether the given number is +ve, -ve or zero begins */

    if (number > 0)
        cout << number << "is positive";
    else if (number < 0)
            cout << number << "is negative";
            else
            cout << "zero";

/* Finding whether the given number is +ve, -ve or zero ends */
    return 0;
}
```

Input-Output:

First-Run:

```
Enter a number
3
3 is positive
```

Second-Run:

```
Enter a number
-4
-4 is negative
```

Explanation

The **number** is declared to be a variable of `int` type. It is to collect a number, the input required by the program.

We accept a number into the variable **number**. To find whether the number entered is positive , negative or zero, we have used else-if ladder. We first check if the number is greater than zero. If it is, then we display that the number is positive. If the number is not greater than zero then only, we check whether it is less than zero. If it is, then we display that the number is negative. If the number is not found to be negative, the default option, it is displayed as zero.

Program 4.8 To Find the Largest of Three Numbers

```
#include <iostream.h>

int main()
{
    int a, b, c, largest;

    cout << "Enter three numbers" << endl;
    cin >> a >> b >> c;

/* Finding the largest begins */

    if ((a > b) && (a > c))
        largest = a;
        else if ((b > a) && (b > c))
            largest = b;
            else
            largest = c;

/* Finding the largest ends */

    cout << "a = " << a << "b = " << b << "c = " << c <<endl;
    cout << "Largest = " << largest;
    return 0;
}
```

```
Input-Output:
Enter three numbers
4
5
6

a = 4 b = 5 c = 6
Largest = 6
```

Explanation

The integer variables **a**, **b** and **c** are to collect the three numbers (inputs), the largest of which is to be found out. The variable **largest** is to collect the largest of the numbers **a**, **b** and **c**.

The program uses the else-if ladder to accomplish the task. If the value in **a** is greater than the values in both **b** and **c**, **a** is assigned to the variable **largest**; if **a** is not greater than both **b** and **c**, **b** is checked against the values of both **a** and **c** . If the value in **b** is greater than the values in both **a** and **c**, **b** is assigned to the variable **largest**. Otherwise the variable **c** is assigned to the variable **largest**. The value of the variable **largest** is then displayed .

Program 4.9 To Accept a Digit and Display it in Word

```
#include <iostream.h>

int main(void)
{
    int digit;

    cout << "Enter a digit" << endl;
    cin >> digit;

    if (digit == 0)
        cout << "Zero";
    else if (digit == 1)
            cout << "One";
    else if (digit == 2)
            cout << "Two";
    else if (digit == 3)
        cout << "Three";
    else if (digit == 4)
        cout << "Four";
    else if (digit == 5)
        cout << "Five";
    else if (digit == 6)
        cout << "Six";
    else if (digit == 7)
        cout << "Seven";
    else if (digit == 8)
        cout << "Eight";
    else if (digit == 9)
        cout << "Nine";
    else
        cout << "Not a digit";
        return 0;
}
```

Input-Output:

First Run:

```
Enter a digit
4
Four
```

Second Run:

```
Enter a digit
5
Five
```

Explanation

`digit` is declared to be a variable of `int` type. It is to collect a digit, the input required by the program.

We accept a digit into the variable and use a series of conditions to match its content with the digits (0, 1 ,2, etc). If matching is found then the digit is displayed in word. Note that anything other than a digit accepted into the variable **digit** causes the program to report that input entered is not a digit. (Even in the case of multiple digit number).

Program 4.10 To Grade a Student

```
#include <iostream.h>

int main(void)
{
   int m1, m2, m3, m4, m5, flag;
   float percent;

   cout << "Enter marks in five subjects" << endl;
   cin >> m1 >> m2 >> m3 >> m4 >> m5;

   cout << "m1 = " << m1 << "\n";
   cout << "m2 = " << m2 << "\n";
   cout << "m3 = " << m3 << "\n";
   cout << "m4 = " << m4 << "\n";
   cout << "m5 = " << m5 << "\n";

   flag = 1;

   if (m1 < 35)
   {
      cout << "Failed in subject1";
      flag = 0;
   }

   if (m2 < 35)
   {
      cout << "Failed in subject2";
      flag = 0;
   }

   if (m3 < 35)
   {
      cout << "Failed in subject3";
      flag = 0;
   }

   if (m4 < 35)
   {
      cout << "Failed in subject4";
      flag = 0;
   }

   if (m5 < 35)
```

```
    {
      cout << "Failed in subject5";
      flag = 0;
    }
    if (flag)
    {
      percent = (float) (m1 + m2 + m3 + m4 + m5) / 5;
      cout << "Percentage = " << percent << "%" << "\n";

      if (percent < 50)
        cout << "Grade : Just Pass";
      else if (percent < 60)
        cout << "Grade : Second class";
      else if (percent < 70)
        cout << "Grade : First class";
      else
        cout << "Grade : Outstanding";
    }
    return 0;
}
```

Input-Output:

```
Enter marks in five subjects
67 78 89 98 95

m1 = 67
m2 = 78
m3 = 89
m4 = 98
m5 = 95

Percentage = 85.400002%
Grade : Outstanding
```

Explanation

m1, m2, m3, m4, m5 and **flag** are declared to be variables of `int` type. The variable **percent** is declared to be a variable of type **float. m1, m2, m3, m4** and **m5** are to collect marks scored by a student in five subjects. The variable **flag** acts as a boolean variable and is used to find whether the student has scored minimum passing marks in each subject or not. **percent** is to collect the percentage of marks.

We accept marks scored by a student in five subjects into the variables **m1, m2, m3, m4** and **m5**. Before grading the student, we first verify whether he has scored passing marks (35) in all the five subjects or not. We use the variable **flag** for this purpose. We start with the assumption that he has passed in all the subjects and assign 1 to **flag**. Each of the subject marks is then checked. If the marks in a subject is below 35 then we display the message that he has failed in the subject and **flag** is set to 0.

If the variable **flag** retains 1, which means that the student has passed in all the five subjects, then only we grade him as just passed, Second class, First class or Outstanding depending on the percentage of marks.

4.6 THE SWITCH STATEMENT

When we need to select one block of statements out of two alternatives, we use `if-else` structure. When we are to select one block of statements for execution out of *n* blocks of statements and associated with each block of statements is a condition and all conditions being mutually exclusive, we tend to use `else-if ladder`. Since the conditions are mutually exclusive, only one condition would evaluate to true at any point of time resulting in the selection of the corresponding block of statements. Even though the programming situation is implementable using else-if ladder, the code becomes more complex when the no. of conditions increase since the degree of readability decreases. Fortunately C++ provides **`switch`** structure, an alternative to else-if ladder, which simplifies the code and enhances readability when we need to implement problems which involve selection of one out of many alternatives.

Syntax of **`switch`** structure is:

```
switch (expression)
{
    case v1:
        statements-1;
        break;
    case v2:
        statements-2;
        break;
        .
        .
    case vn:
        statements-3;
        break;

    default:
        statements;
        break;
}
```

Here, expression is an integer or char expression. It evaluates to either an integer or a character. *v*1, v2, …., *vn* are the case labels. The expression of the switch statement can take any of the case labels. If it takes v_1, `statements-1` will get executed and the break statement following it causes the skipping of the switch structure. The control goes to the statement following the closing brace of the switch structure. If the expression takes *v*2, the corresponding block of statements `statements-2` will get executed and the switch statement is exited and so on. The block of statements to be executed depends on the value taken by the expression. If none of the values is taken by the expression, the statements following the default option will get executed. Thus, the switch statement acts as selector of one block out of many blocks of statements.

Points to remember:

- The case labels should not be float values or boolean expressions.
- The case labels *v*1, *v*2, …, *vn* should be distinct.
- The order of their presence is immaterial.
- After each case, there should be a break statement.
- Default case is optional.

Program 4.11 To Accept a Digit and Display it in Word

```
#include <iostream.h>

int main(void)
```

```
{
   int digit;

   cout << "Enter a number" << endl;
   cin >> digit;

   switch(digit)
   {
       case 0:
          cout << "Zero";
          break;
       case 1:
          cout << "One";
          break;
       case 2:
          cout << "Two";
          break;
       case 3:
          cout << "Three";
          break;
       case 4:
          cout << "Four";
          break;
       case 5:
          cout << "Five";
          break;
       case 6:
          cout << "Six";
          break;
       case 7:
          cout << "Seven";
          break;
       case 8:
          cout << "Eight";
          break;
       case 9:
          cout << "Nine";
          break;
       default:
          cout << "Not a digit";
   }
   return 0;
}
```

Input-Output:

First Run:
```
Enter a digit
4
Four
```

Second Run:
```
Enter a digit
5
Five
```

Explanation

The variable `digit` is declared to be a variable of `int` type and it is to collect a decimal digit (input). During the course of the execution of the program, a digit is accepted into the variable. The variable `digit` forms the expression of the switch structure used in the program. (The expression evaluates to an integer constant) The expression's value is first checked against 0, the label of the first case. If a match takes place, the string "Zero" is displayed by the cout statement corresponding to the label and the `break` statement following it will cause the control of the program to be transferred to the first statement after the closing brace of the `switch` structure. If the expression's value does not match with 0, then it is checked against 1. If a match takes place, the string "One" is displayed and the control is transferred to the first statement after the closing brace of the switch structure. This continues. If none of the values match with the value of the expression then the statements under `default` option would get executed

Program 4.12 To Illustrate Switch Structure

```
#include <iostream.h>
#include <stdio.h>

int main(void)
{
   int a, b, sum, diff, product, rem;
   float quotient;
   char op;

   cout << "Enter two numbers" << endl;
   cin >> a >> b;
   fflush(stdin);
   cout << "Enter an operator" << endl;
   op = getchar();

   switch(op)
   {
      case '+':
         sum = a + b;
         cout << " Sum = " << sum;
         break;
      case '-':
         diff = a - b;
         cout << " Difference = " << diff;
         break;
      case '*':
         product = a * b;
         cout << " Product = " << product;
         break;
      case '/':
         quotient = (float) a / b;
         cout << " Quotient = " << quotient;
         break;
      case '%':
         rem = a % b;
```

```
        cout << " Remainder = " << rem;
        break;
      default:
        cout << "Not a valid operator";
   }

   return 0;
}
```

Input-Output:

First Run:

```
Enter two numbers
6 8

Enter an operator
*
Product = 48
```

Second Run:

```
Enter two numbers
6 7

Enter an operator
+
Sum = 13
```

Explanation

In Program 4.12, a and b are declared to be variables of int type, and op is declared to be a variable of char type. a and b are to collect two numbers and op is to collect an arithmetic operator [+, –, *, /, %]. The variable op forms the expression of the switch structure and it evaluates to a character constant.

During the course of the execution of the program, two numbers are accepted into the variables a and b. An arithmetic operator is accepted into the variable op. Within the switch structure, depending on the operator, the corresponding block of statements would be executed, which display the result of the arithmetic expression after which the control is transferred to the first statement after the closing brace of the switch structure. If none of the case labels match with the value of the expression then the default option gets executed.

In the example programs, we observed that for each case label, there is a separate block of statements. That is, there is one-to-one mapping between the case labels and blocks of statements. When the expression value matches with a case label, the corresponding block of statements would get executed. In addition to this, switch statement enables us to execute a common block of statements for more than one case label value.

Program 4.13 To Accept a Month Number and Display the Maximum No. of Days in the Month

```
#include <iostream.h>

int main(void)
{
   int month, days;
```

```
    cout << "Enter month number" << endl;
    cin >> month;
    switch(month)
{
    case 1:
    case 3:
    case 5:
    case 7:
    case 8:
    case 10:
    case 12: days = 31;
             break;

    case 4:
    case 6:
    case 9:
    case 11:
             days = 30;
             break;
    case 2:
        days = 28;
        break;
    default:
        cout << " Not a valid month number ";
 }
cout << " Maximum no. of days in" << month << "=" << days;
return 0;
}
```

Input-Output:

First Run:

```
Enter month number
4
Maximum no. of days in month 4 = 30
```

Second Run:

```
Enter month number
1
Maximum no. of days in month 1 = 31
```

Third Run:

```
Enter month number
2
Maximum no. of days in month 2 = 28
```

Explanation

In Program 4.13, `month` and days are declared to be variables of `int` type. The variable `month` is to collect the month number (input) of a year [`1-12`] and **`days`** is to collect the number of days in the given month. The variable `month` forms the expression of the switch structure used in the program and it evaluates to an integer constant.

During the course of the execution of the program, month value is accepted. Within the switch structure, the value of month is checked against `1, 3, 5, 7, 8, 10, 12` in a serial manner. If the value of the expression matches with any of these then the variable days is assigned `31`. This segment of the switch structure is equivalent to the following if statement:

```
if ( (month ==1) || (month == 3) || (month == 5) ||(month == 7)|| (month == 8)
||(month == 10)|| (month == 12))
    days = 31;
```

Similarly, if the value of the expression matches with any of the values `4, 6, 9` and `11` then days is assigned `30`. This segment of the switch structure is equivalent to the following if statement:

```
if ( (month ==4) || (month == 6) || (month == 9) ||(month ==11))
    days = 31;
```

If the value of the expression is 2 then days is assigned 28. If none of the labels match with the value of the expression then the default option is executed. After each of the above cases, the control is transferred to the statement after the closing brace of the switch statement.

4.6.1 Nested Switch Statement

On the lines of `if` statement and its variations, even switch statements also can be nested, if required. The following program makes use of this fact. Suppose there are two departments, namely sales and production. Sales department is denoted by the numeric code 1 and production department is denoted by the numeric code 2, and both of these departments have employees with two designations: Manager and Assistant Manager. We will denote Manager by numeric code 1 and Assistant Manager by numeric code 2 for ease of programming.

Dept	Code	Designation	Code
Sales	1	Manager	1
Production	2	Assistant Manager	2

The program is to accept dept_code and dsg_code as inputs, and display the corresponding department name and designation name.

Program 4.14 To Illustrate Nesting of Switch Statements

```
#include <iostream.h>

int main(void)
{
    int dept, dsg;

    cout << "Enter dept code" << endl;
    cin >> dept;
    cout << "Enter dsg code " << endl;
    cin >> dsg;

    switch(dept)
    {
        case 1: switch(dsg)
```

```
          {
            case 1: cout << "Manager in Sales Dept";
                    break;
            case 2: cout <<"Asst.Mgr in Sales Dept";
                    break;
          }
          break;

     case 2: switch(dsg)
          {
            case 1: cout <<"Manager in Production Dept";
                    break;
            case 2: cout <<"Asst. Mgr in Production Dept";
                    break;
          }
          break;
   }
  return 0;
}
```

Input-Output:

First Run:

```
Enter dept code
1

Enter dsg code
2

Asst. Mgr in Sales Dept
```

Second Run:

```
Enter dept code
2
Enter dsg code
1

Manager in Production Dept
```

Explanation

In Program 4.14, the identifiers **dept** and **dsg** are declared to be variables of `int` type. The variable **dept** is to collect the dept_code and it forms the expression for the outer switch statement. The variable **dsg** is to collect dsg_code and it forms the expression for the inner switch statements. Depending on the value taken by the variables, the appropriate combination of designation and department is displayed. It is important to note that the outer switch statement selects the department and the inner switch statement selects the designation of an employee.

4.7 THE GOTO STATEMENT

The goto statement is an unconditional branching statement. It causes the control to be transferred from one part to another part of the same function. The syntax of its usage is as follows:

```
goto label;
```

where `label` is a valid C identifier and it marks the place where the control has to be transferred to in a function. The statement to which the control is to be transferred is preceded by the `label` and a colon.

Forward jumping

```
goto  abc: ──┐
      s1;    │
      s2;    │
abc:  s3; <──┘
      s4;
```

Backward jumping

```
abc:  s1; <───┐
      s2;     │
      s3;     │
      goto abc;┘
```

However, liberal usage of goto statement is not advocated in C++. This is because, its usage makes the programs hard to understand and most of the programming situations can be implemented without using the goto statement. It has to be used very rarely in situations like transferring control out of nested loops from the inner loops.

Jumping out of the innermost loop

```
    for(i = 1; i < 10; i++)
    {
       statements;
       for(j = 0; j < 10; j++)
       for(k = 0; k < 10; k++)
       {
          if (some drastic condition)
          goto abc;   ──────┐
       }                    │
    }                       │
abc: s1; <──────────────────┘
     s2;
```

REVIEW QUESTIONS

4.1 What do you mean by the conditional execution?

4.2 Differentiate between sequential execution and conditional execution.

4.3 What is a test-expression?

4.4 Find out whether the following text-expressions involving the variables **a, b, c** and **d** evaluate to true or false.

a = 3, **b** = 4, **c** = 5, **d** = 7

(a) **a + b > c** (b) **a > b + c** (c) **a > b && a > c** (d) **a + b < c + d**

4.5 Find out errors, if any, in the following:

(a)
```
if (a > b);
{
    g = a;
}
```

(b)
```
if (a > b)
    g = a;
    cout << "g = " << g;
else
    g = a;
    cout << "g = " << g;
}
```

(c)
```
if (c1)
{
    statements-1;
}
    else if (c2)
{
    statements-2;
}
```

4.6 Write the syntax of simple-if structure.

4.7 Explain nested if-else structure.

4.8 What is the need for else-if ladder? Give an example of its requirement.

4.9 Write the syntax of switch structure.

4.10 Compare else-if ladder and switch structure.

4.11 Why is the usage of goto statement not recommended?

4.12 Give the syntax and the usage of goto statement.

True/False Questions

T4.1 The expression of the switch statement can be of any type.

T4.2 The switch statements can be nested.

T4.3 Switch statement is a replacement for else-if ladder in all the cases.

T4.4 Default option is a must in the switch statement.

T4.5
```
a = 6
 if (a)
     cout << "a = 6"; is a valid statement
```

T4. 6 goto is a conditional branching statement.

PROGRAMMING EXERCISES

P4.1 Write a program to validate a given date.

Example

12/3/1998 is valid	
32/3/98 is not valid	Day exceeds 31
30/13/98 is not valid	Month exceeds 12
31/4/98 is not valid	Maximum number of days in the month of April is 30

P4.2 Write a program to find whether one date is earlier than the other or not.

Example

12/3/98 is earlier than 20/4/99

12/3/98 is not earlier than 12/3/98

P4.3 Write a program to accept a number and display whether it is divisible by 5 only or 6 only or by both 5 and 6.

P4.4 Write a program to accept three sides *a*, *b* and *c*. Find whether the sides form a triangle or not. (A triangle can be formed out of *a*, *b*, and *c* if the sum of any two sides is greater than the remaining side.)

P4.5 Write a program to find the value of *y* for the given value of *x*.

$$\begin{aligned} y &= 2 * x + 100 && \text{if } x < 50 \\ &= 3 * x + 300 && \text{if } x = 50 \\ &= 5 * x - 200 && \text{if } x > 50 \end{aligned}$$

P4.6 An electricity supply company charges its consumers according to the following slab rates:

Units	*Charge*
1 – 100	Rs. 1.50 per unit
101 – 300	Rs. 2.00 per unit for excess of 100 units
301 – 500	Rs. 2.50 per unit for excess of 300 units
501 – above	Rs. 3.25 per unit for excess of 500 units

Write a program to accept no. of units. Calculate the total charge and display it.

P4.7 Following are the numeric codes assigned to different colours. Write a program to accept a colour code and display the appropriate colour in word.

Colour code	*Colour*
1	Red
2	Blue
3	Green
4	Yellow
5	Purple

P4.8 Write a program to accept three sides of a triangle and display the type of the triangle. Suppose *a*, *b* and *c* are three sides of the triangle

(a) If all the three sides are equal then the triangle is called an equilateral triangle.

(b) If any two of the sides are equal then the triangle is called an isosceles triangle.

(c) If any one of the angles is an obtuse angle (>90), the triangle is called obtuse angled triangle.

P4.9 Write a program to find the roots of a quadratic equation.

A quadratic equation is of the form $ax^2 + bx + c = 0$

The discriminant $d = \text{sqrt}(b^2 - 4ac)$

The roots of the equation are given by $x_1 = (-b + d)/2 \quad x^2 = (-b - d)/2$

Roots are equal if $d = 0$

Roots are real and distinct if $d > 0$

Roots are complex numbers if $d < 0$

P4. 10 Write a program to accept the three sides of a triangle and find whether the triangle is a right angled triangle or not. (Use Pythagoras theorem)

P4. 11 Write a program to accept a point (x, y) and find whether it lies on the circle or inside the circle or outside the circle. The centre of the circle (0, 0) and radius of the circle is 5.

Equation of a circle with (0,0) as the centre and r as the radius is given by $x^2 + y^2 = r^2$, where r is the radius.

If $x^2 + y^2 < r^2$ then the point (x, y) lies within the circle.

If $x^2 + y^2 > r^2$ then the point (x, y) lies outside the circle.

If $x^2 + y^2 = r^2$ then the point (x, y) lies on the circle.

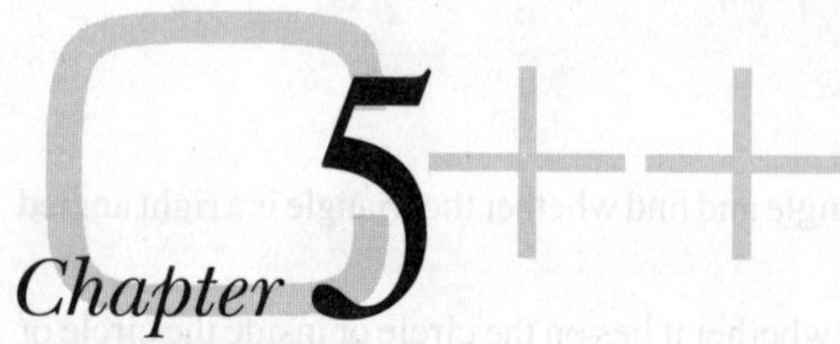

Chapter 5 Iteration

5.1 INTRODUCTION

So far, we have come across two types of execution of statements in our earlier programs: **sequence**, where all the statements from the beginning till the end get executed without fail in the serial order, and **selection** where some statements are executed and some are skipped depending on some condition. The common thing shared by both of these is that statements selected for execution get executed only once.

Under some circumstances, we may need to execute a block of statements repeatedly as long as some condition is true. For instance, suppose we need to find the sum of first n natural numbers 1,2,3,…., n. If a variable **s** expected to collect the sum. Initially 0 is assigned to **s**. First 1 is to be added to **s** then 2 is to be added to **s** then 3 is to be added to **s** and so on. Here, selection of the members of the series and adding them to the variable **s** are to be done repeatedly.

To be precise, the following statements are to be executed repeatedly:

```
s += i
i++;
```

The repetition of execution of a block of statements as long as some condition is true is called **looping**. Looping is also called **iteration**.

Program 5.1 To Find the Sum of First *n* Natural Numbers Using If and Goto Statements

```
#include <iostream.h>

int main(void)
{
    int n, i, sum;

    cout << "Enter a number";
    cin >> n;
```

```
    sum = 0;
    i = 1;
    abc:
        sum += i;
        i++;
        if (i <= n) goto abc;

    cout << "Sum = " << sum;

    return 0;
}
```

Input-Output:

```
Enter a number
8
Sum = 36
```

Explanation

In Program 5.1, **n**, **i** and **sum** are declared to be variables of `int` type. **n** is to collect a natural number; **i** is to collect each natural number starting from `1` to `n`; **sum** is to collect the sum of the natural numbers up to `n`.

First, we accept a number into the variable **n**; initialize **sum** and **i** with `0` and `1` respectively. The initial value of **i**, that is, `1` is added to **sum**. So the first member of the natural numbers series, 1, is added to **sum**. i is incremented by `1`; The value of **i** now becomes `2`, the second member of the natural numbers series. The condition **i <= n** is checked. If it is found to be true, the control is transferred to the statement following the label `abc (Backward jumping)`. The value of **i**, that is, `2` is added to **sum** and **i** is once again incremented. **i** will now become 3. Once again **i <= n** is checked. If it is found to be true, the control is transferred to the statement following the label **abc**. 3 is added to **sum** and **i** is incremented again. This continues as long as **i <= n**. Once **i** exceeds **n**, the control is transferred to the statement cout << `"sum = " << sum;` which displays the sum up to *n* natural numbers.

It is important to note that there are three steps employed to construct a loop:

1. Initialization
2. Checking test-expression
3. Updation

At least one variable should be involved in all these three steps. The variable involved is called **control variable**. In the first step, the control variable is given a value. In the second step, the test-expression involving the control variable is checked to find whether it evaluates to true or false. If the test-expression evaluates to true then only, the statements get repeatedly executed. In the last step, the variable's value gets changed. The updation of the control variable should be such that the test expression evaluates to false at some later point of time so that the loop is exited.

In the Program 5.1, the control variable is **i**. It is assigned the responsibility of selecting the natural numbers one by one. Initialization is **i = 1**. Test-expression is **i <= n** and updation statement is **i++**, which increments `i` by 1.

In the Program 5.1, we have used `if` statement in combination with `goto` statement and effected backward jumping to construct a loop. We need not have to always rely on the combination of `if` and `goto` to construct loops. C++ provides its own looping constructs, which are simple and hence facilitate simplified coding. Let us now get to know the looping structures provided by C++, their syntax and usage.

C++ provides three looping structures. They are:

1. The while loop
2. The for loop
3. The do while loop

We now know that to be able to execute a block of statements repeatedly as long as some condition is true (i.e. , To construct a valid loop) there should be three things: (a) Initialization (b) Test-expression (c) Updation and at least one variable should be involved in all of these. Program 5.1 has thrown light on this account. All these three looping constructs are not exceptions to this fact. They do incorporate the above mentioned three fundamental things in the process of construction of valid loops.

5.2 THE WHILE LOOP

The while loop is the simplest and most frequently used looping structure in C++. The syntax of the looping structure is:

```
while (test-expression)
{
    statements
}
```

As far as the syntax is concerned, it starts with the keyword **while**. The keyword is followed by a test-expression enclosed within a pair of parentheses. The test-expression can be an arithmetic expression, relational expression or a logical expression. The test-expression is then followed by a set of one or more statements, which are expected to be repeatedly executed, enclosed within a pair of braces.

The other two components initialization and updation required for a loop other than test-expression, one of the statements, written before the while loop, acts as initialization statement and one of the statements in the body of the loop acts as updation statement.

Execution sequence effected by the looping construct is as follows: test-expression is evaluated. If test-expression evaluates to true then the statements in the body of the loop get executed. The updation statement in the body of the loop updates the looping variable. Control goes back to the test-expression. The test-expression is again evaluated. If it evaluates to true then once again the statements in the body of the loop would get executed. This is repeated as long as the test-expression remains evaluated to true. Once the test-expression evaluates to false, the loop is exited and the control goes to the first statement following the looping construct.

The execution sequence effected by while looping construct is best illustrated by the following flowchart segment.

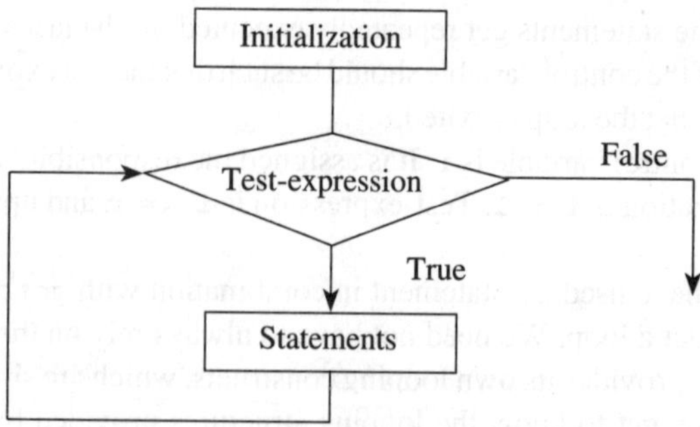

Since the test-expression is first evaluated before entering into the body of the loop, the looping construct is called **entry-controlled or pre-tested** looping construct. Since the test-expression is evaluated in the beginning itself, if it evaluates to false in the beginning itself, the body of the loop is not entered at all. The statements would simply be skipped and the control is transferred to the first statement following the looping construct.

EXAMPLE 1

Consider the following segment of code:

```
i = 1;
sum = 0;
While (i <= 10)
{
    sum += i;
    i++;
}
```

The purpose of the code is to find the sum of first 10 natural numbers.

EXAMPLE 2

Consider the following segment:

```
ch = getchar();
while (ch != '\n')
{
    ch = getchar();
}
```

The segment of code enables us to accept characters one at a time till the new line character is entered, and thus it can be used to accept a line of text.

After getting familiarized with the syntax and examples of the usage of the while loop, we will now write some programs which make use of it.

To find the sum of the digits of an integer: Given a multiple digit integer **n**, in order to find the sum of the digits in it, we need to set up a loop to extract each digit in the number and add it to a variable, say, s repeatedly.

Program 5.2 To Find the Sum of the Digits of an Integer

```
#include <iostream.h>

int main(void)
{
    int n, rem, sum;

    cout << "Enter an integer";
    cin >> n;

    /* Finding the sum of the digits of n begins */
    sum = 0;
    while (n > 0)
    {
        rem = n %10;
```

```
        sum += rem;
        n /= 10;
    }

    /* Finding the sum of the digits of n ends */

    cout << "sum = " << sum;

    return 0;
}
```

Input-Output:

```
Enter an integer
156

Sum = 12
```

Explanation

In Program 5.2, **n**, **rem** and **sum** are declared to be variables of `int` type. The variable **n** is to collect an integer value (input). The variable **sum** is to collect the sum of the digits of the integer value in **n** and it is initialized to zero.

The following segment of the program is responsible for extracting each digit in **n** and adding the digit, collected by the variable **rem**, to the variable **sum**.

```
while (n > 0)
{
    rem = n %10;
    sum += rem;
    n /= 10;
}
```

The loop is exited once the value in **n** becomes zero by which time the variable **sum** has collected the sum of all the digits in it. The value in **sum** is then displayed.

A number is said to be a prime number if it is not divisible by any other number other than 1 and itself.

EXAMPLE

5 is a prime number
7 is a prime number

To find whether a number **n** is prime or not, we need to check whether any number within the range 2 to *n*/2 divides **n** exactly or not. If none of the numbers within the range divides *n*, we conclude that *n* is prime. Otherwise we conclude that *n* is not prime.

Program 5.3 To Find Whether a Number is a Prime Number or Not

```
#include <iostream.h>

int main(void)
{
    int number, k, flag, rem;
```

```
    cout << "Enter a number"<< endl;
    cin >> number;
    k = 2;
    flag = 1;
    while ((k <= number / 2) && (flag == 1))
    {
        rem = number % k;
        if (rem == 0)
            flag = 0;
        k++;
    }

    if (flag == 1)
        cout << number << " is prime" << endl;
    else
        cout << number << "is not prime" << endl;

    return 0;
}
```

```
Input-Output:
First Run:
Enter a number
5
5 is prime

Second Run:
Enter a number
6
6 is not prime
```

Explanation

In Program 5.3, **number, flag, k** and **rem** are declared to be variables of **int** type. Variable **number** is to collect a number, which we have to find whether prime or not. Variable **k** is to select the numbers in the range [2 to number-1]. Variable **flag** is to take a value which is either 1 (true) or 0 (false). The variable **rem** is to collect the remainder after division of **number** by **k**.

First, we accept a number into the variable **number**, and assign 2 to **k** since we need to start dividing **number** from **2**. We start with the assumption that **number** is prime by assigning 1 to **flag** (true). Within the **while** loop, we check whether any value of **k** divides **number** exactly. If any value of **k** is found to divide **number** exactly, **flag** is assigned 0 and the loop is exited. Otherwise the loop completes without altering the value of **flag**. If none of the values of **k** divides **number** exactly, **flag** retains 1 only. If **flag** retains 1 then we conclude that **number** is prime. On the other hand, if **flag** gets 0 then we conclude that **number** is not prime. Thus, the value of **flag** would tell us whether **number** is prime or not.

To generate the members of the Fibonacci series: The first two members of the series are zero and one. The third member is the sum of the first two members, i.e., one. The fourth member is the sum of the second and the third member and so on.

In general, *i*th member of the series, where i > 2, is obtained by adding the (i-1)th and (i-2)th members.

Program 5.4 To Generate Fibonacci Series

```
#include <iostream.h>

int main(void)
{
    int n, i, f1, f2, f3;

    cout << "Enter No. of members to be generated" << endl;
    cin >> n;

    cout << "First" << n << "members of Fibonacci series" << endl;
    f1 = 0;
    f2 = 1;
    cout << f1 << endl;
    cout << f2 << endl;
    i = 3;
    while (i <= n)
    {
        f3 = f1 + f2;
        cout << f3 << endl;
        f1 = f2;
        f2 = f3;
        i++;
    }

    return 0;
}
```

Input-Output:

```
Enter No. of members to be generated
10
First 10 members of Fibonacci series
0
1
1
2
3
5
8
13
21
34
```

Explanation

In Program 5.4, **`n, i, f1, f2`** and **`f3`** are declared to be variables of `int` type. Variable **`n`** collects the no. of members of the Fibonaci series to be generated. **`f1, f2`** and **`f3`** are used in the process of generation of the series. **`i`** is to keep track of the number of members generated during the course of generation.

First, we accept the number of members to be generated into the variable **`n`**. The first two members of the series 0 and `1` are assigned to **`f1`** and **`f2`** respectively. They are displayed. Note that **`i`** is assigned three. This is to indicate that the third member is to be generated.

On the entry into the loop, the third member is found out by summing `f1` and `f2`. It is collected by `f3` and also displayed. Fourth member is then generated by summing up second and third member. Likewise, the loop repeats till the required no. of members of the Fibonacci series are generated by summing up the immediate previous two members to get the next member of the series.

5.3 THE FOR LOOP

The for loop is another looping structure provided by C++ excessively used in many situations because of its inherent simplicity. The simple nature of the loop is evident from its syntax itself.

Following is the syntax of the **for** loop:

```
for(initialization; test-expression; updation)
{
    statements;
}
```

The general form of the looping construct starts with the keyword **for**. The keyword is followed by the three fundamental things to construct a loop, initialization, test-expression and updation all in one place, separated by semicolons and enclosed within a pair of parentheses. (However, initialization, test-expression and updation can be used in different places like the way they are used in while and do-while loop. Usage of them in one line in the for loop increases its simplicity and comprehensibility.) Then the body of the loop follows.

Execution sequence effected by for loop is as follows:

1. Initialization statement is executed.
2. Test-expression is evaluated.
3. If the test-expression evaluates to true, the statements in the body of the loop would get executed.
4. Control goes to the updation statement, the updation statement is executed, which changes the value of the loop variable.
5. Test-expression is again evaluated.
6. If it evaluates to true, again the statements in the body of the loop would get executed.
7. Control goes back to the updation statement, which updates the looping variable.

The sequence is repeated as long as the test-expression evaluates to true. Once the test-expression evaluates to false, the loop is exited and the control is transferred to the first statement following the looping construct.

The execution sequence effected by the while looping construct can best be understood by the following flowchart segment:

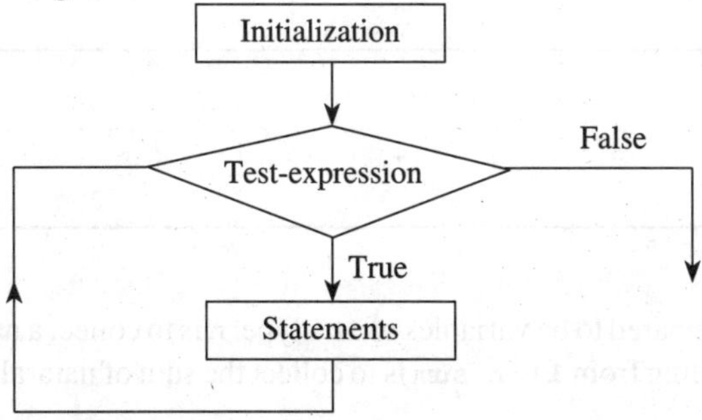

Similar to **while** loop, since the test-expression is evaluated first before entering into the body of the loop, the looping construct is called **entry-controlled or pre-tested** looping construct. If the test-expression evaluates to false in the beginning itself, the body of the loop is not entered at all. The control is transferred to the first statement following the loop.

EXAMPLE 1

The following segment of code finds the sum of the natural numbers up to 10:

```
sum = 0;
for(i = 1; i <= 10; i++)
    sum += i;
```

EXAMPLE 2

The following segment of code finds the factorial of the number 5:

```
fact = 1;
for(i = 5; i >=1; i--)
    fact *= i;
```

After getting familiarized with the syntax and examples of the usage of the for loop, we will now write some programs which make use of it.

Program 5.5 To Find the Sum of First *n* Natural Numbers Using For Loop

```
#include <iostream.h>
#include <iomanip.h>

int main(void)
{
    int n, i, sum;

    cout << "Enter a number" << endl;
    cin >> n;

    sum = 0;
    for(i = 1; i <= n; i++)
        sum += i;

    cout << "Sum = " << sum;

    return 0;
}
```

Input-Output:

```
Enter a number
8
sum = 36
```

Explanation

In Program 5.5, **n**, **i** and **sum** are declared to be variables of `int` type. **n** is to collect a natural number; **i** is to collect each natural number starting from **1** to **n**; **sum** is to collect the sum of natural numbers up to **n**.

First, we accept a number into the variable **n** and initialize **sum** with zero. The following segment finds the sum of the first *n* natural numbers.

```
for(i = 1; i <= n; i++)
    sum += i;
```

The value of sum is then displayed.

To generate multiplication table of a number: Given a number *n*. In order to generate the multiplication table of the number, we definitely need to set up a loop to multiply *n* with the numbers in the range [1–10] and get the product of *n* and each number in the range. Here the multiplication is a repetitive process.

Program 5.6 To Generate Multiplication Table of a Number

```
#include <iostream.h>
#include <iomanip.h>

int main(void)
{
    int number, i, product;

    cout << "Enter a number" << endl;
    cin >> number;

    for(i = 1; i <= 10; i++)
    {
        product = number * i;
        cout << number << "*" << i << "=" << product << endl;
    }

    return 0;
}
```

Input-Output:

```
Enter a number
6

6*1=6
6*2=12
6*3=18
6*4=24
6*5=30
6*6=36
6*7=42
6*8=48
6*9=54
6*10=60
```

Explanation

In Program 5.6, **number, i** and **product** are declared to be variables of `int` type. The variable **number** is to collect a number (input), multiplication table of which is to be generated. The variables **i** and **product** are used in the process of generation of the table.

The segment of the program responsible for generating the table is the following.

```
for(i = 1; i <= 10; i++)
{
    product = number * i;
    cout << number << "*" << i << "=" << product << endl;
}
```

In the **for** loop, the variable **i** ranges from 1 to 10. Initially **i** takes 1. Since `i <= 10` becomes true, the body of the loop is entered and the product of **i** and **number** is found out and is displayed. **i** is then incremented and it becomes 2. Once again since `i <= 10` evaluates to true, the product of **number** and **i** is found out and is displayed. This is repeated till **i** becomes greater than `10`, by which event, the multiplication table of number has been generated.

5.3.1 Variations of For Loop

1. The for loop can have more than one initialization expression separated by comma operator.

   EXAMPLE

   ```
   for(sum = 0, i = 1; i <= 10; i++)
       sum += i;
   ```

   Note the presence of two initialization expressions `sum = 0` and `i = 1` separated by comma operator.

2. The for loop can have more than one updation expression also separated by comma operator.

   EXAMPLE

   ```
       sum = 0;
       for(i = 1; i <= 10; i++, sum += i)
   ```

   Note the presence of two updation expressions `i++` and `sum = i` separated by comma operator.

3. The initialization expression and updation expression can both be displaced as follows. The resulting looping structure resembles while loop.

   EXAMPLE

   ```
   sum = 0;
   i = 1;
   for(;i < =10; )
   {
       sum += i;
       i++;
   }
   ```

4. Consider the following segment of code:

   ```
   sum = 0;
   for(cin >> n; n > 0; n /= 10)
   {
       rem = n % 10;
       sum += rem;
   }
   ```

The segment of code finds the sum of the digits of a number collected by the variable **n**. Note that the `cin >> n;` has been used as the initialization expression. This is perfectly valid and it is executed only once in the beginning similar to the normal initialization expression. Also note the updation expression `n /= 10;` which is different from normal incrementation/decrementation. Since there are two statements to be executed repeatedly they are enclosed within the braces.

5. Consider the following for statement. It does not have any of the three components required for loop. (But the two semicolons are mandatory.)

   ```
   for(; ;)
   ```

   This sets up an infinite loop.

6. Some programming circumstances, require time delay to be set up. The time-delay can be provided with the help of the following loop.

   ```
   for(i=0; i<=10000;i++);
   ```

   The loop is repeated 10000 times without performing anything thereby setting up a time delay.

   Note the presence of a semicolon after the loop, it indicates a null statement.

5.4 THE DO-WHILE LOOP

The do-while loop is another looping structure provided by C++, which is less frequently used when compared to while loop and for loop. Unlike while loop and for loop, this is a post-tested or exit- controlled looping structure. The syntax of the looping structure is as follows:

```
do
{
    statements;
}
while(test-expression);
```

As far as the syntax is concerned, it starts with the keyword **do**. The keyword is followed by a block of one or more statements, which are expected to be executed repeatedly, enclosed within a pair of braces. The set of statements form the body of the loop. The set of statements are then followed by another keyword **while**, which is then followed by a test-expression enclosed within a pair of parentheses. Note the presence of semicolon after the closing parenthesis of the test-expression.

Execution sequence effected by do-while loop is as follows. The statements in the body of the loop get executed once and then the control goes to the test-expression. The test-expression is evaluated. If it evaluates to true then, the body of the loop is re-entered. After the statements in the body of the loop get executed for the second time, the control goes back to the test-expression. Once again the test-expression is evaluated. If it evaluates to true, again the body of the loop gets executed. This is repeated as long as the test-expression evaluates to true. Once the test-expression evaluates to false, the loop is exited and the control goes to the first statement following the looping construct.

The execution sequence effected by do-while looping construct can best be grasped by the following flowchart segment:

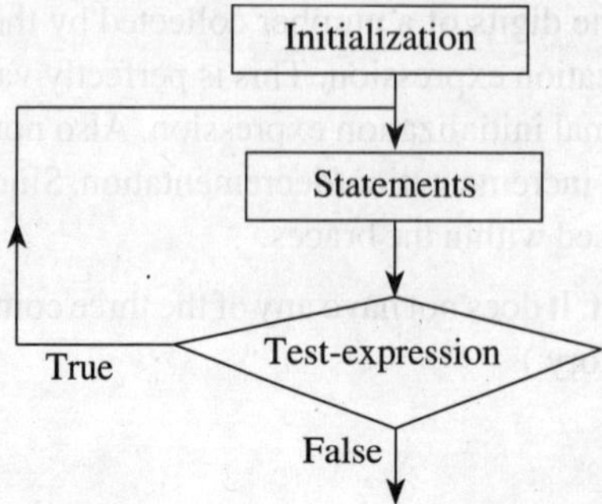

Since the test-expression is evaluated at the end, the looping construct is called **exit-controlled or post-tested** looping construct. The statements in the body of the loop are guaranteed to be executed at least once.

EXAMPLE 1

Consider the following segment:

```
i = 1;
sum = 0;
do
{
    sum += i;
    i++;
}while (i <= 10);
```

The statements in the body of the loop get repeatedly executed as long as `i <= 10` and it finds the sum of the first 10 natural numbers.

EXAMPLE 2

Consider the following segment:

```
ch = 'y';
do
{
    cin >> n;
    cout << "Do you want to continue? y or n " << endl;
    ch = getchar();
}while (ch == 'y');
```

The segment of code enables us to keep accepting integer value into the variable **n** as long as we enter *y* to the variable **ch**. Once we input *n* in response to the statement `ch = getchar();`, the loop is exited.

After getting familiarized with the syntax and examples of the usage of the do-while loop, we will now write some programs which make use of it.

Program 5.7 To Find the Sum of First *n* Natural Numbers using Do-while Loop

```
#include <iostream.h>

int main(void)
```

```
{
    int n, i, sum;

    cout << "Enter a number" << endl;
    cin >> n;

    i = 1;
    sum = 0;
    do
    {
        sum += i;
        i++;
    }
    while (i <= n);
    cout << "Sum = " << sum;

    return 0;
}
```

Input-Output:

```
Enter a number
5
sum = 15
```

Explanation

In Program 5.7, **n**, **i** and **sum** are declared to be variables of `int` type. **n** is to collect a natural number; **i** is to select each natural number starting from `1` to *n*; **sum** is to collect the sum of natural numbers up to *n*.

First, we accept a number into the variable **n** and initialize **sum** with zero. The following segment finds the sum of the first *n* natural numbers:

```
do
{
    sum += i;
    i++;
}
while (i <= n);
```

The sum is collected by the variable **sum**. The value of the variable **sum** is then displayed.

Program 5.8 To Accept Two Numbers and an Arithmetic Operator and Display the Result of the Expression Involving Them

```
#include <iostream.h>
#include <stdio.h>

int main(void)
{
    int a, b;
    char ch, op;

    ch = 'y';
```

```
    do
    {
        cout << "Enter two numbers" << endl;
        cin >> a >> b;
        fflush(stdin);
        cout << "Enter an operator" << endl;
        op = getchar();

        switch (op)
        {
            case '+': cout << "sum = " << a + b << endl;
                      break;
            case '-': cout << "Difference = " << a - b << endl;
                      break;
            case '*': cout << "Product = " << a * b << endl;
                      break;
            case '/': cout << "Quotient = " << a / b << endl;
                      break;
            case '%': cout << "Remainder = " << a % b << endl;
                      break;
            default:  cout << "Not an operator";
        }
        cout << "Do you want to continue y/n?" << endl;
            fflush(stdin);
            ch = getchar();
    }while (ch == 'y');

   return 0;
}
```

Input-Output:

```
Enter two numbers
4
5
Enter an operator
+

sum = 9

Do you want to continue y/n?
y

Enter two numbers
8
9
Enter an operator
*

Product = 72
Do you want to continue y/n?
n
```

Explanation

In Program 5.8, **a** and **b** are declared to be variables of `int` type. These variables are to accept two integer values. **ch** and **op** are the variables of `char` type. The variable **op** is to accept an arithmetic operator symbol [+, –, *, / and %] and the variable **ch** is to accept the characters *y* or *n*.

The program is to accept two numbers and an arithmetic operator repeatedly and interactively as long as the variable `ch` has the value *y*. Thus, the variable **ch** becomes the control variable for the loop used in the program. Initially the variable **op** is assigned the value *y* and the loop is entered. Within the loop, we can accept two numbers into the variables **a** and **b**, and we can accept an arithmetic operator into **ch**. The switch statement incorporated into the loop takes care of evaluating the resultant expression and display the result on the screen. The above procedure is repeated as long as we accept *y* into the variable **ch**. Once we accept **n** into it, the loop is exited and eventually the program also terminates.

5.5 WHICH LOOP TO USE WHEN

As a matter of fact, all the three looping structures can be used in all the situations which require repetition of execution of statements as we have seen before through the programming examples. However, by keeping in mind the nature of the looping structures, we can choose them according to the following guidelines.

If the problem to be programmed requires the test-expression to be checked first before executing the statements and if the statements are to be executed fixed number of times, the **for** loop is ideal (as we have seen in the case of generation of multiplication table of a number).

If the problem to be programmed requires the test-expression to be checked first before executing the statements and if the statements are to be executed unknown number of times, and the loop is to be exited when the specified condition becomes false, the **while** loop is ideal (as we have seen in the case of finding the sum of the digits of an integer value).

If the problem to be programmed requires the test-expression to be checked after executing the statements once and if the statements are to be executed unknown number of times, and the loop is to be exited when the specified condition becomes false, the **do-while** loop is ideal. This looping structure is rarely used.

5.6 JUMPS IN LOOPS

5.6.1 The Break Statement

We know that a loop enables us to execute a block of statements as long as some test-expression is true. Break and continue statements provided by C++ enable us to exercise some kind of control over the working of loops. Let us now understand the need for these statements.

The test-expression of a loop is one of its important components. Under some circumstances, we require the loop be exited even when the loop's test-expression still evaluates to true. Break statement becomes handy in these situations. When used within a loop, it causes the premature exit from the loop. The syntax of its usage is:

```
break;
```

More importantly, a break statement used within a loop is expected to be associated with an if statement. It is when the test-expression of the if statement evaluates to true, the loop is exited prematurely.

```
while (test-expression1)
{
    s1;
    s2;
    if (test-expression2)
        break;
    s3;
    s4;
}
```

Here during the course of iterations, for any iteration, if the test-expression 2 evaluates to true, the control reaches the break statement and the break statement, on its execution, causes the loop to be exited prematurely. Program 5.9 demonstrates the working of the break statement when enclosed in a loop.

Program 5.9 To Illustrate Break Statement

```
#include<iostream.h>

int main(void)
{
    int n, i, sum = 0, number;

    cout << "Enter no. of elements" << endl;
    cin >> n;
    cout << "Enter" << n << "numbers Type -ve number to terminate"
        << endl;
    for(i = 1; i <= n; i++)
    {
        cin >> number;
        if (number < 0)
            break;
        sum += number;
    }
    cout << "sum of" << i-1 << "positive numbers = " << sum << endl;
    return 0;
}
```

Input-Output:

```
Enter no. of elements
5
Enter 5 numbers Type -ve number to terminate
1
2
3
-4
sum of 3 positive numbers = 6
```

Explanation

In Program 5.9, **n**, **i**, **sum** and **number** are declared to be variables of `int` type. The variable **n** is to accept the no. of values to be summed up; the variable **number** is to collect *n* numbers on one by one basis; **i** is to range from 1 to *n* in the loop used and `sum` is to collect the sum of the numbers entered before a negative number is entered.

The segment of the program responsible for the summation is the following:

```
for(i = 1; i <= n; i++)
{
    cin >> number;
    if (number < 0)
        break;
    sum += number;
}
```

Using the above for loop, we try to accept *n* numbers and find their sum. During the course of accepting the numbers, if positive numbers are entered, they are added to the variable **sum**. But if a negative number is entered then the control reaches the break statement, which, when executed causes the loop to be exited prematurely. The value of the variable **sum** is then displayed.

5.6.2 The Continue Statement

The continue statement exercises control over a loop in a slightly different way. When enclosed in a loop, it causes skipping of the statements following it in the body of the loop, and also causes the control to be transeferred back to the beginning of the loop. Similar to break statement, the continue statement is also expected to be associated with an if statement.

```
while (test-expression1)
{
    s1;
    s2;
    if (test-expression2)
        continue;
    s3;
    s4;
}
```

Here for some iteration, when test-expression 2 evaluates to true, the statements s3 and s4 are skipped for those iterations and the control goes to the beginning of the loop. Note that the loop is not prematurely exited as in the case of break statement. Program 5.10 demonstrates this very fact.

Program 5.10 To Illustrate Continue Statement

```
#include <iostream.h>

int main(void)
{
    int n, i, sum = 0, number;

    cout << "Enter no. of numbers" << endl;
    cin >> n;
    cout << "Enter" << n << "numbers" << endl;
    for(i = 1; i <= n; i++)
    {
        cin >> number;
```

```
        if (number < 0)
            continue;
        sum += number;
    }
    cout << " sum of +ve numbers = " << sum;

    return 0;
}
```

Input-Output:

```
Enter no. of numbers
5
Enter 5 numbers
1
2
3
-4
5
sum of +ve numbers = 11
```

Explanation

In Program 5.10, **n**, **i**, **sum** and **number** are declared to be variables of `int` type. The variable **n** is to accept the no. of values to be summed up; the variable **number** is to collect *n* numbers on one by one basis; **i** is to range from 1 to *n* in the loop used and **sum** is to collect the sum of only the positive numbers out of 10 numbers entered.

Following is the segment of the program responsible for the summation:

```
for(i = 1; i <= n; i++)
{
    cin >> number;
    if (number < 0)
        continue;
    sum += number;
}
```

Using the above `for` loop, we accept *n* numbers and find their sum. During the course of accepting the numbers, if positive numbers are entered, they are added to the variable **sum**. But if a negative number is entered , then the control reaches the **continue** statement, which, when executed causes the skipping of the statements following it within the loop, and causes the control to be transferred back to the beginning of the loop, so that the loop continues with its next iteration. This continues as long as the test-expression of the loop evaluates to true. Once it evaluates to false, the loop exits. The value of **sum**, the sum of only positive numbers, is then displayed.

5.6.3 Difference between Break and Continue Statements

The difference between break statement and continue statement is tabulated in Table 5.1.

Table 5.1 Difference between Break and Continue Statements

The Break statement	*The Continue statement*
1. It can be used in switch statement.	1. It can not be used in switch statement.
2. It causes premature exit of the loop enclosing it.	2. It causes skipping of the statements following it in the body of the loop.
3. The control is transferred to the statement following the loop.	3. The control is transferred back to the loop.
4. The loop may not complete the intended no. of iterations.	4. The loop completes the intended no. of iterations.

5.7 NESTING OF LOOPS

We now know that looping refers to repeated execution of a block of statements as long as some condition is true. In all our earlier programs on looping structures, we used a single loop to repeatedly execute a block of statements. There are many programming circumstances which require repeated execution of a block of statements itself to be repeated a known number of times or as long as some other condition is true. In these circumstances, we naturally need to enclose one loop within another loop. C++ allows this. Enclosing one loop within another loop is called **nesting of loops**. The enclosing loop is called **outer-loop** and the enclosed loop is called **inner-loop**.

Suppose we are asked to write a program to generate multiplication table of a number *n*, the program segment would be

```
for(i = 1; i <= 10; i++)
{
   p = n * i;
   cout << p << endl;
}
```

What if we want to generate multiplication tables of numbers of a range of numbers, say, 11 to 20? The direct option would be using the earlier program segment 10 times, one for each number in the range. The problem with this approach is duplication of the program segment, which in turn results in consumption of more memory space. This problem can be solved by embedding the program segment within another loop as follows:

```
for(i = 11; i <= 20; i++)
{
   for(j = 1; j <= 10; j++)
   {
      p = n * i;
      cout << p << endl;
   }
}
```

Here, for loop with the control variable `j` variable (inner loop) is said to be nested within the for loop with the control variable `i` (outer-loop).

Program 5.11 To Generate Multiplication Tables of a Range of Numbers

```
#include <iostream.h>
#include <iomanip.h>
int main(void)
{
    int m, n, i, j, p;

    cout << " Enter Lower limit" << endl;
    cin >> m;
    cout << " Enter Upper limit" << endl;
    cin >> n;

    for(i = m; i <= n; i++)
    {
        for(j = 1; j <= 10; j++)
        {
            p = i * j;
            cout << setw(4) << p;
        }
        cout << endl;
    }

    return 0;
}
```

Input-Output:

```
Enter Lower limit
5
Enter Upper limit
10

 5 10 15 20 25 30 35 40 45 50
 6 12 18 24 30 36 42 48 54 60
 7 14 21 28 35 42 49 56 63 70
 8 16 24 32 40 48 56 64 72 80
 9 18 27 36 45 54 63 72 81 90
10 20 30 40 50 60 70 80 90 100
```

Explanation

The variables **m**, **n**, **i**, **j** and **p** are declared to be variables of **int** type. The variables **m** and **n** are to collect the lower limit and upper limit of the range of values, multiplication tables of which are to be generated. Since the task is to generate multiplication tables of the given range of numbers, we need to nest one loop within another. The outer loop is to select each number in the range and the inner loop is to generate the multiplication table of the number selected by the outer loop. The variables **i** and **j** are used as the control variables in the outer loop and the inner loop respectively. The variable p is used in the process of obtaining the products.

In the outer loop, when **i** takes **m**, the lower limit, the inner loop generates the multiplication table of **m**. Once the inner loop completes, control goes to the outer loop again. **i** gets incremented, it becomes **m+1**. Then the inner loop generates the multiplication table of **m+1**. This continues as long as the test-expression of the outer loop evaluates to true. Once it evaluates to false, the outer loop is exited, by which time, multiplication tables of all the numbers in the range [**m–n**] have been generated.

Program 5.12 To Generate Prime Numbers within a Range of Numbers

```
#include <iostream.h>
int main(void)
{
    int m, n, i, j, k, flag;

    cout << "Enter Lower limit" << endl;
    cin >> m;
    cout << "Enter Upper limit" << endl;
    cin >> n;
    cout << "prime numbers between" << m << "and" << n << endl;
    for(i = m; i <= n; i++)
    {   k = i;
        flag = 1;
        for(j = 2; (j <= k / 2) && flag; j++)
            if ( k % j == 0)
                flag = 0;

    if (flag)
        cout << i << endl;
    }

    return 0;
}
```

Input-Output:

```
Enter Lower limit
10
Enter Upper limit
20

prime numbers between 10 and 20
11
13
17
19
```

Explanation

The variables **m, n, i, j** and **flag** are declared to be variables of **int** type. The variables **m** and **n** are to collect the lower limit and upper limit of the range of values, within which prime numbers are to be generated. Since the task is to generate prime numbers within the given range of numbers, we need to nest one loop within another. The outer loop is to select each number in the range and the inner loop is to find whether the number selected by the outer loop is prime or not. The variables **i** and **j** are used as the control variables in the outer loop and the inner loop respectively. The variable **flag** is used in the process of finding out prime numbers.

In the outer loop, when **i** takes **m**, the lower limit, the inner loop finds out whether *m* is prime or not.

The value of flag tells this. If flag retains 1 then *m* is prime if it gets 0 within the inner loop then it is taken to be not prime. Outside the inner loop, if the value of flag is found to be equal to 1 then *m* is displayed as prime otherwise *m* is not displayed at all. Control goes back to the outer loop again. `i` gets incremented, it becomes `m + 1`. The inner loop finds out whether $m + 1$ is prime or not. if it is found to be prime, it is displayed. This continues as long as the test-expression of the outer loop evaluates to true. Once it evaluates to false, the outer loop is exited, by which time, all the prime numbers in the range [*m*–*n*] have been generated.

5.7.1 Jumps in Nested Loops

The break statement in nested loops: We have understood the working of the break statement in relation to a single loop. Many programming circumstances call for its usage even when the loops are nested. It is important to note that the break statement affects only the loop in which it is enclosed.

```
for(initialization1; test-expression1; updation1)
{
    for(initialization2; test-expression2; updation2)
    {
        if (test-expression3)
            break;
    }
    statements;
}
for(initialization1; test-expression1; updation1)
{
    for(initialization2; test-expression2; updation2)
    {
        statements2;
    }

    if (test-expression3)
        break;
}
statements;;
```

Program 5.13 To Illustrate Break Statement in the Case of Nested Loops

```
#include <iostream.h>
int main(void)
{
    int number, i, j, sum;

    for(i = 1; i <= 2; i++) /* Outer loop */
    {
        sum = 0;
        cout << "Enter five numbers for set-number" << i << endl;
        for(j = 1; j <= 5; j++) /* Inner loop */
        {
            cin >> number;
            if(number < 0)
```

```
            break;
        sum = sum + number;
      }
      cout << "Sum of" << j-1 << "numbers in set-number"<< i
           << "=" << sum << endl;
   }

   return 0;
}
```

Input-Output:

```
Enter five numbers for set-number1
1
2
3
-4

Sum of 3 numbers in set-number1 = 6

Enter five numbers for set-number2
1
2
3
4
-5
Sum of 4 numbers in set-number2 = 10
```

Explanation

In Program 5.13, **`number, i, j`** and **`sum`** are declared to be variables of **`int`** type. The program is to accept two sets of numbers, each set consisting of maximum five numbers and find the sum of +ve numbers in each set before a –ve number is entered. It is important to note that the problem calls for nesting of two loops. The outer loop for selecting each set and the inner loop for enabling us to accept the elements of the set selected by the outer loop. The variables **`i`** and **`j`** act as the control variables of the outer loop and the inner loop respectively. The variable **number** is to collect each number of a set and **sum** is to collect the sum of +ve numbers in the sets before a –ve number is entered.

Initially, the outer loop control variable **`i`** takes **`1`** representing the first set. The inner loop control variable `j` then ranges from **`1`** to **`5`** enabling us to accept up to five numbers of the first set and find the sum of the numbers. Importantly, within the inner loop, break statement is enclosed. It gets executed when the number entered is negative. So once a –ve number is entered for the set, the inner loop is prematurely exited. In which case, the variable **`sum`** would collect the sum of fewer than intended five numbers of the set. This is repeated even for the second set also.

Since break statement is enclosed within the inner loop, we notice that it causes the premature exit of the inner loop only.

The continue statement in nested loops: We have also understood the working of the continue statement in relation to a single loop. Many programming circumstances call for its usage even when the loops are nested. It is important to note that the continue statement also affects only the loop in which it is enclosed.

Continue statement enclosed in inner loop:

```
for(initialization1; test-expression1; updation1)
{
    for(initialization2; test-expression2; updation2)
    {
        if (test-expression3)
            continue;
        statements-2;
    }
    statements-1;
}
```

Continue statement enclosed in outer loop:

```
for(initialization1; test-expression1; updation1)
{
    for(initialization2; test-expression2; updation2)
    {
        statements2;
    }

    if (test-expression3)
    continue;
}
    statements;;
```

Program 5.14 To Illustrate Continue Statement in the Case of Nested Loops

```
#include <iostream.h>
int main(void)
{
   int number, i, j, sum, count;

   for(i = 1; i <= 2; i++)
   {
      sum = 0;
      count = 0;
      cout << "Enter five numbers for set-number" << i << endl;
      for(j = 1; j <= 5; j++)
      {
         cin >> number;
         if (number < 0)
               continue;
         count++;
         sum = sum + number;
      }
      cout << "sum of" << count << "+ve numbers in set-number"
         << i << "=" << sum << endl;
   }
```

```
    return 0;
}
```

Input-Output:

```
Enter five numbers for set-number1
1
2
3
-4
5

sum of4+ve numbers in set-number1=11

Enter five numbers for set-number2
1
2
-3
-4
5

sum of3+ve numbers in set-number2=8
```

Explanation

In Program 5.14, **number, i, j** and **sum** are declared to be variables of **int** type. The program is to accept two sets of numbers, each set consisting of maximum five numbers and find the sum of only +ve numbers in each set ignoring –ve numbers, if any. As in the case of the Program 5.13, the problem calls for nesting of two loops: the outer loop for selecting each set and the inner loop for enabling us to accept the elements of the the set selected by the outer loop. The variables **i** and **j** act as the control variables of the outer loop and the inner loop respectively. The variable **number** is to collect each number of a set and the variable **sum** collects the sum of only +ve numbers in the sets ignoring –ve numbers, if any. Initially, the outer loop control variable **i** takes **1** representing the first set. The inner loop control variable **j** then ranges from **1** to **5** enabling us to accept up to five numbers of the first set and find the sum of the positive numbers. Importantly, within the inner loop, **continue** statement is enclosed. It gets executed when the number entered is negative. So once a –ve number is entered for the set, the statements following it in the inner loop are skipped and the control goes back to the beginning of the inner loop itself. The variable **sum** would collect the sum of fewer than intended five numbers of the set in case negative numbers are entered. This is repeated for the remaining four sets also.

Since continue statement is enclosed within the inner loop, we notice that it affects the inner loop only.

REVIEW QUESTIONS

5.1 What is the need for looping?

5.2 Differentiate between selection and looping.

5.3 How do you construct a loop with the help of if and goto statements?

5.4 Mention the three necessary things required to construct a loop.

5.5 What will be the output of the following program:

```
int main(void)
{
    int i;
    for(i = 1; i < 10; i--)
        cout << i;
    return 0;
}
```

5.6 Explain for loop with its syntax.

5.7 Explain while loop with its syntax.

5.8 Explain do-while loop.

5.9 Differentiate between while loop and do-while loop.

5.10 Why do we need to nest loops?

5.11 Differentiate between break and continue statements.

True/False Questions

T5.1 Initialization, condition and updation all the three are a must to construct a loop.

T5.2 A test-expression is always associated with a loop.

T5.3 Absence of the updation statement leads to infinte loop.

T5.4 While loop executes atleast once.

T5.5 For loop is a post tested looping structure.

T5.6 Do while loop does not execute the block even once.

T5.7 For loop can be nested within while loop.

T5.8 Break statement causes the premature exit of the loop in which it is enclosed.

T5.9 Continue statement can be used only within a loop.

T5.10
```
for(i = 0; i < 9; i++).
{
    continue;
}
```
is a valid statement.

T5.11 Both break and continue statements should be associated with an `if` statement.

T5.12 Continue statement also terminates a loop prematurely.

PROGRAMMING EXERCISES

P5.1 Write a program to find the factorial of a number.

Example
Input = 4, Output = 24

P5.2 Write a program to find whether a number is an Armstrong number or not.
(A number is said to be an Armstrong number if the sum of the cubes of the digits of the number is equal to the number itself. **Example:** $153 = 1^3 + 5^3 + 3^3 = 1 + 125 + 27$)

P5.3 Write a program to find the sum of the digits of a multiple digit integer.

Example

Input = 2345, Output = 14

P5.4 Write a program to generate all the integers in the range m and n divisible by the integer d.

P5.5 Write a program to generate all the divisors of an integer n.

P5.6 Write a program to find the number of occurrences of a digit in a number.

P5.7 Write a program to reverse a given integer.

Example

Input = 2345, Output = 5432

P5.8 Write a program to find the sum of the sequence:

$$1 - \frac{1}{2} + \frac{1}{3} - \frac{1}{4} + \cdots$$

P5.9 Write a program to find the sum of the sequence:

$$\frac{1}{3} + \frac{3}{7} - \frac{5}{11} + \frac{7}{15} + \cdots$$

P5.10 Write a program to evaluate the sine series:

$$\sin(x) = x - \frac{x^3}{3!} + \frac{x^5}{5!} - \frac{x^7}{7!} + \frac{x^9}{9!} - \cdots$$

P5.11 Write a program to evaluate the cosine series:

$$\cos(x) = 1 - \frac{x^2}{2!} + \frac{x^4}{4!} - \frac{x^6}{6!} + \cdots$$

P5.12 Write a program to evaluate the exponential series:

$$e^x = 1 + x + \frac{x^2}{2!} + \frac{x^3}{3!} + \frac{x^4}{4!} + \cdots + \frac{x^n}{n!}$$

P5.13 Write a program to generate Armstrong numbers between two numbers.

P5.14 Write a program to display the following patterns:

(a)
```
123
456
789
```

(b)
```
1
12
123
1234
```

(c)
```
         1
      2  1  2
   3  2  1  2  3
4  3  2  1  2  3  4
```

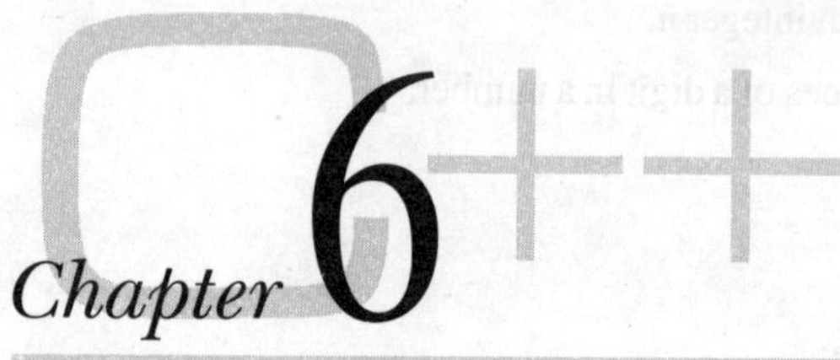

Functions

6.1 INTRODUCTION

One of the important features of C++ is its ability to support structured design (Top-down approach). The basic idea behind which is to divide a big program into a no. of relatively smaller and easily manageable subprograms. So far, in all our earlier programs, we have used only `main()` to solve problems. The algorithms involved in solving the problems were realized in terms of statements embedded in the `main()`. If a problem involves lengthy and complex algorithm, naturally, the length of the `main()` may increase to an extent where keeping track of the steps involved may become an Herculean task. In this case, it would be a nice proposition, if the problem can be divided into a no. of logical units and each logical unit is programmed separately and eventually all the logical units are combined together. This is where the concept of functions comes into picture. Each subprogram in C++ is called a **function**.

A function is defined to be a self-contained program which is written for the purpose of accomplishing some task.

6.2 ADVANTAGES OF FUNCTIONS

Functions offer the following advantages:

Minimization of memory space usage: Suppose we have five sets of numbers, each set consisting of three numbers and suppose we need to find the largest in each of the sets. If we use only `main()` to accomplish this task, we identify that the statements which are used to find the largest of three numbers have to be repeated five times. What if the no. of sets is more than five? Inevitably, we have to repeat the statements as many times as the no. of sets. The repetition of the same code leads to more consumption of memory space. This problem can be avoided by defining a separate function embedding the statements responsible for finding the largest of three numbers within it. The function can then be made to work with each of the sets at different points of time.

Improvization of overall organization of a program: The overall organization of a program is improved by the way of compartmentalization or modularization. Where in, a program is divided into a no. of subprograms depending on the functionality required by each subprogram. Each subprogram is viewed as a separate compartment or a module.

Facilitation of team work: Development of many real life applications calls for involvement of more than one programmer. This is mainly because of the larger size of the projects. The projects will normally be divided into a no. of modules and each module is assigned to a different programmer. Naturally, the programmers implement their modules using functions, which will be integrated together at the final stage.

Simplification of software engineering tasks like testing and debugging: The errors encountered in the code can easily be identified and fixed. Ease of identifying the location of the errors and correcting them is once again attributed to the flexibility provided by functions.

6.3 CLASSIFICATION OF FUNCTIONS

We can categorize functions into two types: (a) Built-in functions and (b) User-defined functions.

Built-in functions are those which are already made available as part of C++ library. They can be used by any programmer. Some of the examples of built-in functions are `sin()`, `cos()`, `strlen()` and `strcpy()`.

Whereas a *user-defined function* is written by a user to solve a problem. The strength of C++ lies in its flexibility in supporting development of user-defined functions at ease. The only user-defined function dealt with so far is `main()`.

Since the built-in functions are already available for use as part of the C++ library, it is enough if we know the purpose of the functions and the syntax of their usage. The list of most commonly used built-in functions, information about the functions like their syntax and their usage and the header file to be included are given in the Appendices towards the end of the book for reference.

We will now delve into the art of defining our own functions to accomplish the tasks which we come across. The general form of defining a function is as follows:

```
return-type   function-name( arguments)
{
    local variables;
    statements;
    return (expression);
}
```

The `return-type` refers to the data type of the value being returned by the function. The `function-name` is the name given to the function which is referred to while using the function. It should be a valid identifier and it is better if it reflects the underlying purpose. The function name is followed by arguments declaration enclosed within a pair of parentheses. The first line consisting of return-type, function-name and arguments declaration enclosed within a pair of parentheses is usually referred to as the **function header**. The function header is followed by the local variables declaration part and a set of executable statements of the function enclosed within a pair of opening brace and closing brace. The local variables declaration part and the set of statements enclosed within the braces is referred to as the **function body**.

Function Header + Function Body = Function Definition

A function, which is defined, can not be executed by itself. It has to be invoked by another function. It can be `main()` or any other function. A function which invokes another function is called **calling function** and the function which is invoked is termed as **called function**.

Sometimes, it is desirable that calling function and called function establish data communication. Arguments facilitate the data communication. Depending on the type of data communication, if any, functions are further classified into four types:

1. Functions with no arguments and no return value
2. Functions with arguments and no return value
3. Functions with arguments and return value
4. Functions with no arguments but with return value

6.4 FUNCTIONS WITH NO ARGUMENTS AND NO RETURN VALUE

Suppose `f()` is a function which does not require arguments to be passed and does not return any value to its calling program. The prototype of the function would be as follows:

```
void f(void);
```

and the function definition will have the form:

```
void f(void)
{
    variables
    statements
}
```

The call to the function `f()` would be like an independent statement as shown hereinafter

```
void fn()
{
    f();
}
```

where `fn()` is the calling function for the function `f()`.

Since the function `f()` does not require arguments to be passed from the calling function `fn()` and does not return any value back to it, there is no data communication between the function `f()` and its calling function. Program 6.1 uses a function which requires no arguments to be passed from the calling program and also does not return any value.

Program 6.1 To Illustrate a Function with No Arguments and No Return Value

```
#include <iostream.h>
void largest(void)
{
    int a, b, c, l;

    cout << "Enter three numbers" << endl;
    cin >> a >> b >> c;

    l = a;
    if (b > l)
        l = b;
    if (c > l)
        l = c;
```

```
    cout << "Largest = " << l;
}

int main(void)
{
    largest();
    return 0;
}
```

Input-Output:

```
Enter three numbers
10
16
20
Largest = 20
```

Explanation

The function `largest()` is to find the largest of three numbers. Its header indicates that it requires no arguments and it does not return any value. In the body of the function, four variables are declared. The variables `a`, `b` and `c` are to collect three numbers. The variable l is to collect the largest of them. The statements, which follow, accept three numbers, find the largest of them and display it.

In the `main()`, `largest()` is invoked by just specifying its name and a pair of parentheses. The actual execution starts from and ends with `main()` only. When `largest();` is encountered in `main()`, control is transferred to the function `largest()`. Upon completion of its execution, the control is regained by the `main()`.

Points to remember:

- A called function can be defined either before or after its calling function. In the Program 6.1, `largest()` (called function) has been defined before `main()` (calling function).
- If called function does not return any value, it has to be used as an independent statement .
- A function can not be defined within the body of another function as it is treated as an external variable.
- If a function `f1()` invokes another function `f2()` then `f2()` is said to have been called by `f1()`.

6.5 FUNCTIONS WITH ARGUMENTS AND NO RETURN VALUE

Suppose `f()` is a function which requires arguments to be passed and does not return any value to its calling program. The prototype of the function would be as follows:

```
void f(arguments);
```

and the function definition will have the form:

```
void f(arguments)
{
    variables
    statements
}
```

The call to the function `f()` would be like an independent statement:

```
void fn()
{
    f(actual-arguments);
}
```

where `fn()` is the calling function for the function `f()`.

Since the function `f()` requires arguments to be passed from the calling function `fn()` and does not return any value back to it, there is one-way data communication between the function `f()` and its calling function, i.e., from `fn()` to `f()` only.

Program 6.2 uses a function which requires arguments but does not return any value.

Program 6.2 To Illustrate a Function with Arguments and No Return Value

```
#include <iostream.h>
void largest(int a, int b, int c);
int main(void)
{
    int a, b, c;
    int x, y, z;

    cout << "Enter values of a , b and c" << endl;
    cin >> a >> b >> c;
    largest(a, b, c);

    cout << "Enter values of x , y and z" << endl;
    cin >> x >> y >> z;
    largest(x, y, z);

    return 0;
}

void largest(int a, int b, int c)
{
    int l;

    l = a;
    if (b > l)
        l = b;
    if (c > l)
        l = c;

    cout << "Largest = " << l;
}
```

Input-Output:

```
Enter values of a , b and c
5
6
7

Largest = 7
```

```
Enter values of x , y and z
5
7
9

Largest = 9
```

Explanation

The function `largest()` is defined with three arguments **a, b** and **c** of `int` type. The arguments **a, b** and **c** are called **formal arguments** of the function. The purpose of the function is to find the largest of the three integer values passed to it. Within the function, one more variable, **l** is declared and it collects the largest of **a, b** and **c**.

In the `main()`, **a, b, c, x, y** and **z** are declared to be variables of `int` type. Initially, the values of **a, b** and **c** are accepted and the function `largest()` is called by passing the values of **a, b** and **c** as `largest (a, b, c);`. As far as the function call `largest(a, b, c);` is concerned, the values of **a, b** and **c** belonging to `main()` are called the **actual arguments** for the function call. Note that **a, b** and **c** specified as formal arguments of `largest()` and **a, b** and **c** (actual arguments) declared in `main()`, even though they have same names are different in terms of storage. As a consequence of the function call `largest(a, b, c);` in `main()`, the values of **a, b** and **c** are copied to the formal arguments of `largest()` **a, b** and **c** respectively as:

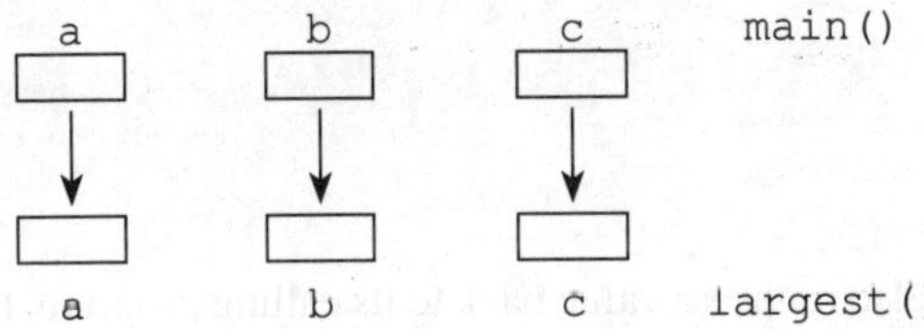

After the formal arguments of `largest()`, **a, b** and **c** get filled up, the function finds the largest of them assigns it to the variable `l`, which is then displayed. Control is regained by `main()`.

Next, three values are accepted into the variables `x`, `y` and `z` and again the function **`largest()`** is called by passing **x, y** and **z** as `largest(x, y, z)`; Now **x, y** and **z** become actual arguments. Similar to the previous case, as a consequence of the call `largest(x, y, z);` the values of `x`, `y` and `z` are copied to the formal arguments **a, b** and **c** respectively as:

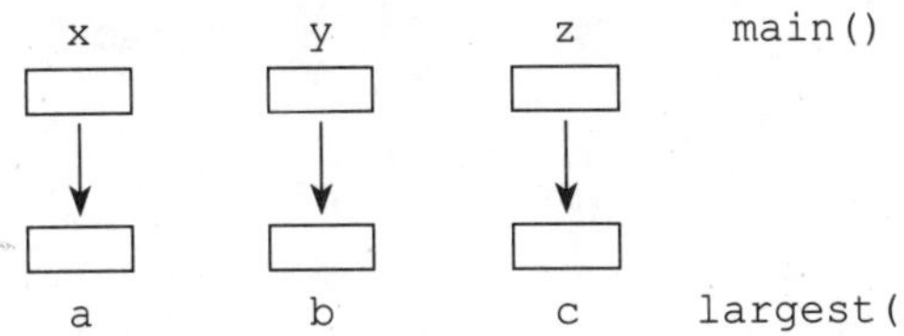

After the formal arguments of `largest()`, **a, b** and **c** get filled up, the function finds the largest of them assigns it to the variable 1, which is then displayed. The control is regained by `main()`.

Points to remember:

- The names of the formal arguments and the names of the actual arguments can be same or different.
- The no. of formal arguments and the actual arguments should be same.

- Types of the actual arguments should be compatible with those of the formal arguments.
- We can even pass constants as actual arguments. That is, `largest(3, 6, 7);` is a valid function call.

6.6 FUNCTIONS WITH ARGUMENTS AND RETURN VALUE

Suppose `f()` is a function which requires arguments to be passed and also returns a value to its calling program. The prototype of the function would be as follows:

```
data-type f(arguments);
```

The function definition will have the form:

```
data-type f(arguments)
{
    variables
    statements
    return (Expression);
}
```

The call to the function `f()` would be like a variable (part of an expression) as shown hereinafter.

```
void fn()
{
    variable = f(actual-arguments);
}
```

where `fn()` is the calling function for the function `f()`.

Since the function `f()` requires arguments and also returns a value back to its calling program, there is two-way data communication between the calling function and the function `f()`. Program 6.3 uses a function which requires arguments and returns a value to its calling program.

Program 6.3 To Illustrate a Function with Arguments and Return Value

```
#include <iostream.h>
int largest(int a, int b, int c);

int main(void)
{

    int a, b, c, lar;
    int x, y, z;

    cout << "Enter values of a, b and c" << endl;
    cin >> a >> b >> c;
    lar = largest(a, b, c);
    cout << " Largest = " << lar;

    cout << "Enter values of x, y and z " << endl;
    cin >> x >> y >> z;
    lar = largest(x, y, z);
```

```
    cout << "Largest = " << lar;
    return 0;
}

int largest(int a, int b, int c)
{
    int largest;

    largest = a;
    if (b > largest)
        largest = b;
    if (c > largest)
        largest = c;

    return (largest);
}
```

Input-Output:

```
Enter values of a, b and c
3
4
5

Largest = 5
Enter values of x, y and z
6
7
8

Largest = 8
```

Explanation

As in the case of previous programs, the `largest()` takes three variables **a**, **b** and **c** of `int` type as formal arguments, and finds the largest of the values collected by the arguments. Unlike in the previous cases, it does not display the largest value, but returns it back to the calling function (`main()`).

In the `main()`, the values of variables **a, b** and **c** are passed in the first call to the function `largest()`. Since `largest()` now returns a value, the function call is used on RHS of an assignment statement as `lar = largest(a, b, c);` the value returned by the function is collected by the variable **lar** and it is displayed.

In the second call to the function `largest()`, the values of **x, y** and **z** are passed.

```
lar = largest(x, y, z);
```

As a result, the function returns the largest of **x**, **y** and **z** and it is assigned to the variable **lar**, which is then displayed.

Points to remember:

- A function can not return more than one value. By default, it returns a value of `int` type.
- If a function returns a value then normally the function call would be like a variable. However, if the value being returned is not required, it can even be called an **independent statement**.

Program 6.4 To Find Whether a Number is Prime or Not Using a Function

```
#include <iostream.h>
int prime(int number)
{
    int k, rem, flag;

    flag = 1;
    k = 2;
    while(k <= number - 1)
    {
        rem = number % k;
        if (rem == 0)
        {
            flag = 0;
            break;
        }
        k++;
    }

    return (flag);
}

int main(void)
{
    int number;

    cout << "Enter a number " << endl;
    cin >> number;

    if (prime(number))
        cout << number<< "is prime" << endl;
    else
        cout << number << "is not prime" << endl;

    return 0;
}
```

Input-Output:

```
Enter a number
5
5 is prime
```

Explanation

The function `prime()` is defined with one formal argument of `int` type and is made to return either 1 or 0. The purpose of the function is to take an integer number and find out whether the number is prime or not. If the number is prime, it returns 1. Otherwise it returns 0.

In the `main()`, an integer number is accepted into the variable **`number`**. A call is made to the function `prime()` by passing the value of **`number`**. Since the function returns either 1 or 0, the function call has been used as a conditional expression as `(prime(number)) in main()`. If `prime(number)` returns 1 then the number is displayed as prime. Otherwise, the number is displayed as not prime.

Point to remember:

- If a function returns a value which is either 0 or 1 (or any non-zero value) can be used as a test-expression.

6.7 FUNCTIONS WITH NO ARGUMENTS BUT WITH RETURN VALUE

We can design functions, which do not require arguments but return a value. There are a number of built-in functions, which belong to this category. The function `getch()` is one such example. The `getch()` function does not require any arguments but it returns the character value it reads from the keyboard.

Program 6.5 To Illustrate a Function with No Arguments but with Return Value

```
#include <iostream.h>
int read_number(void);

int main(void)
{
    int number;

    number = read_number();
    cout << "number = " << number;
    return 0;
}

int read_number(void)
{
    int n;
    cout << "Enter a number" << endl;
    cin >> n;
    return n;
}
```

Input-Output:

```
Enter a number
7
number = 7
```

Explanation

In Program 6.5, the function `read_number()` is defined with no arguments but it is made to return a value. Within the function **n** is declared to be a variable of `int` type and a value is read into it with the statement `cin >> n;` and the value is returned back to the calling program.

In the `main()`, the `read_number()` is invoked in the statement `number = read_number();`. Note that the function call appears on the right hand side of the assignment statement. The variable **`number`** collects the value returned by the function and it is displayed.

6.8 FUNCTIONS RETURNING A NON-INTEGER VALUE

We just learnt that a function, if it returns a value, it will be of type `int` by default. In the real programming situations we may require to write functions which have to return a non-integer value to their calling programs. For instance, most of the built-in mathematical functions return double type values. For example, `sin()`, `cos()`, `tan()`, and `pow()`. In order to force a function to return a non-integer value, the function header should explicitly have the appropriate return-type name specified. If the function call precedes its definition, its prototype should also specify the appropriate return-type. Let us now write a program to illustrate this fact.

Program 6.6 To Illustrate Function Returning a Non-integer Value

```
#include <iostream.h>
float largest(float, float);

int main(void)
{
    float a, b, c;

    cout << "Enter two float values " << endl;
    cin >> a >> b;
    c = largest(a, b);
    cout << " largest = " << c;

    return 0;
}

float largest(float f, float g)
{
    float l;
    l = f;
    if (g > l)
        l = g;
    return (l);
}
```

Input-Output:

```
Enter two float values
4.5
5.6

largest = 5.6
```

Explanation

The function `largest()` is defined with two arguments of **float** type and is made to return value of type **float**. The purpose of the function is to find the largest of the two **float** values passed to it and return the result back to the calling program (`main()` in this case). Since the function is returning a value of **float** type (Non-integer type), the function prototype starts with the keyword **floats**. (function call precedes function definition). Similarly, the keyword **float** is used in the header of the function also while it is defined. These are to force the function to return a value of **float** type.

In the `main()`, two values of **float** type are read into the variables **a** and **b**. The function `largest()` is then called by passing **a** and **b** as the actual arguments as `c = largest(a, b);`. Note that since the function is returning a value, the function call is like a variable or a part of an expression. The value returned by the function `largest()` is assigned to the variable **c** in `main()` and it is displayed.

Points to remember:

- Function prototype is defined to be the declaration of a function, which indicates the no. of arguments, their types and its return-type.
- Prototype for a function is mandatory if the function is defined after its call. However, it is optional if the call is made to the function after defining the function.
- When a function is made to return a value of non-integer type, it is expected to be assigned to a variable of the corresponding type to get the correct value returned by the function.

6.9 RETURN STATEMENT VERSUS EXIT( )

The function exit() is a built-in function available as part of C++ library. The common thing shared by both the `return` statement and the `exit()` is that both are used to exit the function in which they are used. But, the difference lies in where the control is then transferred to after the exit of their corresponding functions. The `return` statement causes the exit of the function in which it is enclosed and transfers the control to the `calling function`. But the `exit()` enclosed within a function, on its execution, terminates the entire program and the control is transferred to the underlying operating system itself.

To be able to use `exit()`, the program should include either **stdlib.h** or **process.h** header files. This is because, the prototype for the function is available in these files.

Program 6.7 To Illustrate Return Statement v/s exit()

```
#include <iostream.h>
#include <process.h>
int fact(int);

int main(void)
{
    int n, f;

    cout << "Enter a number" << endl;
    cin >> n;
    f = fact(n);
    cout << "Factorial = " << f;

    return 0;
}

int fact(int n)
{
    int f = 1, i;
    if (n < 0)
    {
        cout << "The number entered is -ve " << endl;
        exit(0);
    }
    else
```

```
    {
        for(i = 1; i <= n; i++)
            f *= i;
    }
    return (f);
}
```

Input-Output:

First Run:
```
Enter a number
-4
The number entered is -ve (The control goes to the operating system)
```

Second Run:
```
Enter a number
5
Factorial = 120        (The control is transferred to the main())
```

Explanation

In Program 6.7, if the number passed to the function `fact()` is negative, the entire program is terminated because the statement `exit(0);` gets executed and the control is transferred to the operating system. But if a positive integer is passed to the function `fact()`, its factorial is found out and the `return` statement in the function `fact()` on its execution returns the factorial value to the calling function (`main()`).

6.10 RECURSION

Suppose `f1()`, `f2()` and `f3()` are three functions. The function `f1()` can call `f2()`, in turn, `f2()` can call f3(). Likewise, nesting of the function calls can be to any level depending on the requirement. There is one more possibility with regard to functions, which needs to be mentioned. That is, a function `f()` can call itself`()`. The phenomenon of a function calling itself is called **recursion**. The function involved in the process is referred to as a **recursive function**.

There are a number of problems, the solutions of which can be expressed in terms of recursive steps. A solution to a problem is said to be expressible in terms of recursive steps if it can be expressed in terms of its subsolutions. These can be implemented by the use of recursive functions. When a recursive function is employed to solve these problems, care needs to be taken to see to it that the function does not call itself again at some point of time by which the solution for the problem has been arrived at. This is accomplished with the help of a *terminating condition*.

Problem 1 Finding the factorial of a number 4.

Solution: Mathematically, factorial of 4 is denoted by 4!.

$$\begin{aligned} 4! &= 4*3! \\ &= 4*3*2! \\ &= 4*3*2*1! \\ &= 4*3*2*1 \\ &= 24 \end{aligned}$$

In general, factorial of a number n denoted by $n!$ can be written as:

$$
\begin{aligned}
n! &= n * (n-1)! \\
&= n * (n-1) * (n-2)! \\
&\vdots \\
&\vdots \\
&= n * (n-1) * (n-2) \ldots * 1! \\
&= n * (n-1) * (n-2) \ldots * 0!
\end{aligned}
$$

We know that factorial of 0 is 1. Thus, when n takes 0, we do not call the function `fact()` but we simply return 1. This happens to be the terminating condition.

Program 6.8 To Find Factorial of a Number

```
#include <iostream.h>

int fact(int);

int main(void)
{
    int n, f;

    cout << "Enter a number" << endl;
    cin >> n;

    f = fact(n);
    cout << "fact = " << f;

    return 0;
}

int fact(int n)
{
    int f;

    if (n == 0)
        return (1);
    else
        f = n * fact(n - 1);

    return f;
}
```

Input-Output:

```
Enter a number
5
factorial = 120
```

Explanation

Function `fact()` is defined with an argument of `int` type and is made to return a value of `int` type. The purpose of the function is to find the factorial of an integer number passed to it and to return the result back to the calling program [`main()` in this case].

Within the function `fact()`, the task of finding the factorial of `n` is expressed in terms of recursive steps. The function works as follows:

In the simplest case, if the value of `n` is 0, the function returns 1. That is, factorial of 0 is returned back to the `main()`.

If `n > 0` then, as long as `n` > 0, `fact()` is called recursively by passing one less than the previous number. Once argument to `fact()` becomes 0 the function returns 1 to its calling function. In this case, the same function `fact()`, which had the argument as 1 [i.e., (`fact(1)`]. Then the function `fact(1)` returns 1 to its calling function which once again is the `fact()` itself which had the argument as 2 [i.e., `fact(2)`]. Likewise each recently called function `fact ()` returns the value it evaluates, to its calling `fact()` and ultimately, the `fact()` which was called by `main()` returns the factorial of the given number to the `main()`.

Suppose $n = 4$, the function call `fact(4)` in `main()` gives rise to the following sequence:

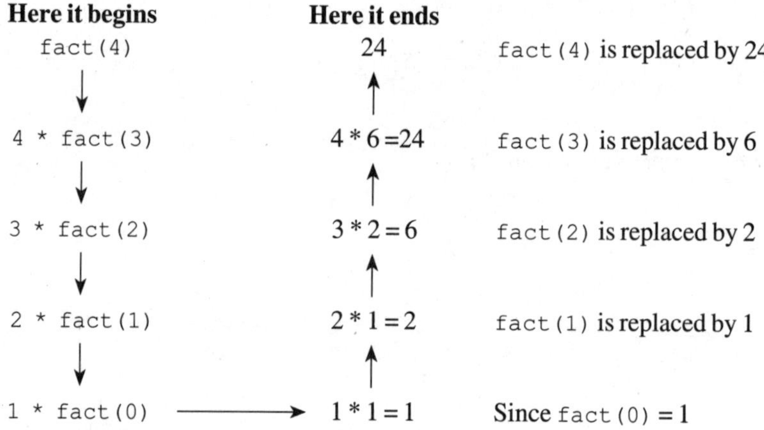

The factorial of 4 = 24 is then collected by the variable **f** in the `main()`.

Suppose we want to find the sum of digits of an integer number, we can see that the task can be expressed in recursive steps as given in the following problem:

Problem 2 To find the sum of the digits of 456.

Solution: If `sum()` is the function defined for this, then

```
sum(456) = 6 + sum(45)
         = 6 + 5 + sum(4)
         = 6 + 5 + 4 + sum(0)
         = 6 + 5 + 4 + 0
         = 15
```

In general, if `sum()` is to find the sum of digits of a number *n*:

`sum(n)` is expanded to $n\,\%10$ + `sum(n/10)` as long as the argument to `sum()` becomes 0. Once the argument becomes 0, `sum(0)` is replaced by 0. This becomes the terminating condition for the problem.

The value of the resultant expression turns out to be the sum of the digits of the given number. Within the function we keep checking the value of the argument passed, if the terminating condition is satisfied, the value 0 is returned.

Program 6.9 To Find the Sum of Digits of a Number

```
#include <iostream.h>

int sum(int);

int main(void)
{
    int number, s;

    cout << "Enter a number" << endl;
    cin >> number;

    s = sum(number);

    cout << " sum =" << s;

    return 0;
}

int sum(int number)
{
    int s;

    if (number == 0)
        return 0;
    else
        s = number % 10 + sum(number / 10);
    return s;
}
```

Input-Output:

```
Enter a number
456
Sum = 15
```

Explanation

The function `sum()` is defined with an argument of `int` type and is made to return a value of `int` type. The purpose of the function is to find the sum of digits of the number passed to it and return the sum back to the calling program. Within the function, the sum of digits of the number passed, is found out using recursive approach as follows. As long as number > 0, remainder after division of number by 10 is extracted and the remaining part of the number is once again passed to the function as in the statement `s = number % 10 + sum(number/10);`. Once the argument to `sum()` becomes 0, the recursive calls to `sum()` are exited in the last in first out order. The first call made by `main()` to `sum()` on its exit returns the sum of the digits to the `main()`. The function `sum()` works as follows:

Suppose $n = 465$, the function call `sum(465)` in `main()` gives rise to the following sequence:

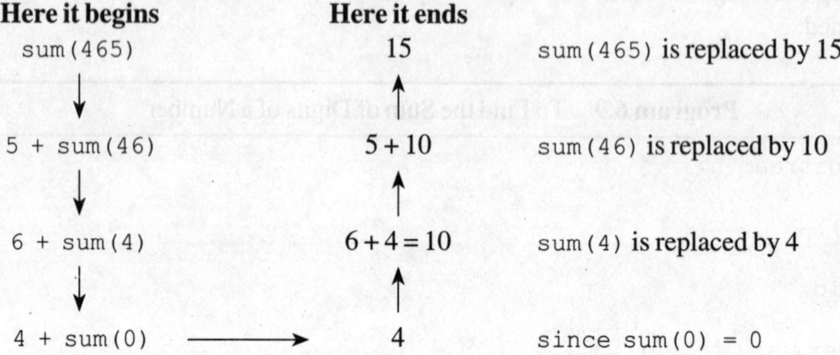

Sum of the digits of the number 465 = 15 is collected by the variable **s** in the `main()`.

Problem 3: Fibonacci series starts with two numbers 0 and 1. The next subsequent member of the series is obtained by summing the immediate previous two. Generation of the series can be recursively expressed as follows:

```
fib(n) = fib(n-1) + fib(n-2)
```

i.e., nth member is the sum of $(n-1)$th and $(n-2)$th member of the series

and `fib(1) = 0, fib(2) = 1`

Thus, we have two terminating conditions. In either of these cases, the function exits without making another call to itself.

Program 6.10 To Generate Fibonacci Series

```
#include <iostream.h>

int fib(int);

int main(void)
{
    int n, i;

    cout << "Enter the number of members to be generated\n" << endl;
    cin >> n;

    for( i = 1; i <= n; i++)
        cout << fib(i) << endl;

    return 0;
}

int fib(int n)
{
    int f;
```

```
    if (n == 1)
        return 0;
    else if (n == 2)
        return 1;
    else
        f = fib(n - 1) + fib(n - 2);
    return f;
}
```

Input-Output:

```
Enter the number of members to be generated
10

0
1
1
2
3
5
8
13
21
34
```

Explanation

The function fib() is defined with one argument of int type and is made to return a value of int type. The purpose of the function is to take an integer number *n* and generate *n*th member of Fibonacci series and return it to the calling program.

The following program segment is responsible for generating *n* members of the Fibonacci series:

```
for( i = 1; i <= n; i++)
    cout << fib(i) << endl;
```

Here when **i** takes the value 1, the function call fib(1) returns 0 the first member of the series and it is displayed. In the next iteration, the control variable **i** takes the value 2, then the function call fib(2) returns 1, the second member of the series and it is displayed.

In the third iteration, i takes 3, the function call becomes fib(3), the function call to fib() with 3 as the argument in turn makes two calls to itself by passing 2 and 1 as the arguments (fib(2) + fib(1)). These function calls return 0 and 1 respectively to the function fib() itself (which was called with 3 as the argument), which in turn returns the sum of them ,which is 1, the third member of the series to the main(). Similarly, when the variable **i** takes 4 the fourth member of the series is obtained and so on.

To find the value of x to the power of y: The task of finding the value of *x* to the power of *y* can also be expressed in terms of recursive steps.

Suppose we need to evaluate 2^3. Let us express 2^3 in recursive terms as follows:

$$\begin{aligned} 2^3 &= 2 * 2^2 \\ &= 2 * 2 * 2^1 \\ &= 2 * 2 * 2 * 2^0 \\ &= 2 * 2 * 2 * 1 \end{aligned}$$

Note that 2^0 is replaced by 1. So the terminating condition for the recursion problem is: if $y = 0$ return 1

Program 6.11 To Find *x* to the Power of *y*

```
#include <iostream.h>

float power(int x, int y)
{
    float p;
    if (y == 0)
        return (1);
    else if (y > 0)
        p =x * power(x, y - 1);
    else
    {
        p = 1 / power(x, -y);
    }
    return (p);
}

int main(void)
{
    int x, y;
    float p;

    cout << "Enter values of x and y \n";
    cin >> x >> y;
    p = power(x, y);
    cout << p;

    return 0;
}
```

Input-Output:

```
Enter values of x and y
2
3

8
Enter values of x and y
4
-1

0.25
```

Explanation

The function `power()` is defined with two arguments *x* and *y* of **int** type and it is also made to return a value of **float** type. The purpose of the function is to find the value of *x* to the power of **y** and return it to its calling program.

When $y = 0$, the function returns one since any number raised to the power of zero is one and this happens to be the terminating condition for the recursive function. If the value of $y > 0$ (i.e., positive), the function is called **recursively** as in the statement `p = x * power(x, y - 1);` note that one less than the previous value of y is passed as the second argument in each successive recursive call till it becomes zero. Once it becomes zero, the function exits in the last in first out manner and ultimately it returns the value of x to the power of y to the calling program (`main()` in this case). If the value of $y < 0$ (i.e., negative), the function is called **recursively** as in the statement `p = 1/ x * power(x, -y);`. This is because mathematically x^{-y} can be written as $1/x^y$. Here the value of x^y is found as in the previous case and the value of $1/x^y$ is returned to the calling program (`main()` in this case).

In the `main()` **x** and **y** are declared to be variables of **int** type and **p** is declared to be a variable of type **float**. The values of **x** and **y** are accepted and the value of x^y is found out with the statement `p = power x, y);` Here **p** collects the value of x^y and it is displayed.

When `x = 2, y = 3.`

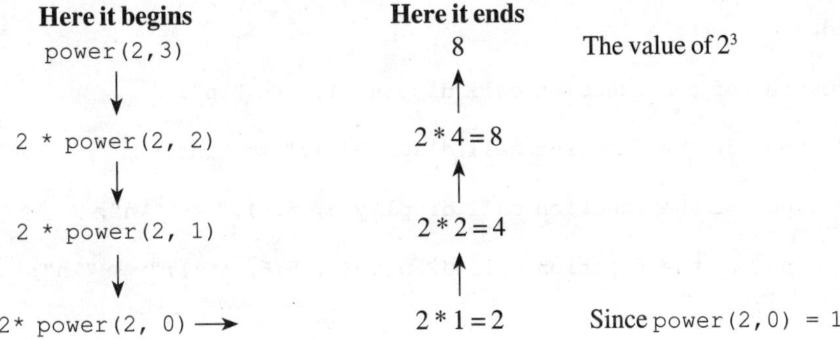

6.10.1 Recursion Versus Iteration

Recursion:

- Near to the problem definition, easy to understand
- Consumes more memory space (Stack memory)
- More CPU overhead
- Less efficient

Iteration:

- Relatively more difficult to understand
- CPU overhead minimal
- Memory consumption minimal
- More efficient

6.11 FUNCTIONS WITH DEFAULT-ARGUMENTS

In C++, we can provide default values to the arguments of functions either in the prototypes or while the functions are defined. Once the default values are specified, the function can be called without passing any actual arguments, in which case, the functions operate on the default values. If actual arguments are provided, the default values are ignored.

EXAMPLE

```
int area(int length = 4, int breadth = 5);
cout << area();
```

Here the function `area()` will operate on the default values 4 and 5.

```
cout << area(6, 7);
```

Here the function `area()` operates on the values 6 and 7 instead of the default values 4 and 5.

Program 6.12 To Illustrate Function Default Arguments

```
#include <iostream.h>

void display(int i = 10, float f = 4.5, char c = 'd');

int main(void)
{
    cout << "Output of the function call display();" << "\n";
    display();
    cout << "Output of the function call display(3);" << "\n";
    display(3);
    cout << "Output of the function call display(3, 5.6);" << "\n";
    display(3, 5.6);
    cout << "Output of the function call display(3, 5.6, 't');" << "\n";
    display(3, 5.6, 't');

    return 0;
}

void display(int i, float f, char c)
{
    cout<<"i = "<< i << "f = " << f << " c = " << c <<"\n\n";
}
```

Input-Output:

```
Output of the function call display();
i = 10 f = 4.5 c = d

Output of the function call display(3);
i = 3 f = 4.5 c = d

Output of the function call display(3, 5.6);
i = 3 f = 5.6 c = d

Output of the function call display(3, 5.6, 't');
i = 3 f = 5.6 c = t
```

Explanation

The function `display()` is defined with three arguments **i, f** and **c** of type `int`, `float` and `char` respectively. The arguments are also given default values in the prototype of the function. The purpose of the function is to display the values passed to it as actual arguments. The function call `display();` displays the default values. The second call to the function `display(3);` displays 3, 4.5 and *d*. Note that the default value 10 for **i** is overridden by the new value 3. In response to the third call to the function `display(3, 5.6);` the values 3, 5.6 and *d* are displayed. The default values of **i** and **f** are overridden by 3 and 5.6. In the fourth call to the function `display(3,5.6,'t');` all the three default values are overridden by the new actual arguments.

Note that the function call `display(6.7);` displays 6, 4.5 and *d*. Here 6.7 is converted to `int` type and it overrides the default value of the `int` argument and the values 4.5 and *d* are taken by default. Thus, if a function is defined with **n** default arguments, we can not override the **i**th argument unless we provide the values for the first $i - 1$ arguments.

6.12 INLINE FUNCTIONS

The concept of functions was invented primarily to modularize programs and save memory space. Once we define a function, it can be invoked anywhere in a program and any number of times. That is the beauty of the functions. Each invocation of a function results in a number of operations to be carried out by the processor. They are: pushing the arguments to the stack(if any), saving the return address in the stack, saving the registers, transferring the control to the called function, after executing the function, cleaning up the stack (arguments), transferring the control back to the calling program. If the functions are reasonably big in size and are required to be called in many places and many times, we should use functions. What if a function is too small (it contains one or two statements) and we infrequently invoke it, even for this function the above operations have to happen. How can we relieve the burden of the processor in regard to these kind of functions? Here comes the concept of inline functions as a remedy.

An inline function is one, which is expanded in line on its invocation. As a result, a call to an inline function does not require the usual function call overhead. A function is made inline by using the keyword inline before the header of a function.

EXAMPLE

```
inline print(char*);
```

Program 6.13 To Illustrate Inline Function

```
#include <iostream.h>

inline void display()
{
    cout << "Welcome" << endl;
}

int main(void)
{
    display();
    display();
    return 0;
}
```

Input-Output:

```
Welcome
Welcome
```

Explanation

Since there are two calls to the inline function `display()`, the calls are replaced by the code of the function in both the places and they get executed resulting in the display of the message "welcome" twice on the screen.

The keyword *inline* is just a request to the compiler to consider a function as an inline function. It is left to the discretion of the compiler to consider or not. If the compiler feels that a function should not be treated as inline, (when a function is too big or too complicated) it flags a warning error and treats the function as a normal function. Following are the functions for which the request for inline status is turned down by the compiler:

(a) Functions with a return statement but do not return values
(b) Functions with loops or a switch statements or goto statements and return values
(c) Functions which contain static variables
(d) Recursive Functions

6.13 FUNCTION OVERLOADING

Function overloading is nothing but retaining the same name for more than one function, which, normally, perform a similar kind of task but over different number and types of operands, thereby enabling us to create a family of functions with the same name. The functions in the family, even though, share a common name, they differ in the number and type of arguments. When the same name is used for multiple functions, the term *function polymorphism* is used to reflect the situation. When the same name is used for multiple functions, the selection of a function for execution depends on the signature of the function being called. The signature of a function is nothing but the number of arguments, their types and their order in the list.

EXAMPLE

Consider the following three functions:

```
int product(int a, int b)
{
    return a * b;
}

int product(int a , int b, int c)
{
    return a * b * c;
}
double product(double a, double b)
{
    return a * b;
}
```

All the three functions have the same name **product**. But they differ in their number and types of arguments, which is enough for the compiler to resolve dispute in the function calls.

```
p = product(3, 6);
```

Invokes the function with the header `int product(int a, int b)`

```
p = product(2, 3, 4);
```

Invokes the function with the header `int product(int a, int b, int c)`

```
p = product(4.5, 5.7);
```

Invokes the function with the header `double product(doublet a, double b)`

Here the function name product is said to have been overloaded. Since the function calls are resolved during compile-time itself, the polymorphism is said to be **compile-time polymorphism**. It is also called **early binding** or **static binding**.

Program 6.14 To Illustrate Function Overloading

```
#include <iostream.h>

void display();
void display(int);
void display(int, float);
void display(int, float, char);
int main(void)
{
    cout << "Call to display()" << endl;
    display();
    cout << "\nCall to display(int)" << endl;
    display(4);
    cout << "\nCall to display(int, float)" << endl;
    display(5, 5.6);
    cout << "\nCall to display(int, float, char)" << endl;
    display(6, 7.8, 'a');

    return 0;
}

void display()
{
    cout << "Function Overloading" << endl;
}

void display(int i)
{
    cout << "i = " << i << endl;
}

void display(int i, float f)
{
    cout << "i = " << i << endl;
    cout << "f = " << f << endl;
}

void display(int i, float f, char c)
{
    cout << "i = " << i << endl;
    cout << "f = " << f << endl;
    cout << "c = " << c << endl;
}
```

Input-Output:

```
Call to display()
Function Overloading

Call to display(int)
i = 4
Call to display(int, float)
i = 5
f = 5.6

Call to display(int, float, char)
i = 6
f = 7.8
c = a
```

Explanation

The program contains four functions with the same name display. It can be noted that the functions differ in both the number of arguments and the types of them, i.e., the signatures of the functions are unique, which is enough for the compiler to distinguish between different functions.

Program 6.15 To Illustrate Function Overloading

```
#include <iostream.h>

float area(int);
float area(int, int);

int main(void)
{
    int radius;
    float cir_area;
    cout << "Enter radius " << endl;
    cin >> radius;
    cir_area = area(radius);
    cout << "Area of Circle = " << cir_area << endl;

    int length, breadth;
    float rect_area;
    cout << "Enter length and breadth " << endl;
    cin >> length >> breadth;
    rect_area = area(length, breadth);
    cout << "Area of Rectangle = " << rect_area << endl;

    return 0;
}

float area(int r)
{
    return 3.14 * r * r;
}

float area(int l, int b)
{
    return l * b;
}
```

Input-Output:

```
Enter radius
5
Area of Circle = 78.5
Enter length and breadth
5 6
Area of Rectangle = 30
```

Explanation

The program contains two functions with the same name area. The function `area()` with one argument of `int` type is to find the area of a circle. The argument represents the radius of the circle. Another function with two arguments of `int` type is to find the area of a rectangle. The arguments represent the length and the breadth of the rectangle.

The function `call area(radius);` invokes the `area()` with one argument and finds the area of the circle and returns it to the calling program. The function `call area(length, breadth);` invokes the `area()` with two arguments and finds the area of the rectangle and returns it to the calling program.

In both the example programs, the selection of a function by the compiler for execution was straightforward because of the exact match between the actual arguments and the formal arguments of a function. There may arise some situations where there may not be exact match. In such cases, the function calls are resolved subject to the following guidelines:

1. The compiler uses default promotions like
   from `char` to `int`
   from `float` to `double` to find a match
2. When no match is found even after checking for default promotions, the compiler then uses the built-in conversions (from the formal arguments to the actual arguments) like `int` to `float` or `float` to `int` to find a unique match.
3. When both of them fail, the compiler uses the user-defined conversions (if any) in combination with the default promotions and the built-in conversions to find a unique match.

The rules are not necessarily mutually exclusive. If there is possibility of multiple matches, the compiler will generate an appropriate message.

Consider the following example:

```
int sum(int);
float sum(float);

 cout << sum(7);
```

Even though an exact match is found there is ambiguity between the two functions since `int` to `float` conversion is a built-in one. The compiler gets confused as to which to select.

But consider the modified `sum()` functions as follows:

```
int sum(int);
double sum(double);
```

Here the function call `sum(4);` invokes the `sum()` with `int` as the argument. Here the signatures of the functions are considered to be distinct.

Now, consider the following two function prototypes:

```
long sqr(long);
double sqr(double);
```

`cout << sqr(4L);` invokes the `sqr()` with `long` as the argument type. Note the presence of the letter **L** after 4. It is to indicate that the value is of type `long`.

`cout << sqr(3.4);` invokes the `sqr()` with `double` as the argument type. Here 3.4 is converted to `double` type by default promotion rule.

No problem is faced by the compiler in selecting the correct function since there were unique matches.

But consider the following statement:

```
cout << sqr(4);
```

Here the compiler gets confused in selecting the correct function. It is because, the value 4 (`int`) can be converted to both `long` as well as `double` type. There are built-in conversions routines available as part of the compiler. As a result, there exist multiple matches. The argument to the function should thus be either 4L or, `(float)` 4 or 4.0 to resolve the ambiguity.

6.14 THE SCOPE RESOLUTION OPERATOR ::

The scope resolution operator :: is used to resolve dispute in regard to scope of local and global variables with same names. Program 6.16 throws light on the usefulness of the operator.

Program 6.16 To Illustrate Scope Resolution Operator

```
#include <iostream.h>

int i = 10;

int main(void)
{
    int i = 20;

    cout << "i inside main() = " << i << "\n";
    cout << "i outside main() = " << ::i << "\n";
    ::i = 25;
    cout << "i outside main() after updation =" << ::i << "\n";
    return 0;
}
```

Input-Output:

```
i inside main() = 10
i outside main() = 20
i outside main() after updation = 25
```

Explanation

In Program 6.16, there are two variables of `int` type with the same name **i**. One is local to the `main()` and the other is the global to the `main()`. Any reference to the variable name **i** in the `main()` would refer to the local variable **i** belonging to it. In order to access the global variable **i**, we have used the scope resolution operator before the variable name as in the statement `cout << "i outside main() =" << ::i << "\n";`. Also note that the value of the global variable **i** is changed to 25 with the statement `::i = 25;`.

6.15 REFERENCE VARIABLES

A reference variable is an alias to an existing variable. It allows us to use multiple names for the same location. Consider the following declarations:

```
int a = 10;
```

a is declared to be a variable of `int` type and is given the value 10.

```
int &b = a;
```

```
 a
┌──────┐
│ 10   │
└──────┘
 b
```

Here, the variable **b** is declared to be a reference variable to the previously declared variable **a**. As a result, **b** becomes another name for the location of the variable **a**. Now, they can be used interchangeably. Note the presence of & symbol before the variable **b**. In this context, it is to indicate that the variable **b** is a reference variable.

Program 6.17 To Illustrate Reference Variables

```
#include <iostream.h>

int main(void)
{
    int i = 10, &j = i;

    cout << "i = " << i << "\n";
    cout << "j = " << j << "\n";
    cout << "Address of i = " << &i << "\n";
    cout << "Address of j = " << &j << "\n";

    return 0;
}
```

Input-Output:

```
i = 10
j = 10
Address of i = 0xfff4
Address of j = 0xfff4
```

Explanation

In Program 6.17, **j** is made a reference variable to the variable **i**. To confirm that both **i** and **j** refer to a common memory location, the values of both **i** and reference **j** are displayed. Not only that, the address of both **i** and its reference **j** are displayed. They are also seen to be same.

Some more examples of reference variables created at the time of declaration are:

```
int x[10];
int &y = x[3];
```

Here, **y** is made a reference variable for the array element `x[3]`.

```
int &m = 5;
```

Here **m** is made a reference variable to the location where the constant 5 is stored.

```
char &c = '\n';
```

Here, **c** is made a reference variable to the unknown location allocated to the new line character. Here **c** refers to a constant.

Reference variables become handy in implementing call by reference, a function call mechanism. Here, the formal arguments to functions are made reference variables. The arguments thus become aliases for the corresponding actual arguments.

6.15.1 Call by Value and Call by Reference

In our earlier programs, which involve functions with arguments, we passed the values of actual arguments. The mechanism of calling a function by passing values is called **call by value**. We now discuss passing reference variables as arguments to functions. The mechanism of calling a function by passing references is called **call by reference**. If a function is to be passed a reference, it has to be reflected in the argument-list of the function prototype (if used) and the header of the function definition.

EXAMPLE

```
void display(int&);
```

The function prototype indicates that the function `display()` requires a reference to `int` as its argument.

```
void display(int& p)
{
    statements;
}
```

Note the type of the formal argument **p** in the definition of the `display()`. It is rightly declared to be a reference to `int` type.

The call to the `display()` would be as follows:

```
display(a);
```

where **a** is a variable of `int` type belonging to the calling program.

Program 6.18 To Illustrate Call by Value and Call by Reference

```
#include <iostream.h>

void inc(int);
void incr(int&);

int main(void)
{
    int a = 10;

    cout << " a = " << a << "\n";
    inc(a);
    cout << "After calling inc() \n";
    cout << "a = " << a << "\n";

    incr(a);
```

```
    cout << "After calling incr() a = " << a << "\n";

    return 0;
}

void inc(int x)
{
    x++;
    cout << "x = " << x << "\n";
}

void incr(int& p)
{
    p++;
}
```

Input-Output:

```
a = 10
x = 11
After calling inc()
a = 10
After calling incr() a = 11
```

Explanation

The function `inc()` is defined with a formal argument **x** of type `int`. The purpose of the function is to increment the value passed to it by one. The function `incr()` is another function defined with one formal argument **p**, which is a reference to `int` type and the purpose of the function is to increment the value of the reference variable.

In the `main()`, **a** and **b** are declared to be variables of `int` type and are initialized with the value 10. To begin with, the value of **a** is displayed to be 10. The function `inc()` is invoked by passing **a** as the actual parameter. As a result, the value of **a** is copied to **x**, the formal parameter of the function and within the function, **x** is incremented by one, it becomes 11and is displayed. After the exit of the `inc()`, the control is transferred back to the `main()`. In the `main()`, the value of **a** is once again displayed. It turns out to be 10 only. The function `inc()` has not been able to change the value of **a**, which belongs to `main()`;. It has acted on **x**, its formal parameter (a copy of **a**).

We now understand the working of `incr()`. The initial value of **b** in `main()` is displayed. Then a call is made to `incr()` by passing the variable **b** to it as `incr(b)`. Within the function `incr()`, **p** is incremented. After the function is exited, the value of **b** is redisplayed and it is seen to be 11. So, the function `incr()` could change the value of the variable **b**, which belonged to `main()`.

Program 6.19 To Illustrate Call by Value and Call by Reference

```
#include <iostream.h>

void swap(int, int);
void swapr(int&, int&);

int main(void)
{
    int a = 5, b = 6;
```

```
    int c = 7, d = 8;

    cout << "a = " << a << "b = " << b << "\n";
    cout << " Call by value\n";
    swap(a, b);
    cout << "After calling swap() \n";
    cout << "a = " << a << "b = " << b << "\n";

    cout << "Call by Reference \n";
    cout << "c = " << c << "d = " << d << "\n";
    swapr(c, d);
    cout << "After calling swapr() \n";
    cout << "c = " << c << "d =" << d << "\n";

    return 0;
}

void swap(int x, int y)
{
    int t;

    t = x;
    x = y;
    y = t;

    cout << "x = " << x << "y = " << y << "\n";
}

void swapr(int& p, int& q)
{
    int t;
    t = p;
    p = q;
    q = t;
}
```

Input-Output:

```
a = 5   b = 6
Call by value
x = 6   y= 5
After calling swap()
a = 5   b = 6
Call by Reference
c = 7   d = 8
After calling swapr()
c = 8   d =7
```

Explanation

The function `swap()` is defined with two formal arguments **x** and **y** of `int` type. The purpose of the function is to interchange the values taken by the formal arguments **x** and **y**. Within the function, the following statements accomplish interchanging of values of **x** and **y**:

```
t = x;
x = y;
y = t;
```

`t` is a local variable of the function, which acts as a temporary variable used to interchange the values.

The function `swapr()` is defined with two formal arguments **p** and **q** which are references `int` type. The purpose of this function is to interchange the values of the reference variables **p** and **q**. Within the function, the following statements accomplish the interchanging:

`t = p;`	The value of **p** is moved to **t**.
`p = q;`	The value of **q** is moved to **p**.
`q = t;`	The value of **t** (the value of **p**) is moved to **q**.

`t` is a local variable of the function, which acts as a temporary variable. It is used to interchange the values.

In the `main()`, the local variables of `int` type **a**, **b** and **c** and **d** are initialized with the values `5, 6, 7` and `8` respectively. The variables **a** and **b** are to be passed as arguments to `swap()`. Before calling `swap()`, the values of **a** and **b** are displayed to be `5` and `6` respectively. Then the function `swap()` is called by passing **a** and **b** as its arguments as `swap(a, b);`. The values of **a** and **b** are copied to **x** and **y**, the formal arguments of the function, respectively. The statements of the function interchange the values of **x** and **y** and they are displayed to be `6` and `5` respectively. After the exit of the function `swap()`, the `main()` function regains the control. The values of **a** and **b** are once again displayed in `main()` and they are seen to be `5` and `6` only, i.e., the values of **a** and **b** are not interchanged by `swap()`. The `swap()` has acted on **x** and **y**, the copies of **a** and **b** respectively not on **a** and **b** themselves.

Let us now understand the working of `swapr()`. The values of **c** and **d** of `main()` are displayed before calling `swapr()`. They are seen to be `7` and `8` respectively. The function `swapr()` is then called by passing **c** and **d** as the arguments. **c** and **d** are taken by the formal arguments of `swapr()`, **p** and **q** respectively. Within the function, the values of **p** and **q** are interchanged. Even within the `swapr()` also, locations of **c** and **d** are the targets. After the exit of the `swapr()`, control is gained by `main()`. In `main()`, the values of **c** and **d** are once again displayed. They are seen to be `8` and `7` respectively, i.e., the function `swapr()` has been able to interchange the values of **c** and **d** themselves.

Program 6.20 To Illustrate Passing both Values and References as Arguments

```
#include <iostream.h>

void lar_seclar(int, int, int, int&, int&);

int main(void)
{
    int a, b, c, l, sl;

    cout << "Enter three numbers \n";
    cin >> a >> b >> c;
    cout << "Given Numbers: a = " << a << "b =" << b << "c = "
            << c << "\n";
    lar_seclar(a, b, c, l, sl);
    cout << " Largest = " << l << "\n";
    cout << "Second largest = " << sl << "\n";
    return 0;
}
```

```
void lar_seclar(int a, int b, int c, int& lp, int& slp)
{
    int l, s, sl;
    l = a;
    if (b > l)
        l = b;
     if (c> l)
        l = c;
    s = a;
    if (b < s)
        s = b;
     if (c < s)
        s = c;
    sl = (a + b + c) - (l + s);
    lp = l;
    slp = sl;
}
```

Input-Output:

```
Enter three numbers
4 5 6

Given Numbers: a = 4 b = 5  c = 6
Largest = 6
Second largest = 5
```

Explanation

In Program 6.20, the function `lar_seclar()` is defined with five formal arguments. The arguments **a, b** and **c** are the plain variables of `int` type, whereas **lp** and **slp** are references to `int` type. The purpose of the function is to find out the largest and the second largest of three numbers collected by the arguments **a, b** and **c** and assign them to the reference variables **lp** and **slp** respectively. The important point being highlighted here is that the function is provided with both values as well as references when it is called.

On execution of the statement `lar_seclar(a, b, c, l, sl);` in the `main()`, the variables **l** and **sl** belonging to the `main()` would collect the largest and the second largest of the numbers in the variables **a, b** and **c** respectively. Table 6.1 highlights the differences between call by value and call by reference.

Table 6.1 Differences between Call by Value and Call by Reference

Call by value	*Call by reference*
Values are passed as arguments.	References are passed as arguments.
The functions operate on the copy of the actual arguments. As a result, no change is seen in the values of the actual arguments in the calling program.	The functions operate on the actual arguments themselves. As a result, the values of the actual arguments are altered.
The functions can not return more than one value.	The effect of changing the values of more than one actual argument in the calling program is equivalent to returning more than one value.

Constants can be passed as arguments.
Example: For the function with the following prototype
`int max(int, int);`
`m = max(5, 6);`
is a valid function call
	Constants can not be passed as arguments.
	Example: For the function with the following prototype:
	`int max(int&, int&);`
	`m = max(5, 6);`
	is an invalid function call.

6.15.2 Return by Reference

A function can return a reference also. If a function is made to return a reference, the function call can appear on both right and left side of an assignment. Consider the following program segment:

```
int& send(int& a)
{
    a++;
    return a;
}
```

The function `send()` takes a reference to `int` type; increments the `int` value by one and returns the reference to it back to its calling program.

```
b = send(a);
```

Here, the function call appears on the right-hand side of the assignment statement and **b** collects the updated value of **a**.

```
if (send(a) > 10)
    send(a) = 1;
```

Here if the value of **a** exceeds 10 it is reinitialized to 1. Note that the function call appears to the left-hand side of the assignment statement.

Program 6.21 To Illustrate Return by Reference

```
#include <iostream.h>

int& set_zero_to_min(int&, int&);

int main(void)
{
    int a, b;

    cout << "Enter a and b \n";
    cin >> a >> b;

    cout << "a = " << a << "\n";
    cout << "b = " << b << "\n";

    set_zero_to_min(a, b) = 0;

    cout << "After calling set_zero_to_min() \n";
    cout << "a = " << a << "\n";
    cout<< "b = " << b << "\n";

    return 0;
}

int& set_zero_to_min(int& a, int& b)
{
    if (a < b)
```

```
        return a;
    else
        return b;
}
```

Input-Output:

```
Enter a and b
10
20
a = 10
b = 20
After calling set_zero_to_min()
a = 0
b = 20
```

Explanation

The function `set_min_to_zero()` is defined with two arguments, which are references to `int` type and is made to return a reference to `int` type. The purpose of the function is to take two integer values by reference and find the minimum of the two and return the reference to the minimum value to the calling program. Since the function returns a reference to a variable it can be used on the left-hand side of an assignment statement, i.e., in the capacity of an L value.

In the `main()`, **a** and **b** are declared to be variables of `int` type and are initialized with values 10 and 20 respectively, and they are displayed. The function `set_min_to_zero()` is then invoked with the statement `set_min_to_zero() = 0;`. As a result of the execution of the function, the variable **a** with the minimum value 10 is assigned zero. It is verified by redisplaying the values of both **a** and **b** after invoking the function.

6.16 STORAGE CLASSES

When we declare a variable of some type, associated with the variable are the variable name and its data type. It is identified by the given variable name and it is capable of storing value of the specified type. In addition to these, two more important factors associated with the variable are: (a) *scope* of the variable and (b) *Lifetime* of the variable.

Scope of a variable is defined to be the area of its existence in a program. That is, parts of the underlying program. Whereas lifetime of a variable is defined to be the duration of time for which the variable exists.

Depending on the scope and the lifetime of the variables, variables are made to fall into the following storage classes:

1. Internal variables
2. External variables

Internal variables (also called **local variables**) are those which are declared within the body of a function. These variables are known only within the body of their enclosing functions.

External variables (also called **global variables**) are those which are declared outside the functions. Global variables are accessible from the point of declaration till the end of the program.

EXAMPLE

```
int k;
int main(void)
```

```
    {
        int j;
    }

    void function1(void)
    {
        int l;
    }
```

j is an internal variable to `main()`. **l** is an internal variable in `function1()` whereas **k** is an external variable. It is available in both `main()` and `function1()`.

Scope of a variable is the area of its existence. Lifetime of a variable is the duration of its availability in a program. Depending on where a variable is allocated required storage, the area of its existence in a program (Scope), and its longevity (Lifetime), variables are classified into what are called **storage classes.**

Following are the four storage classes:

1. Automatic
2. Static
3. Register
4. Extern

Automatic storage class: The variables declared within a function are by default of automatic storage class. The keyword *auto* can also be used to explicitly specify it. For instance,

```
void function(void)
{
    int i;
    auto int j;
}
```

Here, even though the keyword *auto* is not used while declaring `i`. Storage class of `i` would be *auto*, by default. `j` has been explicitly declared with *auto* keyword.

Automatic variables are characterized by the following properties:

1. They get created on entry into their function.
2. They get automatically destroyed on the exit of their function.
3. They are visible within the function only.
4. Their lifetime is the duration of the function only.
5. If not initialized, they will have unpredictable values (garbage values).
6. If initialized, they would be reinitialized on each entry into the function.
7. They can not be declared outside of functions.

Static storage class: Variables can be made to belong to static storage class by explicitly using the keyword *static* while declaring them. Unlike auto variables, the variables of static storage class may be declared either within or outside the functions. Here, let us confine our discussion to the static variables declared within the body of the functions.

```
void function2()
{
    static int a;
}
```

The variable **a** has been declared to be a **static** variable. These **static** variables declared within the body of the functions are characterized by the following properties:

1. They get created on the entry into their enclosing function.
2. They are not destroyed on the function's exit.
3. They are initialized to 0 by default. However, the default can be defeated by initializing them with our own values.
4. They are not reinitialized on the re-entry into the function. The previous values persist.
5. They are visible within the function only.
6. Their lifetime is the duration of the entire program's duration.
7. They can be declared either within or outside of functions.

Register storage class: In order to understand the significance of `register` storage class, it is better to be aware of the roles of memory and CPU in relation to programs and data.

Memory acts as workspace for programs and data. This is where, programs and data are stored. CPU plays the role of instruction executor. CPU needs to fetch instructions and the required data from memory before acting upon them. The `register` storage class enables us to tell the compiler that some variables are to be stored in CPU general purpose registers themselves. CPU can thus act upon these data readily without requiring to fetch from memory resulting in increase in the speed of execution of the program.

Note: Only the local variables of type `int`, `char` can be declared with the keyword ***`register`***.

The no. of register storage class variables is limited by the available no. of general purpose registers. However, if the no. of variables exceeds the limit, C compiler itself converts the remaining as auto variables.

```
void f1()
{
    register int i j;
}
```

variables **i** and **j** are allocated two registers:

Extern storage class: In some situations, some variables need to be accessed by more than one function. Variables belonging to extern storage class serve this purpose. Since the variables are accessible by more than one function, the variables are called **global variables**.

Variables belonging to extern storage class are characterized by the following properties:

1. They are declared outside of functions.
2. The area of their existence is from the point of declaration till the end of the program. That is, all the functions defined after the variables declaration can access the variables. However, there is an exception to this fact. If a function has a local variable with the same name as that of the global variable, as far as the function is concerned, the local variable is given more priority. That is, global variable value can not be accessed.
3. Their lifetime is the duration of the entire program. That is, they are created when the program is launched for execution and destroyed when the program is exited.

```
int i = 10;
void f1()
{
    cout << i;
}
```

```
    void f2()
    {
        cout << i;
    }

    int main(void)
    {
        int i = 5;
        cout << i;

        return 0;
    }
```

Here, variable **i** is declared before all the three functions `f1()`, `f2()` and `main()`. `f1()` and `f2()` can access the value of the variable **i**. But `main()` can not, since it has a local variable with the same name.

Program 6.22 To Illustrate Auto, Static, Extern and Register Storage Classes

```
#include <iostream.h>

extern int i = 10;
void show(void)
{
  cout << " extern i within show() = " << i;
}

void display(void)
{
  int j = 5;
  static int k = 5;

  j++;
  cout << " auto variable j = " << j;
  k++;
  cout << " static variable k = " << k;
}

int main(void)
{
  register int l = 10;

  cout << " register variable l = " << l;
  cout << " extern i in main() = " << i;
  show();
  cout << "After first call to display()\n \n";
  display();
  cout << "\n After second call to display() \n\n";
  display();

  return 0;
}
```

Input-Output:
```
register variable l = 10
extern i in main() = 10
extern i within show() = 10
After first call to display()

auto variable j = 6
static variable k = 6

After second call to display()

auto variable j = 6
static variable k = 7
```

Explanation

In Program 6.22, the variable **i** is declared to be a global variable. The value of the variable can thus be seen by all the functions defined after its declaration. That is, by `show()`, `display()` and `main()`. Within the function `display()`, **j** and **k** are declared to be `auto` and **static** variables respectively. Both the variables are initialized with the value 5. They are displayed after incrementing them. Within the `main()`, `l` is declared to be a register class variable with an initial value and it is displayed. It is important to note that a CPU register is allocated for the variable. The value of the extern variable **i** is then displayed, which implies that the extern variable **i** is accessible even in `main()` also.

Two calls are made to the function `display()` to understand the difference between **auto** and **static** variables. As can be seen from the output, after the first call to it, the values of **j** and **k** are displayed to be 6. But after the second call to the function, the values of **j** and **k** are displayed to be 6 and 7 respectively. This is because, in the second call, the `auto` variable **j** was recreated and initialized with 5 again and redisplayed after incrementation. But the **static** variable **k** persisted even after the exit of the first call and in the second call, **k** was not reinitialized (recreated). The value of **k** now was 6 and after incrementation, when it is displayed, it turned out to be 7.

6.17 MULTIFILE PROGRAMS

So far, each program that we have written was contained in one source file. This was true even in the case of multifunction programs. Many a time, the real programming environment calls for using multiple files. For instance, if a software project is being developed by a team of programmers, it is quite natural that each programmer writes code for the task assigned to him in his own source file. At a later stage, all the source files are combined before being submitted to the compiler. The programs, which are spilt across multiple source files are termed as **multifile programs**.

The multiple source files not only facilitate division of program modules among programmers, but also help in the compilation process, in the sense that if any changes are made in one source file, only that file needs to be recompiled again. The resultant object code can be integrated with the object codes of the remaining files.

Study of static and extern storage classes: When multiple source files are used, we definitely need to deal with the scope of the variables, which are used by the program. Some variables may be required to be shared by all the functions in the entire program or some variables may be required to be shared by all the functions in a specific source file only. The static and extern storage class variables are of use here.

If in a source file, static variables are declared before the definition of all the functions in it, then those variables are accessible by all the functions in that source file only. No other function in other files can access them.

EXAMPLE

```
static int i = 10;
void main()
{
i is accessible
}

void function1()
{
    i is accessible
}
```

file1.c

```
void function2()
{
static i of file1.c is not accessible here
}

void function3()
{
    static i of file1.c is not accessible here
}
```

file2.c

If in a source file, a global variable is declared before the definition of all the functions in it and if the variable is declared as **`extern`** in the beginning of all other source files, then the global variable can be accessed by all the functions in all the source files.

```
int i = 10;
int main(void)
{
    i is accessible
}

void function1(void)
{
    i is accessible
}
```

file1.c

```
extern int i;
void function2(void)
{
    i of file1.c is accessible here also
}

void function3(void)
{
    i of file1.c is accessible here also
}
```

file2.c

REVIEW QUESTIONS

6.1 What is the need for the functions?

6.2 What is a function?

6.3 Explain the general form of defining a function.

6.4 What are formal arguments?

6.5 What are actual arguments?

6.6 What is function header?

6.7 What do you mean by function call?

6.8 Differentiate between built-in functions and user-defined functions. Give examples.

6.9 Define function prototype.

6.10 What is a calling function?

6.11 What is a called function?

6.12 Mention the categories of functions depending on the existence of data communication between calling and called functions.

6.13 How many values can function return?

6.14 What is meant by the scope of a variable?

6.15 What is meant by the lifetime of a variable?

6.16 Mention different storage classes.

6.17 Give an account of characteristics of variables belonging to
(a) Automatic storage class
(b) Static storage class
(c) Register storage class
(d) Extern storage class

6.18 Define recursion and recursive function.

6.19 What is the significance of terminating condition in recursion?

True/False Questions

T6.1 Functions reduce memory space usage.

T6.2 Once a function is defined it can be called anywhere.

T6.3 A function can return any number of values.

T6.4 A function returns float value by default.

T6.5 A function, which does not take any arguments, can not return any value.

T6.6 The names of the formal arguments and the names of the actual arguments should be same.

T6.7 A function whose formal argument is of type int can take a float value as its actual argument.

T6.8 A function whose formal argument is of type char can take an int value as its actual argument.

T6.9 C++ supports recursion.

T6.10 Scope of a variable is the duration of time for which its value is available.

T6.11 Variables declared within functions are by default of static storage class.

T6.12 Automatic variables have default values.

T6.13 An external static variable has the entire file scope.

T6.14 The name of a global variable and that of a local variable can be same.

T6.15 Variables of float type can be made to belong to register storage class.

T6.16 Only local variables can be of register storage class.

T6.17 There is no limit on the number of register variables.

T6.18 Static variables retain their values between function calls.

T6.19 Inline functions can contain loops.

T6.20 `void f(int);`

`void f(float);`

Here the `function f()` is overloaded.

T6.21 `int f(int);`

`double f(nt);`

Here the `function f()` is overloaded.

T6.22 `void f(int = 10, float f = 2.5);`

Here `f(5.6);` is a valid function call.

T6.23 The no. of actual arguments and the no. of formal arguments should be same when a function is called. True/False.

T6.24 One function can be defined within another function. True/False.

PROGRAMMING EXERCISES

P6.1 Write a program to find the reverse of a number using a function.

P6.2 Write a program to grade a student using a function.

P6.3 Write a program to find out the value of an expression v1 op v2 where v1 and v2 are two values of int type and op is an arithmetic operator using a function.

P6.4 Write a program to find out whether a number is a perfect number or not using a function. (A number is said to be a perfect number if the sum of all its divisors (except the number itself) is equal to the number.)

Example: 6 is a perfect number since 6 = 1 + 2 + 3

P6.5 Write a program to find out whether a number is an Armstrong number or not using a function. (A number is said to be an Armstrong number if the sum of the cubes of the digits is equal to the number itself.)

P6.6 Write a program to generate multiplication table of a number using a function.

P6.7 Write a program to calculate

$np_r = n!/(n-r)!$

(Use a function to find out factorial of a number.)

P6.8 Write a program to calculate

$nc_r = n!/n! * (n-r)!$

(Use a function to find out factorial of a number.)

P6.9 Write a program to convert from decimal number to its binary equivalent using a function.

P6.10 Write a program to reverse an integer using a recursive function.

Example: Input: 3456, Output: 6543

P6.11 Given month and year, write a program to find the number of days in the month in the given year using a function.

Example: Month = 4 Year = 2000
Days = 30

Month = 2 Year = 2000
Days = 28

Month = 12 Year = 1999
Days = 31

P6.12 Write a program with a function to calculate the definite integral $\int_b^a f(x)\,dx$ using Simpson's rule with n strips. The approximation to the integral is given by

$h/3\{f(a) + 4f(a+h) + 2f(a+2h) + \cdots + 2f[a+(n-2)h] + 4f[a+(n-1)h] + f(b)\}$

where $h = (b-a)/n$

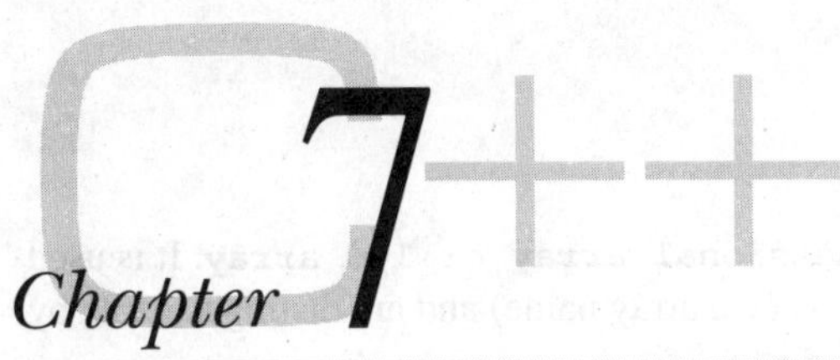

Arrays

7.1 INTRODUCTION

Suppose a C++ program is required to accept five integer values, find their sum and it needs access to each value even after finding their sum. We can declare five variables of `int` type in the program as follows:

```
int a, b, c, d, e;
```

As a result of this declaration, five memory locations get allocated to store these values. The program segment to accept five values into these variables and find their sum is as follows:

```
cin >> a >> b >> c >> d >> e;
s = a + b + c + d + e ;
```

As can be seen, all the five variables have to be explicitly specified both in the `cin` statement and in the arithmetic expression of the assignment statement following it.

What, if the no. of values to be summed up is more than five, say 10 or even 100? If we use ordinary variables to store these, we need to declare so many variables and need to explicitly specify all the variables in the corresponding `cin` statement and the arithmetic expression. Declaration of all of these variables and explicit specification of each of the variables in the `cin` statement and in the required arithmetic expression become laborious.

Here, accepting values into five locations and finding the sum of them are two examples of collective manipulations. A *collective manipulation* over a group of values is one, which requires access to each value in the group or in its selected subgroup. Other collective manipulations include, searching for a value in a list of values and finding the maximum value in a list of values. Collective manipulations, in general, can not be performed over a group of data items stored in ordinary variables in an easier manner.

The problems stated earlier can be overcome, if we can form a group of data items by making them share a common name and use subscripts to indicate a data item. For example, **`a[1]`** to denote first value, **`a[2]`** to denote second value and so on. Here **a** is said to be subscripted or indexed. This is where the concept of arrays comes into picture. We will soon realize that the problems encountered earlier are overcome with the help of one-dimensional array of **`int`** type.

7.2 DEFINITION OF AN ARRAY

An array is defined to be a group of logically related, fixed number of data items of similar type, stored in contiguous memory locations, sharing a common name but distinguished by subscript(s) values.

Depending on the no. of subscripts used, arrays are classified into one-dimensional arrays, two dimensional arrays and so on.

7.3 ONE-DIMENSIONAL ARRAYS

An array with only one subscript is termed as **`one-dimensional array`** `or` **`1-d array`**. It is used to store a list of values, all of which share a common name (1-d array name) and are distinguishable by subscript values.

7.3.1 Declaration of One-dimensional Arrays

The syntax of declaring a one-dimensional array is as follows:

```
data-type variable-name[size];
```

`data-type` refers to any data type supported by C++, **`variable-name`** refers to array name and it should be a valid C++ identifier, **`size`** indicates no. of data items of type **`data-type`** grouped together.

Each element in the array is identifiable by the array name (`variable-name`), followed by a pair of square brackets enclosing a subscript value. The subscript value ranges from 0 to `size-1`. When the subscript value is `0`, first element in the array is selected. When the subscript value is `1`, second element is selected and so on.

EXAMPLE

```
int a[5];
```

Here, **a** is declared to be an array of **`int`** type and of size five. Five contiguous memory locations get allocated as shown below to store five integer values.

2	5	6	8	9
a[0]	a[1]	a[2]	a[3]	a[4]

Each data item in the array **`a`** is identified by the array name followed by a pair of square brackets enclosing a subscript value. The subscript value ranges from `0` to `4`, i.e., **`a[0]`** denotes first data item, **`a[1]`** denotes second data item and so on. **`a[4]`** denotes the last data item.

Since all the five locations share a common name and are distinguishable by index values 0 to 4, to perform a collective manipulation, we can set up a loop (preferably a for loop because of its inherent simplicity) with the control variable of the loop ranging from 0 to 4 to identify the five data items.

EXAMPLE

To accept five values into the array, the following segment can be used.

```
for(i = 0; i < 5; i++)
    cin >> a[i];
```

Here, initially the control variable **i** takes 0. As a result, the value for **a[0]** is accepted. When **i** takes 1, value for the location **a[1]** is accepted and this is continued till the last location **a[4]** of the array gets a value. So when the loop completes, the array **a** gets filled up.

Similarly, to display the elements of the array **a**, the following segment can be used.

```
for(i = 0; i < 5; i++)
    cout << a[i];
```

Here also, initially, the control variable **i** takes 0. As a result, the value in **a[0]** is displayed. When **i** takes 1, value in the location **a[1]** is displayed and this is continued till the value of the last location **a[4]** of the array is displayed. So when the loop completes, all the elements of the array **a** are displayed.

By looking at the declaration of the array variable **a** and, the program segments for accepting values into it and displaying the array elements, we definitely feel the advantage offered by arrays.

Program 7.1 To Accept Values into an Array and Display Them

```
#include <iostream.h>
int main(void)
{
    int a[5], i;

    cout << "Enter five values \n";
    for(i = 0; i < 5; i++)
        cin >> a[i];
    cout << "The values in the array are \n";
    for(i = 0; i < 5; i++)
        cout << "a[" << i << "] = " << a[i] << endl;
    return 0;
}
```

Input-Output:

```
Enter five values
4 5 6 7 8

The values in the array are
a[0] = 4
a[1] = 5
a[2] = 6
a[3] = 7
a[4] = 8
```

7.3.2 Initialization of One-dimensional Arrays

Just as we initialize ordinary variables, we can also initialize one-dimensional arrays if we know the values of the arrays locations in advance, i.e., locations of the arrays can be given values while they are declared.

The syntax of initializing an array of one-dimension is as follows:

```
data-type variable-name[size] = {value0, value1, value2,... };
```

data-type refers to the data type of the array elements. variable-name refers to the name of the array. {value0, value1,..., valuesize-1} are constant values of type data-type or convertible into values of data type data-type. The values {value0, value1,..., valuesize-1} are collectively called initializer-list for the array.

In short, the syntax of initializing a 1-d array can now be written as:

```
data-type variable-name[size] = {initializer-list};
```

EXAMPLE

```
int a[5] = { 2, 5, 6, 8, 9 };
```

as a result of this, memory locations of **a** get filled up as follows:

2	5	6	8	9
a[0]	a[1]	a[2]	a[3]	a[4]

If the no. of values in initializer-list is less than the size of an array, only those many first locations of the array are assigned the values. The remaining locations are assigned zero.

EXAMPLE

```
int a[5] = { 2, 4, 5 };
```

The size of the array **a** is five. initializer-list consists of only three values. As a result of this, only first three locations would get these values. The last two locations get 0 assigned to them automatically, as follows:

2	4	5	0	0
a[0]	a[1]	a[2]	a[3]	a[4]

If a **static** array is declared without initializer-list then all the locations are set to zero.

EXAMPLE

```
static int a[5];
```

0	0	0	0	0
a[0]	a[1]	a[2]	a[3]	a[4]

Program 7.2 To Illustrate Initialization of Arrays of One-dimension

```
#include <iostream.h>

int main(void)
{
    int a[5] = {4, 5, 7, 9, 2};
    int b[5] = {6, 8, 5};
    static int d[5];
    int i;

    cout << "Elements in the array a \n";
    for(i = 0; i < 5; i++)
        cout << "a[" << i << "] = " << a[i] << " ";
    cout << "\n";
```

```
    cout << "Elements in the array b \n";
    for(i = 0; i < 5; i++)
        cout << "b[" << i << "] = " << b[i] << " ";
    cout << "\n";

    cout << "Elements in the static array d \n";
    for(i = 0; i < 5; i++)
            cout << "d[" << i << "] = " << d[i] << " ";
    cout << "\n";

    return 0;
}
```

Input-Output:

```
Elements in the array a
a[0]=4 a[1]=5 a[2]=7 a[3]=9 a[4]=2

Elements in the array b
b[0]=6 b[1]=8 b[2]=5 b[3]=0 b[4]=0

Elements in the static array d
d[0]=0 d[1]=0 d[2]=0 d[3]=0 d[4]=0
```

Points to remember:

1. If the number of values listed within `initializer-list` for an array is greater than the size of the array, the compiler raises an error (Too many initializers).

   EXAMPLE

   ```
   int a[5] = { 2, 3, 4, 5, 6, 7, 8};
   ```

   The size of the array **a** is five. But the no. of values listed within the `initializer-list` is seven. This is illegal.

2. There is no array bound checking mechanism built into C++ compiler. It is the responsibility of the programmer to see to it that the subscript value does not go beyond `size - 1`. If it does, the system may crash.

   EXAMPLE

   ```
   int a[5];
   a[6] = 10;
   ```

   Here, `a[6]` does not belong to the array **a**, it may belong to some other program (e.g. operating system) writing into the location may lead to unpredictable results or even to system crash.

3. Array elements can not be initialized selectively.

   EXAMPLE

   An attempt to initialize only 2nd location is illegal, i.e.,

   ```
   int a[5] = { , 2 }
   ```

   is illegal.

4. If `size` is omitted in a 1-d array declaration, which is initialized, the compiler will supply this value by examining the no. of values in the `initializer-list`.

EXAMPLE

```
int a[] = { 2, 4, 6, 7, 8 };
```

Since the no. of values in the `initializer-list` for the array **a** is five, the size of **a** is automatically supplied as five.

2	4	6	7	8
a[0]	a[1]	a[2]	a[3]	a[4]

Similar to arrays of **int** type, we can even declare arrays of other data types supported by C++, also.

EXAMPLE

```
char s[10];
```

s is declared to be an array of **char** type and size 10 and it can accommodate 10 characters.

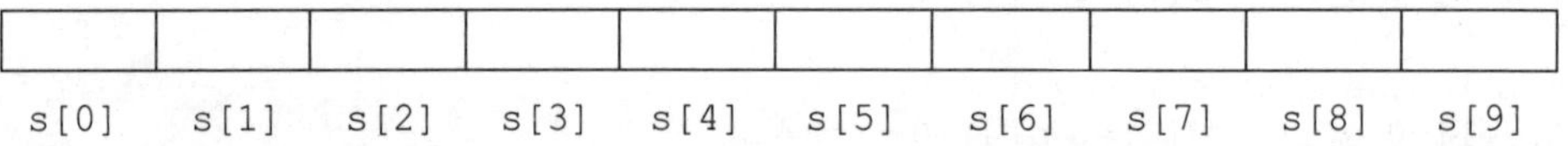

s[0] s[1] s[2] s[3] s[4] s[5] s[6] s[7] s[8] s[9]

An array of **char** is used to store a string. The concept of string manipulations is so important that it deserves to be dealt within detail. So, a separate chapter is meant for discussing this, which is to follow.

```
float f[10];
```

`f` is declared to be an array of **float** type and size 10 and it can accommodate `10` values of **float** type. Following is the scheme of memory allocation for the array `f`.

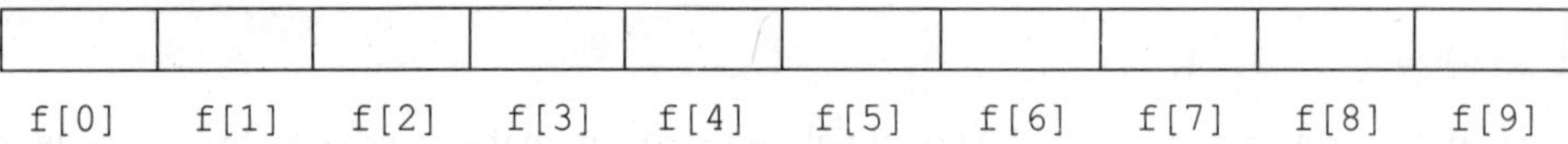

f[0] f[1] f[2] f[3] f[4] f[5] f[6] f[7] f[8] f[9]

Note: A `one-dimensional array` is used to store a list of values. A loop (Preferably, **for** loop) is used to access each value in the list.

7.3.3 Processing One-dimensional Arrays

We have understood that a one-dimensional array is used to store a list of values. The list of values may represent salary of a number of employees or marks obtained by a student in different subjects. The commonly performed operations over lists of values include finding the sum of them, finding the largest or the least among them, arranging the values in the increasing order or decreasing order and so on. Let us now proceed to understand the flexibility provided by one-dimensional arrays in processing lists of values.

To find the sum and average of a list of values: In order to find the sum and average of a list of values, the program should have a one-dimensional array to store the list of values. After accepting the values into the array, we need to set up a loop to select each value and add it to a variable say, **sum**. Once the sum is found out, the sum/no. of values gives the average of the list of values.

Program 7.3 To Find the Sum, Average of the Values in a 1-d Array

```
#include <iomanip.h>
#include <iostream.h>
int main(void)
{
    int a[10], i, n, sum;
    float avg;

    cout << "Enter no. of elements [1-10] \n";
    cin >> n;

    cout << "Enter" << n << "numbers \n";
    for( i = 0; i < n; i++)
        cin >> a[i];

    cout << " The numbers are \n";
    for( i = 0; i < n; i++)
        cout << setw(4) << a[i];

/* Finding the sum and average begins */

    sum = 0;
    for( i = 0; i < n; i++)
        sum += a[i];

    avg = (float) sum / n;

/* Finding the sum and average ends */
    cout << "\n Sum = " << sum << "\n";
    cout << "\n Average = " << avg;

    return 0;
}
```

Input-Output:

```
Enter no. of elements [1-10]
Enter 5 numbers
1 2 3 4 5
The numbers are
1 2 3 4 5
Sum = 15

Average = 3
```

Explanation

a is declared to be an array of **int** type and of size 10. Maximum 10 numbers can be written into the array. The variables **n, i** and **sum** are declared to be variables of **int** type where **n** is to collect the no. of values to be read into the array **a**, which lies within 1 and 10, **i** is to traverse all the values in **a**, and **sum** is to collect the sum of the values in **a**. The variable **avg** is declared to be a variable of **float** type and it is to collect the average of values in **a**.

In the process of finding the sum of all the **n** values, initially **sum** is set to 0. A **for** loop is used to select each number in the array and it is added to **sum** with the statement **sum += a[i]**.

The statement **avg = (float) sum/n**; on its execution, assigns average value to **avg**. Note that we have used type-casting to convert **sum** forcibly to **float** to get the exact result. Otherwise, the expression (**sum/n**) produces only integral part of the quotient since both **sum** and **n** are integers. Both **sum** and **avg** are then displayed.

Program 7.4 To Find the Minimum and the Maximum in a List of Values

```
#include <iostream.h>

int main(void)
{
    int a[10], i, n, min, max;

    cout << "Enter the number of values 1-10 \n";
    cin >> n;

    cout << "Enter" << n << "values \n";
    for(i = 0; i < n; i++)
        cin >> a[i];

    min = a[0];
    for(i = 1; i < n; i++)
        if (a[i] < min)
            min = a[i];

    max = a[0];
    for(i = 1; i < n; i++)
        if (a[i] > max)
            max = a[i];

    cout << "Minimum in the array = " << min << "\n";
    cout << "Maximum in the array = " << max;

    return 0;
}
```

Input-Output:

```
Enter the number of values 1-10
5
Enter 5 values
2 4 6 8 9

Minimum in the array = 2
Maximum in the array = 9
```

Explanation

In Program 7.5, **a** is declared to be an array of `int` type and of size 10. Maximum 10 values can be accepted into the array. The variable **n** is to collect the number of values [1–10]. The variables **min** and **max** are to collect the minimum and the maximum of the values in the array.

The following program segment is for finding the minimum in the array:

```
min = a[0];
for(i = 1; i < n; i++)
    if (a[i] < min)
        min = a[i];
```

Here, we start with the assumption that the first element in the array **a[0]** is the least and then we start comparing the remaining elements with the value of **min**. If any value in the array is found to be less than the value in the variable **min**, min is overwritten by the value in the array. This is repeated till the array elements exhaust. Ultimately the variable **min** collects the minimum of the array elements.

The same logic is used to find the maximum in the array and both min and max are displayed.

To search for a value in a list of values using linear search method: Suppose we are given a list of values and we need to search for a value in the list. In order to program the task, we should use a one-dimensional array to store the list of values and a plain variable of the appropriate type to store the value to be searched.

If **a** is the array having the list of values and **s** is a variable having the value to be searched. To search for **s** in the array **a**, we begin comparing **s** with each of the element in **a** starting from the first element till the element **s** is found or till the list is exhausted. Note that on an average, half the list is traversed during the course of searching. Linear search is also called **sequential search**.

Program 7.5 To Search for a Number in a List of Numbers

```
#include <iostream.h>
#include <iomanip.h>
int main(void)
{
    int a[10], n, i, f, s;

    cout << "Enter the no. of numbers \n";
    cin >> n;

    cout << "Enter" << n << "numbers" << "\n";
    for( i = 0; i < n; i++)
        cin >> a[i];

    cout << "Enter the number to be searched \n";
    cin >> s;

    /* searching for s in a begins */

    f = 0;
    for( i= 0; i < n; i++)
        if ( a[i] == s )
        {
            f = 1;
            break;
        }
    /* searching for s in a ends */
```

```
    cout << "\n List of elements \n";
    for(i = 0; i < n; i++)
    cout << setw(4) << a[i];
    cout << "\n Element to be searched \n";
    cout << "\n s = " << s << "\n";

    if (f == 1)
        cout << s << " is found";
    else
        cout << s << "is not found";

    return 0;
}
```

Input-Output:

```
Enter the no. of numbers
5
Enter5numbers
2 3 4 7 9
Enter the number to be searched
5

List of elements
2 3 4 7 9
Element to be searched
s = 5

5 is not found
```

Explanation

a is declared to be an array of **int** type of size 10. Maximum 10 values can be read into the array. The variables **n, i, s and f** are declared to be variables of **int** type where **n** is to collect the no. of values to be read into **a**, which lies within 1 and 10, **i** is to traverse all the elements of **a**, **s** is to collect a value which is to be searched and **f** is to determine whether **s** is found in **a** or not. It acts as a **flag** variable.

The procedure of searching for **s** in **a** is implemented in the following segment of the program:

```
f = 0;
for(i= 0; i < n; i++)
    if (a[i] == s)
    {
        f = 1;
        break;
    }
```

Before searching begins, **f** is set to zero with the assumption that **s** is not available in **a**. During the course of searching, that is, inside the body of the for **loop**, if **s** is found to match with any element in the array, **f** is set to 1 and the loop is exited. If **f** takes 1 then it means **s** is found in **a**. If **f** retains 0 we conclude that **s** is not found in **a**. The value of **f** would thus tell us whether **s** is found in **a** or not.

Sorting a list of values: Very often we will be required to arrange the values in a list either in the increasing order or in the decreasing order. The procedure of arranging the list of values in the specified order is called **sorting**.

Program 7.6 sorts a list of values of `int` type in the increasing order.

Program 7.6 To Sort a List of Numbers

```
#include <iostream.h>
int main(void)
{
    int a[10], n, i, j, t;

    cout << "Enter the no. of numbers \n";
    cin >> n;

    cout << "Enter "<< n <<" numbers \n";
    for( i = 0; i < n; i++)
        cin >> a[i];

    cout << "Unsorted list \n";
    for( i = 0; i < n; i++)
        cout << a[i] << " ";

    // sorting begins

    for( i = 0; i < n; i++)
    for( j = i+ 1; j < n; j++)
        if ( a[i] > a[j] )
        {
                t = a[i];
                a[i] = a[j];
                a[j] = t;
        }
    // sorting ends
    cout << "Sorted list \n";
    for( i = 0; i < n; i++)
        cout << a[i] << " ";

    return 0;
}
```

Input-Output:

```
Enter the no. of numbers
5
Enter 5 numbers
2 4 3 7 6
Unsorted list
2 4 3 7 6

Sorted list
2 3 4 6 7
```

Explanation

a is declared to be an array of type **int** and of size 10. The variables **n, i, j** and **t** are declared to be variables of **int** type. **n** is to collect the no. of values into the array **a**. The value of **n** has to lie between 1 and 10. **i** and **j** are to traverse the elements of the array **a**. **t** is to collect a value in the array temporarily during the course of sorting.

After accepting a value for **n**, **n** integer values are accepted into the array **a**. The given list (unsorted) is displayed. The list is then sorted by the following program segment:

```
for( i = 0; i < n; i++)
for( j = i + 1; j < n; j++)
    if ( a[i] > a[j] )
    {
        t = a[i];
        a[i] = a[j];
        a[j] = t;
    }
```

Here, when **i** takes 0, the first value in the array is selected. It is compared with the remaining values of the array, which are selected by **j** (**j** ranges from 1 to n-1). If necessary, two values being compared are interchanged. This produces the first least value. The first least value is placed in the location **a[i]**, that is, in **a[0]**.

When i takes 1, second value in the list is taken. It is compared with the remaining values of the list, which are taken by **j** (**j** now ranges from 2 to n-1). If necessary, two values being compared are interchanged. This produces the second least value. The second least value is placed in the location **a[i]**, that is, in **a[1]**. This process continues till the entire array is sorted.

7.4 MULTIDIMENSIONAL ARRAYS

An array with more than one subscript is generally called a **multidimensional array**. We can think of arrays of two dimensions (2-d arrays), arrays of three dimensions (3-d arrays), arrays of four dimensions (4-d arrays) and so on. We do require these in real life situations.

7.4.1 Two-dimensional Arrays (2-d arrays)

An array with two subscripts is termed as **two-dimensional array**. A two-dimensional array can be thought of as a group of one or more one-dimensional array(s), all of which share a common name (2-d array name) and are distinguishable by subscript values. So, a two-dimensional array is essentially, an array of one-dimensional arrays. We know that a one-dimensional array can store a row of elements, so, a two-dimensional array enables us to store multiple rows of elements, that is, **a table of values** or **a matrix**. For this reason two-dimensional arrays are very much associated with matrices and have turned out to be the perfect data structures for storing matrices.

Declaration of two-dimensional arrays: The syntax of declaring a two-dimensional array is as follows:

```
data-type variable-name[rowsize][colsize];
```

data-type refers to any valid C++ data type, variable-name (a valid C++ identifier) refers to the name of the array, rowsize indicates the no. of rows and colsize indicates the no. of elements in each row.

`rowsize` and `colsize` should be integer constants or convertible into integer values. Total no. of locations allocated will be equal to `rowsize * colsize`. Each element in a 2-d array is identified by the array name followed by a pair of square brackets enclosing its row-number, followed by a pair of square brackets enclosing its column-number. Row-number ranges from 0 to `rowsize` – 1 and column-number ranges from 0 to `colsize - 1`.

EXAMPLE

```
int b[3][3];
```

b is declared to be an array of two dimensions and of data type **int**. `rowsize` and `colsize` of **b** are 3 and 3 respectively. Memory gets allocated to accommodate the array **b** as follows. It is important to note that **b** is the common name shared by all the elements of the array.

Column numbers

	0	1	2
0	b[0][0]	b[0][1]	b[0][2]
1	b[1][0]	b[1][1]	b[1][2]
2	b[2][0]	b[2][1]	b[2][2]

Each data item in the array **b** is identifiable by specifying the array name **b** followed by a pair of square brackets enclosing row number, followed by a pair of square brackets enclosing column number. Row-number ranges from 0 to 2. That is, first row is identified by row-number 0. Second row is identified by row-number 1 and so on. Similarly column-number ranges from 0 to 2. First column is identified by column-number 0, second column is identified by column-number 1 and so on.

`b[0][0]` refers to data item in the first row and first column.
`b[0][1]` refers to data item in the first row and second column.
`b[3][3]` refers to data item in the fourth row and fourth column.
`b[3][4]` refers to data item in the fourth row and fifth column.

Program 7.7 To Accept and Display a Matrix

```
#include <iostream.h>
#include <iomanip.h>

int main(void)
{
    int a[3][3], i, j;

    cout << "Enter the elements of a \n";
    for(i = 0; i < 3; i++)
    for(j = 0; j < 3; j++)
        cin >> a[i][j];

    cout << "The matrix a \n";
    for(i = 0; i < 3; i++)
    {
        for(j = 0; j < 3; j++)
                cout << setw(4) << a[i][j];
        cout << "\n";
```

```
    }
    return 0;
}
```

Input-Output:

```
Enter the elements of a
1 2 3 4 5 6 7 8 9

The matrix a
 1 2 3
 4 5 6
 7 8 9
```

Explanation

In Program 7.7, **a** has been declared to be an array of two dimensions, with `rowsize 3`, `colsize 3`, and thus it can accommodate a table of values (matrix) consisting of 3 rows and 3 columns. As can be seen, both while reading into the array and reading from the array to display them, two loops have been used. The outer loop (**i** loop) is used to select each row of the table, the inner loop (`j` loop) is used to select each element in the row selected by **i** loop.

When `i = 0` (First row)
j ranges from 0 to 2 to select all the elements of the first row.
`i = 1` (Second row)
j ranges from 0 to 2 to select all the elements of the second row.
`i = 2` (Third row)
j ranges from 0 to 2 to select all the elements of the third row.

All the elements of the table are thus accessed.

Initialization of two-dimensional arrays: We can initialize a 2-d array also while declaring it, just as we initialize 1-d arrays. There are two forms of initializing a 2-d array:

First form. First form of initializing a 2-d array is as follows:

```
data-type variable-name[rowsize][colsize]={initializer-list};
```

`data-type` refers to any data type supported by C++. `variable-name` refers to array name. `rowsize` indicates the no. of rows, `colsize` indicates the no. of columns of the array. `initializer-list` is a comma separated list of values of type `data-type or` compatible with `data-type`.

If the no. of values in `initializer-list` is equal to the product of `rowsize` and `colsize`, the first `rowsize` values in the `initializer-list` will be assigned to the first row, the second `rowsize` values will be assigned to the second row of the array and so on.

EXAMPLE

```
int a[2][3] = { 2, 3, 4, 5, 6, 7};
```

Since `colsize` is 3, the first 3 values of the `initializer-list` are assigned to the first row of `a` and the next 3 values are assigned to the second row of `a` as shown hereinafter.

2	3	4
5	6	7

Note: If the no. of values in the `initializer-list` is less than the product of `rowsize` and `colsize`, only the first few matching locations of the array would get values from the `initializer-list` row-wise. The trailing unmatched locations would get zeros.

EXAMPLE

```
int a[2][3] = {2, 4, 5};
```

The first row of **a** gets filled with the values in the `initializer-list`. The second row gets filled with zeros.

2	4	5
0	0	0

A static 2-d array is initialized with 0's by default. However, they can be overridden by initializing explicitly.

```
static int a[2][3];
```

0	0	0
0	0	0

While initializing a 2-d array, rowsize is optional but columnsize is mandatory.

EXAMPLE

```
int a[][3] = {1,4,5,3,6,8};
```

Since two rows can be constructed with the elements, rowsize 2 will be provided by the compiler automatically. Memory allocation for the array **a** will be as follows:

1	4	5
3	6	8

Program 7.8 To Illustrate Initialization of a 2-d Array

```
#include <iostream.h>
#include <iomanip.h>

int main(void)
{
    int a[2][2] = { 1, 2, 3, 4};
    int b[2][2] = { 1, 2, 3};
    static int c[2][2];
    int d[][3] = { 1,4,5,3,6,8};
    int i, j;

    cout << "Matrix a \n";
    for(i = 0; i < 2; i++)
    {
        for(j = 0; j < 2; j++)
            cout << setw(4) << a[i][j];
        cout << "\n";
    }
```

```
    cout << "\n";
    cout << "Matrix b \n";
    for(i = 0; i < 2; i++)
    {
        for(j = 0; j < 2; j++)
            cout << setw(4) << b[i][j];
        cout << "\n";
    }
    cout << "\n";

    cout << "Matrix c \n";
    for(i = 0; i < 2; i++)
    {
        for(j = 0; j < 2; j++)
            cout << setw(4) << c[i][j];
        cout << "\n";
    }
    cout << "\n";

    cout << "Matrix d \n";
    for(i = 0; i < 2; i++)
    {
        for(j = 0; j < 3; j++)
            cout << setw(4) << d[i][j];
        cout << "\n";
    }

    return 0;
}
```

Input-Output:

```
Matrix a
 1 2
 3 4

Matrix b
 1 2
 3 0

Matrix c
 0 0
 0 0

Matrix d
 1 4 5
 3 6 8
```

Second form: The second form of initializing a 2-d array has the following general syntax:

```
data-type variable-name[rowsize][colsize] = { {initializer-list1},
                                              {initializer-list2},
                                              ......};
```

The values in `initializer-list1` are assigned to the locations in the first row. The values in `initializer-list2` are assigned to the locations in the second row and so on.

EXAMPLE

```
int a[2][3] = { { 4, 5, 9 },
                {6, 7, 8 }};
```

As a result of this, the array **a** gets filled up as follows:

4	5	9
6	7	8

Note:

1. If the no. of values specified in any `initializer-list` is less than `colsize` of `a`, only those many first locations in the corresponding row would get these values. The remaining locations in that row would get `0`.

EXAMPLE

```
int a[2][3] = { { 3, 4 }, { 4, 5, 6 } };
```

Since the first `initializer-list` has only two values, `a[0][0]` is set to `3`, `a[0][1]` is set to `4`, and the third location in the first row is automatically set to `0`.

3	4	0
4	5	6

Program 7.9 To Illustrate Initialization of a 2-d Array

```
#include <iostream.h>
#include <iomanip.h>

int main(void)
{
   int a[2][2] = { {1, 2}, {3, 4}};
   int b[2][2] = { {1,2}, {3}};
   int i, j;

   cout << "Matrix a \n";
   for(i = 0; i < 2; i++)
   {
      for(j = 0; j < 2; j++)
            cout << setw(4) << a[i][j];
      cout << "\n";
   }
   cout << "\n";
   cout << "Matrix b \n";
   for(i = 0; i < 2; i++)
   {
      for(j = 0; j < 2; j++)
            cout << setw(4) << b[i][j];
```

```
        cout << "\n";
      }

    return 0;
}
```

Input-Output:

```
Matrix a
 1 2
 3 4

Matrix b
 1 2
 3 0
```

Points to remember:

1. If the no. of values specified in any `initializer-list` is more than `colsize` of **a**, Compiler reports an error (Too many initializers).

   EXAMPLE

   ```
   int a[2][3] = {{2, 3, 4, 5},
                  {4 , 6 , 7}};
   ```

   Here `colsize` is `3`, but the no. of values listed in the first row is `4`. This results in compilation error (Too many initializers).
2. Array elements can not be initialized (in each row) selectively.
3. It is the responsibility of the programmer to ensure that the array subscripts do not exceed the rowsize and colsize of the array. If they exceed, unpredictable results may be produced and even the program can result in system crash sometimes.
4. A `2-d` array is used to store a table of values (Matrix).

Similar to 2-d arrays of **`int`** type, we can declare 2-d arrays of any other data type supported by C++, also.

EXAMPLE

```
float s[5][6];
```

`s` is declared to be `2-d` array of **`float`** type with `5` rows and `6` columns.

```
double d[10][20];
```

`d` is declared to be `2-d` array of **`double`** type with `10` rows and `20` columns.

Note: A two-dimensional array is used to store a table of values. Two loops (Preferably **`for`** loops) are used to access each value in the table, first loop acts as a row selector and second loop acts as a column selector in the table.

Processing two-dimensional arrays: We have understood that a two-dimensional array is used to store a table of values (matrix). The table of values may represent marks obtained by a number of students in different subjects (Each row representing a student and each column representing marks in a subject) or sales figures of different salesmen in different months (Each row representing a salesman and each column representing a month). The commonly performed operations over lists of values include finding the sum of each row or column, finding the largest or the least in each row or each column and so on. Let us now proceed to understand the flexibility provided by two-dimensional arrays in processing tables of values.

Program 7.10 To Find the Sum of Each Row and Each Column of a Matrix

```
#include <iostream.h>
#include <iomanip.h>

int main(void)
{
   int a[10][10], i, j, s[10], m, n;

   cout << "Enter no. of rows 1-10 \n";
   cin >> m;
   cout << "Enter no. of columns 1-10 \n";
   cin >> n;

   cout << "Enter the elements of matrix a \n";
   for( i = 0; i < m; i++)
   for( j = 0; j < n; j++)
      cin >> a[i][j];

   cout << " Matrix a \n";

   for( i = 0; i < m; i++)
   {
      for(j = 0; j < n; j++)
         cout << setw(4) << a[i][j];
      cout << "\n";
   }
// Finding sum of each row begins

for( i = 0; i < m; i++)
{
   s[i] = 0;
   for( j = 0; j < n; j++)
      s[i] += a[i][j];
   cout << " sum of values in row number " << i << " = " << s[i]
      << "\n";
}

// finding sum of each row ends

// Finding sum of each column begins

for( i = 0; i < n; i++)
{
   s[i] = 0;
   for( j = 0; j < m; j++)
      s[i] += a[j][i];
```

```
    cout << " sum of values in column number " << i << " = " << s[i]
         << "\n";
}
// finding sum of each column ends

    return 0;
}
```

Input-Output

```
Enter no. of rows 1-10
3
Enter no. of columns 1-10
3
Enter the elements of matrix a
1 2 3 4 5 6 7 8 9

Matrix a
1 2 3
4 5 6
7 8 9
sum of values in row number 0 = 6
sum of values in row number 1 = 15
sum of values in row number 2 = 24
sum of values in column number 0 = 12
sum of values in column number 1 = 15
sum of values in column number 2 = 18
```

Explanation

In Program 7.10, **a** is an array of size `10` and `10`. **m** and **n** are to collect no. of rows and no. of columns respectively, which lie within `1` and `10`. First, the **m * n** elements of the matrix are accepted into the array **a**. The array elements are displayed in matrix form. To find the sum of each row and column, we use a `1-d` array namely **s** of size `10, s[0]` is made to collect the sum of the first row or column, `s[1]` is made to collect the sum of the second row or column and so on.

The following segment is responsible for finding the sum of each row:

```
for( i = 0; i < m; i++)
{
    s[i] = 0;
    for( j = 0; j < n; j++)
        s[i] += a[i][j];
    cout << " sum of values in row number" << i << "=" << s[i]
        << "\n";
}
```

Note that the outer loop is to select each row of the matrix **a**. When `i = 0,` the first row is selected. After the execution of the statements in the body of the loop, `s[0]` collects the sum of the first row and it is displayed. When `i` becomes `1, s[1]` collects the sum of the elements in the second row and it is displayed so on.

Similarly, the sum of the elements in each column are also found out and displayed with the program segment:

```
for( i = 0; i < n; i++)
```

```
{
    s[i] = 0;
    for( j = 0; j < m; j++)
        s[i] += a[j][i];
    cout << " sum of values in column number" << i << "=" << s[i]
         << "\n";
}
```

Note that this time the outer loop selects each column in the matrix.

To find the sum of two matrices: If `a` and `b` represent two matrices with the order `m1*n1` and `m2*n2` respectively, they are said to be compatible for addition, if both of them are of the same order. That is, the no. of rows of `a` is same as that of `b (m1 = m2)` and the no. of columns of `a` is same as that of `b (n1 = n2)`. Addition operation over `a` and `b` produces another matrix `c`, which is also of the same order as `a` and `b`. The element in `i`th row and `j`th column of `c` is obtained by summing the elements in *i*th row and *j*th column of `a` and `b`.

EXAMPLE

$$a = \begin{pmatrix} 2 & 3 & 4 \\ 1 & 2 & 6 \\ 5 & 7 & 8 \end{pmatrix}$$

$$b = \begin{pmatrix} 1 & 4 & 7 \\ 2 & 5 & 9 \\ 2 & 4 & 7 \end{pmatrix}$$

$$\begin{pmatrix} 2+1 & 3+4 & 4+7 \\ 1+2 & 2+5 & 6+9 \\ 5+2 & 7+4 & 8+7 \end{pmatrix}$$

$$a + b = \begin{pmatrix} 3 & 7 & 11 \\ 3 & 7 & 15 \\ 7 & 11 & 15 \end{pmatrix}$$

Program 7.11 To Add Two Matrices

```
#include <iostream.h>
#include <process.h>
#include <iomanip.h>

int main(void)
{
    int a[10][10], b[10][10], s[10][10], m1, n1,m2, n2, i, j;

    cout << "Enter no. of rows and columns of matrix a \n";
    cin >> m1 >> n1;
```

```
cout << "Enter no. of rows and no. of columns of matrix b \n";
cin >> m2 >> n2;

if (( m1 != m2 ) || ( n1 != n2 ))
{
   cout << "Matrices not compatible for addition \n";
   exit(1);
}

cout << "Enter the elements of a \n";
for( i = 0; i < m1; i++)
for( j = 0; j < n1; j++)
   cin >> a[i][j];

cout << "Enter the elements of b \n";
for( i = 0; i < m2; i++)
for( j = 0; j < n2; j++)
   cin >> b[i][j];

// Summation begins

for( i = 0; i < m1; i++)
for( j = 0; j < n1; j++)
   s[i][j] = a[i][j] + b[i][j];

// Summation ends

cout << "Matrix a \n";
for( i = 0; i < m1; i++)
{
   for( j = 0; j < n1; j++)
      cout << setw(4) << a[i][j];
   cout << "\n";
}

cout << "\n\n";

cout << "Matrix b \n";
for( i = 0; i < m1; i++)
{
   for( j = 0; j < n1; j++)
      cout << setw(4) << b[i][j];
   cout << "\n";
}

cout << "\n\n";

cout << "Sum Matrix \n";
for( i = 0; i < m1; i++)
{
   for( j = 0; j < n1; j++)
```

```
        cout << setw(4) << s[i][j];
    cout << "\n";
    }

    return 0;
}
```

Input-Output:

```
Enter no. of rows and columns of matrix a
2 3
Enter no. of rows and no. of columns of matrix b
2 3
Enter the elements of a
1 2 3 4 5 6
Enter the elements of b
6 5 4 3 2 1
Matrix a
 1 2 3
 4 5 6

Matrix b
 6 5 4
 3 2 1

Sum Matrix
 7 7 7
 7 7 7
```

Explanation

In Program 7.11, **a**, **b** and **s** are declared to be arrays of two dimensions of `int` type and size `10 * 10`. **a** and **b** represent the two input matrices, which are to be added. **s** represents the resultant sum matrix. Variables **m1** and **n1** are to collect the no. of rows and columns of **a**. Variables **m2** and **n2** are to collect the no. of rows and columns of **b**. We know that, for **a** and **b** to be added, both **a** and **b** should be of the same order. That is, `m1 = m2` and `n1 = n2`. This compatibility for addition is first checked. If **a** and **b** are not compatible, the program exits reporting the appropriate error. This is accomplished by the following segment of the program:

```
if (( m1 != m2 ) || ( n1 != n2 ))
    {
        cout << "Matrices not compatible for addition \n";
        exit(1);
    }
```

After the matrices are found to be compatible for addition, summation begins. The segment responsible for summation is:

```
/* Summation begins */

    for( i = 0; i < m1; i++)
    for( j = 0; j < n1; j++)
        s[i][j] = a[i][j] + b[i][j];

/* Summation ends */
```

After finding the sum matrix, all the three matrices are displayed.

To find the product of two matrices: Suppose **a** and **b** represent two matrices of order `m1*n1` and `m2*n2` respectively. They are said to be compatible for multiplication, if the no. of columns of **a** is same as the no. of rows of **b**. That is, `n1 = m1`. Multiplication operation over **a** and **b** produces another matrix **c**, which is of the order `m1*n2`. The element in `i`th row and `j`th column of **c** is obtained by summing the products of the pairs of elements in the corresponding positions of `i`th row of **a** and `j`th column of **b**.

EXAMPLE

$$a = \begin{pmatrix} 1 & 4 \\ 2 & 5 \end{pmatrix}$$

$$b = \begin{pmatrix} 4 & 7 \\ 5 & 9 \end{pmatrix}$$

$$a * b = \begin{pmatrix} 1*4+4*5 & 1*7+4*9 \\ 2*4+5*5 & 2*7+5*9 \end{pmatrix}$$

$$= \begin{pmatrix} 24 & 43 \\ 33 & 59 \end{pmatrix}$$

Program 7.12 To Multiply Two Matrices

```
#include <iostream.h>
#include <process.h>
#include <iomanip.h>

int main(void)
{
   int a[10][10], b[10][10], p[10][10], m1, n1, m2, n2, i, j, k;

   cout << "Enter no. of rows and columns of matrix a \n";
   cin >> m1 >> n1;
   cout << "Enter no. of rows and columns of b \n";
   cin >> m2 >> n2;

   if ( n1 != m2 )
   {
      cout << "Matrices are not compatible \n";
      exit(1);
   }

      cout << "Enter the elements of a \n";
      for( i = 0; i < m1; i++)
      for( j = 0; j < n1; j++)
         cin >> a[i][j];

      cout << "Enter the elements of b \n";
```

```
    for( i = 0; i < m2; i++)
    for( j = 0; j < n2; j++)
        cin >> b[i][j];

    /* Multiplication of matrices a & b begins */

    for( i = 0; i < m1; i++)
    for( j = 0; j < n2; j++)
    {
        p[i][j] = 0;
        for( k = 0; k < n1; k++)
            p[i][j] += a[i][k] * b[k][j];

    }

    /* Multiplication of matrices of a & b ends */

    cout << "Matrix a \n";
    for( i = 0; i < m1; i++)
    {
        for( j = 0; j < n1; j++)
            cout << setw(4) << a[i][j];
        cout << "\n";
    }

    cout << "Matrix b \n";
    for( i = 0; i < m2; i++)
    {
        for( j = 0; j < n2; j++)
            cout << setw(4) << b[i][j];
        cout << "\n";
    }
    cout <<"Matrix p \n";
    for( i = 0; i < m1; i++)
    {
        for( j = 0; j < n2; j++)
            cout << setw(4) << p[i][j];
        cout << "\n";
    }

    return 0;
}
```

Input-Output:

```
Enter no. of rows and columns of matrix a
2 3
Enter no. of rows and columns of b
3 2

Enter the elements of a
```

```
1 2 3 4 5 6

Enter the elements of b
1 2 3 4 5 6

Matrix a
1 2 3
4 5 6

Matrix b
1 2
3 4
5 6

Matrix p
22 28
49 64
```

Explanation

In Program 7.12, `a`, `b` and `p` are declared to be arrays of two dimensions of type `int` and size `10 * 10`. `a` and `b` represent two input matrices, which are to be multiplied. `P` represents the resultant product matrix. Variables `m1` and `n1` are to collect the no. of rows and columns of `a`. Variables `m2` and `n2` are to collect the no. of rows and columns of `b`. The no. of rows and columns values for both `a` and `b` are expected to lie within `1` and `10`. Before proceeding to multiply `a` and `b`, we first find whether the matrices are compatible for multiplication. If they are not, the program exits reporting the appropriate error. The following segment does this:

```
if ( n1 != m2 )
{
    cout << "Matrices are not compatible \n";
    exit(1);
}
```

After the matrices `a` and `b` are found to be compatible for multiplication, multiplication proceeds, which is accomplished by the following segment:

```
/* Multiplication of matrices a & b begins */

    for( i = 0; i < m1; i++)
    for( j = 0; j < n2; j++)
    {
        p[i][j] = 0;
        for( k = 0; k < n1; k++)
            p[i][j] += a[i][k] * b[k][j];

    }

/* Multiplication of matrices of a & b ends */
```

After multiplication, all the three matrices **a**, **b** and **p** are displayed.

7.4.2 Three-dimensional Arrays

An array with three subscripts is termed as **three-dimensional array**. A three-dimensional array is a collection of one or more two-dimensional arrays, all of which share a common name and are distinguishable by values of the first subscript of the three-dimensional array. A three-dimensional array is thus an array of two-dimensional arrays. We know that a two-dimensional array is used to store a table of values. So, a three-dimensional array enables us to form a group of tables and perform collective manipulations over them in a fairly easier manner.

Declaration of three-dimensional arrays: Syntax of declaration of a 3-d array is as follows:

```
data-type variable-name[size1][size2][size3];
```

`data-type` refers to any data type supported by C++. `variable-name` refers to the array name. `size1` indicates the no. of tables being grouped together. `size2` indicates the no. of rows of each table. `size3` indicates the no. of columns of each table.

Each element in a 3-d array is identified by the array name followed by a pair of square brackets enclosing a table-number, followed by a pair of square brackets enclosing a row-number, followed by a pair of square brackets enclosing a column number. Table-number ranges from `0` to `size1 minus 1`. When table-number is `0`, first table is selected. When table-number is `1`, second table is selected and so on. Row-number ranges from `0` to `size2 minus -1`. When row-number is `0`, first row is selected. When row-number is `1`, second row is selected and so on. Column-number ranges from `0` to `size3 minus -1`. When column-number is `0`, first column is selected. When column-number is `1`, second column is selected and so on.

EXAMPLE

```
int a[2][4][5];
```

a is declared to be a 3-d array. It can accommodate two tables of values, each table having four rows and five columns. Each element in the array is identified by the array name **a**, followed by a pair of square brackets enclosing a table-number, followed by a pair of square brackets enclosing a row-number, followed by another pair of square brackets enclosing a column-number. Table-number for **a** ranges from `0` to `1`. Row-number ranges from `0` to `3` and column-number ranges from `0` to `4`.

`a[0][0][0]` indicates data item in first table, first row, first column.
`a[1][0][0]` indicates data item in second table, first row, first column.
`a[1][1][2]` indicates data item in second table, second row, third column.

Note: A three-dimensional array is used to store logically related group of tables of values. Three loops (Preferably, `for` loops) are used to access each element in the tables. First loop is to select each table. Second loop is to select each row of the selected table. Third loop is used to access each value in the row and table selected.

Program 7.13 To Accept the Elements of a 3-d Array and Display Them

```
#include <iostream.h>
#include <iomanip.h>

int main(void)
{
```

```
    int a[2][2][2], i, j, k;

    cout << "Enter the elements of a of order 2*2*2 \n";

    for( i = 0; i < 2; i++)
    {
        for( j = 0; j < 2; j++)
        for( k = 0; k < 2; k++)
            cin >> a[i][j][k];
}

    cout << "\n The 3-d array a \n\n";

    for( i = 0; i < 2; i++)
    {
       cout << "a-Table" << i+1 << "\n\n";
       for( j = 0; j < 2; j++)
       {
          for( k = 0; k < 2; k++)
             cout << setw(4) << a[i][j][k];
       cout << "\n";
       }
       cout << "\n\n";
    }

    return 0;
}
```

Input-Output:

```
Enter the elements of a of order 2*2*2
1 2 3 4 5 6 7 8

The 3-d array a

a-Table1

 1 2
 3 4

a-Table2

 5 6
 7 8
```

Explanation

In Program 7.13, **a** has been declared to be a 3-d array of size `2*2*2`. The array **a** can thus accommodate two tables, each with two rows and two columns. The outer most loop (**i** loop) is to select each table. **j** loop is used to select each row of the table selected by **i**. The inner most loop (**k** loop) is used to select the elements of the row selected by **j**.

When i = 0 (First table),
j = 0 (First row in first table),
k ranges from 0 to 1 to select all the elements in the first row of the first table.

j = 1 (Second row in first table),
k ranges from 0 to 1 to select all the elements in the second row of the first table.

All the elements of the first table have now been accessed.

When i = 1 (second table)
j = 0 (First row in the second table),
k ranges from 0 to 1 to select all the elements in the first row of the second table.
j = 1 (Second row in the second table),
k ranges from 0 to 1 to select all the elements in the second row of the second table.

All the elements of the second table have now been accessed.

On the similar lines, we can think of arrays of four dimensions, arrays of five dimensions and so on (An array of *n*-dimension can be thought of as a group of one or more logically related arrays of dimension *n*–1). The limit on the dimensionality is dependent on the C++ compiler being used and availability of memory.

Initialization of three-dimensional arrays: Even the three-dimensional arrays can also be initialized. The following program illustrates this. The initializers' list can have a list of values separated by commas in its simplest form. It can specify the values for each table of the array separately by enclosing them within inner pairs of braces. In Program 7.14, we demonstrate these. It is left as an exercise to the readers to test the other variations on the lines of the variations of two-dimensional arrays initialization.

Program 7.14 To Illustrate Initialization of 3-d Arrays

```
#include <iostream.h>
#include <iomanip.h>
int main(void)
{
   int a[2][2][2] = {1, 2, 3, 4, 5, 6, 7, 8};
   int b[2][2][2] = { {{1, 2}, {3, 4}},
                      {{5, 6}, {7, 8}}};
   int i, j, k;
   cout << "Array a \n";
   for(i = 0; i < 2; i++)
   {
      for(j = 0; j < 2; j++)
      {
         for(k = 0; k < 2; k++)
            cout << setw(4) << a[i][j][k];
         cout << "\n";
      }
      cout << "\n";
   }
   cout << "Array b \n";
```

```
    for(i = 0; i < 2; i++)
    {
        for(j = 0; j < 2 ; j++)
        {
            for(k = 0; k < 2; k++)
                cout << setw(4) << b[i][j][k];
            cout << "\n";
        }
        cout << "\n";
    }
    return 0;
}
```

Input-Output:

```
Array a
  1 2
  3 4

  5 6
  7 8

Array b
  1 2
  3 4

  5 6
  7 8
```

7.5 ARRAYS AND FUNCTIONS

We now know that arrays facilitate collective manipulations over a group of similar data items in a fairly easier way. The collective manipulations may be displaying the elements in an array, summing up the elements in an array, finding the largest element in an array or sorting the elements in an array in some order. So far, the collective manipulations have been accomplished through the statements in `main()` only. If a collective manipulation, say, displaying a list of numbers, has to be repeated for more than one array then, we would be definitely inclined to think of defining a function for the purpose with an array itself as its argument. C++ does permit passing arrays as arguments to functions. Once an array is passed as an argument to a function, all the elements of the array can be operated upon by the statements of the function.

7.5.1 One-dimensional Arrays as Arguments to Functions

To make a function take an array of one dimension as its input to be provided by a calling program, we need to define the function with two formal parameters: (a) Array name with data type specified and (b) the no. of elements of the array being passed, while defining the function as:

```
data-type function-name(data-type array_name[], int size)
{

}
```

EXAMPLE

```
void display(int a[], int n)
{

}
```

Note the presence of a pair of square brackets after array_name. These are required to indicate that we are passing an array.

After the function is defined, while calling it, we need to pass just the array name of actual array belonging to the calling program and the no. of elements in the array.

EXAMPLE

```
int b[10];
```

if `b` is an array declared in the calling program then, invoking `display()` by passing the array `b` is as follows:

```
display(b, 10);
```

Program 7.15 To Display the Elements of a 1-d Array

```
#include <iostream.h>
#include <iomanip.h>

void display(int[], int);

int main(void)
{
    int a[20], i, n;

    cout << "Enter no. of values \n";
    cin >> n;
    cout << "Enter" << n << "Values";
    for(i = 0; i < n; i++)
        cin >> a[i];
    cout << "The elements are \n";
    display(a, n);

    return 0;
}

void display(int a[], int n)
{
    int i;

    for(i = 0; i < n; i++)
        cout << setw(4) << a[i];
}
```

Input-Output:

```
Enter no. of values
5
```

```
Enter 5 Values
1 2 3 4 5
The elements are
1 2 3 4 5
```

Explanation

The function `display()` is defined with two arguments. A pair of square brackets after the name of the first argument **a** indicates an array of `int` type is being passed and the second argument `n` of `int` type indicates the no. of elements in the array. The purpose of the function is to display the elements of the array passed to it.

In the `main()`, **a** is declared to be an array of `int` type and of size 20. Maximum 20 elements can be accepted into the array. **i** and **n** are declared to be variables of `int` type. The variable **i** is to traverse the elements of the array and **n** is to collect the no. of elements of the array which should lie within 1–20.

After accepting the no. of elements into the variable **n**, **n** elements are accepted into the array **a**. The function `display()` is then invoked by passing the array name **a** and the no. of elements of the array **n** (Actual arguments) to it. As a result, control gets transferred to `display()`. The `display()` displays the elements of the array **a**. The function exits after displaying completes and the control is regained by the `main()`.

To find the sum of the elements in a 1-d array:

Program 7.16 To Find the Sum of the Elements in a 1-d Array

```
#include <iostream.h>
#include <iomanip.h>

int sum(int[], int);

int main(void)
{
    int a[20], i, n, s;

    cout << "Enter no. of values \n";
    cin >> n;
    cout << "Enter" << n << "Values \n";
    for(i = 0; i < n; i++)
        cin >> a[i];

    s = sum(a, n);
    cout << "Sum = " << s << "\n";

    return 0;
}


int sum(int a[], int n)
{
    int s = 0, i;

    for(i = 0; i < n; i++)
```

```
        s += a[i];

    return (s);
}
```

Input-Output:

```
Enter no. of values
5
Enter 5 Values
1 2 3 4 5

Sum = 15
```

Explanation

The function `sum()` is defined with two arguments. The first argument indicates that we pass an array of `int` type and the second argument, which is of `int` type, indicates the no. of elements in the array being passed. The function is also made to return a value of `int` type. The purpose of the function as indicated by its name is to find the sum of the elements of the array being passed and return the sum to the calling program (`main()` in this case). Within the `sum()`, two local variables **i, s** of `int` type are declared. If **i** is to traverse the elements of the array **a**, the variable **s** is to collect the sum of the elements in the array. After the sum is found out, the value of **s** is returned back to the calling program `main()`.

Within `main()`, **a** is declared to be an array of `int` type with size 20. Maximum 20 elements can be accepted into the array. **i, n** and **s** are declared to be variables of `int` type. **i** is to traverse the elements of **a**, **n** is to accept the no. of elements of the array **a** and **s** is to collect the sum of the elements in the array returned by the function `sum()`. After accepting **n** elements into the array **a**, `sum()` is called by passing the array name **a** and the size of the array **n** as `s = sum(a, n)`. Upon execution of the `sum()`, the variable **s** in `main()` would collect the sum the array elements which is then displayed.

Note that the variables **n, i** and **s** of `sum()` are different from those in `main()`.

To find the mean, variance and standard deviation of a list of values: Arrays of one dimension are used to store lists of sample values which are then subjected to statistical calculations. We normally come across the statistical terms like **mean, variance** and **standard deviation** of sample values representing some real life data like population in different cities, amount of rainfall in different seasons in a year etc. Mean of a list of values is defined to be the average of the values in it. Variance is defined to be the average of the differences between each element and the mean of the list and standard deviation of a list of values is given by the square root of the variance of the list. We will now write a program to find mean, variance and standard deviation of a list of values.

Program 7.17 To Find Out the Standard Deviation of a List of Values

```
#include <iostream.h>
#include <iomanip.h>

#include <math.h>
void read(int a[], int n);
void display(int a[], int n);
float find_mean(int a[], int n);
float find_variance(int a[], int n);
float find_stddev(int a[], int n);
```

```
int main(void)
{
    int a[10], n;
    float mean, variance, stddev;

    cout << "Enter the number of values \n";
    cin >> n;

    cout << "Enter the values of the array \n";
    read(a, n);

    cout << "The list of values \n";
    display(a, n);

    mean = find_mean(a, n);
    cout<<"mean =" << mean << "\n";
    variance = find_variance(a, n);
    cout << "Variance = " << variance << "\n";

    stddev = find_stddev(a, n);
    cout << "stddev = " << stddev << "\n";
    return 0;
}
void read(int a[], int n)
{
    int i;
    for(i = 0; i < n; i++)
        cin >> a[i];
}

void display(int a[], int n)
{
    int i;

    for(i = 0; i < n; i++)
        cout << setw(4) << a[i];
}
float find_mean(int a[], int n)
{
    float sum = 0, avg;
    int i;

    for(i = 0; i < n; i++)
        sum += a[i];
    avg = (float) sum / n;

    return avg;
}
```

```
float find_variance(int a[], int n)
{
    float mean, sum_sqrs = 0, variance, deviation;
    int i;

    mean = find_mean(a, n);

    for(i = 0; i < n; i++)
    {
        deviation = a[i] - mean;
        sum_sqrs += deviation * deviation;
    }

    variance = sum_sqrs / n;

    return variance;
}

float find_stddev(int a[], int n)
{
    float variance, stddev;

    variance = find_variance(a, n);
    stddev = sqrt(variance);

    return stddev;
}
```

Input-Output:

```
Enter the number of values
5
Enter the values of the array
3 4 5 6 7
The list of values
3 4 5 6 7
mean = 5
Variance = 2
stddev = 1.414214
```

Explanation

In Program 7.17, the function `read()` is defined with two formal arguments **a** and **n**. The formal arguments represent the array name and the number of elements of the array respectively. The purpose of the function is to accept the given number of values into the array specified while calling it.

The function `display()` is also defined with the same two formal arguments **a** and **n.** The formal arguments represent the array name and the number of elements of the array respectively. The purpose of the function is to display the elements of the array specified while calling it. .

The functions `find_mean()`, `find_variance()` and `find_stddev()` are to find the mean, variance and standard deviation of the elements in an array respectively. Note that all these functions are also defined with the two arguments, array name and number of elements.

Also note that the function `find_variance()` calls `find_mean()` and `find_stddev()` in turn calls `find_variance()`.

7.5.2 Passing Two-dimensional Arrays to Functions

To be able to make a function take a two-dimensional array as its argument. We need to specify three formal arguments: (a) Two-dimensional array name followed by two pairs of square brackets with constant enclosed within the second pair of square brackets preceded by the data type of the array (b) The no. of rows in the array (`int`) (c) The no. of columns in the array (`int`). The last two arguments are not required when the function has to deal with the array of the same size as that of the actual argument.

The syntax of the function definition is as follows:

```
data-type function-name(data-type array_name[ ][size2], int rowsize, int
colsize)
{
    local variables
    statements
}
```

Note that the specification of size within the second pair of square brackets for the array is mandatory since the compiler needs to be aware of the size of each row. It is to help the compiler generate appropriate code so that the function selects appropriate elements when it moves to different rows. However, specification of size within the first pair of square brackets is optional.

EXAMPLE

```
void display(int a[ ][10], int m, int n)
{
    local variables
    statements
}
```

The size specified within the second pair of square brackets should be same as that of the actual array to be passed. While calling the function, the calling program needs to pass just the array name (with no square brackets), no. of rows and no. of columns as:

```
display(b, m, n)
```

where **b** is a two-dimensional array declared in the calling program, **m** and **n** provide the no. of rows and no. of columns of the array respectively

Program 7.18 To Display the Elements of a Matrix

```
#include <iostream.h>
#include <iomanip.h>

void display(int[][10], int, int);

int main(void)
{
    int a[10][10], m , n, i, j;

    cout << "Enter the size of the matrix \n";
    cin >> m >> n;
    cout << "Enter the elements of matrix a \n";
    for(i = 0; i < m; i++)
```

```
    for(j = 0; j < n; j++)
        cin >> a[i][j];
    display(a, m, n);

    return 0;
}

void display(int a[][10], int m, int n)
{
    int i, j;

    for(i = 0; i < m; i++)
    {
        for(j = 0; j < n; j++)
            cout << setw(4) << a[i][j];
        cout << "\n";
    }
}
```

Input-Output:

```
Enter the size of the matrix
3 3
Enter the elements of matrix a
2 3 4 6 7 8 8 9 7

2 3 4
6 7 8
8 9 7
```

Note: A function can receive arrays as arguments but can not return an array of automatic storage class to the calling function. However, it can return an array of static storage class declared within it and a dynamically created array within it to the calling function by returning the address of the first element of the array. You can explore the possibility of returning a static array or a dynamically created array to the calling function later after getting an insight into the relationship between arrays and pointers.

Program 7.19 To Subtract One Matrix from Another Matrix

```
#include <iostream.h>
#include <iomanip.h>

void accept(int a[][10],int m, int n);
void display(int a[][10], int m, int n);
void subtract(int a[][10], int b[][10], int c[][10], int m, int n);

int main(void)
{
    int a[10][10], b[10][10], c[10][10], m ,n;
    cout << "Enter the number of rows and columns of the matrices \n";
    cin >> m >> n;
    cout << "Enter the elements of matrix a \n";
    accept(a, m, n);
```

```
    cout << "Matrix a \n";
    display(a, m, n);
    cout << "Enter the elements of matrix b \n";
    accept(b, m, n);
    cout << "Matrix b \n";
    display(b, m, n);
    subtract(a, b, c, m, n);
    cout << "Resultant matrix c\n";
    display(c, m, n);

    return 0;
}

void accept(int a[][10], int m ,int n)
{
    int i, j;

    for(i = 0; i < m; i++)
    for(j = 0; j < n; j++)
        cin >> a[i][j];
}

void display(int a[][10], int m ,int n)
{
    int i, j;

    for(i = 0; i < m; i++)
    {
        for(j = 0; j < n; j++)
            cout << setw(4) << a[i][j];
        cout << "\n";
    }
}

void subtract(int a[][10], int b[][10], int c[][10], int m, int n)
{
    int i, j;

    for(i = 0; i < m; i++)
    for(j = 0; j < n; j++)
        c[i][j] = a[i][j] - b[i][j];
}
```

Input-Output:

```
Enter the number of rows and columns of the matrices
2 2

Enter the elements of matrix a
2 3 4 5

Matrix a
2 3
4 5
```

```
Enter the elements of matrix b
1 2 3 4

Matrix b
1 2
3 4
Resultant matrix c
1 1
1 1
```

Explanation

The function `accept()` is defined with three formal arguments **a** (2-d array name), **m** (`int`) and **n** (`int`). The arguments **m** and **n** represent the number of rows and the number of columns of the 2-d array respectively. The purpose of the function is to accept the elements of a 2-d array.

The function `display()` is also defined with the same types of arguments and it is to display the elements of a 2-d array.

The function `subtract()` is the important part of the program since it serves the purpose of the program. Within the function the matrix represented by the formal argument **b** is subtracted from the matrix **a** and the resultant matrix is collected by **c** with the help of the following segment:

```
for(i = 0; i < m; i++)
for(j = 0; j < n; j++)
   c[i][j] = a[i][j] - b[i][j];
```

It is important to note that all the formal arguments representing 2-d arrays are provided with the value of the second subscript.

7.5.3 Passing Three-dimensional Arrays to Functions as Arguments

To be able to make a function, take a three-dimensional array as its argument. We need to specify four formal arguments: (a) Three-dimensional array name followed by three pairs of square brackets with constants enclosed within the second and third pairs of square brackets preceded by the data type of the array (b) The number of tables (`int`) (c) The no. of rows in the array (`int`) (d) The no. of columns in the array (`int`). The last three arguments are not required when the function has to deal with the array of the same size as that of the actual argument.

The syntax of the function definition is as follows:

```
data-type function-name(data-type array_name[ ][size2][size3], int tabsize,
int rowsize, int colsize)
{
   local variables
   statements
}
```

Note that the specification of size within the second and the third pairs of square brackets for the array are mandatory since the compiler needs to be aware of the size of each table and the size of each row in each table. It is to help the compiler generate appropriate code so that the function selects appropriate elements when it moves to different tables and different rows in each table. However, specification of size within the first pair of square brackets is optional.

EXAMPLE

To display the elements of a three-dimensional array **a**, the function looks as follows:

```
void display(int a[ ][10][10], int t, int r, int c)
{
    local variables
    statements
}
```

The sizes specified within the second and the third pair of square brackets should be same as those of the actual array to be passed. While calling the function, the calling program needs to pass just the array name (with no square brackets), no. of tables , no. of rows and no. of columns as:

```
display(b, t, r, c)
```

where **b** is a two-dimensional array declared in the calling program, **t**, **r** and **c** provide the number of tables, the no. of rows and no. of columns of the array respectively.

Program 7.20 To Illustrate Passing Three-dimensional Arrays to Functions as Arguments

```
#include <iostream.h>
#include <iomanip.h>

void display(int a[][2][2], int t, int r, int c);

int main(void)
{
    int a[2][2][2] ={ 1, 2, 3, 4, 5, 6, 7, 8};
    display(a, 2, 2, 2);
    return 0;
}

void display(int a[][2][2], int t, int r, int c)
{
 int i, j, k;

 for(i = 0;i < t; i++)
 {
    cout << "Table - " << i+1 << "\n";
    for(j = 0; j< r; j++)
    {
        for(k = 0; k < c; k++)
            cout << setw(4) << a[i][j][k];
        cout << "\n";
    }
    cout << "\n";
 }
}
```

Input-Output:

```
Table-1
   1 2
```

```
  3 4

Table-2
  5 6
  7 8
```

REVIEW QUESTIONS

7.1 Explain the need for arrays.

7.2 Define an array.

7.3 What do you mean by dimensionality of an array?

7.4 Explain the syntax of declaring a one-dimensional array with an example.

7.5 Explain the syntax of initializing a one-dimensional array while declaring.

7.6 Write a program segment to accept values through keyboard into an integer array **a** of size 10.

7.7 Find out errors, if any, in the following:

(a) `int a(9);` (b) `float b[ ];` (c) `int c[x];`
(d) `double 1d[10];` (e) `int b c[4];` (f) `int b[10]`

7.8 Explain the syntax of declaring a two-dimensional array with an example.

7.9 Explain the syntax of initializing a two-dimensional array while declaring with an example.

7.10 Write a program segment to accept values through keyboard into an integer array **a** of two dimensions of size 5*4.

7.11 Find out errors, if any, in the following:

(a) `int a(9)(9);` (b) `float b[ ][ ];` (c) `int c[x][y];` (d) `double 1d[10][3];`
(e) `int b c[4][3];` (f) `int b[10][4];` (g) `int [3,4];` (h) `int a(3,4);`

7.12 Explain the syntax of declaring a three-dimensional array with an example.

7.13 Explain the syntax of initializing a three-dimensional array while declaring with an example.

7.14 Write a program segment to accept values through keyboard into an integer array **a** of three dimensions of size 5*4*3.

True/False Questions

T7.1 Arrays facilitate collective manipulations.

T7.2 In an array, there can be data of different types.

T7.3 The size of an array can be a real number.

T7.4 The array index starts with one.

T7.5 Arrays can be initialized.

T7.6 `int a[] = {3, 4, 5};` is a valid initialization.

T7.7 `float f[2] = {3, 5};` is a valid initialization.

T7.8 Any looping structure can be used to access the elements of an array.

T7.9 Two loops are used to access the elements of a 2-d array.

T7.10 `Int a[][] = {1,2,3,4}` is a valid initialization of the 2-d array **a**.

T7.11 Three loops are used to access the elements of a 3-d array.

T7.12 There is a limit on the dimensionality of arrays in C++.

T7.13 Arrays can be passed to functions as arguments.

T7.14 An array can be returned from a function.

T7.15 While passing a 2-d array as an argument to a function, the number of columns should be specified within the second pair of square brackets.

PROGRAMMING EXERCISES

P7.1 Write a program to generate Fibonacci series using an array.
(**Hint:** First two members of the series are 1 and 1.

```
a[0] = 1,
a[1] = 1,
a[i] = a[i-1] + a[i-2],
```

i ranging from 2 to *n*)

P7.2 Write a program to find the sum of odd numbers and sum of even numbers in an integer array.

P7.3 Write a program to display only prime numbers in an integer array.

P7.4 Write a program to insert an element into an array of one dimension.

P7.5 Write a program to delete an integer into an array of one dimension.

P7.6 Write a program to delete duplicates in an array.

P7.7 **a** and **b** are two arrays of one dimension of size 10. Write a program to find the array **c** such that

```
c[0] = a[0] + b[9]
c[1] = a[1] + b[8]
  :
  :
  :
c[8] = a[8] + b[1]
c[9] = a[9] + b[0]
```

P7.8 Write a program to find the intersection of two arrays **a** and **b** with size **m** and **n** respectively.

Example

```
int a[3] = {1, 2, 3, 4, 5};
int b[2] = {1, 4, 6};
```

Result of intersection of **a** and **b** is another array **c** with the elements which are common in both **a** and **b**.

```
c[] = { 1, 4}
```

P7.9 Write a program to find the union of two arrays **a** and **b** with size **m** and **n** respectively.

Example

```
int a[3] = {1, 2, 3, 4, 5};
int b[2] = {1, 4, 6};
```

Result of union of **a** and **b** is another array **c** with the elements which are either in **a** or in **b** or in both.

```
c[] = { 1,2, 3, 4, 5, 6}
```

P7.10 Write a program to find the largest element in an array using a function.

P7.11 Write a program to find the no. of prime numbers in an array using a function.

P7.12 Write a program to search for a number in a list of numbers using linear search method. (Use a recursive function to implement linear search method.)

P7.13 Write a program to search for a number in a list of numbers using binary search method. (Use a recursive function to implement binary search method. For the binary search method to work, the list is expected to be in increasing or decreasing order. Suppose the list is in the increasing order, the number being searched for is compared with the middle element in the list. If the number is less than the middle element, the first half of the list is considered only. If the number is greater than the middle element, the second half of the list is considered. This continues till the number is found or the list gets exhausted.)

P7.14 Write a program to find whether a matrix is symmetric or not.

P7.15 Write a program to find out whether a matrix is an identity matrix or not. (A square matrix is said to be an identity matrix if all the principal diagonal elements are 1's and all the remaining elements are 0's.)

Example

$$\begin{bmatrix} 1 & 0 & 0 \\ 0 & 1 & 0 \\ 0 & 0 & 1 \end{bmatrix}$$

P7.16 Write a program to find whether a matrix is a lower triangular matrix or not. (A square matrix is said to be a lower triangular matrix if all the elements below the principal diagonal elements are non-zero values and the remaining elements are all zeros.)

Example

$$\begin{bmatrix} 0 & 0 & 0 \\ 2 & 0 & 0 \\ 7 & 8 & 0 \end{bmatrix}$$

P7.17 Write a program to find whether a matrix is an upper triangular matrix or not. (A square matrix is said to be an upper triangular matrix if all the elements above the principal diagonal elements are non-zero values and the remaining elements are all zeros.)

Example

$$\begin{bmatrix} 0 & 3 & 5 \\ 0 & 0 & 7 \\ 0 & 0 & 0 \end{bmatrix}$$

P7.18 Write a program to transpose a matrix.

P7.19 Write a program to sort a matrix row-wise.

P7.20 Write a program to sort a matrix column-wise.

P7.21 Write a program to find the trace of a matrix.
(Trace of a matrix is defined to be the sum of the diagonal elements in the matrix.)

P7. 22 Write a program to find the norm of a matrix.
(Norm of a matrix is defined to be the square root of the sum of the squares of the elements of the matrix.)

P7.23 Write a program to check whether a matrix is orthogonal or not.
(A matrix is said to be orthogonal if the product of the matrix and its transpose turns out to be an identity matrix.)

P7.24 Write a program to find the sum of the elements above and below the diagonal elements in a matrix.

P7.25 Write a program to find the saddle points in a matrix.
(A saddle point is one which is the least element in the row and is the largest element in the column.)

P7.26 Write programs to perform the tasks of the Questions P7.20–P7.25 using functions.

Chapter 8

C-Strings

8.1 INTRODUCTION

Consider the statement cout << `"Welcome";` the cout statement displays the message "Welcome" on the screen. Let us now understand how the message "welcome" is stored in memory and how it is displayed. The message "Welcome" is stored in memory as follows:

w	e	l	c	o	m	e	\0

Note that the last location in the memory block has the special character `'\0'`. The special character is automatically appended to the end of the message by the compiler.

In the statement cout << `"Welcome";` the cout statement is provided with the starting address of the memory block. That is, the address of the first character 'w'. It will then continue to pick each character from the block and displays it till the `'\0'` is reached. This is how the message is displayed. Here, the message "Welcome" is a **string**. To be precise, it is a **string constant**.

A string in C is defined to be a sequence of characters terminated by the special character `'\0'`. The special character `'\0'` is called the **null character** and it is to indicate the end of a string.

Strings constitute the major part of data used by many C programs. In real programming environment, we need to perform many more operations over strings like accepting strings through keyboard, extracting a part of a string etc. String I/O operations and other manipulations over strings need variables to store them. The type of the variables inarguably happens to be an arrays of `char` type.

An array of `char` type to store the above string is to be declared as follows:

```
char s[8];
```

s[0]	s[1]	s[2]	s[3]	s[4]	s[5]	s[6]	s[7]
w	e	l	c	o	m	e	\0

An array of `char` is also regarded as a **string variable**, since it can accommodate a string and it permits us to change its contents. In contrast, a sequence of characters enclosed within a pair of double quotes is called a **string constant.**

EXAMPLE

`"Welcome"` is a string constant.

8.2 STRING I/O

The cin and cout statements: Syntax of using `cin` to accept a string into a string variable **s** is as follows:

```
cin >> s;
```

accepts a string into **s** up to a white space character (Blank space, New line character, Tab space). The null character '\0' will be automatically appended to the string. The size of **s** is thus expected to be large enough to collect even the null character also.

EXAMPLE

```
char str[10];
cin >> str;
```

If the input is:

abcd   xyz

only "abcd" would be taken by `str`. Any subsequent `cin` to accept a string would read the string xyz.

EXAMPLE

```
char str1[10], str2[10];
cin >> str1 >> str2;
```

If the user input is:

abcd xyz,

"abcd" would be taken by `str1` and "xyz" would be taken by `str2`.

Syntax of using `cout` to display a string is:

```
cout << s;
```

displays the string contained in **s**. **s** is a string variable the contents of which are to be displayed.

EXAMPLE

```
char s[10];
```

If **s** has the string "abcd xyz",

`cout << s;` would display "abcd xyz".

Program 8.1 To Illustrate String I/O Using cin and cout

```
#include <iostream.h>

int main(void)
{
    char s1[10], s2[20];

    cout << "Enter a string into s1\n";
    cin >> s1;
    cout << "s1 = " << s1 << "\n";
    cout << "Enter a string into s2\n";
    cin >> s2;
    cout << "s2 = " << s2 << "\n";

    return 0;
}
```

Input-Output:

```
Enter a string into s1
Bangalore
s1 = Bangalore
Enter a string into s2
Mysore City
s2 = Mysore
```

The getchar() and putchar() functions: `getchar()` is basically a macro used to read a character through standard input, keyboard. The syntax of its usage is as follows: [macros will be discussed in detail later]

```
c = getchar();
```

where **c** is a variable of char type. As a result of this, a character typed at the keyboard is assigned to the variable **c**.

This can be used iteratively to accept a line of text.

`putchar()` is the counterpart of `getchar()`. It is used to display a character on the standard output device, usually the screen. The syntax of using `putchar()` is as follows:

```
putchar(c);
```

where **c** represents variable of type `char` or a character constant. It displays the character stored in **c** on the screen.

`putchar()` can be used iteratively to display a line of text.

Since both `getchar()` and `putchar()` are defined in the header file stdio.h, the header file has to be included as part of the program which uses them.

Program 8.2 To Accept a Line of Text and Display It Using getchar() and putchar()

```
#include <iostream.h>
#include <stdio.h>
```

```
int main(void)
{
    char text[80], c;
    int i;

    cout << "Enter a line of text \n";
    i = 0;
    c = getchar();
    while( c != '\n')
    {
        text[i] = c;
        c = getchar();
        i++;
    }
    text[i] = '\0'; // The line of text is now available in text
// Displaying the line of text using putchar()

    cout << " The line of text entered is \n";
    for( i = 0; text[i] != '\0'; i++)
    putchar(text[i]);

    return 0;
}
```

Input-Output:

```
Enter a line of text
Bangalore is the IT capital of India.

The line of text entered is
Bangalore is the IT capital of India.
```

The gets() and puts() functions: The purpose of `gets()` is to accept a string up to a new line character into a string variable. It automatically appends the null character `'\0'` to the end of the string. Prototype of `gets()` is as follows:

```
char* gets(char*);
```

The function accepts a pointer to `char` type and returns a pointer to `char` type.

EXAMPLE

```
        char str[40];

gets(str);
```

Enables us to accept a string up to a new line character into **str**. If the string given is `"I am going"`, the entire string gets accepted by **str**.

The purpose of `puts()` is to display a string contained in a string variable. It also adds the new-line character `'\n'` to the string automatically, as a result of which the cursor is moved down by one line after the string is displayed.

The prototype of `puts()` is as follows:

```
int puts(char*);
```

EXAMPLE

```
char str[20];
```

If **str** has the string `"I am going"`, `puts(str)` would display the entire string `"I am going"` and moves the cursor to the beginning of the next line. Since both the functions are declared in the header file **stdio.h,** the header file has to be included as part of the program.

Program 8.3 To Accept a Line of Text Using gets() and Display It Using puts()

```
#include <iostream.h>
#include <stdio.h>
int main(void)
{
    char str[40];

    cout << "Enter a line of text  \n";
    gets(str);
    cout << "The line of text entered is \n";
    puts(str);

    return 0;
}
```

Input-Output:

```
Enter a line of text
Mumbai is the Commercial Capital of India.

The line of text entered is
Mumbai is the Commercial Capital of India.
```

The sprintf() and sscanf() functions: The syntax of the `sprintf()` is similar to that of the `printf()` except the presence of buffer address as its first parameter and it is as follows:

```
void sprintf(char *s, char *fmt, arguments);
```

The argument **s** is the buffer address, **fmt** represents the control string. The function writes the values of the arguments into the memory area identified by **s**.

The syntax of the `sscanf()` is similar to that of the `scanf()` except the presence of buffer address as its first parameter and it is as follows:

```
void sscanf(char *s, char *fmt, arguments);
```

The argument **s** is the buffer address, **fmt** represents the control string. The function reads the values in **s** into the arguments.

Program 8.4 To Illustrate sscanf() and sprintf() Functions

```
#include <iostream.h>
#include <stdio.h>
int main(void)
```

```
{
    char str[100];
    int a;
    float f;
    char s[10];

    sprintf(str, "%d %f %s", 12, 23.4, "Mysore");
    cout << s;
    sscanf(str, "%d %f %s", &a, &f, s);
    cout << "a = " << a << "f = " << f << "s =" <<  s << "\n";
    return 0;
}
```

Input-Output:

```
12 23.400000 Mysore
a = 12    f = 23.4    s = Mysore
```

8.3 INITIALIZATION OF ARRAYS OF CHAR TYPE

The syntax of initializing a string variable has two variations:

Variation 1:

```
char str1[5] = {  'a', 's', 'd',  'f', '\0' };
```

Here, `str1` is declared to be a string variable with size five. It can accommodate maximum five characters. The `initializer-list` consists of comma separated character constants. Note that the null character `'\0'` is explicitly listed. This is required in this variation.

Variation 2:

```
char str2[5] = { "asdf" };
```

Here, `str2` is also declared to be a string variable of size five. It can accommodate maximum five characters including null character. The `initializer-list` consists of a string constant. In this variation, null character `'\0'` will be automatically appended to the end of string by the compiler.

In either of these variations, the size of the character array can be skipped, in which case, the size, the no. of characters in the `initializer-list` would be automatically supplied by the compiler.

EXAMPLE

```
char s1[] = { "abcd" };
```

The size of `s1` would be five, four characters plus one for the null character `'\0'`.

```
char s2[] = { 'a', 'b', 'c', '\0'};
```

The size of `s2` would be four, three characters plus one for null character '`\0`'.

The strings being initialized can have white spaces (blank spaces, new line character and tab space character etc).

```
char s[20] = { "Programming with strings \n"};
```

Note the presence of the blank spaces and a new line character as part of the string.

Program 8.5 To Illustrate Strings Initialization

```
#include <iostream.h>

int main(void)
{
    char s1[10] = { "welcome" };
    char s2[10] = { 'a', 'd', 'f', 'g', '\0' };
    char s3[] = { "Welcome" };
    char s4[] = {"Programming with strings \n"};

    cout << "s1 = " << s1 << "\n";
    cout << "s2 = " << s2 << "\n";
    cout << "s3 = " << s3 << "\n";
    cout << "s4 = " << s4 << "\n";

    return 0;
}
```

Input-Output:

```
s1 = welcome
s2 = adfg
s3 = Welcome
s4 = Programming with strings
```

8.4 ARITHMETIC AND RELATIONAL OPERATIONS ON CHARACTERS

Character variables and character constants can be included as part of arithmetic and relational expressions. When included, the ASCII values of the characters participate during their evaluation. For example, consider the arithmetic expression 5 + 'a'. This is certainly valid in C++. The value of the expression would be 5 + 97 = 104 where 97 is the ASCII value of 'a'.

Now, consider the arithmetic expression 'b' – 'a'. The value of this expression turns out to be 1. Since ASCII value of 'b' is 98 and that of 'a' is 97.

Similarly, consider the relational expression 'a' > 50. The expression evaluates to true since the ASCII value of 'a' is 97 and 97 > 50 is certainly true. Consider another relational expression 'a' > 'z'. This expression evaluates to false since the ASCII value of 'z' is 122.

We know that a string is nothing but an array of `char` type. Similar to arrays of numeric type (`int`, `float`), individual characters of a string can be accessed by using the array name and the appropriate subscript values. The characters can be subjected to arithmetic and relational operations.

Program 8.6 To Encrypt and Decrypt a String

```
#include <iostream.h>

int main(void)
{
    char name[20];
    int i;
```

```
    cout << "Enter a name \n";
    cin >> name;
    cout << name << "\n";
    for(i = 0; name[i] != '\0'; i++)
        name[i] = name[i] + 1;
    cout << "Encrypted name = " << name << "\n";

    for(i = 0; name[i] != '\0'; i++)
        name[i] = name[i] - 1;
    cout << "Decrypted name = " << name << "\n";

    return 0;
}
```

Input-Output:

```
Enter a name
Nishchith
Encrypted name = Ojtidijui
Decrypted name = Nishchith
```

Explanation

name is declared to be a string variable. It can accommodate maximum 20 characters. It is to collect a name (input). **i** is declared to be a variable of `int` type and it is to access each character of the input string. In the body of the first for loop, one is added to the ASCII value of each character of the string, i.e., `name[i] = name[i] + 1`. As a result, each character in the string is replaced by its next character in the alphabet of C++. Encrypted name is displayed.

In the body of the second for loop, one is subtracted from the ASCII value of each character of the string, i.e., `name[i] = name[i]- 1`. As a result, each character in the string is replaced by its preceding character in the alphabet of C++. As a result, the original name is obtained and it is displayed.

To find the number of occurrences of a character in a string: There are two inputs to the program: (a) String of characters (b) A single character. We use an array of `char` type to collect a string and a variable of type `char` to collect a character, and we keep a counter which is incremented when a character in the string is found to match with the given character during the course of traversing of the string from the first character till the last character is encountered.

Program 8.7 To Find the No. of Occurrences of a Character in a String

```
#include <iostream.h>
#include <stdio.h>

int main(void)
{
    char str[20], ch;
    int i, count;

    cout << "Enter a character \n";
    cin >> ch;
    fflush(stdin);
    cout << "Enter a string \n";
    cin >> str;
```

```
    // Finding the no. of occurrences of c in str begins

    count = 0;
    for( i = 0; str[i] != '\0'; i++)
        if (str[i] == ch)
            count++;

    // Finding the no. of occurrences of c in str ends

    cout << "No. of Occurrences of " << ch << " in " << str << " = " << count;
        return 0;
}
```

Input-Output:

```
Enter a character
m
Enter a string
Programming
No. of Occurrences of m in Programming = 2
```

Explanation

`str` is declared to be a string variable of size 20. It can thus accommodate 20 characters and is to collect a string (input). **`ch`** is declared to be a variable of `char` type and it is to collect a character (input), the no. of occurrences of which in **`str`** is to be found out. `i` and `count` are declared to be variables of `int` type. The variable `i` is to traverse the characters in **`str`** and **`count`** is to collect the no. of occurrences of **`ch`** in **`str`** (output).

After a string is accepted into **`str`**, a for loop is set up to traverse each character of the string. Within the body of the loop, each character of the string is checked against **`ch`** for equality. In case of a match, the variable **`count`** is incremented. When the loop exits, the variable **`count`** will have the no. of occurrences of the given character in the given string.

To count the no. of upper case, lower case letters, digits and special characters in a string: There is only one input to the program, i.e., a string of characters. We use an array of `char` type to collect a string and we keep separate counters which are incremented when a character in the string is found to lie within the range of respective category of characters during the course of traversing of the string from the first character till the last character is encountered.

Program 8.8 To Count the No. of Upper Case, Lower Case Letters, Digits and Special Characters in a String

```
#include <iostream.h>
#include <ctype.h>
#include <string.h>

int main(void)
{

    char str[40];
    int uc, lc, dc, sc, length, i;
```

```
    cout << "Enter a string \n";
    cin >> str;

    lc = uc = dc = sc=0;
    length = strlen(str);
    for(i = 0; i < length; i++)
    {
        if ((str[i] >= 'a') && (str[i] <= 'z'))
            lc++;
        else if ((str[i] >= 'A') && (str[i] <= 'Z'))
            uc++;
        else if((str[i] >= '0') && (str[i] <= '9'))
            dc++;
        else
            sc++;
    }
    cout << "No. of Upper Case Letters = " << uc << "\n";
    cout << "No. of Lower Case Letters = " << lc << "\n";
    cout << "No. of Digits = " << dc << "\n";
    cout << "No. of Special characters = " << sc << "\n";

    return 0;
}
```

Input-Output:

```
Enter a string
Object_Oriented123

No. of Upper Case Letters = 2
No. of Lower Case Letters = 12
No. of Digits = 3
No. of Special characters = 1
```

Explanation

In Program 8.8, **str** is declared to be a string variable of size 40. The variables **lc**, **uc**, **dc**, **sc**, **l** and **i** are declared to be of `int` type. **str** is to collect a line of text. Maximum 39 characters can be accepted into it. **lc** is to collect no. of lower case letters; **uc** is to collect no. of upper case letters; **dc** is to collect no. of digits; **sc** is to collect no. of special characters in the given line of text.

First, a line of text is accepted into the string variable **str**. The length of **str** is then found out and is assigned to the variable **l**. **lc**, **uc**, **dc** and **sc** are set to 0. The **for** loop is to traverse each character in the line of text. As each character is taken, it is checked whether it is a lower case letter with the condition `str[i] >= 'a' && str[i] <='z'`. If the condition is found to be true, **lc** is incremented. Similarly, for upper case letters, digits and special characters, the corresponding variable is incremented.

To find whether a string is palindrome or not: A string is said to be a palindrome if the string and its reverse are the same.

EXAMPLE

"madam" is a palindrome.

The string "liril" is another example of a palindrome.

Program 8.9 To Find Out Whether a String is Palindrome or Not

```
#include <iostream.h>
#include <string.h>

int main(void)
{
    char str[20];
    int l, i, flag;

    cout << "Enter a string \n";
    cin >> str;
    l = strlen(str);
    flag = 1;
    for(i = 0; i <= l/2; i++)
        if ( str[i] != str[l - i - 1])
        {
            flag = 0;
            break;
        }
    if (flag)
        cout << str << "is a palindrome \n";
    else
        cout << str << "is not a palindrome \n";

    return 0;
}
```

Input-Output:

First Run:

```
Enter a string
madam
madam is a palindrome
```

Second Run:

```
Enter a string
karan
karan is not a palindrome
```

Explanation

In Program 8.9, **str** is declared to be a string variable and it is to collect a string (input). **i** and **l** are declared to be variables of `int` type. The variable **i** is to scan through the string and the variable **l** is to collect the length of the string.

After accepting a string into the variable **str**, it is subjected to the test of palindrome property. The segment of the program responsible for finding out whether the string in **str** is palindrome or not is the following:

```
l = strlen(str);
flag = 1;
for(i = 0; i <= l/2; i++)
    if ( str[i] != str[l - i - 1])
```

```
    {
        flag = 0;
        break;
    }
```

The length of the string is found out and it is assigned to the variable **l**. The variable **flag** is assigned one before the loop is entered and we assume that the string is palindrome. Within the body of the loop, the first character `s[0]` is checked against the last character `s[l-1]`. If they match, the second character `s[1]` is matched against the last but one character `s[l-2]`. If they also match, the third character `s[2]` is checked against the last but two character `s[l-3]` and this is repeated till a mismatch is found or till the half of the string is traversed, whichever occurs first. If there is any mismatch, the variable **flag** is assigned 0 and the loop is exited prematurely. Ultimately the value of **flag** determines whether the string in **str** is palindrome or not. If **flag** retains 1, the string is displayed to be "palindrome". Otherwise it is displayed to be "not a palindrome".

8.5 STRING MANIPULATIONS

The most commonly performed operations over strings are:

1. Finding the length of a string
2. Copying one string to another string
3. Concatenation of two strings
4. Comparing two strings
5. Searching substring in a string

All these operations are to be performed on a character by character basis. Let us now try to understand the logic involved and the built-in functions provided by C to perform these operations. Each of these operations is implemented using the underlying logic and using the built-in functions in the programs to follow. Since the string manipulation built-in functions are declared in the header file **string.h**, this file has to be included in all the programs which use these functions with the help of preprocessor directive #include.

Finding the length of a string: Length of a string is defined to be the no. of characters in it excluding the null character `'\0'`. To find the length of a string, we need to scan through the string; count the no. of characters till the null character is reached. C provides a built-in function namely `strlen()` to find the length of a string. The prototype of `strlen()` is as follows:

```
int strlen(s );
```

Argument **s** represents a string. It can be a string constant or a string variable. The function returns an integer value, which is the length of the string.

EXAMPLE

```
    char s[20] = { "anbfdd" };
    int l;
    l = strlen(s);
```

`l` collects the length of **`s`**.

Program 8.10 To Find the Length of a String

```
#include <iostream.h>
#include <string.h>

int main(void)
{
    char str[20];
    int i, length;

    cout << "Enter a string \n";
    cin >> str;

/* Finding the length of s without using strlen()begins */

    length = 0;
    for( i = 0; str[i] != '\0'; i++)
        length++;
    cout << "Length of" << str << "=" << length << "\n";

/* Finding the length of str without using strlen()ends */

    length = strlen(str);
    cout << "Length of" << str << "using strlen() = " << length << "\n";

    return 0;
}
```

Input-Output:

```
Enter a string
Harshith
Length of Harshith = 8
Length of Harshith using strlen() = 8
```

Explanation

str is declared to be an array of **char** type and of size 20. **Length** and **i** are declared to be variables of **int** type. **str** is to collect the input string. Variable **length** is to collect the length of the string in **str**. The variable **i** is to scan through the string accessing each character.

A string is read into **str** through the keyboard. The following segment finds the length of **str** without using `strlen()`:

```
length = 0;
for( i = 0; str[i] != '\0'; i++)
    length++;
```

length is initialized to 0 before scanning through the string begins. When the loop is entered, scanning through the string begins. During the course of scanning, if the character is found to be not null character `'\0'`, **length** is incremented by one. The loop is exited when the null character is reached. So when the loop completes, **length** collects the length of **str**.

The length of **str** is found out using `strlen()` built-in function also.

Copying one string to another string: Suppose `s1` and `s2` are two string variables and `s1` has the string "abcd". If we want to make a copy of `s1` in `s2`, we can not use the assignment statement `s2 = s1`. The assignment operator = is not defined over strings. Copying `s1` to `s2` should be done on a character by character basis. First character in `s1` should be assigned to first location of `s2`, second character in `s1` should be assigned to second location of `s2` and so on till the null character in `s1` is encountered. C provides `strcpy()` built-in function to copy one string to another. The prototype of `strcpy()` is as follows:

```
strcpy(s2, s1);
```

copies string contained in `s1` to `s2`.
`s1` can be string constant or a string variable. But `s2` should be a string variable and it should be large enough to collect the string in `s1`.

EXAMPLE

```
char s1[20]={"abcd"}, s2[20];

strcpy(s2, s1);
```

As a result of this, `s1` gets copied to `s2`. `s2` now contains "abcd".

```
strcpy(s1, "xyz");
```

Here, the string constant "xyz" gets copied to `s1`. `s1` now contains "xyz".

Program 8.11 To Copy One String to Another String

```
#include <iostream.h>
#include <string.h>

int main(void)
{
   char str1[20]="abcd", str2[20], str3[20], str4[20];
   int i;

   cout << "String in str1 = " << str1 << "\n";

   // Copying str1 to str2 without using strcpy() begins

   for( i = 0; str1[i] != '\0'; i++)
       str2[i] = str1[i];
   str2[i] = '\0';
   cout << "string in str2 = " << str2 << "\n";

   // Copying str1 to str2 without using strcpy() ends

   strcpy(str3, str1); // copying string in a string variable
   cout << "string in str3 = " << str3 << "\n";
   strcpy(str4, "mno");          // Copying a string constant
   cout << "string in str4 = " << str4 << "\n";

   return 0;
}
```

Input-Output:

```
String in str1 = abcd
string in str2 = abcd
string in str3 = abcd
string in str4 = mno
```

Explanation

str1, **str2**, **str3** and **str4** are declared to be string variables of size 20. Each of the variables can thus accommodate up to 20 characters including the null character '\0'. The variable **i** is to scan through the strings. String variable **str1** is initialized to "abcd" and it is displayed. The following segment of the program copies **str1** to **str2** without using strcpy():

```
for( i = 0; str1[i] != '\0'; i++)
    str2[i] = str1[i];
str2[i] = '\0';
```

The for loop is to scan through the string in **str1** and assign its each character to the corresponding position in **str2**. When **i** takes 0, the first character in **str1** is assigned to the first position in **str2**. When **i** takes 1, the second character in **str1** is assigned to the second position in **str2** and so on. The loop is terminated when the null character in **str1** is encountered. Note that the null character '\0' is assigned to the last position in **str2**. This is required to mark the end of the string in it.

strcpy() is then used to copy string in **str1** to **str3** and a string constant "mno" to **str4**. The contents of both **str3** and **str4** are then displayed.

Comparing two strings: Comparison of two strings is another most commonly performed operation over strings. We require this while searching for a string in a list of strings or sorting a list of strings. Suppose s1 and s2 are two strings. To find whether s1 is alphabetically greater than s2, we can not use relational expression s1 > s2. To find whether s1 is alphabetically lower than s2, we can not use relational expression s1 < s2. Similarly s1 == s2 can not be used to find whether s1 and s2 are equal or not. The relational operators are not defined over strings. So, comparison of two strings also should be done on a character by character basis. That is, comparison of first pair of characters of s1 and s2, comparison of second pair of characters and so on. C provides strcmp() built-in function to compare two strings.

The prototype of strcmp() is as follows:

```
int strcmp(s1, s2);
```

s1 and s2 represent two strings being compared. s1 can be a string constant or a string variable. Similarly, s2 also. The function returns the numerical difference between the first non-matching pair of characters of s1 and s2. It returns a positive value when s1 is alphabetically greater than s2. It returns a negative value when s1 is alphabetically lower than s2. It returns 0 when s1 and s2 are equal.

EXAMPLE

```
char s1[20]={ "abc"}, s2[20]={"aac"};
int i;
i = strcmp(s1,s2);
```

i gets 1 since the numerical difference between the first non-matching pair 'b' of s1 and 'a' of s2 is 1.

```
char s1[20]={ "aac"}, s2[20]={"abc"};
int i;
i = strcmp(s1,s2);
```

i gets -1 since the numerical difference between the first non-matching pair 'a' of s1 and 'b' of s2 is -1.

```
char s1[20]={ "abc"}, s2[20]={"abc"};
int i;
i = strcmp(s1,s2);
```

i gets 0 since both the strings are equal.

Program 8.12 To Compare Two Strings

```
#include <iostream.h>
#include <string.h>

int main(void)
{
    char str1[20] = {"abc"} , str2[20] = {"aac"}, str3[20] = {"abc"};
    int i, diff;

    cout << " str1 = " << str1 << "\n";
    cout << "str2 = " << str2 << "\n";

/* comparing str1and str2 without using strcmp() begins */

    i = 0;
    while  ((str1[i] == str2[i])&& (str1[i] != '\0')&& (str2[i]!='\0'))
        i++;
    diff = str1[i] - str2[i];
    cout << " Difference between" << str1 << "and" << str2 << "=" << diff <<
    "\n";
/* comparing str1 and str2 without using strcmp() ends */

    diff = strcmp(str1, str2); /* comparison using strcmp() */
    cout << "Difference between" << str1 << "and" << str2 << "=" << diff <<
    "\n";

    diff = strcmp(str2, str1);
    cout << " Difference between" << str2 << "and" << str1 << "=" << diff <<
    "\n";

    diff = strcmp(str1, str3);
    cout << " Difference between" << str1 << "and" << str3 << "=" << diff <<
    "\n";

    return 0;
}
```

Input-Output:

```
str1 = abc
str2 = aac
Difference between abc and aac=1
Difference between abc and aac=1
Difference between aac and abc=-1
Difference between abc and abc=0
```

Explanation

str1, str2 and **str3** are declared to be arrays of `char` type and all have been initialized. the integer variable **i** is to scan through the strings. **diff** is to collect the numeric difference of the ASCII values of the first non-matching pair of characters of two strings. The following segment of the program is to compare the strings **str1** and **str2** without using `strcmp()`.

```
i = 0;
while((str1[i] == str2[i])&& ((str1[i] != '\0')&& (str2[i] != '\0')))
        i++;
diff = str1[i] - str2[i];
```

The while loop repeats as long as the pairs of characters in **str1** and **str2** are same or the end of any of the strings is not reached. Once mismatch is found or the end of any of **str1** and **str2** is reached, the loop is terminated and the numerical difference between the non-matching pair of characters is assigned to **diff**.

Then, three calls are made to `strcmp()`. In the first call, strings **str1** and **str2** are passed to `strcmp()`. The function returns `1`, the numerical difference between the first non-matching pair `(b, a)` of **str1** and **str2** respectively indicating that **str1** is alphabetically greater than **str2**.

In the second call, the strings **str2** and **str1** are passed to `strcmp()`. The function returns `-1`, the numerical difference between the first non-matching pair `(a, b)` of **str2** and **str1** respectively indicating that **str2** is alphabetically lower than **str1**.

In the third call, the strings **str1** and **str3** are passed to `strcmp()`. The function returns `0`, indicating that both the strings are same.

Concatenation of two strings: The process of appending one string to the end of another string is called **concatenation**. If `s1` and `s2` are two strings and when `s2` is appended to the end of `s1`, `s1` and `s2` are said to be concatenated. The string `s1` then contains its original string plus the string contained in `s2`. Similar to copying and comparing, appending `s2` to `s1` should be done on a character by character basis. C provides `strcat()` built-in function to concatenate two strings.

The prototype of `strcat()` is as follows:

```
strcat(s1,s2);
```

appends `s2` to `s1`. `s2` can be a string variable or a string constant. But `s1` should be a string variable and the size of `s1` should be large enough to collect even `s2` also in addition to its own string.

EXAMPLE

```
char s1[10] = {"abc"}, s2[10] = {"xyz"};
strcat(s1,s2);
```

`s1` will now collect "abcxyz".

Program 8.13 To Concatenate Two Strings

```
#include <iostream.h>
#include <string.h>

int main(void)
{
        char str1[20] = { "abc" }, str2[20] = { "def" }, str3[20]={ "ghi"};
```

```
    int i, j;

    cout << " str1 = " << str1 << "\n";
    cout << "str2 = " << str2 << "\n";

 /* Concatenation of str1 and str2 without using strcat() begins */

    for( i = 0; str1[i] != '\0'; i++);

    for( j = 0; str2[j] != '\0'; j++)
        str1[i + j] = str2[j];

    str1[i+j] = '\0';
    cout << "After concatenation str1 = " << str1 << "\n";

 /* Concatenation of str1 and str2 without using strcat() ends */

    strcat(str1, str3);
    cout << " str1 = " << str1 << "\n";
    strcat(str1, "jkl");
    cout << " str1 = " << str1 << "\n";

    return 0;
 }
```

Input-Output:

```
str1 = abc
str2 = def
After concatenation str1 = abcdef
str1 = abcdefghi
str1 = abcdefghijkl
```

Explanation

str1, **str2** and **str3** are declared to be arrays of `char` type and all are initialized strings. The integer variables **i** and **j** are to traverse the strings. String in **str2** is appended to the end of the string in **str1** by following segment of the program:

```
for( i = 0; str1[i] != '\0'; i++);

for( j = 0; str2[j] != '\0'; j++)
    str1[i + j] = str2[j];

str1[i + j] = '\0';
```

The first for loop is to simply scan through the string **str1**. When the loop completes, the variable **i** points to the position of null character `'\0'` in **str1**. The second loop is to scan through the second string **str2** till end of it is reached. When **j** takes 0, the first character in **str2** is assigned to the position of null character in **str1**. So, the null character in **str1** is overwritten by the first character in **str2**. Subsequently, the remaining characters in **str2** are appended to **str1** and lastly, the null character `'\0'` is assigned to the last position of **str1**. The string in **str1**, "abcdef" is then displayed.

Then two calls are made to `strcat()`. In the first call, `strcat(`**`str1`**`, `**`str3`**`)`, **`str3`** is appended to **`str1`**. Since **`str3`** had “ghi”, **`str1`** now becomes “abcdefghi” and is displayed. In the second call, `strcat(str1, "jkl")`, the string constant “jkl” is appended to **`str1`**. The new string “abcdefghijkl” in **`str1`** is again displayed.

To find the position of one string in another string (Indexing): We will now write a program to find the position of occurrence of one string in another string. The C library provides a built-in function by name `strstr()` to perform this task. The program would thus simulate the working of the function.

Program 8.14 To Find the Position of One String in Another String (Indexing)

```
#include <iostream.h>
#include <string.h>
#include <process.h>

int main(void)
{
   char str1[20], str2[20];
   int len_str1, len_str2, i, j, flag;

   cout << "\n Enter first string \n";
   cin >> str1;
   cout << "\n Enter second string \n";
   cin >> str2;

   len_str1 = strlen(str1);
   len_str2 = strlen(str2);

   if (len_str2 > len_str1)
   {
      cout << str2 << "can not be found in" << str1 << "\n";
      exit(0);
   }

   for(i = 0; i < (len_str1 - len_str2 + 1); i++)
   {
      flag = 1;
      for(j = 0; j < len_str2; j++)
         if (str1[i + j] != str2[j])
         {
            flag = 0;
            break;
         }
         if (flag)
         break;
   }
   if (flag)
      cout << str2 << "is found in" << str1 << "at position" <<
         i << "\n";
```

```
  else
     cout << str2 << " is not found in " << str1 << "\n";

  return 0;
}
```

Input-Output:

```
Enter first string
Ravikumar

Enter second string
kumar  is found in Ravikumar at position 4
```

Explanation

str1 and **str2** are declared to be string variables of size 20. Both can collect strings consisting of maximum 19 characters. **str1** is to collect main string; **str2** is to collect a string, the position of occurrence of which in **str1** is to be found. **len_str1** and **len_str2**, **i**, **j** and **flag** are declared to be variables of **int** type. **len_str1** and **len_str2** are to collect the lengths of **str1** and **str2** respectively. **i** and **j** are to traverse the strings in **str1** and **str2** character by character.

len_str1 and len_str2 are assigned the lengths of the strings str1 and str2 respectively with the following statements :

```
len_str1 = strlen(str1);
len_str2 = strlen(str2);
```

For the string str2 to be a part of str1, essentially the length of str2 should be less than or equal to that of str1. Otherwise the question of occurrence of str2 in str1 does not arise. So the following segment of the program causes the program to exit gracefully with a proper message:

```
if (len_str2 > len_str1)
{
    cout << str2 << "can not be found in" << str1 << "\n";
    exit(0);
}
```

If the above condition is not true, then the procedure of finding the occurrence of str2 in str1 starts with the following segment:

```
for(i = 0; i < (len_str1 - len_str2 + 1); i++)
{
    flag = 1;
    for(j = 0; j < len_str2; j++)
        if (str1[i + j] != str2[j])
        {
            flag = 0;
            break;
        }
        if (flag)
        break;
}
```

Note that there are two loops one nested within the other. The outer loop is to select the characters of the string str1 and the inner loop is to select the characters of the string str2. Also note the usage of the variable `flag`. During each iteration of the outer loop, it is assigned the value 1. When the inner loop is entered and if a mismatch occurs between the characters of `str1` and `str2`, the **flag** variable is assigned 0 and the inner loop is prematurely exited. If the string `str2` is found in `str1` the **flag** variable, the inner loop completely executes and the variable **flag** retains 1. Once the value of **flag** is not changed to 0 within the inner loop, the outer loop is exited prematurely indicating that the string `str2` is found in `str1`.

8.6 TWO-DIMENSIONAL ARRAY OF CHAR TYPE

We now know that we can use a character array to store a string. Suppose we need to deal with a list of five strings, even though we can use five character arrays to store them by declaring them as follows:

```
char s1[20], s2[20], s3[20], s4[20], s5[20];
```

It would not be a wise idea. This is because the list of strings can not be treated as a group in the programming environment. Therefore, we can not perform collective manipulations over the list of names. The ideal data structure would be an array of character arrays, in other words, an array of two dimensions of `char` type which would be declared as follows:

```
char s[5][10];
```

Here, s is declared to be a 2-d array of `char` type and it can accommodate 5 strings with each string having maximum 10 characters including the null character `'\0'`. Each string is identifiable by the array name followed by a pair of square brackets enclosing a subscript value. `s[0]` represents the first string, `s[1]` represents the second string and so on. As observed, all the five strings share a common name and are distinguishable by a subscript value.

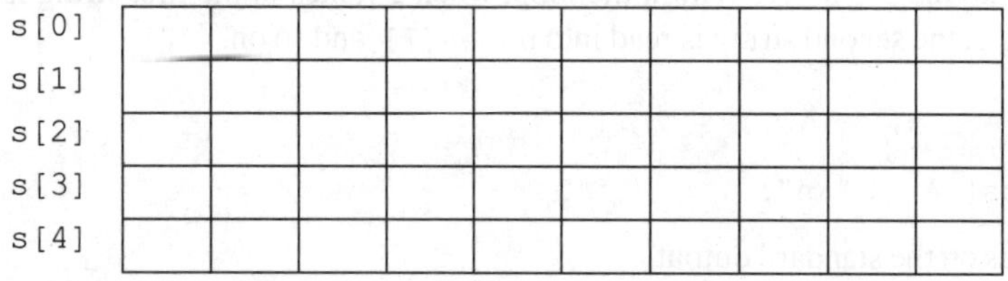

s[0]										
s[1]										
s[2]										
s[3]										
s[4]										

Program 8.15 To Accept a List of Names and Display Them

```
#include <iostream.h>

int main(void)
{
    char names[5][20];
    int i;

    cout << "Enter five names \n";
    for( i = 0; i < 5; i++)
        cin >> names[i];

    cout << "List of Names \n";
    for( i = 0; i < 5; i++)
        cout << names[i] << "\n";
```

```
    return 0;
}
```

Input-Output:

```
Enter five names
Harshith
Nishchith
Darshan
Prashanth
Pooja

List of Names
Harshith
Nishchith
Darshan
Prashanth
Pooja
```

Explanation

Here, **names** is declared to be two-dimensional array of `char` type of size `5*20`. At maximum , it can accommodate five names and no. of characters in each name can be up to `20` characters. The following segment of the program:

```
    for( i = 0; i < 5; i++)
        cin >> names[i];
```

is to accept five names into the 2-d array. Within the loop, when `i` takes `0`, the first string is read into `names[0]`, when `i` takes `1`, the second string is read into `names[1]` and so on.
Similarly, the segment:

```
    for( i = 0; i < 5; i++)
        cout << names[i] << "\n";
```

displays all the five names on the standard output.

8.6.1 Initialization of a 2-d Array of char Type

Just as we initialize arrays of two-dimensions of numeric type, we can even think of initializing two-dimensional arrays of `char` type. We know that a two-dimensional array of `char` type is used to store a collection of strings. The initializer-list contains string constants separated by commas and the number of string constants should not exceed the size specified within the first pair of square brackets.

Note that the size within the second pair of square brackets is a must and the size within the first pair of square brackets is optional.

Program 8.16 To Illustrate Initialization of Strings

```
#include <iostream.h>
int main(void)
{
    char names[5][10] = {"Raghav", "Nishu", "Harshith", "Asha", "Veena"};
    int i;
```

```
    cout << "List of Names \n";
    for(i = 0; i < 5; i++)
        cout << names[i] << "\n";

    return 0;
}
```

Input-Output:

```
List of Names
Raghav
Nishu
Harshith
Asha
Veena
```

Note that in Program 8.16, the initialization statement could have been written as:

```
char names[][10] = {"Raghav", "Nishu", "Harshith", "Asha", "Veena"};
```

where the size within the first pair of square brackets is omitted. In which case the compiler finds the size by looking at the number of strings enclosed within the braces. Note also that the size specified within the second pair of brackets should be large enough to collect the largest string in the list and a null character.

To search for a name in a list of names: We use a two-dimensional array of `char` type to accommodate a list of names and a one-dimensional array of type `char` to store a name to be searched. We employ the linear search method to search for the name in the given list of names.

Program 8.17 To Search for a Name in a List of Names

```
#include <iostream.h>
#include <string.h>

int main(void)
{
    char names[5][20], sname[20];
    int i, flag;

    cout << "Enter 5 Names \n";
    for( i = 0; i < 5; i++)
        cin >> names[i];

    cout << "List of Names \n";
    for( i = 0; i < 5; i++)
        cout << names[i] << "\n";

    cout << "Enter name to be searched \n";
    cin >> sname;

/* Searching for s in names begins */

    flag = 0;
    for( i = 0; i < 5; i++)
    if(strcmp(names[i], sname) == 0)
```

```
    {
        flag = 1;
        break;
}

/* Searching for s in names ends */

    if (flag)
        cout << sname << "is found \n ";
    else
        cout << sname << "is not found \n";

    return 0;
}
```

Input-Output:

```
Enter 5 Names
Raja
Gopal
Vishesh
Arjun
Nishanth

List of Names
Raja
Gopal
Vishesh
Arjun
Nishanth

Enter name to be searched
Vishesh
Vishesh is found
```

Explanation

names is declared to be two-dimensional array of `char` type of size 5 `* 20`. Maximum 5 names can be stored in it and each name can have up to `20` characters including the null character `'\0'`. **sname** is declared to be one-dimensional array of `char` type. It can accommodate a single name with the maximum length of `19` characters. Five names are read into **names**. The name to be searched is read into **sname**. The following segment of the program is to search for `sname` in `names`:

```
    flag = 0;
    for( i = 0; i < 5; i++)
    if(strcmp(names[i], sname) == 0)
    {
        flag = 1;
        break;
}
```

The variable **flag** acts as a Boolean variable. Before searching for **sname** in **names** begins (Before the for loop is entered), **flag** is set to 0. The for loop is to select each name in **names** and try to match them with **sname** by calling `strcmp()`. If any name in **names** is found to be matching with **sname**, **flag** is set to 1 and the loop is prematurely exited. The value of **flag** would thus determine whether **sname** is found in **names** or not. If **flag** retains 0 then it means that **sname** is not found in **names**. On the other hand, if **flag** gets 1 then it means that **sname** is found in **names**.

To sort a list of names alphabetically in the increasing order: Here also, we should use a two-dimensional array of `char` type to accommodate a list of names. After accepting a list of names into the 2-d array, we can use any sorting technique to sort the list. Let us employ the exchange sort method to arrange the names alphabetically in the increasing order. We know that the sorting requires comparison and swapping of the names, if need be, to be done repeatedly till the list is sorted. We use the built-in functions `strcmp()` and `strcpy()` to perform comparison and swapping respectively.

Program 8.18 To Sort a List of Names Alphabetically in the Increasing Order

```
#include <iostream.h>
#include <string.h>

int main(void)
{
    char names[5][20], tname[20];
    int i, j;

    cout << "Enter 5 Names \n";
    for( i = 0; i < 4; i++)
        cin >> names[i];

    cout << "Unsorted List of Names \n";
    for( i = 0; i < 5; i++)
        cout << names[i] << "\n";

    /* Sorting begins */

    for( i = 0; i < 4; i++)
    for( j = i + 1; j < 5; j++)
    if (strcmp(names[i], names[j])>0)
    {
        strcpy(tname, names[i]);
        strcpy(names[i], names[j]);
        strcpy(names[j], tname);
    }

    /* Sorting ends */

    cout << "Sorted List \n";
    for( i = 0; i < 5; i++)
        cout << names[i] << "\n";

    return 0;
}
```

Input-Output:

```
Enter 5 Names
Raghav Devaraj Babu Rajith Vinay

Unsorted List of Names
Raghav
Devaraj
Babu
Rajith
Vinay

Sorted List
Babu
Devaraj
Raghav
Rajith
Vinay
```

Explanation

names is declared to be a two-dimensional array of `char` type of size `5 * 20`. Maximum five names can be read into it and each name can have up to `20` characters including the null character `'\0'`. **tname** is declared to be one-dimensional array of `char` type. It is used to store a name temporarily while sorting the list of names. Five names are read into the array `names` and they are displayed. The following segment of the program sorts the list of names:

```
for( i = 0; i < 5; i++)
for( j = i + 1; j < 5; j++)
if (strcmp(names[i], names[j])>0)
{
    strcpy(tname, names[i]);
    strcpy(names[i], names[j]);
    strcpy(names[j], tname);
}
```

The outer for loop is to select each name from the list one by one starting from the first name till the last but one, as indicated by the range of values `[0-3]` taken by **i**. The inner for loop is to select the next remaining names in the list of names. When **i** takes `0`, first name is selected. It is compared with all the remaining names, which are selected by **j** with the help of `strcmp()`. If necessary, the pair of strings being compared are interchanged. This produces the first least name, and it is placed in the first position of the array names. Note that three calls are made to `strcpy()` to interchange a pair of names. This is because, the assignment operator = is not defined over strings. This is repeated for all values of **i**. As a result, the list of names gets sorted. The sorted list is then displayed.

8.7 STRINGS AND FUNCTIONS

Strings can be passed as arguments to functions and within the body of the functions the strings can be subjected to required kind of manipulation. Later we understand that when we pass a string as an argument to a function, what we are passing is the address of the first character of the string. A function can even return a string to the calling program. This is done by returning the starting address of the string.

8.7.1 Passing 1-d Arrays of char Type as Arguments to Functions

Arrays of `char` type can also be passed to functions as arguments on the lines of passing arrays of numeric type. Following are some examples of the functions which require strings as arguments:

Program 8.19 To Simulate `strlen()`

```
#include <iostream.h>
int str_len(char s[]);

int main(void)
{
    char str[20];
    int i, length;

    cout << "Enter a string into str \n";
    cin >> str;
    length = str_len(str);
    cout << "Length of" << str << "=" << length ;

    return 0;
}

int str_len(char s[])
{
    int i, l = 0;

    for(i = 0; s[i] != '\0'; i++)
        l++;
    return (l);

}
```

Input-Output:

```
Enter a string into str
Ramesh

Length of Ramesh=6
```

8.7.2 Passing 2-d Arrays of char to Functions

Passing 2-d arrays of char type is similar to passing 2-d arrays of numeric type. Specification of the size within the second pair of square brackets is a must for the array argument in the function prototype and in the function definition.

Program 8.20 To Display a List of Strings Using a Function

```
#include <iostream.h>
void display(char names[][20], int n);
```

```
int main(void)
{
    char names[10][20];
    int n, i;

    cout << "Enter the number of names [1-10]\n";
    cin >> n;
    cout << "Enter" << n << "names \n";
    for(i = 0; i < n; i++)
        cin >> names[i];

    cout << "The names are \n";
    display(names, n);

    return 0;
}

void display(char names[][20], int n)
{
    int i;

    for(i = 0; i < n; i++)
        cout << names[i] << "\n";
}
```

Input-Output:

```
Enter the number of names [1-10]
3
Enter 3 names
Nitin
Raghu
Girish

The names are
Nitin
Raghu
Girish
```

Explanation

The function `display()` is defined with a two-dimensional array of `char` type names and an integer value ***n*** as its formal arguments. The purpose of the function is to display ***n*** names in the list of names represented by the 2-d array names. Note that the size within the second pair of square brackets for the array is specified. This is required since the function should know the starting address of each name in the list of names. Within the function a loop is set up to access each name in the list of names and it is displayed. In the `main()`, the function `display()` is called with the name of the 2-d array of `char` type and the number of names to be displayed as the actual arguments as `display(names, n);`.

REVIEW QUESTIONS

8.1 Define a string.

8.2 What data structure is used to store a string?

8.3 Give an account of different functions used to input strings.

8.4 Give an account of different functions used to output strings.

8.5 Define the length of a string.

8.6 Explain the syntax and working of `strcpy()`.

8.7 Explain the syntax and working of `strcat()`.

8.8 Explain the syntax and working of `strcmp()`.

8.9 Explain the syntax and working of `strchr()`.

True/False Questions

T8.1 A string is a sequence of characters terminated by the null character `'\0'`.

T8.2 C++ supports string built-in data type.

T8.3 `cin` accepts even white spaces while accepting strings.

T8.4 `gets()` reads a line of text terminates on encountering `'\n'`.

T8.5 `cout` will stop displaying a string on encountering a white space.

T8.6 `Puts()` replaces `'\0'` by `'\n'` on displaying a string.

T8.7 We can pass strings to functions as arguments.

T8.8 We can return a string from a function.

T8.9 The function prototype void `display(char names[][], int n);` is valid.

T8.10 `strchr()` returns the position of the first occurrence of a character in a string.

PROGRAMMING EXERCISES

P8.1 Write a program to count the number of words in a line of text.

P8.2 Write a program to accept a string and display the ASCII character equivalent of each character in the string.

P8.3 Write a program to convert a decimal integer number into its hexadecimal number equivalent.

Example

Decimal number	126
Hexadecimal number	7E

P8.4 Write a program to convert an hexadecimal integer number into its decimal number equivalent.

Example

Hexadecimal number	7E
Decimal number	126

P8.5 Modify Program P8.3 to convert a decimal real number into its hexadecimal number equivalent.

P8.6 Modify Programs P8.4 to convert a hexadecimal real number into its decimal number equivalent.

P8.7 Write a program to convert as hexadecimal number into its binary equivalent.

Example

Hexadecimal number	A23
Equivalent binary number	1010 0010 0011

Note that each hexadecimal digit is replaced by its four bit binary equivalent.

P8.8 Write a program to convert a binary number into its hexadecimal equivalent.

Example

Equivalent binary number	1010 0010 0011
Hexadecimal number	A23

Note that each group of four bits in the binary number is replaced by a hexadecimal digit.

P8.9 Write a program to delete a given character in a string.

Example

Given string	"abcdebfd"
Given character	'b'
New string	"acdefd"

P8.10 Write a program to extract left part of a string and display it. Inputs to the program are a string and the number of characters.

Example

Given string	"Bangalore"
No. of characters	4
Extracted string	Bang

P8.11 Write a program to extract right part of a string and display it. Inputs to the program are a string and the number of characters.

Example

Given string	"Bangalore"
No. of characters	4
Extracted string	"lore"

P8.12 Write a program to extract a part of a string and display it. Inputs to the program are a string, starting position of the string and the number of characters.

Example

Given string	"Bangalore"
Starting position	3
No. of characters	4
Extracted string	"ngal"

P8.13 Write a program to find the no. of occurrences of a substring in a string.

Example

Given string	"abcdefcd"
Substring	"cd"

Number of occurrences of "cd" in the given string = 2

P8.14 Write a program to insert a substring at the specified position into a string.

Example

Given string	"abcde"
Substring	"xyz"
Position	2
Output string	"abxyzcde"

P8.15 Write a program to delete a given substring from a string.

Example

Given string	"abcde"
Substring	"bc"
Output string	"ade"

P8.16 Write a program to search for a name in a list of names using binary search method.

P8.17 Write a program to simulate `strcmpi()`.
The function `strcmpi()` ignores case of the letters while comparing. For example the strings "abc" and "ABC" are treated to be equal.

P8.18 Write a program to simulate `strncpy()`.
The function `strncpy()` copies the specified number of characters of the source string to the target string.

P8.19 Write a program to simulate `strncat()`.
The function `strncat()` concatenates the specified number of characters of the source string to the target string.

P8.20 Accept dates in 'dd-mm-yyyy' format into string variables and perform the following:

(a) Validate the given date.

(b) Find the difference between two dates.

(c) Find whether date d1 is earlier than or later than or equal to the date d2.

Chapter 9

Structures and Unions

9.1 INTRODUCTION

Each entity in the world is described by a no. of characteristics. These descriptive characteristics of an entity are called its **attributes**. For instance, the entity, employee is characterized by the attributes empno, name, designation, salary, etc. The entity, book is characterized by its author, title, publisher, number of pages and price. It can be noticed that the attributes of an entity may be of different types. If we consider the entity book, author, title and publisher are strings; number of pages is of `int` type and price may be of `float` type. To store the details of a book, no doubt, we can declare the following variables and use them.

```
char author[20], title[20], publisher[20];
int pages;
float price;
```

Even though these variables can be used to store a book's details, the problem is, these variables are not treated as a single unit and hence do not necessarily reflect the fact that all these describe a single book. What if we have to deal with more than one book? Say, 10 books. This approach turns out to be prohibitive since it is difficult to establish mapping between a book and its details.

We now know that an array enables us to identify a group of similar data items by a common name and thus facilitates easier collective manipulation. In many programming situations such as discussed earlier, we do require to identify a group of data items, which may be of dissimilar types, also by a common name with a provision for accessing individual data items.

The concept of structures accomplishes this. The concept of structures is analogous to the concept of records, a database terminology, and helps in coining new user-defined data types or derived types.

9.2 DEFINITION OF STRUCTURE TEMPLATE

Structure template definition helps in creating a format or prototype of the user-defined data type. The format or prototype of the user-defined data type allows us to logically relate a group of data items which may be of different types.

The syntax of defining a structure template is as follows:

```
struct tag-name
{
    data-type  member1;
    data-type  member2;
    .
    .
    data-type   member n;
};
```

Here **struct** is a keyword. tag-name is a user defined name, it is the name of the structure, a valid C++ identifier. data-type refers to any valid data type supported by C++ and member1, member2,..., member n are the members of the structure. It is important to note that member1, member2, ..., membern are not variables by themselves. So, no memory locations get allocated at this juncture. Memory locations get allocated only when variables of the structure are declared.

9.3 DECLARATION OF STRUCTURE VARIABLES

Syntax of declaring a variable of structure type:

```
tag-name variable-name;
```

As a result of this, n memory locations get allocated. Each location is identified by the structure variable name followed by a dot followed by the member name. Dot is used to access each individual member and it is called **member operator**. The dot operator expects the structure variable name to the left of it and member name to the right of it. variable-name.member1 is used to access the value of member1, variable-name.member2 is used to access value of member2 of the structure and so on.

EXAMPLE

```
struct emp
{
    int empno;
    char name[20];
    float salary;
};
```

empno, name and salary are now logically grouped.

```
emp e;
```

e is declared to be a variable of emp type. This results in allocation of three locations which are contiguous in nature, as follows:

e.empno	e.name	e.salary

All the three data items share the common name e, and are distinguishable by members empno, name and salary. The operator dot (.) called **member operator,** enables us to access each data item separately. A data item is referred to by structure variable name followed by a dot (.), followed by the corresponding member name `e.empno` refers to employee number, `e.name` refers to employee name and `e.salary` refers to the salary of employee.

It is important to note that `e.empno` is a variable of `int` type, `e.name` as an array of `char` type and `e.salary` is a variable of `float` type when taken in isolation.

We can even declare variables of structure type while defining the structure template itself. The syntax of this kind of declaration is as follows:

```
struct  tag-name
{
    data-type    member1;
    data-type    member2;
    data-type    member3;
    .
    .
    .
    data-type    membern;
}  variable_1, variable_2,..., variable_n;
```

EXAMPLE

```
    struct emp
    {
        int empno;
        char name[20];
        float salary;
    } e1, e2;
```

where **`e1`** and **`e2`** are variables of `emp` type.

Definition of structure: A structure can be defined to be a group of logically related data items, which may be of different types, stored in contiguous memory locations, sharing a common name, but distinguished by its members.

The following statements can be used to provide values to members of the structure variable:

```
e.empno  =  121;
strcpy( e.name,  "Raghav");
e.salary  =  12000;
```

The locations allocated for `e` get filled up as follows:

e.empno	e.name	e.salary
121	Raghav	12000

The following statements are used to accept and display an employee's details:

```
cin >> e.empno >> e.name >> e.salary;
cout << e.empno << e.name << e.salary;
```

Program 9.1 To Accept and Display Two Employees Details

```
#include <iostream.h>
#include <iomanip.h>
struct emp
{
    int empno;
    char name[20];
    float salary;
};

int main(void)
{
    emp e;

    cout << "Enter empno, name and salary of the employee \n";
    cin >> e.empno >> e.name >> e.salary;
    cout << "Details of the employee \n";
    cout << setw(6) << e.empno << setw(15) << e.name
         << setw(8) << e.salary << "\n";

    return 0;
}
```

Input-Output:

```
Enter empno, name and salary of the employee
123      Nishchith   45000
Details of the employee
123      Nishchith   45000
```

The `setw()` is a facility to display values within the specified width. To use this the header file **iomanip.h** has to be included. We will learn more about it later.

9.4 INITIALIZATION OF STRUCTURE VARIABLES

If we know the values of structure variables in advance, we can even think of initializing structure variables also. The syntax of initializing a structure variable is as follows:

```
tag-name variable-name = { member1-value, member2-value,...,
                                          membern-value };
```

If a member is of `char` type, its value should be enclosed within single quotes. If a member is an array of `char` type, its value should be enclosed within double quotes.

EXAMPLE

To initialize a variable of type `struct emp`:

```
emp e = { 121, "Anju", 20000 };
```

e.empno	e.name	e.salary
121	Raghav	12000

If the no. of values listed in the `initializer-list` is less than the no. of members of the structure, trailing members that are unmatched to initializers are implicitly initialized to zero (null character in the case of strings).

EXAMPLE

```
emp e = {124};
```

Here only the first member empno gets the value. The other two remaining members name and salary are set to null character and 0 respectively as shown hereinafter.

e.empno	e.name	e.salary
124	0	0

The members of a structure variable belonging to static storage class are automatically initialized with 0's in the case of numeric data types and null character's in the case of strings.

EXAMPLE

```
static emp e;
```

e.empno	e.name	e.salary
0	/0	0

Program 9.2 To Illustrate Initialization of Structure Variables while Declaring

```
#include <iostream.h>
#include <iomanip.h>
struct emp
{
    int empno;
    char name[20];
    float salary;
};

int main(void)
{
    emp e1 = {123, "Harshith", 23456};
    emp e2 = {124};
    static emp e3;

    cout << "Details of the employee e1 \n";
    cout << setw(6) << e1.empno << setw(15) << e1.name
         << setw(8) << e1.salary << "\n";
    cout << "Details of the employee e2 \n";
    cout << setw(6) << e2.empno << setw(15) << e2.name
         << setw(8) << e2.salary << "\n";
    cout << "Details of the employee e3 \n";
    cout << setw(6) << e3.empno << setw(15) << e3.name
         << setw(8) << e3.salary << "\n";
```

```
    return 0;
}
```

Input-Output:

```
Details of the employee e1
   123        Harshith    23456
Details of the employee e2
   124                        0
Details of the employee e3
     0                        0
```

Note: The members of a structure variable can not be initialized selectively.

9.5 OPERATIONS ON STRUCTURES

The no. of operations which can be performed over structures is limited. Following are the permissible operations:

1. Accessing the individual members of a structure variable with the help of member operator (Dot operator).

   EXAMPLE

   In the case of a variable of type emp,

   ```
         emp e;
      e.empno   =   10;
   ```

   `10` is assigned to empno member of e .

   ```
      strcpy(e.name, "Ram");
   ```

   The string "`Ram`" is copied to `name` member of e.
2. Assigning one structure variable to another of the same type.

   EXAMPLE

   ```
      emp e1= { 12, "Ram", 2900}, e2;
      e2 = e1;
   ```

   `e1` has been assigned to `e2`.
3. Retrieving the size of a structure variable using `sizeof()` operator.

   ```
   emp e;
   int s;
   s = sizeof(e);
   ```
4. Retrieving the address of a structure variable using `& (address of)` operator.

   ```
   emp e;
   ```
   `&e` gives the address of e.
5. Passing and returning a structure variable value to and from a function.
6. Checking whether two structure variables of same type are equal using == if **s1** and **s2** are two variables of the same structure type, `s1==s2` returns 1 if all the members of **s1** are equal to the corresponding members of **s2,** otherwise it returns 0.

7. Checking whether two structure variables of same type are not equal using != if **s1** and **s2** are two variables of the same structure type, `s1!=s2` returns 1 if all the members of **s1** are not equal to the corresponding members of **s2,** otherwise it returns 0.

Note that not all compilers support the last two operations. In which case, each pair of the corresponding members should be compared separately.

Program 9.3 To Illustrate the Concept of Structures and Permissible Operations Over Them

```
#include <iostream.h>
#include <iomanip.h>

struct emp
{
   int empno;
   char name[20];
   float salary;
};

int main(void)
{
   emp e1, e2;
   int size;

   cout << "Enter empno, name and salary \n";
   cin >> e1.empno >> e1.name >> e1.salary;
   size = sizeof(e1);
   cout << "\n No. of bytes required for e1 =" << size << "\n";
   e2 = e1;
   cout << "After assigning e1 to e2 \n\n";
   cout << "e2.empno = " << e2.empno << "\n";
   cout << "e2.name = " << e2.name << "\n";
   cout << "e2.salary = " << e2.salary << "\n";
   cout << "Address of e1 = " << &e1 << "\n";

   return 0;
}
```

Input-Output:

```
Enter empno, name and salary
121 Harsha 34000

No. of bytes required for e1 =26
After assigning e1 to e2

e2.empno = 121
e2.name = Harsha
e2.salary = 34000
Address of e1 = 0xffda
```

Explanation

e1 and **e2** are declared to be variables of `emp` type. Both can accommodate details of an employee. Details of an employee are accepted into the variable **e1**. The no. of bytes occupied by a variable of emp type is found out with the help of the operator `sizeof()` by passing **e1** to it. The value returned by `sizeof()` is then displayed. To illustrate the fact that structure variables assignment is permissible, **e1** is assigned to **e2**. The contents of **e2** are then displayed. The address of operator & is used with **e1** to obtain its address and it is then displayed.

9.6 ARRAYS AND STRUCTURES

Arrays can be treated in conjunction with the concept of structures in two different ways: (a) By arraying structures themselves and (b) By making arrays as members of structures.

Array of structures: So far, we have dealt with arrays of fundamental data types (e.g. **int**, **float**, **char**) supported by C++. Let us now explore the need for and possibility of using arrays of user-defined data type, structures, as well.

We know that a variable **e** of type `emp` can accommodate details (empno, name and salary) of a single employee. If we are required to deal with more than one employee's details, say 5 or even `10`, declaration of so many variables of `emp` type and using those variables would not be a wise idea. This is because collective manipulations can not be performed over them easily. We would naturally be inclined to use the concept of array of `emp` type because of the flexibility provided by arrays in performing collective manipulations. C++ does support arraying of structures.

Suppose 5 employees' details are to be dealt with, we would declare an array of `emp` of size `5` as follows:

```
emp e[5];
```

Memory for the array gets allocated as follows:

	empno	name	salary
e[0]			
e[1]			
e[2]			
e[3]			
e[4]			

Here, the array elements `e[0], e[1], ..., e[4]` are variables of `emp` type and thus each can accommodate an employee's details. Since all the variables share a common name **e** and are distinguishable by subscript values [0–4], collective manipulation over the structure elements becomes easy.

Program 9.4 To Illustrate an Array of Structures

```
#include <iostream.h>
#include <iomanip.h>
struct emp
{
    int empno;
```

```
    char name[20];
    float salary;
};

int main(void)
{
    emp e[10];
    int i, n;

    cout << "Enter no. of employees [1-10]\n";
    cin >> n;

    cout << "\n Enter" << n << "employees' details \n";
    for( i = 0; i< n; i++)
        cin >> e[i].empno >> e[i].name >> e[i].salary;
    cout << "\n Employees' details \n";
    for( i = 0; i < n; i++)
        cout << e[i].empno << e[i].name << e[i].salary << "\n";

    return 0;
}
```

Input-Output:

```
Enter no. of employees [1-10]
2

Enter 2 employees' details
121 Nishu 35000
122 Harsha 29000

Employees' details
121    Nishu    35000
122    Harsha   29000
```

Explanation

In Program 9.4, **e** is declared to be an array of emp type and size 10, maximum 10 employees' details can be stored in it. The variable **n** is to collect the no. of employees which should lie between 1 and 10 inclusive. **i** ranges from 0 to n-1 in the for loop used, thereby selecting each employee one by one. After accepting the no. of employees to be stored in **e** into the variable **n**, **n** employees' details are accepted and they are displayed by the program segments:

```
for( i = 0; i < n; i++)
    cin >>e[i].empno >>e[i].name >> e[i].salary;
```

and

```
for( i = 0; i < n; i++)
    cout << e[i].empno << e[i].name << e[i].salary << "\n";
```

respectively.

Initialization of arrays of structures: Just as we initialize arrays of built-in type, we can initialize arrays of structure also. Program 9.5 illustrates initializing the elements of arrays of structures:

Program 9.5 To Illustrate Initialization of Arrays of Structures

```
#include <iostream.h>
#include <iomanip.h>

struct emp
{
    int empno;
    char name[20];
    float salary;
};

int main(void)
{
    emp e[2] = { {121, "Nishu", 2345},
                 {122, "Harshith", 23498}};

    cout << "Employee details \n";
    for(int i = 0; i < 2; i++)
        cout << setw(6) << e[i].empno << setw(15) << e[i].name <<
            setw(9) << e[i].salary << "\n";
    return 0;
}
```

Input-Output:

```
Employee details
 121          Nishu      2345
 122       Harshith     23498
```

Suppose we have a list of employees' details and we are to search for an employee in the list with the help of the value of any field (like empno, name) of the employees' details. Here, in the program that we develop, we use the concept of array of structures to store the employees' details and a variable of appropriate type to collect the field value and employ the procedure for searching the required employee in the list of employees. Program 9.6 accomplishes the task.

Program 9.6 To Search for an Employee in a List of Employees

```
#include <iostream.h>
#include <string.h>

struct emp
{
    int empno;
    char name[20];
    float salary;
};

int main(void)
{
    emp e[10];
```

```
    int i, n, flag;
    char sname[20];

    cout << "Enter the no. of employees \n";
    cin >> n;

    cout << "Enter" << n << "employees' details \n";
    for( i = 0; i < n; i++)
       cin >> e[i].empno >> e[i].name >> e[i].salary;
    cout << "Enter name of the employee to be searched \n";
    cin >> sname;

    cout << n << "employees' details \n";
    for( i = 0; i < n; i++)
       cout << e[i].empno << e[i].name << e[i].salary << "\n";

    cout << "\n Enter the name of the employee to be searched \n";
    cout << sname;

    // Searching begins

    flag = 0;
    for( i = 0; i < n; i++)
    if (strcmp(e[i].name, sname)==0)
    {
       flag = 1;
       break;

    }
    // Searching ends

    if (flag == 1)
       cout << "found";
    else
       cout << "Not found";

    return 0;
}
```

Input-Output:

```
Enter the no. of employees
3
Enter 3 employees' details
121 Nishu   23000
122 Harsha  45000
123 Darshan 32000

3 employees' details
121 Nishu   23000
122 Harsha  45000
```

```
123 Darshan  32000

Enter the name of the employee to be searched
Nishu found
```

Explanation

e is declared to be an array of emp type and of size 10. It is to store a list of employees. Maximum 10 employees' details can be accepted into it. **sname** is declared to be an array of `char` type and this is to collect the name of an employee to be searched in the list. **i**, **n** and **flag** are declared to be variables of `int` type. **n** is to collect the no. of employees, **i** is to traverse the structure elements and **flag** is to collect 1 (true) or 0 (false) depending on whether the employee being searched is found in the list or not.

After accepting the no. of employees into the variable **n, n** employees' details are accepted into the variable **e**. The list of employees' details is now available in **e.** The name of the employee to be searched is accepted into the string variable **sname.** Searching for an employee with the name **sname** in the list is accomplished by the following segment of the program:

```
flag = 0;
for( i = 0; i < n; i++)
if (strcmp(e[i].name, sname)==0)
{
   flag = 1;
   break;

}
```

Initially, **flag** is set to 0 (false) assuming that employee with the name in **sname** is not found in the list. The for loop selects each employee one by one and the selected employee's name is compared with the name in **sname** (note the use of `strcmp()`). If there is found to be match, **flag** is set to 1 (true) and the loop is exited. So **flag** is set to 1 (true) only when a match is found between the name of an employee in the list and **sname,** otherwise **flag** retains 0 (false) only. Thus, the value of **flag** determines whether the employee being searched is found in the list or not. After the searching process, depending on the value of the variable **flag**, the result is displayed.

The concept of array of structures is useful even when we need to arrange a list of records in some order. Suppose we have a list of employees' details and we are to sort the records in the increasing order of salary, we tend to use an array of structure with the structure template having the members like empno, name, salary, designation, etc. and work on it. Program 9.7 sorts the employees' details in the increasing order of salary.

Program 9.7 To Sort a List of Employees in the Increasing Order of Salary

```
#include <iostream.h>
#include <iomanip.h>

struct emp
{
   int empno;
   char name[20];
   float salary;
};
```

```
int main(void)
{
   emp e[10], temp;
   int i, j, n;

   cout << "Enter no. of employees [1-10]\n";
   cin >> n;

   cout << "Enter" << n << "employees' details \n";
   for( i = 0; i < n; i++)
      cin >> e[i].empno >> e[i].name >> e[i].salary;

   cout << "Unsorted list of employees' details \n";
   for( i = 0; i < n; i++)
      cout << setw(6) << e[i].empno << setw(10) << e[i].name <<
         setw(9) << e[i].salary << "\n";

   // sorting begins

   for( i = 0; i < n - 1; i++)
   for( j = i + 1; j < n; j++)
      if ( e[i].salary > e[j].salary)
      {
         temp    = e[i];
         e[i] = e[j];
         e[j] = temp;
      }

   // sorting ends

   cout << "sorted List \n";
   for( i = 0; i < n; i++)
      cout << setw(6) << e[i].empno << setw(10) << e[i].name <<
         setw(9) << e[i].salary << "\n";

   return 0;
}
```

Input-Output:

```
Enter no. of employees [1-10]
3
Enter 3 employees' details
121  Raghu   20000
122  Nishu   23000
123  Ashok   34000

Unsorted list of employees'  details
121        Raghu     20000
122        Nishu     23000
123        Ashok     34000
```

```
Sorted List
121        Raghu     20000
122        Nishu     23000
123        Ashok     34000
```

Explanation

e is declared to be an array of `emp` type with size 10. Maximum 10 employees' details can be accepted and stored in it. So **e** is to store the details of a list of employees, which are to be sorted in the increasing order of salary. **temp** is also declared to be a variable of `emp` type and it is used to temporarily collect details of an employee during the process of sorting. **i**, **j** and **n** are declared to be variables of `int` type. **i** and **j** are to traverse the structure elements and **n** is to collect the no. of employees.

After accepting the no. of employees into the variable **n**, details of **n** employees are accepted into the array variable **e** and are displayed. The employee records are sorted in the increasing order of salary by the following segment of the program:

```
for( i = 0; i < n - 1; i++)
for( j = i + 1; j < n; j++)
    if ( e[i].salary > e[j].salary)
    {
        temp   = e[i];
        e[i] = e[j];
        e[j] = temp;
    }
```

Sorting proceeds as follows:
When **i** takes 0, first employee in the list is selected. Salary of the first employee is compared with that of the remaining employees. The remaining employees are selected by the inner loop. **j** ranges from 1 to $n - 1$. If needed, employees records being compared are interchanged. When the inner loop completes, employee record with the lowest salary is made available in the first position, i.e. `e[0]`. When **i** takes 1, the second employee is selected, his salary is compared with that of the remaining employees. During the process, if needed, two employees records being compared are interchanged. When the inner loop completes, employee record with the second lowest salary is made available in the second position of the array, i.e. `e[1]`. This is repeated till the outer loop completes.

Arrays within structures: We have already explored the need for and the possibility of using arrays within structures. In the previous programs, we used an array of `char` type as a member of `emp` to store name of an employee. However, the array was treated in its entirety. The array name was used to refer to the entire sequence of characters forming a name.

Now, let us try to make an array of `int` type as a member of a structure, where we need to deal with each integer value of the array. Suppose we need to maintain a list of students' details (reg-no, name, marks in five subjects), the structure template definition will be as follows:

```
struct student
{
     int regno;
     char name[20];
     int marks[5];
};
```

Program 9.8 To Create a List of Students' Details and Display Them

```
#include <iostream.h>
#include <iomanip.h>

struct student
{
  int reg_no;
  char name[20];
  int marks[5];
  int total;
  float percent;
};

int main(void)
{
   student s[10];
   int i, n, j;

   cout << "Enter no. of students \n";
   cin >> n;
   for( i = 0; i < n; i++)
   {
      cout << "Enter reg_no, name of student-" << i+1 << "\n";
      cin >> s[i].reg_no >> s[i].name;
      cout << "Enter marks in five subjects of " << s[i].name << "\n";
      for( j = 0; j < 5; j++)
         cin >> s[i].marks[j];
   }

   /* Finding the total and percentage begins */

      for( i= 0; i < n; i++)
      {
         s[i].total = 0;
         for( j = 0; j < 5; j++)
            s[i].total += s[i].marks[j];
         s[i].percent = (float)s[i].total/5;
      }
   /* Finding the total and percentage ends */
   cout << "\n Reg-No      Name      Percentage \n";
   for( i = 0; i < n; i++)
      cout << setw(6) << s[i].reg_no << setw(12) << s[i].name <<
         setw(9) << s[i].percent << "\n";

   return 0;
}
```

Input-Output:

```
Enter no. of students
2
```

```
Enter reg_no, name of student-1
1234 Nishu
Enter marks in five subjects of Nishu
76 74 75 73 77
Enter reg_no, name of student-2
1235 Harsha
Enter marks in five subjects of Harsha
86 84 85 83 87

 Reg-No      Name      Percentage
  1234      Nishu         75
  1235     Harsha         85
```

Explanation

The structure type `student` is defined with members **`regno`** (`int`), **`name`** (array of `char`), **`marks`** (an array of `int` with size 5), **`total`** (`float`), **`percent`** (`float`). A variable of `student` can thus capture register number, name, marks scored in five subjects, total marks and percentage of marks of a student.

In `main()`, **`s`** is declared to be an array of `student` type with size 10. It can thus maximum accommodate 10 students' details. **`n`** and **`i`** are declared to be variables of `int` type. **`n`** is to accept the no. of students [1–10]. **`i`** is to traverse the structure elements.

After accepting the no. of students into the variable **`n`**, **`n`** students' details are accepted into the array variable **`s`** by the segment of the program:

```
for( i = 0; i < n; i++)
{
    cout << "Enter reg_no, name of student-" << i+1 << "\n";
    cin >> s[i].reg_no >> s[i].name;
    cout << "Enter marks in five subjects of " << s[i].name << "\n";
    for( j = 0; j < 5; j++)
        cin >> s[i].marks[j];
}
```

Note the nesting of two loops. The outer loop (i loop) is to select each student. The inner loop (j loop) is to select marks in five subjects for each student.

After the details are fed into the array **`s`**, total marks and percentage of each student are found out by the following segment of the program:

```
for( i= 0; i < n; i++)
{
    s[i].total = 0;
    for( j = 0; j < 5; j++)
        s[i].total += s[i].marks[j];
    s[i].percent = (float)s[i].total/5;
}
```

when **`i`** takes 0, first student is selected. **`s[0].total`** is set to 0 initially. Then the inner loop selects marks of the first student in five subjects and adds them to **`s[0].total`**. Percentage of marks of the student is then assigned to **`s[0].percent`**. This is repeated for all values of **`i`**.

Register number, name, total marks and percentage of marks of all the students are then displayed in tabular form.

9.7 STRUCTURE WITHIN STRUCTURE

We know that structure enables us to make a group of heterogeneous types of data items. So far, our discussion was confined to heterogeneity with respect to fundamental data types `int, float, char,` etc. Let us now explore the possibility of making a group of data items of user-defined types also in addition to data items of built-in type. This is where the concept of nesting one structure within another comes into picture. Structures of one type are made the members of another structure.

EXAMPLE

```
struct date
{
    int day, month, year;
};

struct emp
{
    int empno;
    char name[20];
    date doj;
    float salary;
};
```

Here, the structure template for `date` includes three members `d`, `m` and `y`. A variable of `date` type can be used to store a date. Within the structure template for employee, a variable of type `date doj` has been used as a member. A variable of `emp` type thus can accommodate empno, name, date of joining and salary of an employee.

```
emp e;
```

Here, `e` can represent the details of an employee with `e.empno, e.name, e.salary` and `e.doj` representing empno, name, salary and date of joining of the employee respectively. Since `e.doj` becomes a variable of `date` type, `e.doj.day, e.doj.month` and `e.doj.year` represent day, month and year part of `doj`. Note the use of two dots.

```
e.empno
e.name
```

`e.doj` is a variable of `date` type.

Program 9.9 To Illustrate the Concept of Structure within Structure

```
#include <iostream.h>

struct date
{
   int day, month, year;
};
```

```
struct emp
{
    int empno;
    char name[20];
    date doj;
    float salary;
};

int main(void)
{
    emp e;

    cout << "Enter empno, name, doj and salary \n";
    cin >> e.empno >> e.name >> e.doj.day
        >> e.doj.month >> e.doj.year >> e.salary;

    cout << "Empno = " << e.empno << "\n";
    cout << "Name = " << e.name << "\n";
    cout << "DOJ = " << e.doj.day << "/" << e.doj.month << "/"
        << e.doj.year << "\n";
    cout << "Salary = " << e.salary << "\n";

    return 0;
}
```

Input-Output:

```
Enter empno, name, doj and salary
12345 Nagesh 12 3 1980 35000

Empno = 12345
Name = Nagesh
DOJ = 12/3/1980
Salary = 35000
```

Explanation

The structure type `date` is defined with three members **day**, **month** and **year** all of `int` type. A variable of `date` type can thus represent a date. Another structure type, `emp` is defined with members **empno** (`int`), **name** (array of `char`), **doj** (`struct date`) and **salary** (`float`). A variable of `emp` type can thus accommodate employee number, name, date of joining and salary of an employee.

In `main()`, **e** is declared to be an array of `emp` type. The previously discussed details of an employee are accepted into it and then they are displayed.

In Program 9.9, we saw that we can nest one structure within another structure and understood how the members of the nested structure are accessed (two dots). In fact, nesting of structures can be to any level. If need be, we can nest structure A within structure B, in turn structure B can be nested within another structure C and so on.

Initialization of a structure containing another structure: Just as we initialize the variables of some structure type when the members of the structure are of basic type, we can even initialize the variables of structures which themselves contain some other structures as members (Nesting of structures). Program 9.10 demonstrates this.

Program 9.10 To Illustrate Initialization of a Structure Containing Another Structure

```
#include <iostream.h>
#include <iomanip.h>

struct date
{
    int day, month, year;
};

struct emp
{
    int empno;
    char name[20];
    date doj;
    float salary;
};

int main(void)
{
emp e1 = {123, "Raghav", 12,04,1998, 13450};
emp e2 = {124, "Madhav", {12,05,1999}, 23450};

cout << setw(6) << e1.empno << setw(12) << e1.name << setw(9) << e1.salary;
cout << " " << e1.doj.day << "/" << e1.doj.month << "/" << e1.doj.year <<
"\n";

cout << setw(6) << e2.empno << setw(12) << e2.name << setw(9) << e2.salary;
cout <<  " " << e2.doj.day << "/" << e2.doj.month << "/" << e2.doj.year <<
"\n";

    return 0;
}
```

Input-Output:

```
123     Raghav    13450 12/4/1998
124     Madhav    23450 12/5/1999
```

Explanation

In Program 9.10, a structure with the tag name **date** is defined with three members **day, month** and **year,** all of `int` type. Any variable of type **date** would thus represent a date. Another structure with tag name **emp** is defined with the members **empno** (`int`), **name** (array of `char`) , **doj** (`struct date`) and **salary** (`float`). Any variable of `emp` type would thus denote the details of an employee, which include `empno`, `name`, `date` of joining and salary. While initializing a variable of `emp` type the members of date may be listed one after the other separated by commas as in the following statement:

```
emp e1 = {123, "Raghav", 12,04,1998, 13450};
```

or the members of **date** type can be enclosed within a pair of braces as in the statement:

```
emp e2 = {124, "Madhav", {12,05,1999}, 23450};
```

Consider the following example:

```
struct measure
{
    int feet;
    float inches;
};

struct room
{
    measure length, breadth;
};

struct building
{
    room r1, r2;
};
```

Let us declare a variable of type `building`.

```
building b;
```

`b` represents a building.
`b.r1` and `b.r2` represent two rooms of the building `b`.

`b.r1.length` represents the length of room `r1` of building `b`
`b.r1.breadth` represents the breadth of room `r1` of building `b`

`b.r1.length.feet` represents feet part of length of room `r1` of building `b`
`b.r1.length.inches` represents inches part of length of room `r1` of building `b`
`b.r1.breadth.feet` represents feet part of breadth of room `r1` of building `b`
`b.r1.breadth.inches` represents inches part of breadth of room `r1` of building `b`

Similarly,

`b.r2.length.feet` represents `feet` part of `length` of room `r2` of building `b`
`b.r2.length.inches` represents `inches` part of `length` of room `r2` of building `b`
`b.r2.breadth.feet` represents `feet` part of `breadth` of room `r2` of building `b`
`b.r2.breadth.inches` represents `inches` part of `breadth` of room `r2` of building `b`

Note that the nesting of structure within structure increases the readability of the variable names.

9.8 STRUCTURES AND FUNCTIONS

The concept of structures can be treated in combination with the concept of functions in two different ways. One, passing structures as arguments to functions. Two, returning a structure from a function.

There are three approaches to passing a structure to a function:

1. Passing members of a structure individually
2. Passing entire structure at once
3. Passing address of structure

Passing members of a structure individually: Passing the members of a structure individually boils down to passing basic types of data to a function which we have dealt with so far. If `f()` is a function which requires the members of a variable of some structure type, the fact that we are passing the members of it individually to the function `f()` should be indicated both while declaring and defining the function.

EXAMPLE

If the `f()` requires a variable of type `emp` as its argument, the declaration of the function would be as:

```
void f(int empno, char name[], float salary);
```

and the function definition would be as:

```
void f(int empno, char name[], float salary)
{
    statements;
}
```

and the function call would be as:

```
f(e.empno, e.name, e.salary);
```

where **e** is a variable of type `emp`.

Note that the individual members are explicitly specified in the function declaration, function definition and the function call.

Program 9.11 To Illustrate Passing the Individual Members of a Structure to a Function

```
#include <iostream.h>

struct student
{
    int reg_no;
    char name[20];
    float percent;
};

void display(int, char[], float);

int main(void)
{
    struct student s;

    cout << "Enter reg_no, name and percent \n";
    cin >> s.reg_no >> s.name >> s.percent;
    display(s.reg_no, s.name, s.percent);

    return 0;
}

void display(int reg_no, char name[], float percent)
{
    cout << reg_no << name << percent << "\n";
}
```

Input-Output:

```
Enter reg_no, name and percent
1234
Nishu
95

1234 Nishu 95
```

The limitations encountered in this approach are: (a) If the no. of members of the structure to be passed is more, this method turns out to be prohibitive. (b) If some changes are made to the members of the structure by the called function, the called function can not be made known about the changes (Only one value can be returned by a function).

Passing entire structure at once: Passing an entire structure as an argument is another way of passing the structure values to a function. If `f()` is a function which requires a variable of some structure type as its argument, the fact that we are passing the entire structure to the function `f()` should be indicated both while declaring and defining the function.

EXAMPLE

If the `f()` requires a variable of type `emp` as its argument, the declaration of the function would be as:

```
void f(emp e);
```

and the function definition would be as:

```
void f(emp e)
{
   statements;
}
```

and the function call would be as:

```
f(e);
```

where **e** is the actual argument, a variable of type `emp`.

Program 9.12 To Illustrate Passing Entire Structure to a Function

```
#include <iostream.h>
#include <iomanip.h>
struct student
{
   int reg_no;
   char name[20];
   float percent;
};

void display(student);

int main(void)
{
   student s;
```

```
    cout << "Enter reg_no, name and percent \n";
    cin >> s.reg_no >> s.name >> s.percent;
    display(s);

    return 0;
}

void display(student s)
{
    cout << setw(6)  << s.reg_no << setw(10)  << s.name << setw(5)
        << s.percent << "\n";
}
```

Input-Output:

```
Enter reg_no, name and percent
1234
Harshith
87

1234  Harshith   87
```

Explanation

The structure **student** is defined with the three members `reg_no, name, percent;`. Any variable of the structure type would thus denote a student. The function `display()` is defined with an argument of type **student**. The purpose of the function is to display the details of a student. In the `main()` a student's details are accepted into the variable **s** and the variable is passed as the actual argument to the function `display()` with the statement `display(s);`. The function on its execution displays the contents of **s** and returns to the `main()`.

Passing address of a structure variable: Passing the address of a structure variable is another and efficient way of passing the members of a structure variable to a function. If `f()` is a function which requires the address of a variable of some structure type, the fact that we are passing the address of the variable to the function `f()` should be indicated both while declaring and defining the function.

EXAMPLE

If the `f()` requires the address of a variable of type `emp` as its argument, the declaration of the function would be as:

```
void f(emp*);
```

and the function definition would be as:

```
void f(emp *ep)
 {
    statements;
}
```

and the function call would be as:

```
f(&e);
```

where **e** is a variable of type `emp`.

Program 9.13 To Illustrate Passing the Address of a Structure to a Function

```
#include <iostream.h>
#include <iomanip.h>

struct student
{
   int reg_no;
   char name[20];
   float percent;
};

void display(student*);

int main(void)
{
   student s;

   cout << "Enter reg_no, name and percent \n";
   cin >> s.reg_no >> s.name >> s.percent;
   display(&s);

   return 0;
}

void display(student *sp)
{
   cout << setw(5) << sp->reg_no << setw(10) << sp->name
        << setw(5) << sp->percent << "\n";
}
```

Input-Output:

```
Enter reg_no, name and percent
1234
Harshith
87

1234  Harshith   87
```

In fact, we can read values into a structure variable with the help of a function by passing the address of the structure variable.

```
void read(student *sp)
{
   cin >> sp->reg_no >> sp->name >> sp->percent;
}


read(&s);
```

enables us to accept reg_no, name and percent of a student into the variable **s**.

Passing a structure variable v/s passing address of a structure variable: If a structure variable itself is passed to a function, the function operates on a copy of the structure variable thereby protecting its original contents. Passing a structure variable amounts to passing all the members of the structure, which is tedious. If any changes are made to the members of the structure variable in the called function, the entire structure needs to be returned to the calling function if it wants to manipulate on the changed values.

Passing address of a structure variable to a function is quite simple since only one value (address) needs to be passed. However, by means of the address all the members of the structure variable can be accessed in the calling function. We do not need to return the structure to the calling function even if any changes made to the members of the structure by the called function since the changes made are visible to the calling function also. The disadvantage of this approach is that there is always a chance of altering the contents of the structure inadvertently.

Passing arrays of structure to functions: Similar to the way, we pass arrays of basic type (`char`, `int`, `float`, etc) to functions, we can even think of passing arrays of structures to functions as arguments. We know that to be able to pass an array of basic type to a function, we need to pass the array name (address of the first element in the array) and the no. of elements in the array. Same is true even in the case of arrays of structure type. The prototype of the function which takes an array of structure type as an argument and the header of the function should reveal the argument type.

Program 9.14 To Illustrate Passing an Array of Structures to a Function

```
#include <iostream.h>
#include <iomanip.h>
struct emp
{
    int empno;
    char name[20];
    float salary;
};

void display(emp e[], int);

int main(void)
{
    emp e[10];
    int i, n;


    cout << "Enter no. of employees \n";
    cin >> n;
    cout << "Enter" << n << "employees' details \n";
    for(i = 0; i < n; i++)
        cin >> e[i].empno >> e[i].name >> e[i].salary;
    cout << "The list of employees \n";
    display(e, n);

    return 0;
}

void display(emp e[], int n)
```

```
{
    int i;
    for(i = 0; i < n; i++)
        cout << setw(6) << e[i].empno << setw(10) << e[i].name
            << setw(8) << e[i].salary << "\n";
}
```

Input-Output:

```
Enter no. of employees
2

Enter 2 employees' details
123 Nishu    23000
124 Harshith 45000

The list of employees
123      Nishu            23000.00
124      Harshith         45000.00
```

Explanation

We have defined a structure by name `emp`. It involves three members empno, name and salary. A variable of `emp` type can accommodate empno, name and salary of an employee. An array of `emp` type can thus accommodate details of a list of employees. The function `display()` is to display the details of a list of employees passed to it. The prototype of `display()` indicates that it requires two arguments (a) Array name (b) No. of structure elements.

In the `main()`, **`e`** is declared to be an array of `struct emp` type and of size 10. Maximum 10 employees' details can be accepted. **`i`** and **`n`** are declared to be variables of `int` type. **`i`** is to traverse the structure elements and **`n`** is to collect the no. of employees. After accepting the no. of employees into the variable **`n`**, we accept **`n`** employees details into the array **`e`**. The array name **`e`** and **`n`** are passed to `display()`, which in turn displays the list of employees' details.

When a function is made to accept and return a structure from and to the calling program, the function declaration and its definition should reflect the same. We will now write a program which illustrates not only passing a structure to a function but also illustrates returning a structure from the function.

Program 9.15 To Illustrate Passing and Returning Structure to and from a Function

```
#include <iostream.h>
#include <iomanip.h>
struct book
{
    char author[20];
    char title[20];
    int pages;
    float price;
};

book update(book b, int p, float pr);

int main(void)
```

```
{
    book b = {"M.T. Somashekara", "Programming in C", 308, 225}, ub;
    int p;
    float pr;

    cout << "Enter the number of pages increased by \n";
    cin >> p;
    cout << "Enter the price increased by \n";
    cin >> pr;
    ub = update(b, p, pr);
    cout << "Updated book details \n";
    cout << "Author = " << ub.author << "\n";
    cout << "Title = " << ub.title << "\n";
    cout << "Pages = " << ub.pages;
    cout << "Price = " << ub.price;

    return 0;
}

book update(book b, int p, float pr)
{
    b.pages += p;
    b.price += pr;

    return b;
}
```

Input-Output:

```
Enter the number of pages increased by
150
Enter the price increased by
50

Updated book details
Author = M.T. Somashekara
Title = Programming in C
Pages = 458
Price = 275
```

Explanation

The structure **book** is defined with four members: author (array of `char`), title (array of `char`), pages (`int`) and price (`float`). A variable of `book` type would thus represent the details of a book. The function `update()` is defined with three formal arguments **b** of `book` type , **p** of `int` type and **pr** of `float` type representing the details of a book, the number of pages increased by and the price increased by, respectively. The purpose of the function is to update the values of the members pages and price of the book passed to it and return the updated structure value back to the calling program.

In the `main()`, the structure variable **b** is initialized with values and the number of pages and the price increased by, are accepted into the local variables **p** and **pr** respectively. A call is made to the function `update()` through the statement `ub = update(b, p, pr);` after the execution of the statement, the variable **ub** gets the updated values and they are displayed.

9.9 UNION

The concept of union is derived from the concept of structure. The common thing shared by both structure and union is that both enable us to identify a group of data items which may be of different types by a common name. But the difference lies in their storage allocation scheme. In the case of structure, the no. of locations allocated would be equal to the no. of members in the structure. Whereas in the case of union, only one location which is large enough to collect the largest data type member in the union gets allocated. This single location can accommodate values of different type at different points of time one at a time. This feature provided by union has helped in a big way while developing system software.

Before instantiating variables of some union type, the data items which are to share a common name should be grouped together. This is done with the help of union template. The syntax of defining a union template is as follows:

```
union tag_name
{
    data-type member1;
    data-type member2;
              :
              :
              :
    data-type membern;
};
```

union is a keyword. tag-name is any user-defined name, which should be a valid C++ identifier. `data-type` is any valid data type supported by C++ or user-defined type. `member1, member2...` `membern` are the members of the union. Note the similarity between a union template and a structure template except the keyword **union** in the former and the keyword **struct** in the latter.

The syntax of declaring a variable of union type is as follows:

```
tag_name variable_name;
```

As a result of this, a memory location gets allocated, the size of which is equal to that of the largest of the members `member1, member2, member3,..., membern.` Accessing the members of a union is similar to accessing the members of a structure. Dot operator is used to access each individual member. Dot operator expects union variable to its left and member name to its right.

EXAMPLE

```
union temp
{
    int i;
    float f;
    char c;
};
```

union `temp` makes a group of three data items of type `int`, `float` and `char`.

```
temp t;
```

A variable **t** is declared to be of type `temp`. As a result of this, only one memory location gets allocated. It can be referred to by any one individual member at any point of time. Note that the size of the memory location is four bytes, which happens to be the size of the largest sized data type `float` in the member-list. Figure 9.1 depicts the sharing of one location by the member of union temp.

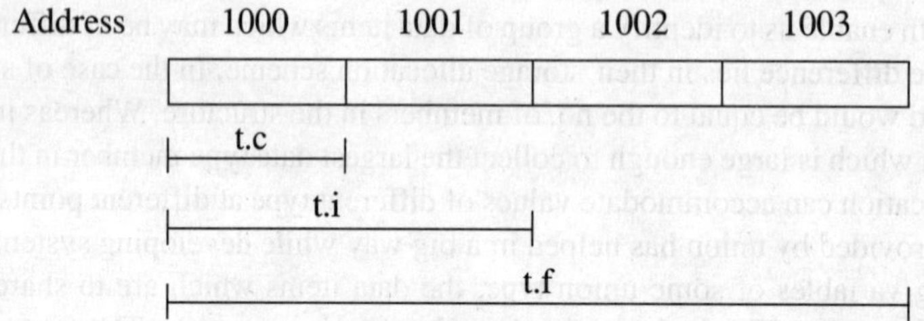

Fig. 9.1 Sharing of space by members of union temp.

Program 9.16 To Differentiate between Structure and Union

```
#include <iostream.h>

struct temp
{
   int i;
   float f;
   char c;
};
union utemp
{
   int i;
   float f;
   char c;
};

int main(void)
{
   temp st;
   utemp ut;

   cout << " size of temp = " << sizeof(st) << "\n";
   cout << " size of utemp = " << sizeof(ut) << "\n";

   st.i = 10;
   st.f = 3.45;
   st.c = 's';

   cout << " st.i = " << st.i << "\n";
   cout << " st.f = " << st.f << "\n";
   cout << " st.c = " << st.c << "\n";

   ut.i = 10;
   cout << " ut.i = " << ut.i << "\n";
   ut.f = 3.45;
   cout << " ut.f = " << ut.f << "\n";
```

```
    ut.c = 's';
    cout << " ut.c = " << ut.c << "\n";

    return 0;
}
```

Input-Output:

```
size of temp = 7
size of utemp = 4
st.i = 10
st.f = 3.45
st.c = s
ut.i = 10
ut.f = 3.45
ut.c = s
```

Explanation

In Program 9.16, structure template `temp` logically relates three data items **`i`**, **`f`** and **`c`** of type `int`, `float` and `char` type respectively. **`st`** is declared to be a variable of type `temp`. Intentionally, the same three types of data items are grouped together even in the union template `utemp`. and **`ut`** is declared to be a variable of type `utemp`.

First, the size of **`st`** is displayed. It turns out to be seven bytes, the sum of the size of its members, then the size of **ut** is displayed. Note that it turns out to be only four bytes, the size of the largest data type, **`float`** member in the union.

Values of corresponding type are assigned to the members of **`st`** and they are displayed. An integer value is assigned to **`ut.i`** and it is displayed. Then a float value is assigned to **`ut.f`** and it is also displayed. It is important to note that when **`ut.f`** is assigned a value, **`ut.i`** ceases to exist since it is overwritten by **`ut.f`**. Lastly, **`ut.c`** is assigned a character. Now, **`ut.f`** ceases to exist, since **`ut.c`** overwrites it. So at any point of time, only one of **`ut.i`**, **`ut.f`** and **`ut.c`** is accessible.

9.9.1 Union within Structure

Unions can be made as members of structures as well. Program 9.17 illustrates this concept.

Program 9.17 To Illustrate Union within Structure

```
#include <iostream.h>
#include <iomanip.h>

union utemp
{
    int i;
    float f;
    double d;
};

struct stemp
{
    int type;
    char name[20];
    union utemp u;
};
```

```
int main(void)
{
    stemp s[3];
    int i, t;

    for(i = 0; i < 3; i++)
    {

        cout << "Enter type [1 for int, 2 for float, 3 for double \n";
        cin >> t;
        cout << "Enter name \n";
        cin >> s[i].name;
        if (t == 1)
        {
            cout << "Enter an integer value \n";
            cin >> s[i].u.i;
        }
        else if (t == 2)
        {
            cout << "Enter a float value \n";
            cin >> s[i].u.f;
        }
        else
        {
            cout << "Enter a double value \n";
            cin >> s[i].u.d;
        }
        s[i].type = t;
    }
    for(i = 0; i < 3; i++)
    {
        if (s[i].type == 1)
            cout << "integer" << setw(10) << s[i].name
                    << setw(5) << s[i].u.i << "\n";
        else if (s[i].type == 2)
            cout << "float " << setw(10) << s[i].name
                    << setw(5) << s[i].u.f << "\n";
        else
            cout << "double" << setw(10) << s[i].name
                    << setw(5) << s[i].u.d << "\n";
        cout << "\n";
    }

    return 0;
}
```

Input-Output:

```
Enter type [1 for int, 2 for float, 3 for double ]
1
Enter name
counter
Enter an integer value
10
Enter type [1 for int, 2 for float, 3 for double
```

```
2
Enter name
salary
Enter a float value
23000
Enter type [1 for int, 2 for float, 3 for double
3
Enter name
Total
Enter a double value
2340000.00

integer   counter    10
float     salary    23000.00
double    total     2340000.00
```

Explanation

The union template `utemp` is defined with three members **i, f** and **d** of type `int`, `float` and `double` respectively. We know that a variable of union **utemp** type can store any one of the types of values at a given point of time. The structure **struct stemp** is defined with three members type, name and u of type `int`, `char` array and union `utemp` type respectively. So a variable of type **struct stemp** would thus store a record of the symbol table with three fields integer value (type), name of the variable (name) and its value (*u*). Note that in the array **s** of type **struct stemp** the member *u* of different records stores either an integer or a float value or a double value and the type of the value stored in *u* is remembered by storing the numeric codes assigned to the types (1 for integer, 2 for float and 3 for double).

9.9.2 Structure within Union

On the lines of embedding unions within structure, we can even think of making structures as members of unions. The following example illustrates this:

```
struct date
{
    int day, month, year;
};

union emp
{
    int age;
    date dob;
};
```

A variable of `emp` type can be used to store either the age of a person or his date of birth.

9.9.3 Arrays within Unions

The following example illustrates the fact that we can have arrays as members of unions:

```
union student
```

```
{
    int reg_no;
    char name[20];
};
```

In a variable of `student` type, either reg_no or name of a student can be stored.

9.9.4 Anonymous Unions

We know that the concept of union enables us to use a single memory location for multiple members, which may be of different types, accessible one at a time. Each member is accessed with the help of the dot operator with the tag name of the union to its left and the member name itself to its right. C++ allows us to define unions without the tag name. These unions are called **anonymous unions**. The members of the anonymous unions are then accessed without the help of the dot operator.

```
union
{
    type m1;
    type m2;
    type m3;
    :
    :
    type mn;
};
```

Here, for example, the statement `m1 = 10;` is valid. Note the absence of the tag name and the dot operator with the member `m1` of the union.

Program 9.18 To Illustrate Anonymous Unions

```
#include <iostream.h>

int main(void)
{
    union
    {
        int qty_in_stock;
        int qty_balance;
    };
    int qty_sold;

    qty_in_stock = 100;
    cout << "Enter the quantity sold \n";
    cin >> qty_sold;

    qty_in_stock -= qty_sold;

    cout << "Qty_balance =" << qty_balance << "\n";

    return 0;
}
```

Input-Output:

```
Enter the quantity sold
25
Qty_balance =75
```

Explanation

The union is defined with two members of `int` type `qty_in_stock` and `qty_balance`. There is no tag name associated with the union. The members of the union can now be used like any other variable of `int` type. The statement `qty_in_stock = 100;` assigns the value `100` to the member. After accepting the value of `qty_sold`, the local variable of `int` type in the `main()`, the statement `qty_in_stock -= qty_sold;` is executed. After which `qty_in_stock` is reduced by `100`. The value of the member is then displayed with the member `qty_balance`, more intuitive name to the content of the memory location. A global anonymous union should be declared as static.

9.10 BIT-FIELDS

Suppose a variable in a program takes a value, which is either 0 or 1. Since both 0 and 1 are integers, we may be inclined to declare a variable of `int` type. A variable of `int` type consumes 2 bytes of memory space. A careful look at the values to be taken by the variable reveals that only one bit is enough. When a variable of `int` type is used, only one bit out of 16 bits (2 bytes = 16 bits) would be used. The remaining 15 bits go waste! But we do not have a say in determining the no. of bits to be allocated for a variable. Is there a way out, where the remaining 15 bits can be put to use? The concept of bit-fields answers this question

A bit-field is basically a set of adjacent bits in a word of memory. Members of structure can include bit-fields. By making bit-fields as the members of a structure, we can pack several items of information into a single word. Thereby optimizing the memory usage. This is how the low level instructions consisting of opcode, addressing mode specifiers and operand addresses are packed into single words.

The syntax of defining structure template using bit-fields is as follows:

```
struct tag_name
{

    data-type m1 : size;
    data-type m2 : size;
    .
    .
    .
    data-type mn : size;

};
```

`data-type` can be either `int` or `unsigned int` only. Size can vary from 1 to 16, the word size of memory.

Points to observe:

1. Bit-fields can not be arrayed.
2. We can not retrieve the address of a bit-field. Consequently, the concept of pointer to a bit-fields does not arise.

3. If a bit-field does not fit into a word, the bit-field is placed into the next word.
4. Some members in the structure can be of normal data type also.

Program 9.19 To Illustrate the Concept of Bit-fields

```
#include <iostream.h>

struct temp
{
   int a : 3;
   int b : 3;
   unsigned int c :2;
};

int main(void)
{
   temp t;

   t.a = 3;
   t.b = 2;
   t.c = 3;
   cout << "t.a = " << t.a << "\n";
   cout << "t.b = " << t.b << "\n";
   cout << "t.c = " << t.c << "\n";

   cout << "size = " << sizeof(struct temp);

   return 0;
}
```

Input-Output:

```
t.a = 3
t.b = 2
t.c = 3
size = 1
```

Explanation

The structure `temp` is defined with three bit-field members **a, b** and **c**. The members **a** and **b** are of `int` type and are of size three bits. The range of values represented by **a** and **b** thus is –4 to 3 (-2^2 to 2^2-1). The bit-field member **c** is of `unsigned int` type and is of size three bits. The range of values which can be stored in **c** is thus 0 to 3 (0 to 2^2-1). A variable of `temp` type requires one byte memory. As can be seen, three pieces of data can be stored in one byte of memory.

Program 9.20 To Illustrate Bit-fields

```
#include <iostream.h>
#include <iomanip.h>

struct date
{
```

```
    unsigned int day : 5;
    unsigned int month : 4;
    unsigned int year : 7;
};

struct emp
{
    date doj;
    unsigned mar_status : 2;
    unsigned grade   : 2;
    int empno;
    char name[20];
    float salary;
};

int main(void)
{
    emp e;
    unsigned int day, month, year, mar_status, grade;

    cout << "Enter empno, name and salary \n";
    cin >> e.empno >> e.name >> e.salary;

    cout << "Enter date of joining \n";
    cin >> day >> month >> year;
    e.doj.day = day;
    e.doj.month = month;
    e.doj.year = year;

    cout << "Enter marital status [1-3] \n";
    cin >> mar_status;
    e.mar_status = mar_status;

    cout << "Enter grade [1-3] \n";
    cin >> grade;
    e.grade = grade;
    cout << setw(6) << e.empno << setw(10) << e.name << setw(9) << e.salary;
    cout << e.doj.day << "/" << e.doj.month << "/" << e.doj.year; cout <<
    e.mar_status << e.grade;

    return 0;
}
```

Input-Output:

```
Enter empno, name and salary
121
Raghav
2345

Enter date of joining
12
```

```
3
1998
Enter marital status [1-3]
1
Enter grade [1-3]
2

121 Raghav          2345.00 12/3/98  1  2
```

Explanation

The structure **date** is defined with three bit-field members day, month and year of `unsigned int` type with the sizes five, four and seven bits respectively. The member day can store a value in the range 0 to 31; the member month can store a value in the range 0 to 15 and the member year can store a value in the range 0 to 127. Thus, a variable of `struct date` type can represent a date [day 1-31, month 1-12, year 1 to 127 an offset value after the year 2000.

The structure `emp` is defined with a member `doj` of type `date` which represents the date of joining of an employee. Two bit-fields `mar_status` and `grade` are of size two bits, which are to collect the marital status and grade of an employee, each denoted by a value in the range 0 to 3. empno, name and salary are the normal members. So a variable of type `emp` would thus pack several pieces of information.

9.11 ENUMERATED DATA TYPE

Enumerated data type offers us a way of inventing our own data type. The invented new data type enables us to assign symbolic names to integer constants, thereby increasing the degree of readability and maintainability of programs. Variables of enumerated data type are very often used in conjunction with structures and unions.

Like unions, enumerated data type also resembles structures as far as its template definition and declaration of its variables are concerned The syntax of defining an enumerated type is as follows:

```
enum  tag_name
{

    enumerator-1,
    enumerator-2,
    enumerator-3,
    .
    .
    .

    enumerator-n
};
```

`enum` is a keyword. `tag_name` is any user-defined name. It is better if the `tag-name` happens to a collective name reflecting the set of enumerators. `enumerator-1`, `enumerator-2` etc. are the symbolic names representing the integer constants 0, 1 etc. by default. However, the default integer constants of the enumerators can be overridden by assigning our own values.

The syntax of declaring a variable of `enum` type is similar to that used while declaring variables of structure or union type.

```
enum tag_name variable;

enum boolean
{
    false,
    true
};

enum boolean f;

f = false;
```

Program 9.21 To Illustrate Enumerated Data Type

```
#include <iostream.h>

enum subjects
{
    kannada,
    english,
    physics,
    maths,
    computers
};


int main(void)
{
    int marks[5];
    enum subjects subject;

    cout << "Enter marks in five subjects \n";
    for(subject = kannada; subject <= computers; subject++)
        cin >> marks[subject];

    cout << "Marks in Different Subjects \n";

    cout << "Kannada : " << marks[kannada] << "\n";
    cout << "English : " << marks[english] << "\n";
    cout << "Physics : " << marks[physics] << "\n";
    cout << "Maths   : " << marks[maths] << "\n";
    cout << "Computers : " << marks[computers] << "\n";

    return 0;
}
```

Input-Output:

```
Enter marks in five subjects
45 67 87 76 98

Marks in Different Subjects
Kannada   : 45
```

```
English   : 67
Physics   : 87
Maths     : 76
Computers : 98
```

Explanation

In Program 9.21, an enumerated data type with the name `enum subjects` is defined with the enumerators Kannada, English, Physics, Maths and Computers. **marks** is declared to be an array of `int` type of size five. The array is to collect the marks obtained by a student in five subjects mentioned earlier. **subject** is declared to be a variable of type `enum subjects` and it can take any one of the enumerators listed within the definition of `enum subjects`. Since the enumerators will have the values starting from 0, they are used as the indices with the array in the following program segment:

```
for(subject = kannada; subject <= computers; subject++)
           cin >> marks[subject];
```

which accepts marks in five subjects.

Here, `marks[kannada]` (Marks obtained in Kannada) is same as `marks[0]`. `marks[english]` (Marks obtained in English) is same as `marks[1]` and so on. Note the increase in the degree of readability.

Program 9.22 To Illustrate the Concept of Enumerated Data Type

```
#include <iostream.h>

enum week_day
{
   sunday    = 1,
   monday    = 2,
   tuesday   = 3,
   wednesday = 4,
   thursday  = 5,
   friday    = 6,
   saturday  = 7
};

int main(void)
{
   int n;

   cout << "Enter  the day number [1-7] \n";
   cin >> n;

   switch(n)
   {
      case sunday:
            cout << "Sunday";
            break;
      case monday:
            cout << "Monday";
            break;
```

```
        case tuesday:
                cout << "Tuesday";
                break;
        case wednesday:
                cout << "Wednesday";
                break;
        case thursday:
                cout << "Thursday";
                break;
        case friday:
                cout << "Friday";
                break;
        case saturday:
                cout << "Saturday";
                break;
        default: cout << "Invalid day number ";
    }
    return 0;
}
```

Input-Output:

```
Enter  the day number [1-7]
4
Wednesday
```

Explanation

In Program 9.22, note that the enumerators [Sunday-Monday] are assigned the integer values starting from 1 to 7 overriding the default values which range from 0 to 6. So , the program not only illustrates that the enumerators can be assigned our own values but also it illustrates that the enumerators can be used as case labels in the switch structure.

9.12 typedef

typedef, a facility provided by C++, enables us to rename existing built-in data types and user-defined data types and thereby helps in increasing the degree of readability of source code. The syntax of its usage is as follows:

```
typedef old-name new-name;
```

where `old-name` is the name of the existing data type and `new-name` is the new name given to the data type identified by old-name.

EXAMPLE 1

```
    typedef unsigned int TWOWORDS;
```

We can now declare variables of `unsigned int` type using the new name as:

```
TWOWORDS i;
```

`i` has been declared to be a variable of `unsigned int` type.

EXAMPLE 2

```
struct emp
{
    int empno;
    char name[20];
    float salary;
};
```

```
typedef struct emp EMP;
```

variables of `struct emp` can now be declared using EMP as the type specifier as:

```
EMP e;
```

e has been declared to be a variable of `struct emp` type.

Program 9.23 To Illustrate the Usage of Typedef

```
#include <iostream.h>

struct book
{
    char author[20];
    char title[20];
    int pages;
    float price;
};

typedef struct book BOOK;
int main(void)
{
    BOOK b;

    cout << "Enter the details of a book \n";
    cin >> b.author;
    cin >> b.title;
    cin  >> b.pages >> b.price;
    cout << "Author : " << b.author << "\n";
    cout << "Title : " << b.title << "\n";
    cout << "Pages : " << b.pages << "\n";
    cout << "Price : " << b.price << "\n";

    return 0;
}
```

Input-Output:

```
Enter Author, Title, Pages and Price of a book
MT_Somashekara
Programming_in_C
308
225
```

```
Author : MT_Somashekara
Title : Programming_in_C
Pages : 308
Price : 225
```

Explanation

In Program 9.23, a structure with the name **`book`** is defined with four fields **`author`**, **`title`**, **`pages`** and **`price`**. A variable of type **`book`** thus denotes a book. The facility *typedef* is used to rename the type struct book as BOOK. A variable **b** is declared to be of type struct book with the new name **BOOK**. The details of a book are then accepted into **b** and they are displayed.

REVIEW QUESTIONS

9.1 Explain the need for the concept of structure.

9.2 What is structure template?

9.3 Explain syntax of defining structure template with an example.

9.4 Define structure.

9.5 Explain the syntax of declaring a structure variable.

9.6 Can we initialize structure variables while they are declared? If yes, explain the syntax with an example.

9.7 Give an account of the operations which can be performed over structure variables.

9.8 What is the need for array of structures? Give an example.

9.9 Can we make an array as a member of a structure? If yes, give an example of its requirement.

9.10 Can we nest one structure within another structure? If yes, give an example of its requirement.

9.11 How do we pass a structure variable as an argument to a function? Give an example.

9.12 What is union?

9.13 Differentiate between structure and union.

9.14 What is the need for bit-fields? Give an example of their usage.

9.15 What is enumerated data type? Give an example of its usage.

9.16 Give the syntax of defining enumerated data type.

9.17 What is the significance of typedef? Give an example.

True/False Questions

T9.1 In a structure the member data should be of different types.

T9.2 Structure variables can be initialized.

T9.3 Arrays can be made as members of structures.

T9.4
```
union temp
{
    int i;
    float f;
};
```

The size of the union is six bytes.

T9.5 Unions can be used as members of structures and vice-versa.

T9.6 Structures can be nested.

T9.7 The keyword typedef is to create new data type.

T9.8 The enumerators in the enumerated data type are of float type.

T9.9 Structures can be passed and returned to and from functions.

T9.10 The default values of the enumerators in the enumerated data type can not be changed.

T9.11 Unions can not be arrayed.

T9.12 Strings can not be used as members of unions.

PROGRAMMING EXERCISES

P9.1 Write a program to create a list of books' details. The details of a book include title, author, publisher, publishing year, no. of pages, price.

P9.2 Perform the following with respect to the list of books created in Exercise P9.1.

(a) Display the details of books written by a given author.

(b) Sort the details of books in the increasing order of price.

(c) Display the details of books published by a given publisher in a given year.

(d) Sort the list of books in the increasing order of two fields, author and title of the books.

P9.3 Define a structure by name date with members day, month and year of int type. Perform the following:

(a) Validate a date

(b) If d1 and d2 are two dates, find whether d1 is earlier than d2 or d1 is later than d2 or both are equal.

(c) Find the difference between two dates. If d1 and d2 are two dates, difference between d1 and d2 is the no. of days between them.

(d) Increment a date by one day, that is, to get next date for a given date.

(e) If d is a date and n is the no. of days, to get the next date after adding n days to the date d.

P9.4 Define a structure by name time with members seconds, minutes and hours of int type. A variable of the structure type would thus represent time. If t1 and t2 are two variables of the structure type, write a program to find the sum of the two times using a function.

P9.5 Write a program to search for an employee in a list of employees by means of empno using binary search method. (Use structure concept with empno, name and salary are the fields)

P9.6 A complex number is of the form $a + ib$, where a is the real part and b is the imaginary part. Define a structure with real part and imaginary part of a complex number as its member data. Write a program to perform the following operations over two complex numbers:

(a) Addition

(b) Subtraction

(c) Multiplication

(d) Division

P9.7 Given the co-ordinates (x, y) of 10 points, write a program which will output the co-ordinates of all the points which lie inside or on the circle with unit radius with its centre (0, 0).

Hint: Define a structure by name **point** with the **x** and **y** of **int** type as its members. Each variable of the structure type represents a point. The equation of a circle with the centre (0,0) is given by

$$x^2 + y^2 = r^2$$

The point (x, y) lies on the circle if $x^2 + y^2 = r^2$.

The point (x, y) lies inside the circle if $x^2 + y^2 < r^2$.

Chapter 10

Pointers

10.1 INTRODUCTION

Pointers are a powerful concept in C++ (and C) and add to its strength. Mastery over pointers empowers a C++ programmer to deal with system level jargons. Let us begin by enumerating the advantages offered by pointers.

1. Enable us to write efficient and concise programs
2. Enable us to establish inter-program data communication
3. Enable us to dynamically allocate and de-allocate memory
4. Enable us to optimize memory space usage
5. Enable us to deal with hardware components
6. Enable us to pass variable no. of arguments to functions

It would be wise idea to get to know the organization of memory before stepping into the concept of pointers. This is because understanding of pointers and their significance depends on understanding of this.

Memory is organized as an array of bytes. A byte is a basic storage and accessible unit in memory. Each byte is identifiable by a unique number called **address.** Suppose we have 1 kB of memory. Since 1 kB = 1024 bytes, the memory can be viewed as an array of locations of size 1024 with the subscript range [0–1023]. 0 represents the address of the first location; 1 represents the address of the second location and so on. The location is identified by the address 1023.

Address	Location
0	
1	
2	
:	:
:	:
1022	
1023	

We know that variables are to be declared before they are used in a program. Declaration of a variable tells the compiler to perform the following:

1. Allocate a location in memory. The no. of bytes in the location depends on the data type of the variable.
2. Establish a mapping between the address of the location and the name of the variable.

EXAMPLE

The declaration `int i;` tells the compiler to reserve a location in memory. We know that the size of a variable of `int` type is two bytes. So the location would be two bytes wide. If the location is:

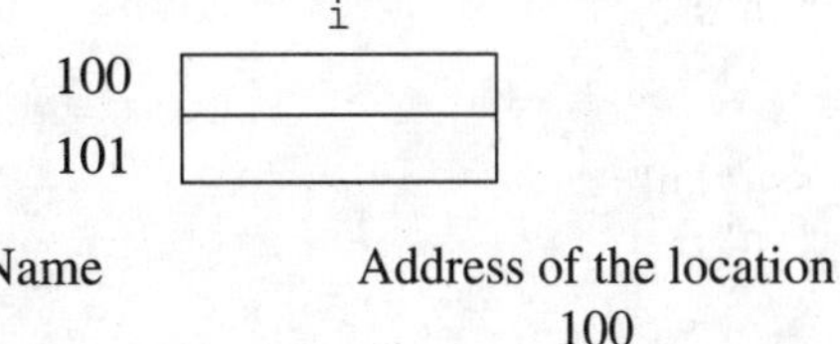

Variable Name	Address of the location
i	100

A mapping between the variable name and the address of the location is established. Note that the address of the first byte of the location becomes the address of the variable. The address of a variable is also a number, numeric data item. It can also be retrieved and stored in another variable. A variable which can store the address of another variable is called a **pointer**.

10.2 POINTER OPERATORS— &, *

C++ provides two special operators known as **pointer operators**. They are **&** and *****. & stands for `'Address of'` and it is used to retrieve the address of a variable. * stands for `'value at address'` and it is used to access the value at a location by means of its address.

Since a pointer is also a variable, it also should be declared before it is used. The syntax of declaring a pointer variable is as follows:

```
data-type *variable_name;
```

`data-type` is any valid data type supported by C++ or any user-defined type and `variable-name` is the name of the pointer variable. The presence of * before `variable_name` indicates that it is a pointer variable.

EXAMPLE

```
int *ip;
```

`ip` is declared to be a pointer variable of `int` type.

```
float *fp;
```

`fp` is declared to be a pointer variable of `float` type.

Program 10.1 To Illustrate the Concept of Pointers and Pointer Operators [&, *]

```
#include <iostream.h>

int main(void)
```

```
{
    int i = 10, *ip;
    float f = 3.4, *fp;
    char c = 'a', *cp;

    cout << "i = " << i << "\n";
    cout << "f = " << f << "\n";
    cout << "c = " << c << "\n";

    ip = &i;
    cout << "\n Address of i = " << ip << "\n";
    cout << "Value of i = " << *ip << "\n";

    fp = &f;
    cout << "\nAddress of f = " << fp << "\n";
    cout << "Value of f = " << *fp << "\n";

    cp = &c;
    cout << "\n Address of c = " << cp << "\n";
    cout << "value of c = " << *cp << "\n";

    return 0;
}
```

Input-Output:

```
i = 10
f = 3.4
c = a

Address of i = 0xfff4
Value of i = 10

Address of f = 0xfff0
Value of f = 3.4

Address of c = aš™Y@

value of c = a
```

Explanation

In Program 10.1, **i**, **f** and **c** are declared to be variables of `int`, `float` and `char` type respectively. **ip**, **fp** and **cp** are declared to be pointer variables of type `int`, `float` and `char` respectively.

The initial values of **i**, **f** and **c** are displayed. The pointer variable **ip** is assigned the address of **i** using the statement `ip = &i;` the address of **i** and its value are displayed through the pointer variable. The same thing is repeated for `char` and `float` variables.

10.3 POINTER ARITHMETIC

Following are the operations that can be performed over pointers:

1. We can add an integer value to a pointer.
2. We can subtract an integer value from a pointer.
3. We can compare two pointers if they point the elements of the same array.
4. We can subtract one pointer from another pointer if both point to the same array.
5. We can assign one pointer to another pointer provided both are of same type.

But the following operations are not possible:

1. Addition of two pointers
2. Subtraction of one pointer from another pointer when they do not point to the same array.
3. Multiplication of two pointers
4. Division of one pointer by another pointer

Suppose **p** is a pointer variable to integer type. The pointer variable **p** can be subjected to the following operations:

1. We can increment it using increment operator ++.

   Suppose the address stored in **p** initially is 100. After the statement `p++;` is executed, the content in **p** gets incremented by 2, the size of int type. So it becomes 102.
2. We can decrement it using decrement operator --.

   Suppose the address stored in **p** initially is 100. After the statement `p--;` is executed, the content in **p** gets decremented by 2, the size of `int` type. So it becomes 98.

   In general, if a pointer variable is incremented using ++, it gets incremented by the size of its data type. i.e., a `char` pointer gets incremented by 1, the size of `char` type. A float pointer gets incremented by 4, the size of `float` data type. In the case of decrement operator, a pointer variable gets decremented by the size of its data type.
3. An integer value can be added to it, i.e.,

   p = **p** + integer value

   The content of **p** will now get incremented by the product of integer value and the size of `int` type.
4. An integer value can be subtracted from it, i.e.,

   p = **p** – integer value

   The content of **p** will now get decremented by the product of integer value and the size of `int` type.

Program 10.2 To Illustrate the Concept of Pointer Arithmetic

```
#include <iostream.h>

int main(void)
{
    int i, *ip;

    ip = &i;
    cout << "ip = " << ip << "\n";
    ip++;
    cout << "After ip++     ip = " << ip << "\n";
    ip--;
    cout << "After ip--     ip = " << ip << "\n";
```

```
    ip = ip + 2;
    cout << "After ip=ip+2   ip = " << ip << "\n";
    ip = ip - 2;
    cout << "After ip=ip-2   ip = " << ip << "\n";

    return 0;
}
```

Input-Output:

```
ip = 0xfff4
After ip++          ip = 0xfff6
After ip--          ip = 0xfff4
After ip=ip+2       ip = 0xfff8
After ip=ip-2       ip = 0xfff4
```

Explanation

In Program 10.2, **i** is declared to be a variable of `int` type and **ip**, a pointer to `int` type. Initially, the address of **i** is assigned to **ip** and it is displayed. The pointer variable **ip** is incremented using ++ operator. As can be seen, the value in **ip** gets incremented by two, the size of `int` type. The pointer variable **ip** is then decremented using – operator. Now, the value in **ip** is decremented by two, the size of `int` data type. Then, an integer constant 2 is added to **ip**. As a result, the value of **ip** gets incremented by 4, i.e., 2*size of `int` type. On the execution of the statement `ip = ip - 2;` the value of **ip** gets decremented by 4, i.e., 2 * `sizeof(int)`.

10.3.1 Pointer Expressions

Once we assign the address of a variable to a pointer variable, the value of the variable pointed to can be made to participate in all the manipulations by means of the pointer itself. This is required when we pass the addresses of variables to functions as arguments. Let us now write a program to illustrate performing manipulations over variables' values by means of their pointers.

Program 10.3 To Illustrate Pointer Expressions

```
#include <iostream.h>

int main(void)
{
    int a = 4, b = 2, *ap, *bp, *sp;
    int s, d, p, q, r, t;

    ap = &a;
    bp = &b;

    s = *ap + *bp;
    d = *ap - *bp;
    p = *ap * *bp;
    q = *ap / *bp;
    r = *ap % *bp;
```

```
    sp = &t;
    *sp = *ap + *bp;
    cout << "sum = " << s << "\n";
    cout << "Difference = " << d << "\n";
    cout << "Product = " << p << "\n";
    cout << "Quotient = " << q << "\n";
    cout << "Remainder = " << r << "\n";
    cout << "Sum = " << t << "\n";

    return 0;
}
```

Input-Output:

```
sum = 6
Difference = 2
Product = 8
Quotient = 2
Remainder = 0
Sum = 6
```

Explanation

In Program 10.3, **a** and **b** are declared to be variables of `int` type and they are initialized also. **ap** and **bp** are declared to be pointers to `int` type. The pointer variables **ap** and **bp** point to the integer variables **a** and **b** respectively because of the statements `ap = &a;` and `bp = &b;`. All the five basic arithmetic operations are performed over the values of **a** and **b** by means of **ap** and **bp** respectively and the results of the operations are assigned to the variables of `int` type. Here ***ap** and ***bp** represent the values of **a** and **b** respectively.

The fact that the de-referencing expression (i.e., `*ptr`) can be used on the left-hand side of an assignment statement is also illustrated with the statement `*sp = *ap + *bp;` Here the sum of the values of **a** and **b** is assigned to the variable pointed to by **sp** i.e., **s**. Here we say that the de-referencing expression is used as an **Lvalue**. (Lvalue is one which has a location and which can be assigned a value)

10.4 POINTERS AND ARRAYS

We are now acquainted with both arrays and pointers. In our earlier discussions, we treated them as separate entities. But in C++, there is a close relationship between them. Elements of an array are accessed through pointers internally. Let us now try to unravel the bonding between them.

10.4.1 Pointers and One-dimensional Arrays

Let us first consider the relationship between one-dimensional arrays and pointers. Suppose **a** is a one-dimensional array of `int` type and of size 10, which is declared as follows:

```
int a[10];
```

We know that a block of memory consisting of 10 contiguous locations gets allocated and all the locations share common name **a** and are distinguishable by subscript values `[0-9]`.

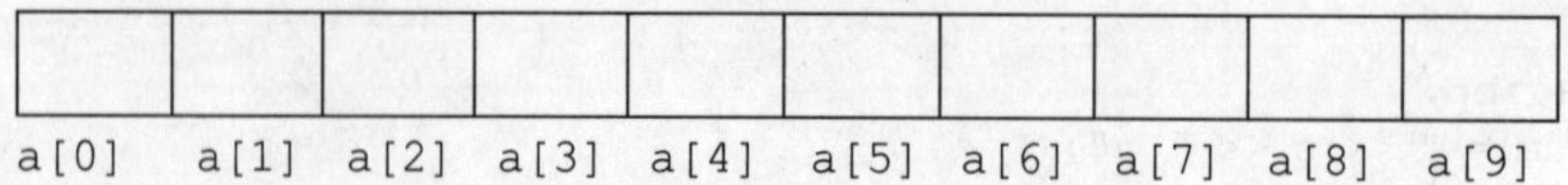

Here, the array name **a** gives the base address of the array. That is, the address of the first element `a[0]` of the array. So **a** being equivalent to `&a[0]` can be regarded as a pointer to integer but in the capacity of a constant pointer. That is, **a** can not be incremented or decremented.

Since **a** is the address of **a[0]**, ***a** is the element stored in the first location. Since **a** is a constant pointer, it can not be incremented to point to the next location. But the expression `(a + 1)` gives the address of the second element `a[1]` of the array. `*(a + 1)` gives the element itself stored at `a[1]`. Similarly, `(a + 2)` is the address of `a[2]` and `*(a + 2)` is the value at `a[2]`.

```
*a =    *(a + 0)  =  a[0]
        *(a + 1)  =  a[1]
        *(a + 2)  =  a[2]
        *(a + 3)  =  a[3]
        *(a + 4)  =  a[4]
               .
               .
               .
        *(a + i)  =    a[i]
```

In general, `(a + i)` gives the address of `i`th element in the array **a** and `*(a + i)` is the element stored in the `i`th location of the array.

Program 10.4 To Illustrate Processing One-dimensional Arrays Using Pointers

```
#include <iostream.h>

int main(void)
{
    int a[10], n, i;

    cout << "Enter no. of elements \n";
    cin >> n;

    cout << "Enter" << n << "elements \n";
    for(i = 0; i < n; i++)
        cin >> *(a + i);

    cout << "The list if elements \n";
    for(i = 0; i < n; i++)
        cout << *(a + i) << "\n";

    return 0;
}
```

Input-Output:

```
Enter no. of elements
5
```

```
Enter 5 elements
1 2 3 4 5
The list if elements
1 2 3 4 5
```

Explanation

a is declared to be an array of `int` type of size 10. **n** and **i** are declared to be variables of `int` type. The variable **n** is to accept the no. of elements to be accepted into the array **a**, the value of which should lie within 1 and 10 and the variable **i** is to select each location of the array. We know that the array name **a** gives the address of the first location of the array and the expression **a + i** gives the address of **i**th location of the array. The following segment of Program 10.4 enables us to accept **n** values into the array:

```
for(i = 0; i < n; i++)
    cin >> *(a + i);
```

`*(a + 0)` gives the value at the first location of the array and in general, `*(a + i)` gives the value at **i**th location of the array **a**. The following segment of Program 10.4 displays the `n` values stored in the array.

```
for(i = 0; i < n; i++)
    cout << *(a + i) << "\n";
```

Note that the expression `*(a + i)` is equivalent to `a[i]`.

Program 10.5 To Access the Elements of an Array through a Pointer Variable

```
#include <iostream.h>

int main(void)
{

    int a[5] = { 4, 6, 7, 5, 2};
    int *p1, *p2;

    p1 = a;
    p2 = &a[4];
    cout << "The elements of the array a \n";
    while (p1 <= p2)
    {
        cout << *p1 << "\n";
        p1++;
    }

    return 0;
}
```

Input-Output:

```
The elements of the array a
4
6
7
5
2
```

Explanation

a has been declared to be an array of `int` type and it is also initialized. **p1** and **p2** are declared to be pointers of `int` type. **p1** is assigned the address of the first element of the array with the statement `p1 = a;`. The pointer variable **p2** is assigned the address of the last element of the array with the statement `p2 = &a[4];`. Since the pointers **p1** and **p2** point to the elements of the same array, they can be compared. The while loop is to traverse the elements of the array and display them. As long as `p1 <= p2`, the loop repeats and displays the value pointed to by **p1**. Since **p1** is getting incremented each time, once it exceeds the address in **p2**, the test-expression `p1<= p2` evaluates to false and the loop is exited.

Because of the same reason, `p2 - p1` is also a valid expression.

10.4.2 Pointers and Two-dimensional Arrays

Suppose **a** is an array of two dimensions of `int` type, which is declared as follows:

```
int a[2][3];
```

We know that a 2-d array is essentially an array of 1-d arrays. So each element in a 2-d array happens to be a 1-d array.

Here also, the array name **a** gives its base address. That is, the address of its first element. First element in this case is the first 1-d array. So **a** is the address of its first 1-d array. Hence **a** is a pointer to its first 1-d array. As we have seen earlier, since 1-d array itself is a pointer, **a** can now be regarded as a pointer to pointer of `int` type. Note the two levels of indirections.

`a + 1` is the address of the second 1-d array of **a** and so on.

`(a + 0)` is the address of first 1-d array — `*(a + 0)` is the first 1-d array
`(a + 1)` is the address of second 1-d array — `*(a + 1)` is the second 1-d array
`(a + 2)` is the address of third 1-d array — `*(a + 2)` is the third 1-d array
⋮ — ⋮
`(a + n-1)` is the address of nth 1-d array — `*(a + n-1)` is the nth 1-d array

Now, `*(a + i)`, (i € 1)th 1-d array of **a** is similar to any 1-d array, say **b**, which is declared as follows:

```
int b[10];
```

Here, we know that the array name **b** gives the address of its first element. On the similar lines,

`*(a + 0)`
`= *(a + 0) + 0` gives the address of the first element in the first 1-d array of **a**.

`*(a + 0) + 1` gives the address of the second element in the first 1-d array of **a**
`*(a + 0) + 2` gives the address of the third element in the first 1-d array of **a** and so on.

`* (* (a + 0) + 0)` gives the first element in the first 1-d array — `a[0][0]`
`* ( *(a + 0) + 1)` gives the second element in the first 1-d array — `a[0][1]`
`* ( *(a + 0) + 2)` gives the third element in the first 1-d array — `a[0][2]`

Similarly,

`* (* (a + 1) + 0)` gives the first element in the second 1-d array — `a[1][0]`

`* ( *(a + 1) + 1)` gives the second element in the second 1-d array `a[1][1]`
`* ( *(a + 1) + 2)` gives the third element in the second 1-d array `a[1][2]`

In general, `a[i][j]` can be written as `*(*(a + i) + j)`.

Program 10.6 To Illustrate Processing 2-d Arrays Using Pointer Notations

```
#include <iostream.h>
#include <iomanip.h>

int main(void)
{
    int a[10][10], m, n, i, j;

    cout << "Enter the order of the matrix a \n";
    cin >> m >> n;

    cout << "Enter elements of the matrix a of order" << m << "*" << n << "\n";
    for(i = 0; i < m; i++)
    for(j = 0; j < n; j++)
        cin >> *(*(a + i) + j);

    cout << "Matrix a \n";
    for(i = 0; i < m; i++)
    {
        for(j = 0; j < n; j++)
            cout << setw(4) << *(*(a + i) + j);
        cout << "\n";

    }

    return 0;
}
```

Input-Output:

```
Enter the order of the matrix a
3 3
Enter elements of the matrix a of order 3*3
1 2 3 4 5 6 7 8 9

Matrix a
1  2  3
4  5  6
7  8  9
```

Explanation

a is declared to be an array of two dimensions and of size 10 * 10. The variables **m**, **n**, **i** and **j** are declared to be variables of `int` type. The variables **m** and **n** are to collect the no. of rows and the no. of columns of the 2-d array. The variables **i** and **j** are to select rows and columns of the array respectively. The segment of the program responsible for accepting the elements into the array **a** is as follows:

```
for(i = 0; i < m; i++)
for(j = 0; j < n; j++)
    cin >> *(*(a + i) + j);
```

The following segment of the program is responsible for displaying the elements of the array **a**:

```
for(i = 0; i < m; i++)
{
    for(j = 0; j < n; j++)
        cout << *(*(a + i) + j);
    cout << "\n";
}
```

Note that the expression `*(*(a + i) + j)` is same as `a[i][j]`.

10.5 POINTERS AND STRINGS

In the previous section, we learnt that pointers and arrays are close associates. They are so close to each other that arrays are processed using pointers internally. Strings also being arrays enjoy the same kind of relation with pointers. We know that a string is a sequence of characters terminated by a null character '\0'. The null character marks the end of the string. We also know that the name of an array gives the base address of the array, that is, the address of the first element of the array. This is true even in the case of strings. Consider the string variable `char s[20]`; here **s** gives the base address of the array, that is, the address of the first character in the string variable and hence can be regarded as a pointer to character. Since each string is terminated by a null character, it is enough for us to know the starting address of a string to be able to access the entire string. In view of these observations, we conclude that a string can be denoted by a pointer to character.

```
char s[20];
char *cp;
cp = s;
```

s is declared to be an array of `char` and it can accommodate a string. To be precise, **s** represents a string. **cp** is declared to be a pointer to `char` type. Assignment of **s** to **cp** is perfectly valid since **s** is also a pointer to `char` type. There is type compatibility. Now, **cp** also represents the string in **s**.

Let us now consider a string constant "abcd". We know that a string constant is a sequence of characters enclosed within a pair of double quotes. The string constant is stored in some part of memory and it requires five bytes of space. Here also the address of the first character represents the entire string. The value of the string constant thus is the address of the first character 'a'. So it can be assigned to a pointer to `char` type.

If **cp** is a pointer to `char` type, **cp** = "abcd" is perfectly valid and **cp** now represents the entire string "abcd".

Program 10.7 To Illustrate Pointers to Strings

```
#include <iostream.h>
int main(void)
{
    char str[20], *cp;
```

```
    cout << "Enter a string \n";
    cin >> str;
    cp = str;
    cout << "string in str = " << cp << "\n";

    cp = "abcd";
    cout << cp << "\n";

    return 0;
}
```

Input-Output:

```
Enter a string
Program
string in str = Program
abcd
```

Explanation

In Program 10.7, **str** is declared to be a string variable of size 20. Maximum 20 characters can be stored in it. **cp** is declared to be a pointer to `char` type. A string is accepted into the variable **str** using the statement `cin >> str`. The pointer variable **cp**, being a pointer to `char` type is then assigned **str**. It is perfectly correct since **str**, the array name, gives the base address of the array and hence is a pointer to `char` type. Pointer assignment is permissible. After the assignment of **str** to **cp**, **cp** will also represent the string in **str**. It is confirmed by the statement `cout << cp;`, which displays the string in **str**. **cp** is then assigned a string constant "abcd" and the string constant is displayed by the statement `cout << cp;`.

Thus, a pointer to `char` type can represent a string and it can be made to represent different strings at different points of time. But an array of `char` type can represent only one string throughout the program. It is because of the fact that the name of a string variable is a constant pointer and it can not be assigned any other address.

In the case of an array of `char` type, a string can be accepted into it through console. But in the case of a pointer to `char` type, we can only assign a string but can not accept a string through the console. Table 10.1 shows the differences between an array of `char` and a pointer to `char` type.

Table 10.1 Comparison between an Array of char and a Pointer to char

Array of char	*Pointer to char*
We can initialize a string during declaration `char str[20] = "abcd".`	We can initialize a string during declaration `char *cp = "abcd".`

A string variable or a string constant can not be assigned to an array of `char` type
`char str[20];`
`str = "abc"`
is invalid.
	A string variable or a string constant can be assigned to a pointer to `char` type
	`char *p;`
	`P = "abcd";.`

The no. of bytes allocated for a string variable is determined by the size of the array.	The no. of bytes allocated for a string is determined by the no. of characters within the string.
An array of `char` refers to the same string (storage area).	A pointer to `char` can represent different strings (storage area) at different points of time.

10.5.1 Array of Pointers to Strings

We now know that a pointer variable to `char` type can represent a string. If we are to deal with more than one string, then we can use an array of pointers to `char` type to represent the strings. An example of the declaration of an array of pointers to `char` type is:

```
char *ptr[10] ;
```

Here, `ptr[0], ptr[1],...., ptr[9]` are all pointers to `char` type and each of them can denote a string.

Program 10.8 To Illustrate Array of Pointers to Strings

```
#include <iostream.h>

int main(void)
{
   char *names[5] = { "Nishu", "Harsha", "Shobha", "Devaraj", "Asha" };
   int i;

   cout << "The list of five Names \n";
   for(i = 0; i < 5; i++)
      cout << names[i] << "\n";
   return 0;
}
```

Input-Output:

```
The list of five Names

Nishu
Harsha
Shobha
Devaraj
Asha
```

Explanation

`names` is declared to be an array of pointers to `char` type and of size 5. The array of pointers is initialized with five strings. **`names[0]`** denotes the string "Nishu"; **`names[1]`** denotes the string "Harsha", and so on. **`i`** is declared to be a variable of `int` type. It is to select each string in the list of strings. A for loop is used to display the strings represented by the pointers of the array **`names`**.

Program 10.9 To Sort a List of Names Using Array of Pointers to Strings

```
#include <iostream.h>
#include <string.h>

int main(void)
{
char *t, *names[5] = { "Nishu", "Harsha", "Shobha", "Devaraj", "Pooja" };
   int i, j;
```

```
    cout << "Unsorted list of five Names \n";
    for(i = 0; i < 5; i++)
        cout << names[i] << "\n";

    // sorting begins
    for(i = 0; i < 4; i++)
    for(j = i + 1; j < 5; j++)
        if (strcmp(names[i], names[j])>0)
        {
            t = names[i];
            names[i] = names[j];
            names[j] = t;
        }
    // sorting ends
    cout << "Sorted list of names \n";
    for(i = 0; i < 5; i++)
        cout << names[i] << "\n";

    return 0;
}
```

Input-Output:

```
Unsorted list of five Names
Nishu
Harsha
Shobha
Devaraj
Pooja

Sorted list of names
Devaraj
Harsha
Nishu
Pooja
Shobha
```

Explanation

names is declared to be an array of pointers to `char` type and of size 5. It is initialized with five strings. **t** is another pointer to `char` type and it is used as a temporary variable to represent a string during sorting process (swapping). The integer variables **i** and **j** are to be used to traverse the list of names. Initially, the unsorted list of strings is displayed. The following segment of the program accomplishes the task of sorting the list of strings:

```
for(i = 0; i < 4; i++)
for(j = i + 1; j < 5; j++)
    if (strcmp(names[i], names[j])>0)
    {
        t = names[i];
        names[i] = names[j];
        names[j] = t;
    }
```

Note that during the process of sorting, swapping of strings is done by just interchanging the pointers. (without calling `strcpy()`).

10.6 POINTERS AND STRUCTURES

The concept of pointers can be used in combination with structures in two ways: (a) Since the address of a structure variable can be retrieved using & operator, we can think of pointers to structures (b) Having pointers to different data types as members of structures.

10.6.1 Pointers to Structures

Similar to pointers to basic type like `int`, `float` and `char` etc., we can have pointers to structures also. The pointer variables should be declared to be the corresponding type. We use & operator to retrieve the address of a structure variable.

EXAMPLE

```
struct temp
{
    int i;
    float f;
    char c;
};

struct temp t, *tp;
```

`t` is declared to be variable of `struct temp` type. **`tp`** is declared to be a pointer to `struct temp` type. The statement `tp = &t;` assigns the address of **`t`** to **`tp`**. The pointer variable **`tp`** is now said to point to **`t`**. The members of **`t`** are accessed through **`tp`** with the help of operator -> known as **structure-pointer operator**. -> expects the pointer variable to its left and member name to its right. `tp -> i`, `tp -> f` and `tp -> c` represent **`t.i`**, **`t.f`** and **`t.c`** respectively.

Program 10.10 To Illustrate Pointers to Structures

```
#include <iostream.h>

struct temp
{
    int i;
    float f;
    char c;
};

int main(void)
{
    struct temp t = {123, 34.56, 'p'}, *tp;
    tp = &t;
    cout << "t.i = " << tp->i << "\n";
    cout << "t.f = " << tp->f << "\n";
```

```
    cout << "t.c = " << tp->c;

    return 0;
}
```

Input-Output:

```
t.i = 123
t.f = 34.560000
t.c = p
```

Explanation

The structure variable **t** is initialized with values 123, 34.56 and the character constant 'p'. The memory locations allocated for **t** will be filled with the given values as follows:

123	34.560000	p
t.i	t.f	t.c

The pointer variable **tp** is then assigned the address of **t**. The members of **t** are then accessed by means of **tp** with the use of the operator ->.

10.6.2 Structures Containing Pointers

Structures can have pointers as their members as well. Consider the following example:

```
struct temp
{
    int i;
    int *ip;
};
```

The structure definition includes **ip**, a pointer to **int** type as one of its members.

Program 10.11 To Illustrate Structure Containing Pointer

```
#include <iostream.h>

struct temp
{
    int i;
    int *ip;
};

int main(void)
{
    struct temp t;
    int a = 10;

    t.i = a;
    t.ip = &a;
```

```
    cout << "Value of a = " << t.i << "\n";
    cout << "Address of a = " << t.ip;

    return 0;
}
```

Input-Output:

```
Value of a = 10
Address of a = 65520
```

Explanation

The definition of the structure `struct temp` includes two members **`i`** and **`ip`**. The member **`i`** is of type `int` and the member **`ip`** is a pointer to `int` type. In the `main()`, **`t`** is declared to be a variable of `struct temp` type. The storage for the variable **t** is as follows:

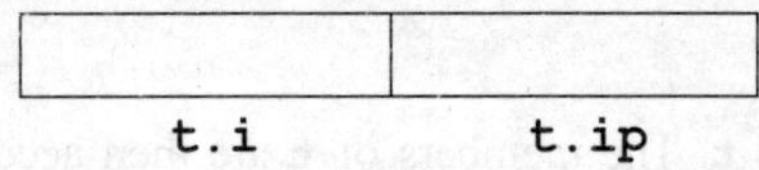

`t.i` is a variable of `int` type whereas **`t.ip`** is a pointer variable to `int` type. **`a`** is declared to be a variable of `int` type and it is initialized with the value 10. The value of **`a`** is assigned to **`t.i`** and the address of **`a`** is assigned to **`t.ip`**, a pointer to `int` type. The value of **`a`** and its address are displayed through **`t.i`** and **`t.ip`** respectively.

10.7 POINTERS AND UNIONS

The concept of pointers can be used in combination with unions in two ways. One, since the address of a union variable can be retrieved using & operator, we can think of pointers to unions. Two, having pointers to different data types as members of unions.

10.7.1 Pointers to Unions

Similar to the concept of pointers to structures, we can think of pointers to unions as well. The address of (&) operator used with a union variable gives the address of the variable, and it can be assigned to a pointer declared to be of the union type. Program 10.12 demonstrates this:

Program 10.12 To Illustrate Pointer to Unions

```
#include <iostream.h>
union temp
{
    int i;
    float f;
};

int main(void)
{
    union temp t, *tp;
```

```
    tp = &t;
    t.i = 10;
    cout << "t.i = " << tp -> i << "\n";
    t.f = 12.35;
    cout << "t.f = " << tp -> f;
    return 0;
}
```

Input-Output:

```
t.i = 10
t.f = 12.35
```

10.7.2 Pointers as Members of Unions

Pointers also can be made members of unions. Program 10.13 reveals this fact.

Program 10.13 To Illustrate Unions Containing Pointers

```
#include <iostream.h>
union temp
{
    int i;
    int *ip;
};

int main(void)
{
    union temp t;
    int a = 20;

    t.i = a;
    cout << "t.i = " << t.i << "\n";
    t.ip = &a;
    cout << "*(t.ip) = " << *(t.ip);
    return 0;
}
```

Input-Output:

```
t.i = 20
*(t.ip) = 20
```

10.8 POINTERS AND FUNCTIONS

Here, we explore the possibility of the following:

- Passing pointers as arguments to functions
- Returning a pointer from a function
- Pointer to a function
- Passing one function as an argument to another function

10.8.1 Passing Pointers as Arguments to Functions

We can even implement call by reference by passing pointers to functions as arguments. Earlier we used the concept of reference variables to implement call by reference. We will now understand passing pointers as arguments. If a function is to be passed a pointer, it has to be reflected in the argument-list of the function prototype (if used) and the header of the function definition.

EXAMPLE

```
void display(int*);
```

The function prototype indicates that the function `display()` requires a pointer to `int` as its argument.

```
void display(int *p)
{
    statements;
}
```

Note the type of the formal argument **p** in the definition of the `display()`. It is rightly declared to be a pointer to `int` type.

While calling the function `display()`, it needs to be passed the address of an integer variable as follows:

```
display(&a);
```

where **a** is a variable of `int` type.

Program 10.14 To Illustrate Call by Reference Using Pointers

```
#include <iostream.h>

 void incr(int*);

int main(void)
{
    int a = 10;

    cout << "Before calling incr() \n";
    cout << "a = " << a << "\n";
    incr(&a);
    cout << "After calling incr() \n";
    cout << "a = " << a << "\n";

    return 0;
}

void incr(int *p)
{
    *p = *p + 1;
}
```

Input-Output:

```
Before calling incr()
a = 10
After calling incr()
a = 11
```

Explanation

The function `incr()` is defined with a formal argument **p**, a pointer to `int` type. The purpose of the function is to increment the value pointed to by the address by one.

In the `main()`, **a** is declared to be a variable of `int` type and is initialized with the value 10. To begin with, the value of **a** is displayed. The function `incr()` is invoked by passing the address of **a** as the actual parameter. Now what happens is, the address of **a** is copied to **p**, the formal parameter of `incr()`. Within the function `incr()`, the value at address in **p** is incremented by one, i.e., `*p = *p + 1;` which turns out to be the variable **a** of `main()` itself. After the function is exited, the value of **a** is redisplayed and it is seen to be 11. So, the function `incr()` could change the value of the variable **a**, which belonged to `main()`.

Pointers versus reference variables: Table 10.2 highlights the differences between pointers and reference variables.

Table 10.2 Differences between Pointers and Reference Variables

Pointers	*References variables*
A pointer can collect the address of a memory block.	A reference variable can not collect the address of a memory block.
When specified as a formal argument, the actual argument should be the address of the variable of the same type as the formal argument.	When specified as a formal argument, the actual argument is the name of the variable of the same type as the formal argument.

Need not be initialized when declared as an auto variable
`int *p;`
is valid.
	Should be initialized when declared as an auto variable
	`int &i;`
	is not valid
	`int i, &j = i;`
	is valid.

The symbol * follows the data type while a pointer is declared.	The symbol & follows the data type while a pointer is declared.

10.8.2 Returning a Pointer from a Function

Under some circumstances, we require functions to return a pointer. The declaration and definition of the functions should indicate that they return a pointer.

The syntax of declaration of a function returning a pointer is as follows:

```
data-type *function_name (arguments);
```

Note the presence of * before function_name. It is to indicate that the function returns a pointer to data-type.

EXAMPLE

```
int *sum(int, int);
```

The function `sum()` is declared to indicate that it requires two parameters of `int` type and it returns a pointer to `int` type.

Program 10.15 To Illustrate a Function Returning a Pointer

```
#include <iostream.h>

int *sum(int, int);

int main(void)
{
    int a, b, *s;

    cout << "Enter two numbers \n";
    cin >> a >> b;
    cout << "a = " << a << "b =" << b << "\n";
    s = sum(a, b);
    cout << "sum = " << *s;

    return 0;
}

int* sum(int a, int b)
{
    int s;
    s = a + b;
    return (&s);
}
```

Input-Output:

```
Enter two numbers
4 5

a = 4  b = 5
s = 9
```

Explanation

The function `sum()` is defined with two arguments of type `int` and it is made to return a pointer to `int` type. The purpose of the function is to find the sum of the values passed to it and return the address of the variable, which stores the sum of the values.

In the `main()`, values are accepted into the variables **a** and **b**. A call is then made to `sum()` by passing **a** and **b** as its actual arguments as `s = sum(a, b);`. Note that **s** is declared to be a pointer to `int` type. The value pointed to by **s**, the sum of **a** and **b**, is then displayed.

10.8.3 Pointers to Functions

In the case of arrays, we know that name of an array gives its base address (address of the first location) and thus acts as a pointer to the first location of the array. This is true even in the case of functions. Name of a function also gives its starting address. Thus, we can use a pointer to invoke a function before which the pointer has to be declared appropriately and assigned the address of the function.

The syntax of declaring a pointer to a function is as follows:

```
data-type (*variable_name)(argument_types);
```

`variable_name` is declared to be a pointer to a function, which returns a value of type `data-type`.

EXAMPLE

```
int (*fnp)(int, int);
```

`fnp` is declared to be a pointer to a function, which takes two arguments of `int` type and returns a value of type `int`. **`fnp`** can now be assigned the address of a function returning a value of `int` type.

```
int sum(int, int);
fnp = sum;
```

`fnp` now points to the function `sum()`.

Program 10.16 To Illustrate Pointers to Functions

```
#include <iostream.h>

int sum(int, int);

int main(void)
{
    int a, b, s, (*fnp)(int, int);

    cout << "Enter two numbers \n";
    cin >> a >> b;
    cout << "a = " << a << "b = " << b << "\n";
    fnp = sum;
    s = (*fnp)(a, b);
    cout << "sum = " << s;

    return 0;
}

int sum(int a, int b)
{
    int s;
    s = a + b;
    return s;
}
```

Input-Output:

```
Enter two numbers
4 6
a = 4  b = 6
sum = 10
```

Explanation

The function `sum()` is defined with two arguments of type `int` and it is made to return value of `int` type. The purpose of the function is to find the sum of the values passed to it and return the sum of the values.

In the `main()`, **a**, **b** and **s** are declared to be variables of `int` type. **fnp** is declared to be a pointer to a function which returns a value of `int` type. Values are accepted into the variables **a** and **b**. The variable **fnp** is assigned the address of the function `sum()` with the statement `fnp = sum;` then, a call is made to `sum()` through the pointer **fnp** with the statement `s = (*fnp)(a, b);` the variable **s** collects the value returned by the function and it is displayed.

10.8.4 Passing One Function as an Argument to Another Function

We know that the name of a function always gives the starting address of the function and thus it is a pointer to the function. We also know that we can pass pointers to data types as arguments to functions. These facts lead us to think of the possibility of passing a pointer to a function to another function. This is certainly possible. Program 10.17 illustrates this.

Program 10.17 To Illustrate Passing One Function as an Argument to Another Function

```
#include <iostream.h>

int lessthan(int, int);
int greaterthan(int, int);
void sort(int a[], int n, int (*fnp)(int, int));

int main(void)
{
    int a[10], i, n;

    cout << "Enter no. of values \n";
    cin >> n;
    cout << "Enter" << n << "values \n";
    for(i = 0; i < n; i++)
        cin >> a[i];

    cout << "Unsorted List \n";
    for(i = 0; i < n; i++)
        cout << a[i] << "\n";

    sort(a, n, lessthan);
    cout << "sorted in decreasing order  \n";
    for(i = 0; i < n; i++)
        cout << a[i] << "\n";

    sort(a, n, greaterthan);
    cout << "sorted in increasing order  \n";
    for(i = 0; i < n; i++)
        cout << a[i] << "\n";
```

```
   return 0;
}

int lessthan(int a, int b)
{
   return (a < b);
}

int greaterthan(int a, int b)
{
   return (a > b);
}

void sort(int a[], int n, int (*fnp)(int, int))
{
   int i, j, t;

   for(i = 0; i < n - 1; i++)
   for(j = i + 1; j < n; j++)
   if (fnp(a[i], a[j]))
   {
        t = a[i];
        a[i] = a[j];
        a[j] = t;
   }

}
```

Input-Output:

```
Enter no. of values
5
Enter 5 values
1 3 4 2 6
Unsorted List
1 3 4 2 6
sorted in decreasing order
6 4 3 2 1
sorted in increasing order
1 2 3 4 6
```

Explanation

The function `lessthan()` is defined with two formal arguments **a** and **b** of `int` type and it is made to return a value of `int` type. The purpose of this function is to collect two numbers into **a** and **b** and return 1 if **a** is found to be less than **b** otherwise 0.

The function `greaterthan()` is also defined with two formal arguments **a** and **b** of `int` type and it is made to return a value of `int` type. The purpose of this function is to collect two numbers into **a** and **b** and return 1 if **a** is found to be greater than **b** otherwise 0.

The function `sort()` is defined with three formal arguments **a**, **n** and **fnp**. The argument **a** is a pointer to integer type; **n** is of `int` type and **fnp** is a pointer to a function which returns an integer value. The purpose of the function is to take an array of integers and sort the elements of the array in the order determined by the function pointed to by **fnp**.

In the `main()`, **a** is declared to be an array of `int` type and of size 10. Maximum 10 elements can be accepted into the array. **i** and **n** are declared to be variables of `int` type. The variable **n** is to collect the no. of elements to be accepted into the array **a** and the variable **i** is to select each location of the array.

After accepting a value for the variable **n**, **n** values are accepted into the array **a** and they are displayed. The list is then sorted in the decreasing order with the call `sort(a,n,lessthan)`. Within the function `sort()`, the function `lessthan()` is invoked to compare two numbers which returns true when the first number is less than the second number being compared. Thus, the list is sorted in the decreasing order. The sorted list is then displayed.

The list is then sorted in the increasing order with the call `sort(a, n, greaterthan)`. Within the function `sort()`, this time, the function `greaterthan()` is invoked to compare two numbers which returns true when the first number is greater than the second number being compared. Thus the list is sorted in the increasing order. The sorted list is once again displayed.

A list of **n** numbers is accepted into the array **a**. The unsorted list is displayed. The function `sort()` is invoked by passing the array **a**, **n** and `lessthan` as the actual arguments (Note that `lessthan` is the address of the function `lessthan()`, which is mapped onto the third argument **fnp** of `sort()`) as `sort(a, n, lessthan);` the function call sorts the elements in the array **a** in the decreasing order and then the function call `sort(a, n, greaterthan);` sorts the elements in the array **a** in the increasing order. (Note that this time, `greaterthan`, the address of the function `greaterthan()` is passed and it is mapped onto **fnp**, the third parameter of the function `sort()`).

10.9 POINTERS TO POINTERS

We now know that a pointer is a special type of variable and it can collect the address of another variable. Once a pointer is assigned the address of a plain variable, the value of the plain variable can then be accessed indirectly through the pointer with the help of * (value at address) operator. Since the pointer is also a variable, it is also allocated memory space of size two bytes and its address also is retrievable. The address of the pointer variable itself can also be stored in another appropriately declared variable. The variable which can store the address of a pointer variable itself is termed as **Pointer to Pointer**. Note that a pointer to pointer adds a further level of indirection. The syntax of declaring a pointer to pointer is as follows:

```
data-type **variable;
```

Note the usage of two *'s before the pointer variable name. They are to indicate that the variable is a pointer to a pointer to a variable of type `data-type`.

Consider the following declarations:

```
int a = 10, *ap, **app;
```

Here, **a** is a plain integer variable. The variable **ap** is a pointer to `int` type and the variable **app** is declared to be a pointer to pointer to `int` type (Note that two *'s are used). Now, **ap** can be assigned the address of the variable **a**. The variable **app** can be assigned the address of **ap**. The following statements accomplish these assignments:

```
ap = &a;
app = &ap;
```

To access the value of **a** through **ap** , we use ***ap**.

To access the value of **a** through **app** , we use ****ap**.

Program 10.18 To Illustrate a Pointer to a Pointer

```
#include <iostream.h>

int main(void)
{
   int a = 10, *ap, **app;

   ap = &a;
   app = &ap;

   cout << "Address of a = " << ap << "\n";
   cout << "Address of ap = " << app << "\n";
   cout << "value of a through ap = " << *ap << "\n";
   cout << "value of a through app = " << **app;

   return 0;
}
```

Input-Output:

```
Address of a = 0xfff4

Address of ap = 0xfff2

value of a through ap = 10

value of a through app = 10
```

Explanation

In Program 10.18, we have seen that there are two levels of indirection to access the value of the variable **a**. This was accomplished through a pointer to pointer. Theoretically, the levels of indirection can be further extended. There is no constraint imposed on this. Further levels of indirection like three levels and four levels are rarely used because of the following fact: Higher the level of indirection, lesser will be the degree of comprehensibility.

10.10 DYNAMIC MEMORY ALLOCATION

We know that the variables are named memory locations and they are to hold data to be manipulated by the programs. So far, in all our programs, memory locations for the variables were allocated during compilation time itself. For instance, the declarations `int a;` `float f;` and `char c;` direct the compiler to allocate two bytes, four bytes and one byte of memory to hold integer value, float value and char value respectively. The quantum of memory is determined by the compiler itself depending on the type of variables. This type of memory allocation is termed as **static memory allocation**. Consider the declaration of arrays in C++.

```
int a[10];
```

declares **a** to be an array of `int` type and size 10. The compiler thus allocates 10 contiguous memory locations as follows:

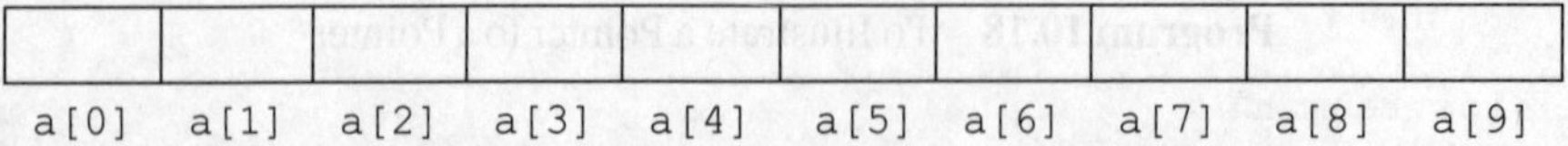

a[0] a[1] a[2] a[3] a[4] a[5] a[6] a[7] a[8] a[9]

Memory locations are allocated for the array statically. Here we identify two shortcomings. Firstly, what if we need to deal with more than ten values of `int` type during runtime of the program, we can not increase the size of the array during runtime. Secondly, many a time, not all the locations are used, when this is the case, we can not decrease the size of the array. As a result, memory goes wasted. This is where the concept of **dynamic memory allocation** comes into picture. As the name itself indicates, memory can be allocated dynamically, i.e., during runtime of the programs. While allocating, we can specify the size of the memory block to be allocated and also we can release the unwanted memory blocks for later use.

10.10.1 New and Delete Operators

C++ has the following operators to deal with dynamic memory allocation and deallocation:

1. new
2. delete

The new operator is to allocate the required amount of memory dynamically. The syntax of its usage is as follows:

```
ptr = new data-type;
```

where **`ptr`** is a pointer to the `data-type` specified after the keyword *new* and it collects the address of the memory block allocated by the new operator.

EXAMPLE

```
int *ip;
ip = new int;
```

The amount of memory required to store an integer gets allocated and its address is assigned to the pointer variable **ip**.

```
struct emp
{
    int eno;
    char name[20];
    float salary;
};

emp *ep;

ep = new emp;
```

The amount of memory required to store a variable of type **emp** gets allocated and its address is assigned to the pointer variable **ep**.

The delete operator is to release the memory which was earlier allocated by the new operator.

The syntax of its usage is as follows:

```
delete ptr;
```

where `ptr` is the pointer to memory block being released.

EXAMPLE

```
delete ip;
```

releases the memory pointed to by the integer pointer **ip**.

```
delete ep;
```

releases the memory pointed to by the pointer **ep** of **emp** type.

Every usage of new operator should be matched by a delete operator usage.

Using the new operator, we can create arrays dynamically, i.e., we can specify the number of elements of the required type during run time and allocate the required amount of memory. The syntax of using new operator to dynamically allocate arrays is:

```
ptr = new data-type[size];
```

where **ptr** is a pointer to data-type and size is the number of elements of the array to be allocated. Size can be either a constant or a variable.

EXAMPLE 1

```
int *a;
a = new int[5];
```

allocates memory for an integer array of size five and the address of the first element is assigned to the variable **a**.

Program 10.19 To Allocate an Array Dynamically

```
#include <iostream.h>

int main(void)
{
    int *a, n, i;

    cout << "Enter no. of elements \n";
    cin >> n;
    a = new int[n];

    cout << "Enter" << n << "elements \n";
    for(i = 0; i < n; i++)
        cin >>  a[i];
    cout << "The list of elements \n";
    for(i = 0; i < n; i++)
        cout <<  a[i];
    delete a; // Release the allocated memory

    return 0;
}
```

Input-Output:

```
Enter no. of elements
5
Enter 5 elements
1 2 3 4 5
The list of elements
1 2 3 4 5
```

Explanation

In Program 10.19, the variable **a** is declared to be a pointer to `int` type. **n** and **i** are declared to be plain variables of `int` type. The purpose of the program is to create an array dynamically by specifying the size of the array during runtime. The pointer variable **a** is to collect the address of the first integer. The variable **n** is to accept the size of the array during runtime. The variable **i** is used as the array index.

After accepting the size of the array, the required amount of memory space is allocated with the statement `a = new int[n];`. On successful execution of the statement, a block of memory large enough to accommodate *n* integers is allocated in the memory heap and the address of the first element of the array is assigned to the pointer variable **a**. Now, the array is filled with integer values and they are displayed. Then the statement `delete a;` releases the block of memory pointed to by the variable **a**.

Program 10.20 To Allocate Memory for Employee Details Dynamically

```
#include <iostream.h>

struct emp
{
    int empno;
    char name[20];
    float salary;
};
int main(void)
{
    emp *ep;
    int n, i;

    cout << "Enter the number of Employees \n";
    cin >> n;

    ep = new emp[n];
    cout << "Enter" << n << "employees details \n";
    for(i = 0; i < n; i++)
        cin >> ep[i].empno >> ep[i].name >> ep[i].salary;
    cout << "Employees Details \n";
    for(i = 0; i < n; i++)
        cout << ep[i].empno << ep[i].name << ep[i].salary << "\n";
    delete ep;

    return 0;
}
```

Input-Output:

```
Enter the number of Employees
2
Enter 2 employees details
121    Nishu      23000
124    Harsha     34500

Employees Details
121      Nishu         23000.00
124      Harsha        34500.00
```

Explanation

The statement `ep = new emp[n];` allocates memory for storing *n* employees' details and the address of the first block is assigned to the variable **ep**. Using array notation, the data for the employees are accepted and they are displayed.

REVIEW QUESTIONS

10.1 What is a pointer?

10.2 What are the advantages offered by pointers?

10.3 Give the significance of & and * operators.

10.4 Give an account of pointer arithmetic.

10.5 Explain how one-dimensional array elements are accessed using pointer notation.

10.6 Explain how two-dimensional array elements are accessed using pointer notation.

10.7 `a[i]` and `i[a]` are equivalent. Justify.

10.8 What is call by value?

10.9 What is call by reference?

10.10 Differentiate between call by value and call by reference.

10.11 Explain the concept of passing one function as the argument to another function with an example.

10.12 Explain the concept of pointers to functions.

10.13 Differentiate between static memory allocation and dynamic memory allocation.

10.14 Mention the operators supported by C++ to deal with dynamic memory allocation.

10.15 What is a self-referential structure?

10.16 Explain the concept of pointers to structures.

True/False Questions

T10.1 Pointers facilitate static memory allocation.

T10.2
```
int *p1;
float *p2;
p1 = p2;
```
is a valid statement.

T10.3 `int *p;`
`p += 2;`
is a valid statement.

T10.4 `int *p1, *p2;`
`p1 < p2`
is a valid test-expression.

T10.5 We can have a pointer to a pointer to an integer.

T10.6 Pointers enable us to write efficient programs.

T10.7 We can access array elements using pointers.

T10.8 We can use pointers as members of structures.

T10.9 We can pass one function as argument to another function.

T10.10 There is no way of protecting the variables from altering which are passed by reference.

PROGRAMMING EXERCISES

P10.1 What is the output of the following programs?

(a)

```
int main(void)
{
    int a[10], *ap, *bp;
    ap = a;
    bp = &a[0];
    cout << ap-bp;
    return 0;
}
```

(b)

```
int main(void)
{
    int a[10] = {1, 2, 5, 7}, *ap, *bp;
    ap = a;
    bp = &a[3];
    cout << *ap << *bp;

    return 0;
}
```

P10.2 Write a program to sort a list of numbers using pointers notation.

P10.3 Write a program to create a list of students' details using a dynamic array.

P10.4 Write a function to extract a part of a string using pointers.

P10.5 Write a program to sort a matrix row-wise using pointer notation for the elements of the matrix.

P10.6 Write a program to find the LCM and GCD of two numbers using a function.
The function call should be as follows: `lcm_gcd(a, b, &i, &g);` where `a` and `b` are two numbers (Inputs) and **i** and **g** are two variables collecting the LCM and the GCD of the two numbers.

P10.7 Write a program using a function to accept an amount in figures and display the amount in words.

Example:

Amount in figures:	478
Amount in words:	Four hundred seventy eight only

P10.8 Write a program using a function to accept an amount and format it using commas for better readability.

Example:

Unformatted amount	: 45678765
Formatted amount	: 4,56,78,765

Chapter 11

The C++ Preprocessor

11.1 INTRODUCTION

The preprocessor is another distinctive feature of C++ (and C). In other higher level languages, the source program is submitted directly to the corresponding language compiler, which in turn produces object code. But in C++, the source program is first passed to the program called **preprocessor**, the preprocessor acts on the source program according to the instructions specified to it in the source program and the output produced by the preprocessor is then submitted to C++ compiler. The instructions specified in the source program to the preprocessor are called the **preprocessor directives**. The preprocessor plays a very important role in enhancing the readability, modifiability, and portability of the C++ programs.

Source-program ⟶ Preprocessor ⟶ Expanded source program ⟶ C++ compiler

Following are the general rules governing the preprocessor directives:

1. All preprocessor directives should start with the symbol #. ANSI allows the symbol to be preceded by spaces or tabs.
2. Only one directive can appear in a line.
3. The directives are not terminated by semicolons.
4. The preprocessor directives can be placed anywhere in a source program. The directives apply to the source code, which follows them.

The preprocessor directives are broadly classified into three types based on the purposes for which they are used.

1. Files Inclusion Directives
2. Macros Definition Directives
3. Conditional Compilation Directives.

11.2 FILES INCLUSION DIRECTIVE [#INCLUDE]

The #include preprocessor directive has already been used in all our programs and we know that it is used to include a file as part of the source program file. For example, in response to the directive #include <stdio.h>, the preprocessor expands the source file by embedding the contents of the header file stdio. h, before the source program is submitted to the C++ compiler. In all our earlier programs, #include has been used to include the header files. As a matter of fact, contents of any text file can be included as part of a source program with the help of the directive. If the file name is enclosed within double quotes then the file is expected to be available in the current working directory. Suppose a file by name functions. c in the current working directory, contains the definitions for the functions used by a program, the file functions.c can be included as part of the source program with the directive #include "functions.c".

```
#include <iostream.h>
#include "functions.c"
int main(void)
{
   return 0;
}
```

Here, the preprocessor embeds the contents of the header file **stdio.h** and contents of the file **functions.c** into the source program before the program is passed onto the compiler.

11.3 MACROS DEFINITION DIRECTIVES [#DEFINE, #INDEF]

A macro is defined to be a symbolic name assigned to a segment of text. The preprocessor directive #define is used for defining macros. The syntax of its usage is as follows:

```
#define MACRO_NAME segment_of_text
```

Here, `MACRO_NAME` is the name of a macro; it should conform to the rules, which are used to construct valid identifiers and normally it is written using upper case letters just to distinguish it from the identifiers. `segment_of_text` is actually the string referred to by the `MACRO_NAME`. Once a symbolic name (`MACRO_NAME`) is assigned to a segment of text, throughout the program, the symbolic name can be used in place of the segment of text. The preprocessor then replaces all the occurrences of the `MACRO_NAME` by the `segment of text.`

EXAMPLES

1. `#define COUNT 10`

COUNT becomes the symbolic name for the constant **10.**

2. `#define NO_OF_STUDENTS 100`

NO_OF_STUDENTS becomes the symbolic name for the constant **100.**

Program 11.1 To Illustrate Macros Definition

```
#define PI 3.14
#include <iostream.h>

int main(void)
{
```

```
    int r;
    float area, circum;

    cout << "Enter radius of a circle \n";
    cin >> r;

    area = PI * r * r;
    circum = 2 * PI * r;
    cout << "Area = " << area << "\n";
    cout << "Circumference = " << circum<< "\n";

    return 0;
}
```

The preprocessor acts on the source program and produces the following output. Note that the macro `PI` has been replaced by the value `3.14` by the preprocessor. The process of replacement of macros by their corresponding segments of texts is termed as **macros substitution**. The output produced by the preprocessor is then submitted to the compiler for compilation.

```
#define PI 3.14
#include <iostream.h>

int main(void)
{
    int r;
    float area, circum;

    cout << "Enter radius of a circle \n";
    cin >> r;

    area = 3.14 * r * r;
    circum = 2 * 3.14 * r;
    cout << " Area = " << area << "\n";
    cout << "Circumference = " << circum << "\n";

    return 0;
}
```

Input-Output:

```
Enter radius of a circle
4

Area = 50.240002
Circumference = 25.120001
```

In Program 11.1, the segment of text happened to be a numeric value. In fact, it can be a string enclosed within double quotes or a C++ statement.

EXAMPLE

```
#define ACCEPT cout << "Enter two numbers \n"
```

Here, the macro `ACCEPT` is assigned a C++ statement `cout << "Enter two numbers \n"`.

Program 11.2 To Illustrate a Macro Definition

```
#define ACCEPT cout << "Enter two numbers \n"
#include <iostream.h>

int main(void)
{
    int a, b;

    ACCEPT;

    /* Expanded to cout << "Enter two numbers \n" by the preprocessor */
    cin >> a >> b;
    cout << "a = " << a << "b = " << b << "\n";
    return 0;
}
```

Input-Output:

```
Enter two numbers
4 5
a = 4 b = 5
```

Note: We can use **const** qualifier also to define constants.

11.3.1 Macros with Arguments

The preprocessor permits us to pass arguments to macros in much the same way as we pass arguments to functions. Let us now explore the possibility of passing arguments to macros and understand how macros with arguments are helpful.
Consider the following C++ statement:

```
if ( a > 0) a = a + 1
```

If we are to assign a symbolic name for this, we would define a macro INCREMENT_A as follows:

```
#define INCREMENT_A if ( a > 0) a = a + 1
```

Consider another C++ conditional statement:

```
if ( b > 0) b = b + 1
```

If we are to assign a symbolic name for the statement, we can define another macro INCREMENT_B as follows:

```
#define INCREMENT_B if ( b > 0) b = b + 1
```

As can be seen, both the statements have the same structure except the variable names. Here, we can define only one macro by name `INCREMENT` with an argument and it can represent both the conditional statements considered earlier. The macro is defined as follows:

```
#define INCREMENT(x) if ( x > 0 ) x = x + 1
```

Now,

INCREMENT(a) would be expanded to the statement if (a > 0) a = a + 1

INCREMENT(b) would be expanded to the statement if (b > 0) b = b + 1

INCREMENT(c) would be expanded to the statement if (c > 0) c = c + 1

and so on.

Program 11.3 To Illustrate a Macro with Arguments

```
#include <iostream.h>
#define INCREMENT(x) if (x > 0) x = x + 1

int main(void)
{
    int a, b;

    cout << "Enter the value of a \n";
    cin >> a;
    cout << "Given value of a = " << a << "\n";
    INCREMENT(a);      /* would expand to if ( a > 0) a = a + 1 */
    cout << "New Value of a = " << a << "\n";

    cout << "Enter the value of b \n";
    cin >> b;
    cout << "Given value of b = " << b << "\n";
    INCREMENT(b);      /* would expand to if ( b > 0) b = b + 1 */
    cout << "New Value of b = "<< b << "\n";
    return 0;
}
```

Input-Output:

```
Enter the value of a
4

Given value of a = 4
New Value of a = 5

Enter the value of b
6

Given value of b = 6
New Value of b = 7
```

Consider the preprocessor directive #define SQUARE(x) x * x. The macro SQUARE(x) is to find the square of the argument x. Now, the macro SQUARE(3) expands to 3 * 3 . We would get the square of 3, which is 9. To find the square of the expression a + 2, we would use the macro SQUARE(a + 2). The macro SQUARE(a + 2) expands to a + 2 * a + 2, the value of the expression will not be the square of a + 2. This problem is eliminated by enclosing the argument within parentheses in the replacement string as (x) * (x). New definition of the macro would then be

```
#define SQUARE(x) (x) * (x)
```

Now, SQUARE(a + 2) is expanded to (a + 2) * (a + 2), which evaluates correctly to the square of a + 2.

It is always better to enclose each occurrence of the argument in the replacement string within a pair of parentheses so that the corresponding macros are expanded to correct forms of expressions.

Now, consider the expression 100/SQUARE(2). Here, the expression expands to 100/(2) * (2). According to the associativity rule the value of the expression would be 50 * 2 = 100. But actually square of 2 , which is 4, should divide 100 and the result should be 25. We would be able to get the correct expression after expansion by the preprocessor if we enclose the entire replacement string within a pair of parentheses. The correct way of defining the macro would thus be

```
#define SQUARE(x) ((x) * (x))
```

Now, the expression 100 / SQUARE(2) is expanded to 100/((2) * (2)). This expression would evaluate correctly to 100 / 4 = 25. Thus, it is even better to enclose the replacement string itself within a pair of parentheses if the replacement string happens to be an expression.

Program 11.4 To Find the Square of a Number—Macro with Argument

```
#include <iostream.h>
#define SQUARE(x) ((x) * (x))

int main(void)
{
    int a = 5, sqr, b;

    sqr = SQUARE(4);
    cout << "Square of 4 = " << sqr << "\n";
    sqr = SQUARE(a+2);
    cout << "Square of a+2 = " << sqr << "\n";
    b = 100 / SQUARE(2);
    cout << "b = " << b << "\n";

    return 0;
}
```

Input-Output:

```
Square of 4 = 16
Square of a+2 = 49
b = 25
```

Explanation

In Program 11.4, the macro SQUARE is defined with an argument **x**. It is important to note that the argument **x** is enclosed within a pair of parentheses in the substitution string. It is to ensure that the argument in the macro call is expanded correctly when the argument is an expression. During the preprocessing:

The statement `sqr = SQUARE(4);` is expanded to `sqr = ((4) * (4))`

The statement `sqr = SQUARE(a + 2);` is expanded to `sqr = ((a+2) * (a+2))`

And the statement `b = 100 / SQUARE(2);` is expanded to `b = 100/((2) * (2))`

The expanded code is then passed on to the compiler to generate the appropriate code.

Some more examples of macros with arguments

1. `#define CUBE(x)          (x) *(x) *(x)`
   Finds the cube of *x*.

2. `#define MAX(x, y)        ((x) >(y)) ? (x) : (y)`
   Finds the maximum of *x* and *y*.

3. `#define SI(p, t, r)      ((p) * (t) *(r) ) / 100`
   Finds the simple interest given the principle, rate of interest and time period.

4. `#define AREA(b, h)       0.5 * (b) * (h)`
   Finds the area of a triangle whose base is *b* and height is *h*.

5. `#define AREA(l, b)       (l) * (b)`
   Finds the area of a rectangle whose length is *l* and breadth is *b*.

Macros can even be extended into multiple lines. In this case each line except the last line must be terminated by a backslash \.

EXAMPLE

```
#define MSG    Learning C++ \
is quite interesting
```

Here the segment of text "`Learning C++ is quite interesting`" is a replacement string for the macro `MSG`. Note that there is a backslash \ at the end of the first line.

Note: We can use **inline** functions also in place of macros with arguments also.

11.3.2 Macros vs Functions

A macro is a symbolic name assigned to a segment of text. The segment of text can be merely a sequence of digits or it can be a string enclosed within double quotes or it can even be a C++ statement. Whereas a function is a self-contained program by itself. As far as usage of the macros with arguments and functions in programs is concerned, they look alike. But there are significant differences between them. We will now try to figure out the differences between macros and functions with the help of Program 11.5.

Program 11.5 To Illustrate the Differences between Macros and Functions

```
#include <iostream.h>
#define SQUARE(x) ((x) * (x))

int square(int x)
{
   return (x * x);
}

int main(void)
{
   int a = 6, sqr_of_a;
   cout << " a = " << a << "\n";
   sqr_of_a = SQUARE(a);
   cout << " Square of a through the macro SQURE(a) = " << sqr_of_a
<< "\n";
   sqr_of_a = square(a);
   cout << " Square of a through the function square(a) = " << sqr_of_a
<< "\n";

   return 0;
}
```

Input-Output:

```
a = 6
Square of a through the macro SQUARE(a) = 36
Square of a through the function square(a) = 36
```

Explanation

In Program 11.5, the preprocessor directive `#define SQUARE(x) ((x) * (x))` defines the macro `SQUARE` with an argument **x** to represent the replacement string **((x) * (x))**. The purpose of the macro definition is to find the square of a number.

The function `square()` is defined with an argument **x** of type and it is made to return a value of `int` type. The purpose of the function is also to find out the square of an integer passed to it and return it to the calling program.

In the `main()`, **a** and **sqr_of_a** are declared to be variables of `int` type. The variable **a** is to collect a number, square of which is to be found out and the variable **sqr_of_a** is to collect the square of **a**. The variable **a** is passed as an argument to the macro `SQUARE` in the statement `sqr_of_a = SQUARE(a)` and to the function `square()` in the statement `sqr_of_a = square(a);`. During the preprocessing stage, the statement `sqr_of_a = SQUARE(a)` is expanded to `sqr_of_a = ((a) * (a))`. But no change is made to the statement `sqr_of_a = square(a);` by the preprocessor. The expanded source code is passed on to the compiler. The compiler generates the appropriate sequence of instructions for both the statements.

Table 11.1 highlights the differences between macros and functions.

Table 11.1 Differences between Macros and Functions

Macros	*Functions*
Macros are expanded to their replacement strings during preprocessing.	Function calls are not affected during preprocessing.
Arguments to macros are merely string tokens. No data type is associated with the arguments.	Arguments to functions should be declared to be of some data type(Built-in or user-defined).
During compilation, no type checking of arguments takes place.	During compilation, type checking of arguments takes place. If the actual arguments are not compatible with formal arguments, the compiler reports an error.
More occurrences of a macro in a program lead to consumption of more memory space. This is because of the fact that each occurrence of the macro in the program is replaced by its replacement string by the preprocessor.	More calls to a function does not lead to consumption of more memory space. This is because of the fact that only one copy of the function will be available in the memory and whenever the function is called, the program control itself is transferred to the function; the instructions in the function are executed and after the execution of the function, the control is transferred back to the calling program.
A macro name does not evaluate to an address.	The function name evaluates to the address of the function and thus can be used in the contexts requiring a pointer.
Macro definitions can be nested.	Function definitions can not be nested.
No CPU overhead involved.	Considerable amount of CPU time is consumed in tracking the transfer of control from a calling function to a called function and from the called function back to the calling function and also in establishing data communication between the functions like passing actual parameters to called function and returning a value from the called function.

11.3.3 Advantages of Macros

When macros are used as symbolic names for some replacement strings, which are used quite often in a program, following are the advantages offered by macros definition:

1. The macros definition increases the degree of readability of programs since the names selected for the macros are normally selected to be reflective of the meaning of the replacement strings.
2. The macros definition enhances easier modifiability since any change made in the replacement string in the macro definition will be effected in all its occurrences throughout the program.

EXAMPLE

Consider the following macro definition:

```
#define NO_OF_STUDENTS 100
```

Here, quite obviously, the symbolic name `NO_OF_STUDENTS` to the constant 100 is more readable than the constant itself. Suppose the macro NO_OF_STUDENTS has been used in our program in, say, 10 different places. Later, if the number of students changes, say, to 200, then only one change is to be made in the program. That is, in the macro definition, we replace 100 by 200 as:

```
#define NO_OF_STUDENTS 200
```

Thus, modification becomes simple. Once this is done, the preprocessor takes care of replacing all the occurrences of the macro by 200.

3. Sometimes, macros can be used in place of functions, thereby eliminating the CPU overhead involved in the execution of functions. Macros can be used in place of functions when the number of calls to macros is less.

11.3.4 The Stringizing Operator

The stringizing operator serves the purpose of converting an argument in a macro to a string.

EXAMPLE

```
#define macro(a)   cout << #a;
```

Here the argument **a** to the macro is converted into the string "a".

Program 11.6 To Illustrate Stringizing Operator #

```
#include <iostream.h>
#define prod(x) cout << #x "=" << x;

int main(void)
{
    int a = 8, b = 7;
    prod(a * b);
    return 0;
}
```

Input-Output:

```
a * b = 56
```

Explanation

In Program 11.6, the statement `prod(a * b)` expands to cout << `"a * b" " =" << a * b;` which in turn gets transformed to cout << `"a * b =" << a * b;`. Note that the strings `"a * b"` and `" ="` are concatenated to produce `"a * b ="`.

As a result, the product of the values of **a** and **b** is calculated and displayed.

11.3.5 The Token Pasting Operator

The token pasting operator supported by ANSI standard enables us to merge two tokens into a single token.

EXAMPLE

Suppose **t1** and **t2** are two tokens, which are to be merged together to form a single token **t1t2**, the following preprocessor directive can be used:

```
#define paste(t1, t2) t1##t2
```

Now, all appearances of **paste(t1, t2)** in a program will be replaced by **t1t2** by the preprocessor.

Program 11.7 To Illustrate the Token Pasting Operator ##

```
#include <iostream.h>
#define DISPLAY(i) cout << "b" #i "= " << b##i

int main(void)
{
    int b1 = 10, b2 =20;

    DISPLAY(1);
    DISPLAY(2);

    return 0;
}
```

Input-Output:

```
b1 = 10
b2 = 20
```

Explanation

In Program 11.7, the macro DISPLAY has been defined with an argument. The replacement string contains a cout statement which in turn contains both the stringizing operator # and the token pasting operator ## within the control string and the argument respectively. As a result, DISPLAY(1) is expanded to cout << `"b1 = " << b1;` and similarly DISPLAY(2) also is expanded to cout << `"b2 = " << b2;`

11.3.6 The #undef Directive

The #undef directive is used to remove a macro which has been previously defined using #define. The syntax of its usage is as follows:

```
#undef MACRO_NAME
```

EXAMPLE

```
#undef COUNT
```

As a result of this directive, the macro `COUNT` loses its existence.

11.4 CONDITIONAL COMPILATION DIRECTIVES [#IFDEF, IFNDEF, #ENDIF, #IF, #ELSE]

Conditional compilation, as the name itself indicates, offers us a way for compiling only the required sections of code in a source program. Conditional compilation of source programs is necessitated by the following reasons:

1. To make the programs portable so that they can be compiled according to the machines being used.

2. To make the programs suit different situations without the need for rewriting the programs from scratch.

Conditional compilation is accomplished with the help of the following conditional compilation directives:

11.4.1 #ifdef - #endif Directives

The `#ifdef - #endif` directives check for the definition of a macro. The syntax of their usage is as follows:

```
#ifdef MACRO_NAME
        statements
#endif
```

Here, the statements will be considered for compilation only when `MACRO_NAME` has been defined. Otherwise the statements will be ignored by the compiler.

11.4.2 #ifdef - #else - #endif Directives

```
syntax:
#ifdef MACRO_NAME
    statements-1
#else
    statements-2
#endif
```

Here, if `MACRO_NAME` has been defined previously, `statements-1` will be compiled. Otherwise, `statements-2` will be compiled.

Program 11.8 To Illustrate Conditional Compilation: Usage of #ifdef - #else - #endif

```
#include <iostream.h>
#define SUM

int main(void)
{
    int a = 1, b = 5, r;

    #ifdef SUM
        r = a + b;
        cout << " Sum = " << r << "\n";
    #else
        r = a - b;
        cout << "Difference = " << r << "\n";
    #endif

    return 0;
}
```

Input-Output:

```
Sum = 6
```

Explanation

In Program 11.8, a macro by name SUM has been defined with the directive #define SUM. In the `main()`, since `#ifdef SUM` evaluates to true, the statements `r = a + b; cout << "sum = " << r;` are selected for compilation. The statements between `#else` and `#endif` are ignored by the compiler. As a result, when the program is run, the program finds the sum of the variables **a** and **b**, and displays it.

If we remove the definition of the macro SUM and compile and run the program, the program finds the difference between **a** and **b**, and displays it. This is because, in the absence of the macro SUM, the statements between `#else` and `#endif` are compiled.

11.4.3 #ifdef - #elif - #else - #endif Directives

```
Sintax:
#ifdef macro1
    statements-1
#elif defined(macro2)
    statements-2
#elif defined(macro3)
    statements-3
#elif defined(macro4)
    statements-4
#else
    statements-5
endif
```

Here, only one out of many alternative blocks of code will be considered for compilation depending on what macro has been defined previously.

Program 11.9 To Illustrate Conditional Compilation: Usage of #ifdef - #elif defined() - #else - #endif

```
#include <iostream.h>
#define MULT

int main(void)
{
    int a = 10, b = 5, r;

    #ifdef SUM
        r = a + b;
        cout << " Sum = " << r << "\n";
    #elif defined(DIFF)
        r = a - b;
        cout << "Difference = " << r << "\n";
    #elif defined(MULT)
        r = a * b;
        cout << "Product = " << r << "\n";
    #elif defined(DIVIDE)
        r = a / b;
        cout << "Quotient = " << r << "\n";
    else
```

```
    r = a % b;
    cout << "Remainder = " << r << "\n";
    #endif

    return 0;
}
```

Input-Output:

```
Product = 50
```

Explanation

In Program 11.9, since the macro defined is MULT, the statements:

```
r = a * b;

cout << "Product = " << r << "\n";
```

only will be compiled and other alternative blocks are skipped by the compiler. As a result, when the program is run, it displays the product of the values of the variables **a** and **b**.

11.4.4 #ifndef Directive

The `#ifndef` directive is just the negative of the `#ifdef` directive. It is normally used to define a macro after ascertaining that the macro has not been defined previously. The syntax of the directive for the purpose is as follows:

```
#ifndef macro
    #define macro
#endif
```

EXAMPLE

```
#ifndef SUM
    #define SUM
#endif
```

#if directive: The `#if` directive is to select a block of code for compilation when a test-expression (rather than a macro) evaluates to true. Otherwise to ignore the block of code for compilation.

```
#if - #endif
#if - #else - #endif
#if - #elif defined() - #else - #endif
```

are similar to their `#ifdef` counterparts except the fact that, here macros are replaced by test-expressions.

The example programs, which were written to illustrate conditional compilation, were just to highlight the fact that the compilation can be done selectively with respect to blocks of code. When we compiled and ran the programs, we understood this fact. In real life programming environments, we need to prepare programs in such a way that the programs run on different types of machines or the programs should cater to different clients. The facility of conditional compilation plays an important role since the same programs are made to suit to the differing environments by conditionally compiling the required sections of code for a particular environment.

EXAMPLE

Suppose a program being written is targeted to two types of machines: 1. IBMPC and 2. VAX 8810.

Since the word length, memory size and other architectural details vary between the two systems, the sections of code in the program, which are dependent on these, should be selectively compiled. The following code accomplishes this:

```
#ifdef IBMPC
    statements for IBMPC
#else
    statements for VAX 8810
#endif
```

IBMPC is a macro.

11.4.5 The #error Directive

The `#error` directive when it is encountered displays some error message and terminates the compilation process.

The syntax of its usage is as follows:

```
#error message
```

Program 11.10 demonstrates the usage of the directive

Program 11.10 To Illustrate #error Directive

```
#if !defined(M)
#error M NOT DEFINED
#endif

#include <iostream.h>
int main(void)
{
    cout << "Welcome";
    return 0;
}
```

Since the macro `M` has not been defined, `!defined(M)` evaluates to true and the control reaches the `#error` directive which when executed displays the message `M NOT DEFINED` and terminates the compilation process.

11.5 OTHER STANDARD DIRECTIVES

The standard C++ provides the following two directives:

11.5.1 The #pragma Directive

The `#pragma` directive is an implementation specific directive and it allows us to specify various instructions to the compiler.

The syntax of its usage is as follows:

```
#pragma name
```

where `name` refers to a kind of instruction to the compiler supported by the C++ implementation. The `name` can vary from one C++ implementation to another. If a particular name is not supported by a C++ implementation, it is simply ignored. Some examples of #pragma directives include

```
#pragma startup <function name>
```

which indicates that the function identified by the function name is to be executed before the `main()`

```
#pragma exit <function name>
```

which indicates that the function identified by the function name is to be executed after the program terminates.

```
#pragma argsused
```

which suppresses the error message "parameter not used" in case parameters are not used within the functions.

11.5.2 The #line Directive

The `#line` directive informs the line number of the next line in the current source file. The syntax of the directive is as follows:

```
#line constant "source_file"
```

EXAMPLE

```
#line 5 "fact.cpp"
```

REVIEW QUESTIONS

11.1 What is the role of preprocessor during compilation?

11.2 What are preprocessor directives?

11.3 Mention the need for #define.

11.4 What is the need for #include?

11.5 Define a macro.

11.6 Why do we need macros with arguments?

11.7 Differentiate between functions and macros.

11.8 Explain the concept of nesting of macros.

11.9 What is the need for conditional compilation?

11.10 Explain conditional compilation related directives.

True/False Questions

T11.1 Macro is a symbolic name assigned to a segment of text-expression.

T11.2 Macros can be defined with arguments.

T11.3 There can be a space or tab space between # and define.

T11.4 The symbol # can appear in any column.

T11.5 Macros can be multiline.

T11.6 A macro with arguments is just like a function with the same arguments.

PROGRAMMING EXERCISES

P11.1 Write a program to find the maximum of two numbers using a macro.

P11.2 Write a program to find the smallest of three numbers using the concept of nesting of macro calls. (Use a macro to find the maximum of two numbers)

P11.3 Define a macro by name RECT with two arguments length and breadth. Write a program to find the area of a rectangle for the given values of length and breadth.

P11.4 Define a macro by name SI with three parameters *p*, *t* and *r* (*p*-Principle amount, *t*-Time period, *r*-Rate). Write a program to find the simple interest for two sets of values of *p*, *t* and *r* using the macro.

P11.5 Define a macro by name SWAP with two arguments **a** and **b** which swaps the arguments and write a program to call the macro.

P11.6 Write a program to illustrate conditional compilation.

Chapter 12

Classes and Objects

12.1 INTRODUCTION

We discussed the structure concept at length earlier and we used the concept of structure to logically group data items, which may or may not be of different types. One more important feature supported by the concept of structures, which was not mentioned earlier, is that we can even have functions as members within them. The functions defined within the structure are called the **member functions** of the structure. The member functions are to perform the required manipulations over the member data of the structure.

The syntax of the structure template is as follows:

```
struct tag-name
{
    member-data declaration;

    member-functions definition
};
```

EXAMPLE

```
struct emp
{
    int empno;
    char name[20];
    float salary;

    void get()
    {
        cin >> empno >> name >> salary;
    }

    void display()
```

```
    {
        cout << empno << name << salary;
    }

};
```

In this example, the structure `emp` has two member functions `get()` and `display()`. The purpose of the function `get()` is to accept the member data values and that of the `display()` is to display the member-data values of variables of the structure type.

Let us now declare a variable of `emp` type

```
emp e;
```

Here **e** comes with the member data empno, name and salary. Now, we can accept the values of the member-data of **e** using the member function `get()` with the function call `e.get();` and the values are displayed using the member function `display()` with the function call `e.display();`. Note that the member functions `get()` and `display()` can not be called by themselves. They have to be invoked with a variable of `emp` type.

Program 12.1 To Illustrate the Concept of Structure

```
#include <iostream.h>
#include <iomanip.h>

struct emp
{
    int empno;
    char name[20];
    float salary;

    void get(void)
    {
        cin >> empno >> name >> salary;
    }

void display(void)
    {
        cout << setw(6) << empno << setw(12) << name << setw(8)
             << salary << "\n";
    }
};

int main(void)
{
    emp e;
    cout << "Enter empno, Name and Salary \n";
    e.get();
    cout << "Details of the employee \n";
    e.display();

    return 0;
}
```

Input-Output:

```
Enter empno, Name and Salary
121
Kishan
45000

Details of the employee
121    Kishan    45000
```

12.2 CLASS DEFINITION AND ACCESS SPECIFIERS (PRIVATE, PUBLIC)

Class is defined to be a group of data items and functions, which perform manipulations over the data items. An object is defined to be an instance of a class. The syntax of defining the class is as follows:

```
class tagname
{
    private:
        member data
        member functions
    public:
        member data
        member functions
};
```

class is the keyword. The tagname is any user-defined name (Valid C++ identifier). **private** is another keyword which indicates that the members declared under it are not accessible outside the class. The keyword **public** is to indicate that the members declared under it are accessible even outside the class also. The class definition looks similar to that of a structure. There is no substantial syntactical difference between them. The only difference is that the members of a structure are public by default and those in a class are private by default. If the keywords private and public are used explicitly in both of them, they can be used interchangeably. But for the sake of brevity, we use structure when we need to deal with only data items and use classes when we need to deal with both data items and functions.

The class definition allows the member functions also under the private section and member data under the public section. In the normal situations the member data are declared under private and the member functions are declared under the keyword public. Declaring member data under private access specifier ensures that the data are accessible only by the member functions of the class. No other functions (including `main()`) can access the member data of the class. The ability to shield the member data of a class from outside functions leads to **data hiding** and thus provides security to the data members. One of the important features of OOPs concept. Each object of a class will have its own copy of member data and it can invoke the member functions of the class, which are ready available, to perform operations over the data. So each object gets both data and functions encapsulated into it. The phenomenon is called **data encapsulation**.

Program 12.2 To Illustrate the Concept of Class and Object

```
#include <iostream.h>

class integer
```

```
{
    private:
        int x;
    public:
        void get()
        {
            cin >> x;
        }

        void display()
        {
            cout << x << "\n";
        }

        void increment()
        {
            x++;
        }
    };


int main(void)
{
    integer a;

    cout << "Enter the value of a \n";
    a.get();
    cout << "The value of a =";
    a.display();
    a.increment();
    cout << "After incrementation \n";
    cout << "The value of a =";
    a.display();
    return 0;
}
```

Input-Output:

```
Enter the value of a
5
The value of a = 5
After incrementation
The value of a = 6
```

Explanation

The class **integer** is defined with a member data **x** of `int` type. The functions `get()`, `display()` and `increment()` are three member functions defined as part of the class. The purposes of the member functions `get()` and `display()` are to accept and display the member data of an object of type **integer** respectively. The member function `increment()` is to increment the value of the member data of an object by one.

In the `main()`, **a** is declared to be an object of type `integer`. The function call `a.get();` enables us to accept a value to the member data of the object **a**. The member data of the object is displayed with the function call `a.display();`. The function call `a.increment();` increments the value of **a** and it is redisplayed by calling `display()` again with the object **a**.

The member functions defined within a class are by default inline functions. There is another approach, which is normally used to define classes, i.e., to have member functions declarations within the classes and define them outside the class definitions. Once the member functions are defined outside the classes, they are treated as normal functions.

```
#include <iostream.h>

class integer
{
    private:
        int x;
    public:
        void get();
        void display();
        void increment():
};

void integer :: get()
{
    cin >> x;
}

void integer :: display()
{
    cout << x << "\n";
}

void integer :: increment()
{
    x++;
}
```

Note the presence of **integer ::** before the member function names. This is required to indicate to the compiler that the functions are the members of the class **integer**. We will follow both the approaches in defining classes throughout the text.

Program 12.3 To Illustrate the Concept of Classes and Objects

```
#include <iostream.h>

class measure
{
    private:
        int feet;
        float inches;
    public:
```

```
    void get();
    void display();
};

void measure :: get()
{
    cin >> feet >> inches;
}
void measure :: display()
{
    cout << feet << "-" << inches << "\n";
}

int main(void)
{
    measure m;

    cout << "Enter feet and inches of m \n";
    m.get();
    m.display();

    return 0;
}
```

Input-Output:

```
Enter feet and inches of m
4
5

4-5
```

Explanation

The class **measure** is defined with two member data **feet** and **inches** of type `int` and `float` respectively. An object of type **measure** represents a measurement in terms of feet and inches. The member function `get()` is to accept the values of the member data and the member function `display()` is to display the measurement.

In the `main()`, an object **m** is declared to be of type **measure**. Values for feet and inches are accepted into it with the function call `m.get();` and they are displayed with the function call `m.display();`.

12.3 PASSING OBJECTS AS ARGUMENTS

We know that a function can take structures as arguments. The structures can either be passed by value or by reference. On the similar lines, we can also think of passing objects of some class type to functions as arguments. If a function takes an object of some class type as the argument, it has to be indicated not only in the function prototype but also in the function header. We follow the approach of passing objects by reference to functions.

Program 12.4 To Find the Sum of Two Integers

```
#include <iostream.h>

class integer
{
   private:
      int x;
   public:
      void get();
      void display();
      void sum(integer&);
};

void integer :: get()
{
   cin >> x;
}

void integer :: display()
{
   cout << x << "\n";
}

void integer :: sum(integer& b)
{
   x += b.x;
}

int main(void)
{
   integer a, b;

   cout << "Enter the value of a \n";
   a.get();
   cout << "Enter the value of b \n";
   b.get();
   cout << "The value of a =";
   a.display();
   cout << "The value of b =";
   b.display();

   a.sum(b);

   cout << "The sum of a and b = ";
   a.display();

   return 0;
}
```

Input-Output:

```
Enter the value of a
4
Enter the value of b
5
The value of a = 4
The value of b = 5
The sum of a and b = 9
```

Explanation

The function prototype `void sum(integer&);` in the class **integer** indicates that the function takes an argument, which is a reference to integer type and the function does not return any value to its calling program. The purpose of the function is to find the sum of the member data of two objects of the **integer** class. The two objects are: (a) The object passed as the actual argument to the function (b) The object with which the function is called.

The definition of the function is as follows:

```
    void integer :: sum(integer& b)
    {
        x += b.x;
    }
```

The member data of the object **b,** the formal argument**,** is added to that of the object with which the function `sum()` is called. As a result, the object which invokes the member function collects the sum of the member data of the object passed as the actual argument to the function and the member data of its own.

In the `main()`, **a** and **b** are declared to be objects of type `integer`. The member data of both the objects are accepted with the function calls `a.get();` and `b.get();`. The member data values of **a** and **b** are displayed with the function calls `a.display()` and `b.display();`. The sum of **a** and **b** is found with the function call `a.sum(b);`. Here the sum is collected in the object **a** itself and it is displayed.

Let us write one more program, which deals with passing an object as a function argument. This time we find the sum of two measurements.

Program 12.5 To Find the Sum of Two Measurements

```
#include <iostream.h>

class measure
{
    private:
        int feet;
        float inches;
    public:
        void get();
        void display();
        void sum(measure&);
};

void measure :: get()
```

```
{
    cin >> feet >> inches;
}
void measure :: display()
{
    cout << feet << "-" << inches << "\n";
}

void measure :: sum(measure& m)
{
    feet += m.feet;
    inches += m.inches;
    if (inches >= 12)
    {
        feet++;
        inches -= 12;
    }
}

int main(void)
{
    measure m1, m2;

    cout << "Enter feet and inches of m1 \n";
    m1.get();
    cout << "Enter feet and inches of m2 \n";
    m2.get();

    m1.sum(m2);
    cout << "Sum =";
    m1.display();

    return 0;
}
```

Input-Output:

```
Enter feet and inches of m1
3
5

Enter feet and inches of m2
5
8

Sum =9-1
```

Explanation

The function prototype `void sum(measure&);` in the class `measure` indicates that the function takes an argument, which is a reference to `measure` type and the function does not return any value to its calling program. The purpose of the function is to find the sum of the member data of two objects of the `measure` class. The two objects are: (a) The object passed as the actual argument to the function (b) The object with which the function is called.

The definition of the function is as follows:

```
void measure :: sum(measure& m)
{
    feet += m.feet;
    inches += m.inches;
    if (inches >= 12)
    {
        feet++;
        inches -= 12;
    }
}
```

The feet parts and the inches parts of the two objects are separately summed up with the statements:

```
feet += m.feet;
inches += m.inches;
```

As a result of the summation of the inches part since inches may exceed 12, we have incorporated the segment:

```
if (inches >= 12)
{
    feet++;
    inches -= 12;
}
```

which increments feet by one and decrements inches by 12 if inches is found to be greater than or equal to 12.

In the `main()`, **m1** and **m2** are declared to be objects of type `measure` and they represent two measurements in terms of feet and inches. The member data of both the objects are accepted with the function calls `m1.get();` and `m2.get();`. The member data values of **m1** and **m2** are displayed with the function calls `m1.display();` and `m2.display();`. The sum of the measurements **m1** and **m2** is found with the function call `m1.sum(m2);`. Here the sum is collected in the object **m1** itself and it is displayed.

12.4 RETURNING AN OBJECT FROM A FUNCTION

We know that a function can take structures as arguments and it also can return a structure to its calling program. On the similar lines it is also possible for a function to return an object of some class type. The function prototype and the function header should indicate that the function returns an object of the required class type. Let us now write a program to illustrate this concept.

Program 12.6 To Find the Sum of Two Integers

```
#include <iostream.h>

class integer
```

```
{
   private:
      int x;
   public:
      void get();
      void display();
      integer sum(integer&);

};

void integer :: get()
{
   cin >> x;
}

void integer :: display()
{
   cout << x << "\n";
}

integer integer :: sum(integer& b)
{
   integer t;

   t.x = x + b.x;
   return t;
}

int main(void)
{
   integer a, b;
   cout << "Enter the value of a \n";
   a.get();
   cout << "Enter the value of b \n";
   b.get();
   cout << "The value of a =";
   a.display();
   cout << "The value of b =";
   b.display();

   integer s;
   s = a.sum(b);
   cout  <<  "Sum =";
   s.display();

   return 0;
}
```

Input-Output:

```
Enter the value of a
4
Enter the value of b
5
The value of a =4
The value of b =5
Sum =9
```

Explanation

The function prototype `integer sum(integer&);` indicates that the function `sum()` requires a reference to `integer` type as its argument and it also returns an object of type `integer` type. The purpose of the function is to find the sum of the member data of two objects of `integer` type and return an object with the sum as its member data value.

The function definition is as follows:

```
integer integer :: sum(integer& b)
{
    integer t;

    t.x = x + b.x;
    return t;
}
```

Within the body of the function **t** is declared to be an object of type `integer`. The sum of the member data of the argument **b** and that of the object with which the function is called is assigned to **t.x**. The object **t** is then returned to the calling program. Note that we have used a local object to enable returning an object from the function. Also note that the member data of the object with which the function is called is not changed here.

In the `main()` **a** and **b** are declared to be objects of type `integer`. The member data of both the objects are accepted with the function calls `a.get();` and `b.get();`. The member data values of **a** and **b** are displayed with the function calls `a.display()` and `b.display();`. The sum of **a** and **b** is found and is assigned to the object **s** with the function call `s = a.sum(b);`. Here the sum collected in the object **s** is displayed.

Program 12.7 To Find the Sum of Two Measurements

```
#include <iostream.h>

class measure
{
    private:
        int feet;
        float inches;
    public:
        void get();
        void display();
        measure sum(measure&);
};
```

```
void measure :: get()
{
   cin >> feet >> inches;
}
void measure :: display()
{
   cout << feet << "-" << inches << "\n";
}

measure measure :: sum(measure& m)
{
   measure t;

   t.feet = feet + m.feet;
   t.inches = inches + m.inches;
   if (t.inches >= 12)
   {
      t.feet++;
      t.inches -= 12;
   }
   return t;
}

int main(void)
{
   measure m1, m2;

   cout << "Enter feet and inches of m1 \n";
   m1.get();
   cout << "Enter feet and inches of m2 \n";
   m2.get();

   measure s;
   s = m1.sum(m2);
   cout << "Sum =";
   s.display();

   return 0;
}
```

Input-Output:

```
Enter feet and inches of m1
3
4

Enter feet and inches of m2
5
6

Sum =8-10
```

Explanation

The function prototype `measure sum(measure&);` indicates that the function `sum()` requires a reference to `measure` type as its argument and it also returns an object of type `measure` type. The purpose of the function is to find the sum of the member data of two objects of `measure` type and return an object with the sum as its member data value.

The function definition is:

```
measure measure :: sum(measure& m)
{
    measure t;

    t.feet = feet + m.feet;
    t.inches = inches + m.inches;
    if (t.inches >= 12)
    {
        t.feet++;
        t.inches -= 12;
    }
    return t;
}
```

Within the body of the function **t** is declared to be an object of type `measure`. As in the earlier case the sum of the two measurements is found out and assigned to the object **t**. The object **t** is then returned to the calling program. Note that we have used a local object to enable returning an object from the function. Here also note that the member data of the object with which the function is called are not altered.

In the `main()` **m1** and **m2** are declared to be objects of type **measure**. Two measurements are accepted into the objects with the function calls `m1.get();` and `m2.get();`. The measurements are displayed with the function calls `m1.display()` and `m2.display();`. The sum of **m1** and **m2** is found, and is assigned to the object **s** with the function call `s = m1.sum(m2);`. Here the sum collected in the object **s** is displayed.

12.5 ARRAYS OF OBJECTS

We know that an array is a group of variables of similar type sharing a common name and we also know the flexibility offered by arrays while performing collective manipulation. We have dealt with arrays of basic type and arrays of structures. On the similar lines we can think of having arrays of objects of some class type. The syntax of declaring an array of objects is no different from that of the basic types and structures. The class type replaces the data type.

```
class_type array_name[size];
```

Here `class_type` is the tagname of the class under consideration; `array_name` is any valid C++ identifier and `size` is an integral value.

Program 12.8 To Find the Sum of a List of Integers

```
#include <iostream.h>

class integer
```

```
{
    private:
        int x;
    public:
        void get();
        void display();
        void sum(integer&);

};


void integer :: get()
{
    cin >> x;
}

void integer :: display()
{
    cout << x << "\n";
}

void integer :: sum(integer& b)
{

    x += b.x;
}

int main(void)
{
    integer a[10], s;
    int n, i;

    cout << "Enter the number of objects \n";
    cin >> n;
    cout << "Enter" << n << "Integers" << "\n";
    for(i = 0; i < n; i++)
        a[i].get();

//  Finding the sum begins

    s = a[0];
    for(i = 1; i < n; i++)
        s.sum(a[i]);

    cout << "Sum =";
    s.display();

    return 0;
}
```

Input-Output:

```
Enter the number of objects
5
Enter 5 Integers
1
3
5
6
8

Sum =23
```

Explanation

In Program 12.8, **a** is declared to be an array of `integer` type of size 10. The array **a** can thus accommodate 10 objects of `integer` type. The `int` type variables **n** and **i** are to collect the number of objects to deal with [1–10] and to traverse the objects in the array respectively. The purpose of the program is to find the sum of **n** objects which is collected by the object **s**.

After accepting the number of objects into the variable **n**, **n** objects values are entered with the segment:

```
for(i = 0; i < n; i++)
    a[i].get();
```

The following segment accomplishes the process of finding the sum:

```
s = a[0];
for(i = 1; i < n; i++)
    s.sum(a[i]);
```

Note that the object **s** is assigned the object **a[0]**, the first object in the list. The member function `sum()` is called with the object **s** by passing the remaining objects in the array **a**. Once the loop completes, the object **s** would collect the sum of the member data of the **n** objects in the array and it is displayed.

Program 12.9 To Find the Sum of a List of Measurements

```
#include <iostream.h>

class measure
{
    private:
        int feet;
        float inches;
    public:
        void get();
        void display();
        void sum(measure&);
};

void measure :: get()
{
    cin >> feet >> inches;
}
```

```
void measure :: display()
{
    cout << feet << "-" << inches << "\n";
}

void measure :: sum(measure& m)
{
    feet += m.feet;
    inches += m.inches;
    if (inches >= 12)
    {
        feet++;
        inches -= 12;
    }
}

int main(void)
{
    measure m[10], s;
    int n, i;

    cout << "Enter the number of measurements \n";
    cin >> n;
    cout << "Enter" << n << "measurements \n";
    for(i = 0; i < n; i++)
        m[i].get();
    // Summation begins

    s = m[0];
    for(i = 1; i < n; i++)
        s.sum(m[i]);

    // Summation ends

    cout << "Sum of the measurements \n";

    s.display();

    return 0;
}
```

Input-Output:

```
Enter the number of measurements
3
Enter 3 measurements
2 3
4 5
6 7

Sum of the measurements
13-3
```

Explanation

In Program 12.9, **m** is declared to be an array of `measure` type of size 10. The array **m** can thus accommodate 10 measurements. The `int` type variables **n** and **i** are to collect the number of measurements to deal with [1–10] and to traverse the objects in the array respectively. The purpose of the program is to find the sum of **n** measurements, which is collected by the object **s**.

After accepting the number of measurements into the variable **n**, they are accepted with the segment:

```
for(i = 0; i < n; i++)
    m[i].get();
```

The following segment accomplishes the process of finding the sum:

```
s = a[0];
for(i = 1; i < n; i++)
    s.sum(a[i]);
```

Note that the object **s** is assigned the object **m[0]**, the first measurement in the list. The member function `sum()` is called with the object **s** by passing the remaining objects in the array **m**. Once the loop completes, the object **s** would collect the sum of all the **n** measurements in the array and it is displayed.

12.6 ARRAYS AS MEMBERS OF CLASSES

So far we considered scalar types of data as members of classes. Similar to the way we use arrays within the structures, we can use arrays as member data of class types as well. We will examine this in the following programs.

Program 12.10 To Illustrate Arrays as Members of Classes

```
#include <iostream.h>

class vector
{
    private:
        int a[5];
    public:
        void get();
        void display();
};

void vector :: get()
{
    int i;

    for(i = 0;i < 5; i++)
        cin >> a[i];
}

void vector :: display()
```

```
{
    int i;

    for(i = 0; i < 5; i++)
        cout << a[i] << "\n";
}

int main(void)
{
    vector v;

    cout << "Enter 5 values of int type \n";
    v.get();
    cout << "The vector elements are \n";
    v.display();

    return 0;
}
```

Input-Output:

```
Enter 5 values of int type
3 4 6 9 8
The vector elements are
3
4
6
9
8
```

Explanation

The class `vector` is defined with an array **a** of `int` type and of size 10 as its member data. An object of the class type would thus accommodate 10 values of `int` type. The member functions `get()` and `display()` are to accept and display the array elements of the vector respectively.

In the `main()`, **v** is declared to be an object of type vector and the memory for the object gets allocated as follows:

	v
a[0]	
a[1]	
a[2]	
a[3]	
a[4]	
a[5]	
a[6]	
a[7]	
a[8]	
a[9]	

The statement `v.get();` accepts the values into all the 10 locations of the vector **v** and the statement `v.display();` displays them. Note that each `a[i]` belongs to the vector **v**.

Program 12.11 To Illustrate Arrays as Members of Classes

```
#include <iostream.h>
#include <iomanip.h>

class matrix
{
    private:
        int a[3][3];
    public:
        void get();
        void display();

};

void matrix :: get()
{
    int i, j;

    for(i = 0; i < 3; i++)
    for(j = 0; j < 3; j++)
        cin >> a[i][j];
}

void matrix :: display()
{
    int i, j;

    for(i = 0; i < 3; i++)
    {
        for(j = 0; j < 3; j++)
            cout << setw(4) << a[i][j];
        cout << "\n";
    }
}

int main(void)
{
    matrix m;

    cout << "Enter the elements of the matrix m \n";
    m.get();
    cout << "The matrix is \n";
    m.display();

    return 0;
}
```

Input-Output:

```
Enter the elements of the matrix m
1 2 3 4 6 5 7 8 9

The matrix is
  1  2  3
  4  6  5
  7  8  9
```

Explanation

The class matrix is defined with a two-dimensional array **a** of `int` type and of size `3*3` as its member data. An object of the class type would thus accommodate a matrix of size `3*3`. The member functions `get()` and `display()` are to accept and display the array elements of the matrix respectively.

In the `main()` **m** is declared to be an object of type matrix and the memory for the object gets allocated as follows:

m

a[0][0]	a[0][1]	a[0][2]
a[1][0]	a[1][1]	a[1][2]
a[2][0]	a[2][1]	a[2][2]

The statement `m.get();` accepts the values into the two-dimensional array **a**, the member data of **m**. The statement `m.display();` displays it. Note that each **a[i][j]** belongs to the matrix **m**.

12.7 STATIC MEMBER DATA

Suppose **A** is a class with **x** as its normal member data of type `int`. The number of copies of member data would be equal to the number of objects of the class type declared, i.e., each object will have its own copy of the member data **x**.

Let us declare three objects of **A** type as follows:

```
A a, b, c;
```

Here **a**, **b** and **c** are the three objects of **A** type. Memory gets allocated for the three objects as follows:

a.x

b.x

c.x

Under some rare conditions, we want only one copy of member data irrespective of the number of objects instantiated. This is accomplished with the use of the qualifier static for the member data. Static Member Data are characterised by the following properties:

- Only one copy of the member data is maintained irrespective of the number of objects that are created and all the objects can see it. The static member data are also called **class variables**.
- It is initialized to zero by default once the first object is instantiated. However, the default value can be changed by explicitly assigning our own value.
- The scope of the private static member is the class only and that of the public static member is the entire program.

Program 12.12 To Illustrate Static Member Data

```
#include <iostream.h>

class emp
{
   private:
       int empno;
       static int count;
   public:
       void get()
       {
           cout << "Enter empno \n";
           cin >> empno;
           count++;
       }

           void display_count()
       {
           cout << "Number of employees = " << count << "\n";
       }
};

int emp :: count; // Initializes count to zero

int main(void)
{
    emp a, b;

    a.get();
    b.get();

    a.display_count();
    b.display_count();
    return 0;
}
```

Input-Output:

```
Enter empno
123
```

```
Enter empno
125
Number of employees = 2
Number of employees = 2
```

Explanation

The class `emp` is defined with a normal member data `empno` of type `int` and a static member data `count`. Each object of `emp` type would thus collect the employee number of an employee. The purpose of the static member `count` is to keep track of the number of employees being dealt with. The unusual thing about the static member is that it needs two separate statements for declaration and definition. The statement `static int count;` within the class tells the compiler about the name and the type of the member. The statement `int emp::count;` outside the class is responsible for the allocation of memory space and defining it.

In the `main()`, **a** and **b** are declared to be objects of `emp` type. The statement `a.get();` enables us to accept empno of the first employee and increments count by one. The statement `b.get()` would enable us to accept the employee number of the second employee and increments the static member count by one. As a result, the value of the variable `count` would become two. Note that both the objects **a** and **b** can access the memory location allocated for `count`.

12.8 STATIC MEMBER FUNCTIONS

We now are aware of the characteristic of the static member data of a class that only one copy of it is maintained irrespective of the number of objects of the class and all the objects can see the copy. For this reason a static member data is also called the **class variable** since it relates to the entire class. Similar to the concept of static member data, we can have static member functions also. A member function is made a static member by preceding the prototype of the function by the keyword *static*.

A static member function is characterised by the following properties:

1. It can access only the static member data of the class.
2. It can be invoked with the use of the class name and the scope resolution operator.

```
class_name :: function();
```

This kind of function call mechanism does make sense since the function can access only the static member data, which relates to the entire class.

Program 12.13 To Illustrate Static Member Functions

```
#include <iostream.h>

class emp
{
   private:
       int empno;
       static int count;
   public:
       emp()
       {
          count++;
```

```
    }

    void get()
    {
        cout << "Enter empno \n";
        cin >> empno;
    }

        void display()
    {
        cout << "Empno = " << empno ;
    }
        static void show_count()
    {
        cout << "Number of employees = " << count << "\n";
    }
};

int emp :: count;

int main(void)
{
    emp a, b;

    a.get();
    b.get();

    a.display();
    b.display();
    emp :: show_count();
    return 0;
}
```

Input-Output:

```
Enter empno
121
Enter empno
124

Empno = 121
Empno = 124
Number of employees = 2
```

Explanation

The class **emp** is defined with the member data **empno** and a static member data **count** of `int` type. The purpose of the static member data is to keep track of the number of objects of **emp** type created. Within the constructor, we intentionally use the statement `count++;`. As a result, whenever an object is created, the static member **count** is incremented. The member functions `get()` and `display()` are to accept and display the details of an employee. Whereas the static member function `show()` is to display the value of the static member **count**.

In the `main()`, two objects **a** and **b** are declared. Since the constructor gets called twice the static member **count** would get the value two. The member data of both **a** and **b** are accepted and displayed by invoking the member functions `get()` and `display()` respectively with the objects. The statement `emp :: show();` displays the value of **count**, the static member data of the class. Note that the function is not invoked with an object since the function accesses only the static member data, which belong to the entire class. C++ enables us to call the function with the class name followed by the scope resolution operator (::).

Note also that a static member data can be accessed by member functions also.

12.9 FRIEND FUNCTIONS

We know that the private member data of a class can be accessed by the member functions of the class only. Under some circumstances, we may need even non-member functions also to be able to access the private member data of some classes. This is where the concept of *friend functions* comes into play a role. Even though this defeats the very spirit of data hiding, one of the important concepts of Object Oriented Programming. It becomes inevitable under some special programming situations. Let us get to know the intricacies of these functions.

Suppose **A** is a class. **x** is a member data and, `f1()` and `f3()` are the member functions of the class. If `f3()` is another function which is not a member of the class **A** and it still needs to manipulate the member data of the class. Here the function `f3()` is made a friend of the class by embedding the prototype for the function within the class definition which is preceded by the keyword *friend* as shown hereinafter.

```
class A
{
    private:
        int x;
    public:
        void f1(void);
        void f2(void);
        friend void f3(A&);
};
```

The definition of the function `f3()` will be like any other C++ function.

```
void f3(A& a)
{
    int c;

    c = a.x;
    .................
    .................
}
```

Note that the keyword *friend* is not used in the header of the function (The keyword has to be used only with the function prototype placed within the class definition) and the scope resolution operator :: is not used while defining the function. This is simply because the function `f3()` is not a member of the class.

Also note that a reference to the class type is passed as the formal argument. The function then manipulates over the object passed as the actual argument. This is required since the function can not be called with an object of the class type. Within the function the member data of the object passed as the argument is accessed with the use of the dot operator.

A friend function of a class is one, which is not a member of the class but still is able to access the private member data of the class.

Program 12.14 To Illustrate Friend Function

```
#include <iostream.h>

class temp
{
    private:
    int x;

    public:
        void get();
        friend void display(temp&);
};

void temp:: get()
{
    cin >> x;
}

void display(temp &t)
{
    cout << t.x;
}


int main(void)
{
    temp t;

    cout << "Enter the value of t \n";
    t.get();
    cout << "The value of t = ";
    display(t);

    return 0;
}
```

Input-Output:

```
Enter the value of t
8
The value of t = 8
```

Explanation

The class `temp` is defined with a private member data **x** of type `int`. The function `get()` is a member function of the class and it is to accept the value of an object. The function `display()` is made as the friend of the class by embedding the prototype `friend void display(temp&);` within the class. The purpose of the friend function is to display the value of an object of the class `temp`.

Note the differences between the definitions of the functions `get()` and `display()`. The header of the function `get()` is preceded by the class name and the scope resolution operator ::. These are required because `get()` is a member function of the class. Whereas in the case of `display()`, these are not required since it is a friend function.

Within the `main()`, **t** is declared to be an object of type `temp`. `t.get();` enables us to accept a value for **t** and the function call `display(t)` displays the value of **t**. Note that `display()` is not called with an object to its left with the dot operator. But it is called like a normal function with an object as the argument.

We will now consider an example where a non-member function is made to access the private member data of two classes. The function should undoubtedly be made a friend of both the classes. Program 12.15 illustrates this.

Program 12.15 To Illustrate Friend Function as a Bridge between Two Classes

```
#include <iostream.h>

class beta;
class alpha
{
   private:
      int a;
   public:
      void get();
      void display();
      friend int sum(alpha&, beta&);
};

void alpha :: get()
{
   cin >> a;
}

void alpha :: display()
{
   cout << a << "\n";
}


class beta
{
   private:
      int b;
   public:
      void get();
      void display();
      friend int sum(alpha&, beta&);
};
```

```
void beta :: get()
{
   cin >> b;
}

void beta :: display()
{
   cout << b << "\n";
}


int sum(alpha& a1, beta& b1)
{
   return (a1.a + b1.b);
}

int main(void)
{
   alpha a1;
   beta b1;

   cout << "Enter the value of a1 \n";
   a1.get();
   cout<< "Enter the value of b1 \n";
   b1.get();

   cout << "The value of a1 = ";
   a1.display();
   cout << "The value of b1 = ";
   b1.display();

   int s;

   s = sum(a1, b1);

   cout << "Sum  = " << s;

   return 0;
}
```

Input-Output:

```
Enter the value of a1
4
Enter the value of b1
5
The value of a1 = 4
The value of b1 = 5
Sum  = 9
```

Explanation

The class `alpha` is defined with a member data **a** of `int` type. The member functions `get()` and `display()` of the `alpha` class type are to accept and display the member data of an object of the class type. Similarly, the class `beta` is defined with a member data **b** of `int` type. The member functions `get()` and `display()` of the `beta` class type are to accept and display the member data of an object of the class type.

The function `sum()`, which is neither a member of `alpha` and nor a member of `beta`, is made a friend of both the classes by embedding the line of code `friend int sum(alpha&, beta&);` in both the classes. The purpose of the function is to find the sum of the member data of an object of `alpha` type and that of an object of `beta` type and return it to the calling program as indicated by its declaration. Also note the presence of the keyword *friend* with the prototype.

The friend function `sum()` forms the core part of the program, the definition of which is as follows:

```
int sum(alpha& a1, beta& b1)
{
    return (a1.a + b1.b);
}
```

The function is provided with two formal arguments **a1** and **b1** which are references to `alpha` and `beta` respectively and it returns the sum of the member data of the objects. Note the absence of the keyword *friend* in the function header. It has to be used only with the prototype of the function.

In the `main()`, **a1** and **b1** are declared to be objects of type `alpha` and `beta` respectively. After accepting their member data through the function `get()`, they are displayed with the help of the member function `display()`. Then the friend function `sum()` is invoked by passing **a1** and **b1** as the actual arguments with the statement `s = sum(a1, b1);` . The variable **s** would collect the value returned by the function `sum()`, which happens to be the sum of the member data of the objects **a1** and **b1** and it is displayed.

12.10 FRIEND CLASS

We are now aware of the concept of friend functions. A friend function of a class is not a member function of the class but it is still able to access the private member data of the class. We will now explore the possibility of making an entire class itself to be a friend of another class.

Suppose **A** and **B** are two classes. Class **B** itself can be made a friend of class **A** and if class **B** is made a friend of class **A** then all the member functions of class **B** can access the private member data of class **A**.

Program 12.16 To Illustrate Friend Class

```
#include <iostream.h>

class beta;

class alpha
{
    private:
        int x;
    public:
```

```
        alpha(int y)
        {
            x = y;
        }
    friend beta;
};

class beta
{
    public:
        void display(alpha a)
        {
            cout << "In display() a.x =" << a.x << "\n";
        }

        void show(alpha a)
        {
            cout << "In show() a.x =" << a.x << "\n";
        }
};

int main(void)
{
    alpha a(10);
    beta b;

    b.display(a);
    b.show(a);

    return 0;
}
```

Input-Output:

```
In display() a.x = 10
In show() a.x = 10
```

Explanation

In Program 12.16, the class `beta` is made a friend of the class `alpha`. As a result, the private member data of the `alpha` class are made accessible to all the member functions of the `beta` class. Both the member functions `display()` and `show()` of `beta` are provided with an object of `alpha` class and within them the member data of the object is displayed.

The line of code `class beta;` before the definition of `alpha` class is significant since it resolves forward reference of the class `beta`. Note that the class name `beta` is used within the `alpha` class and later it is defined.

12.11 CONSTANT MEMBER FUNCTIONS

A constant member function of a class is one, which can not change the member data of the class. The keyword ***const*** is appended to both prototype and the header of the member function. Once a member function is made a const member function, any attempt within the function to change the member data of the class gives rise to a compile time error.

Program 12.17 To Illustrate Constant Member Function

```
#include <iostream.h>

class emp
{
    private:
        int empno;
        char name[20];
        float salary;

    public:
        void get();
        void display() const;
};

void emp:: get()
{
    cin >> empno >> name >> salary;
}

void emp :: display() const
{
    cout << empno << name << salary;
}
int main(void)
{
    emp e;

    e.get();
    e.display();

    return 0;
}
```

Input-Output:

```
125 Kishan 25000
```

Explanation

The class `emp` is defined with three member data `empno`, `name` and `salary` of type `int`, array of `char` and `float` respectively. Any object of `emp` type would thus store empno, name and the salary of an employee. The member functions `get()` and `display()` are to accept and display the details of an employee respectively. Since the purpose of the member function `display()` is only to display the details of an employee, it is declared as a constant member function by appending the prototype and the header of the function by the keyword *const*. Note that the member function `get()` can not be declared as a constant member function. If it is made then we can not accept the values of the member data of an object.

12.12 CONSTANT OBJECTS

The keyword *const* can be used to qualify variables as constants to prevent modification inadvertently.

Consider the following declaration:

```
const int count = 10;
```

Here, the variable **count** would get the capacity of a constant. Any attempt to change the value of the variable raises compiler error.

On the similar lines, we can use the keyword while declaring objects of classes as well.

```
const integer a(10);
```

a is declared to be a **const** object of `integer` class and the member data **10** of the object can not be altered.

```
const measure m(4, 6.7);
```

m is declared to be a **const** object of `measure` class and the member data 4 and 6.7 can not be altered.

A **const** object can call const member functions only.

12.13 THIS POINTER

Suppose `B` is a class with some member data and `f()` as its public member function, and `b1` is an object of the class. The statement `b1.f();` is a valid function call and here the member function `f()` manipulates on the object `b1`. Careful understanding of the function call sequence reveals that the member function `f()` is passed the address of the object `b1` as the implicit argument by the calling program and this is how the member function is given the access to the object. The address of the object `b1` within the function `f()` is given by the special keyword *this* and hence the keyword *this* is the pointer to the object.

Now, consider the statement `b2.f();` where `b2` is another object of the class `B`. As a part of the function call sequence, the address of `b2` is passed as the argument to `f()` implicitly and the function manipulates on the object `b2`. Now, within `f()` the keyword *this* represents the address of `b2`.

In general, the keyword *this* used in a member function of a class gives the address of the object which invokes the function. The special pointer can be put to use like any other pointer to objects. The member data of the object can be accessed through the pointer by the use of the operator -> with the general form as **`this`** `-> member_data.`

Let us now deal with some programs which make use of the special pointer.

Program 12.18 To Illustrate This Pointer

```
#include <iostream.h>

class integer
{
    private:
        int x;
    public:
```

```
        void show_address();
};

void integer :: show_address()
{
    cout << "My object's address is = " << this << "\n";
}

int main(void)
{
    integer a, b, c;

    a.show_address();
    b.show_address();
    c.show_address();

    return 0;
}
```

Input-Output:

```
My object's address is = 0xfff4
My object's address is = 0xfff2
My object's address is = 0xfff0
```

Explanation

The member function `show_address()` defined as part of the class `integer` is to display the address of the object, which invokes the function. Note that we have used the keyword *this* in the `cout` statement in the function.

In the `main()` **a, b** and **c** are declared to be objects of `integer` type. Each of the objects will have its own address in the memory. The statements:

```
a.show_address();
b.show_address();
c.show_address();
```

display the address of the objects **a**, **b** and **c** respectively.

We can put **this** pointer to use in two situations: (a) To distinguish between the members of the class and the formal arguments when they have the same names. (b) To make a member function return the object, which invokes it. We will explore these possibilities in Program 12.19.

Program 12.19 To Return an Object from a Function

```
#include <iostream.h>

class measure
{
    private:
        int feet;
        float inches;

    public:
```

```
        void setdata(int feet, float inches)
        {
            this -> feet = feet;
            this -> inches = inches;
        }

        void display()
        {
            cout << feet << "-" << inches << "\n";
        }

        measure sum(measure m)
        {
            feet += m.feet;
            inches += m.inches;
            if (inches >= 12)
            {
                feet++;
                inches -= 12;
            }
            return *this;
        }
};
int main(void)
{
    measure m1, m2;

    m1.setdata(3, 4.5);
    m2.setdata(7, 6.3);

    cout << "m1 = ";
    m1.display();
    cout << "m2 = ";
    m2.display();
    measure s;

    s = m1.sum(m2);
    cout << "Sum =" ;
    s.display();
    return 0;
}
```

Input-Output:

```
m1 = 3 - 4.5
m2 = 7- 6.3
Sum = 10-10.8
```

Explanation

Consider the code in the following member function:

```
        setdata(int feet, float inches)
        {
```

```
        this -> feet = feet;
        this -> inches = inches;
    }
```

We can see that the names of the formal arguments and those of the members of the class are same. In order to distinguish between them, the members of the class measure are denoted by `this->feet` and `this->inches`. The value of the formal argument `feet` is assigned to `this -> feet`, the feet member data of the class measure, and the value of the formal argument `inches` is assigned to `this->inches`, the inches member data of the class.

In the member function `sum()`, the sum of two objects is found out and the sum is collected by the object which invokes the function.The object is returned with the statement `return *this`. Note that this is a pointer to the object which invokes the function `sum()` and the expression `*this` gives the object itself.

12.14 NESTING OF MEMBER FUNCTIONS

A member function of a class can invoke another member function of the class. If this is the case, the called member function is said to have been nested in the calling member function. Consider Program 12.20 to understand the concept.

Program 12.20 To Illustrate Nesting of Member Functions in a Class

```
#include <iostream.h>

class permutation
{
    private:
        int n, r;
        int n_fact();
        int nr_fact();
    public:
        void get_nr();
        void display_npr();

};

void permutation :: get_nr()
{
    cout << "Enter the values of n and r \n";
    cin >> n >> r;
}


int permutation :: n_fact()
{
    int i, f = 1;
    for(i = 1; i <= n; i++)
        f *= i;
```

```
    return f;
}

int permutation :: nr_fact()
{
    int i, f = 1;
    for(i = 1; i <= n - r; i++)
        f *= i;
    return f;
}

void permutation :: display_npr()
{
    int npr;

    npr = n_fact()/ nr_fact();
    cout << "npr = " << npr << "\n";
}

int main(void)
{
    permutation p;

    p.get_nr();
    p.display_npr();

    return 0;
}
```

Input-Output:

```
Enter the values of n and r
4
3
npr = 24
```

Explanation

The class permutation is defined with two member data **n** and **r** of `int` type. The member function `get_nr()` is to accept the values of the member data: The private member functions `n_fact()` and `nr_fact()` are to find the factorials of **n** and **n** – **r** respectively. The member function `display_npr()` is to display the value of $\mathbf{n_pr}$, number of permutations of **r** elements out of **n** elements. It is important to note that both the member functions `n_fact()` and `nr_fact()` are private members of the class and they are invoked in the other member function `display_npr()` of the class.

Since the member functions `n_fact()` and `nr_fact()` are not required to be called outside the class, they are made private members. This program has thus not only illustrated the fact that we can have member functions under private section but the fact that one member function can be called by another member function.

REVIEW QUESTIONS

12.1 Define a class.

12.2 What is an object?

12.3 Why do we use private, public access specifiers?

12.4 Write the general syntax of defining a class.

12.5 Mention the differences between structure and class.

12.6 What is data hiding?

12.7 Can we pass objects of a class to a member function? Explain with an example.

12.8 Can we return an object from a function? Explain with an example.

12.9 What is the significance of static member data? Give an example of its usage.

12.10 Static member data are also called class variables. Why?

12.11 Why do we use a static member function? How do we invoke it?

12.12 What is a friend function? Why do we use it?

12.13 What is a friend class? Give an example.

12.14 Explain the significance of this pointer.

12.15 Explain the concept of constant member function.

12.16 Explain constant objects.

True or False Questions

T12.1 Structures can not have member functions.

T12.2 Members of a structure are public by default.

T12.3 The keyword *struct* should be used while declaring structure variables.

T12.4 Classes can have both data and functions.

T12.5 The members of classes are also public by default.

T12.6 The member functions of a class should be called with an object of the class.

T12.7 There is no difference between structures and classes.

T12.8 The keywords private and public should be used in classes.

T12.9 The member data should be declared under private and the member functions should be declared under public access specifier.

T12.10 The member functions of a class can be defined even outside the class.

T12.11 The member functions defined within the classes are inline by default.

T12.12 We can not pass objects as arguments to functions.

T12.13 We can return an object from a function.

T12.14 Each object of a class will have its own copy of its member data.

T12.15 Only one copy of a static member data exists.

T12.16 The static member data will have garbage values by default.

T12.17 A non-static member function can access the static member data.

T12.18 The keyword *this* refers to the pointer to the current object within a member function.

T12.19 We can use this pointer to return the current object from a function.

T12.20 A constant object can call any member function of its class.

PROGRAMMING EXERCISES

P12.1 Write a program to find whether one object of integer class is less than the other.

P12.2 Write a program to find the least object in a list of objects of integer class.

P12.3 Write a program to sort a list of objects in the increasing order of their member data.

P12.4 Write a program to find whether one measurement is less than the other (measure class).

P12.5 Write a program to find the longest measurement in a list of measurements.

P12.6 Write a program to sort a list of measurements in the decreasing order.

P12.7 A complex number is of the form $x + iy$ where x is the real part and y is the imaginary part of the number. Design a class by name complex representing a complex number with member data x (real part) and y (imaginary part) of the number. Provide member functions to perform the following:

(a) To accept and display a complex number

(b) To find the sum of two complex numbers

$c1: x1 + iy1 \quad c2: x2 + iy2$

Sum of $c1$ and $c2 = (x1 + x2) + i\,(y1 + y2)$

(c) To find the difference between two complex numbers

$c1: x1 + iy1 \quad c2: x2 + iy2$

Difference of $c1$ and $c2 = (x1 - x2) + i\,(y1 - y2)$

(d) To find the product of two complex numbers

(e) To divide one complex number by the other

P12.8 Create a class by name triangle with the three sides *a*, *b* and *c* as its member data. Include member functions to perform the following:

(a) To accept the sides of a triangle

(b) To display the sides of a triangle

(c) To find whether the triangle is an equilateral triangle

(d) To find whether the triangle is an isosceles triangle

(e) To find whether the triangle is a right angled triangle

P12.9 Create a class by name date with the member data day, month and year. Include member functions to perform the following:

(a) To accept a date

(b) To display a date

(c) To find whether the date is valid or not
(d) To check whether one date is earlier than the other
(e) To increment a date
(f) To find the next date after adding a number of days

P12.10 Create a class by name emp with the member data empno, name, deptname, designation, age and salary and perform the following by including the member functions in the class:
(a) To accept the details of an employee
(b) To display the details of an employee
(c) To search for an employee in a list of employees by means of empno
(d) To find the youngest employee in a list of employees
(e) To find the highest paid employee
(f) To sort the list of employees in the increasing order of names

P12.11 Create a class by name account with the member data accno, name, balance. Perform the following:
(a) To accept the details of an account
(b) To display the details of an account
(c) To credit the account with some amount
(d) To debit the account with some amount

P12.12 Provide the required member functions in the vector class to perform the following:
(a) To add two vectors
(b) To subtract one vector from the other
(c) To search for an element in the vector
(d) To sort the elements in the vector in the decreasing order

P12.13 Provide the required member functions in the matrix class to perform the following:
(a) To add two matrices
(b) To multiply two matrices
(c) To sort each row of a matrix
(d) To find whether the matrix is identity matrix or not
(e) To find whether the matrix is symmetric or not

Chapter 13

Constructors and Destructors

13.1 INTRODUCTION

When we know the values of variables of built-in type in advance, we initialize them while they are declared.

EXAMPLE

```
int i = 10;
float f = 18.9;
char c = 'd';
```

As a result, we do not need to accept the values through the keyboard while the program is being run.

Now the question to be answered is: "Is it possible to initialize the objects of classes while they are declared on the lines of built-in types?" The answer is yes. This chapter tells how it is possible. This is where the concept of constructors comes into picture.

13.2 CONSTRUCTORS AND THEIR CHARACTERISTICS

A **constructor** is defined to be a special member function, which helps in initializing an object while it is declared. It is characterized by the following characteristics:

- It should be a public member.
- The name of the constructor should be as that of the class name.
- It can take arguments (Even the default arguments) but it does not return any value.
- No return type should be specified including void .
- It is invoked implicitly at the time of creation of the objects.
- The addresses of the constructors can not be retrieved.

13.3 TYPES OF CONSTRUCTORS

Depending on how the member data of objects are provided with values while they are declared, we classify the constructors into the following four types:

1. Default constructor
2. Parameterized constructor
3. Copy constructor
4. Dynamic constructor

13.3.1 Default Constructor

A constructor which does not take any arguments is called the **default constructor**. Suppose **A** is a class, the default constructor in the class takes the following form:

```
A()
{
    statements;
}
```

The statements within the body of the function assign the values to the member data of the class. Note that the name of the constructor is same as the class name and no return type is specified not even **void**. In line with the definition, the constructor is not provided with any arguments.

Now, when we declare an object of **A** type as `A a;` the member data of **a** are filled with the values specified in the body of the constructor.

EXAMPLE

Following is the default constructor in the integer class:

```
integer()
{
    x = 0;
}
```

Once the constructor is made available in the class integer. When an object is created the member data `x` of the object is set to 0.

```
integer a;
```

Here the value of `a.x` would be zero.

Program 13.1 Default Constructor in Integer Class

```
#include <iostream.h>

class integer
{
    private:
        int x;

    public:
```

```
        integer()
        {
            x = 10;
        }

        void display()
        {
            cout << x << "\n";
        }
};

int main(void)
{
    integer a, b;

    cout << "The member data of a =";
    a.display();
    cout << "The member data of b =";
    b.display();

    return 0;
}
```

Input-Output:

```
The member data of a = 10
The member data of b = 10
```

Explanation

Because of the presence of the default constructor in the integer class in which zero is assigned to the member data **x** of the class, each object will have zero to its member data. We have two objects **a** and **b** of type integer in the `main()`. The member data of both of the objects are displayed to be zero.

Suppose we need to assign default values to the members of an object of measure class. The default constructor in the measure class will do the job. Program 13.2 uses default constructor in the class.

Program 13.2 Default Constructor in Measure Class

```
#include <iostream.h>

class measure
{
    private:
        int feet;
        float inches;
    public:
        measure()
        {
            feet = 5;
            inches = 5.25;
        }
```

```
    void display()
    {
        cout << feet << "-" << inches << "\n";
    }
};

int main(void)
{
    measure m;

    cout << "m =" ;
    m.display();
    return 0;
}
```

Input-Output:

```
M = 5 - 5.25
```

Explanation

The `measure` class is provided with the default constructor in which the value `5` is assigned to **feet** and `5.25` to **inches** member data of the class. So any object declared will have these values to its corresponding members. In the `main()`, we have declared **m** to be an object of `measure` type. Because of the default constructor, which gets called during the creation of the object, the object will have `5` and `5.25` to its **feet** and **inches** members. They are displayed with the statement `m.display();`.

13.3.2 Parameterized Constructor

When a default constructor is used in a class, all the objects of the class will have the same default values (which are specified within the body of the constructor) for their member data.

For instance, consider three objects of integer class which are declared as follows:

```
integer a, b, c;
```

Here all the three objects will have zero to their member data. What if we want to initialize different objects of the class with different values? Default constructor does not solve the problem. To be able to initialize objects with different values while they are declared, we will be forced to provide the values with the objects themselves like `integer a(3), b(4), c(7);` in the form of parameters to the objects. This is possible through parameterized constructors.

A constructor, which takes arguments, is called **parameterized constructor**. The arguments are then assigned to the members of the class.

The general form of a parameterized constructor in class **A** is as follows:

```
A(type arg1, type arg2,..., type argn)
{
    member1 = arg1;
    member2 = arg2;
    :
    :
    membern = argn;
}
```

If a member is of string type then `strcpy()` is used to copy the corresponding argument to it. We can have more than one parameterized constructor with different number of arguments. When this is the case, the constructors are said to be **overloaded constructors**. Recall the definition of function overloading.

EXAMPLE

Parameterized constructor in `integer` class would be as follows:

```
integer(int y)
{
    x = y;
}
```

Once the constructor is made available as part of the `integer` class we can declare objects as follows:

```
integer a(3), b(5);
```

Here the member data of **a** is assigned 3 and that of **b** is assigned 5.

Program 13.3 Parameterized Constructor in Integer Class

```
#include <iostream.h>

class integer
{
    private:
        int x;

    public:

        integer(int y)
        {
            x = y;
        }

        void display()
        {
            cout << x << "\n";
        }
};

int main(void)
{
    integer a(15), b(25);

    cout << "The member data of a = ";
    a.display();
    cout << "The member data of b = ";
    b.display();
```

```
    return 0;
}
```

Input-Output:

```
The member data of a = 15
The member data of b = 25
```

Explanation

Because of the presence of the constructor with argument we can declare integer objects with a value. The constructor would thus enable us to declare objects with different values for their member data.

Also note that we can even provide default values to the arguments in the parameterized constructors.

```
integer(int y = 0)
{
    x = y;
}
```

If this is included as part of the class, we can declare objects with or without specifying initial values

```
integer a, b(7);
```

Here the member data of **a** would be 0, the default value of the argument in the constructor and that of the object **b** would be 7.

Program 13.4 Parameterized Constructor in Measure Class

```
#include <iostream.h>

class measure
{
    private:
        int feet;
        float inches;
    public:
        measure(int f, float i)
        {
            feet = f;
            inches = i;
        }

        void display()
        {
            cout << feet << "-" << inches << "\n";
        }
};

int main(void)
{
    measure m1(3, 4.5), m2(8, 5.7);

    cout << "m1 =";
```

```
    m1.display();
    cout << "m2 =";
    m2.display();

    return 0;
}
```

Input-Output:

```
m1 = 3-4.5
m2 = 8-5.7
```

Explanation

Because of the presence of the constructor with two arguments in the class `measure`, we could declare object of the class with initial values. In response to the declaration `measure m1(3, 4.5), m2(8, 5.7);` the **feet** member data of **m1** is assigned `3` and the **inches** member data of the object is assigned `4.5`. Similarly, the **feet** member data of **m2** is assigned `8` and the **inches** member data of the object is assigned `5.7`.

Here also, the arguments in the constructor can have default values. Constructor with default values for its arguments is as follows:

```
    measure(int f = 0, float i = 0)
    {
        feet = f;
        inches = i;
    }
```

In this case, we can declare objects with or without initial values.

`measure m1;` Here, both **feet** and **inches** of **m1** would be 0, the default value.

`measure m2(4, 7.8);` Here, **feet** and **inches** of **m2** are assigned 4 and 7.8 respectively.

13.3.3 Copy Constructor

Many a time, we require to create objects which are duplicates of other objects already available. This is done with the help of special constructor called **copy constructor**.

A copy constructor in class **B** takes the following form:

```
B(B& b)
{
    Statements;
}
```

The constructor takes a reference to the class type and the values of the members of the referenced object are assigned to the members of the class.

A constructor which initializes an object with another object is called the **copy constructor**.

Copy constructor in integer class:

```
integer(integer& b)
{
    x = b.x;
}
```

Copy constructor in measure class:

```
measure(measure& m)
{
    feet = m.feet;
    inches = m.inches;
}
```

13.3.4 Dynamic Constructor

Sometimes we may require to dynamically allocate memory for objects of classes during their creation. This is done with the help of dynamic constructors. The dynamic constructors use the **new** operator to allocate memory for objects during runtime. A constructor which allocates memory and initializes an object during runtime is called a **dynamic constructor**.

Consider the following example:

```
class vector
{
    private:
        int *a;
    public:
        vector(int n)
        {
            a = new int[n];
        }
};
```

Here, the member data **a** of the class vector is a pointer to `int` type. The constructor takes an argument **n** of `int` type and allocates memory for *n* integers. The address of the first element in the dynamic array is assigned to the pointer **a**.

Program 13.5 illustrates dynamic constructor in string class.

Program 13.5 To Illustrate Dynamic Constructor

```
#include <iostream.h>
#include <string.h>

class string
{
    private:
        char *str;
        int length;
    public:
        string()
        {
            length = 0;
            str = new char[length + 1];
            strcpy(str,"");
        }
```

```
    string(char *cp)
    {
        length = strlen(cp);
        str = new char[length + 1];
        strcpy(str, cp);
    }

    void display()
    {
        cout << str << "\n";
    }
};

int main(void)
{
    string s1, s2("Welcome");

    s1.display();
    s2.display();

    return 0;
}
```

Input-Output:

```
Welcome
```

Explanation

The class **string** is defined with the member data **str**, a pointer to `char` type and **length**, which is of `int` type. An object of **string** type would thus collect a string and its length in the members **str** and **length** respectively. The class has two dynamic constructors:

Consider the constructor

```
string()
{
    length = 0;
    str = new char[length + 1];
    strcpy(str,"");
}
```

The statement `str = new char[length + 1];` allocates memory for a character (one byte) and assigns the address of the location to the pointer **str**, and the statement `strcpy(str,"");` copies the empty string (only null character) to **str**. This constructor gets invoked when we declare an object of string type without any value.

Consider the following constructor:

```
string(char *cp)
{
    length = strlen(cp);
    str = new char[length + 1];
    strcpy(str, cp);
}
```

Here, the constructor takes **cp**, a pointer to `char` type, as its argument. Within the function, the length of the string passed to it is found using the statement `length = strlen(cp);`. Now, the function knows how much of memory space to allocate and it allocates the required amount of memory space using the statement `str = new char[length + 1];`. Once the required amount of memory for the string is allocated, the string is copied to the block pointed to by **str**. This constructor gets invoked when we declare an object of **string** type with a string as an initial value.

Note that in both the constructors `length + 1` bytes allocated since one extra byte is for the null character '`/0`'.

Let us write one more program to understand dynamic constructor better. Here we construct objects with two-dimensional array as their member data. We know that a two-dimensional array is an array of one-dimensional arrays and we also know that a pointer to the first element of the array denotes the one-dimensional array. Consider the following declaration `int b[10];` Here **b** represents the array and it is a pointer to the first element in the array. Having said that a two-dimensional array is an array of one-dimensional arrays, to allocate memory dynamically we need to first allocate memory for the pointers to the required number of one-dimensional arrays (rows). The variable, which collects the starting address of the block thus, allocated should be a pointer to pointer to the given type. Hence the member data of the class matrix defined below consists of a pointer to pointer to `int` type.

Program 13.6 To Illustrate Dynamic Constructor

```
#include <iostream.h>
#include <iomanip.h>

class matrix

{
    private:
        int **a;
        int r, c;
    public:
        matrix()
        {
        }
        matrix(int r1, int c1)
        {
            int i;

            r = r1;
            c = c1;
            a = new int*[r];
            for(i = 0; i < r; i++)
                a[i] = new int[c];
        }

        void read()
        {
            int i, j;

            for(i = 0; i < r; i++)
```

```
            for(j = 0; j < c; j++)
                cin >> a[i][j];
        }

    void display()
    {
        int i, j;

        for(i = 0; i < r; i++)
        {
            for(j = 0; j< c; j++)
                cout<< setw(4) << a[i][j];
            cout << "\n";
        }
    }
};

int main(void)
{
    matrix m;
    int rows, cols;

    cout << "Enter rows and cols \n";
    cin >> rows >> cols;
    m = matrix(rows, cols);
    m.read();
    m.display();

    return 0;
}
```

Input-Output:

```
Enter rows and cols
3 4
Enter the elements of the matrix
1 2 3 4 5 6 7 8 9 3 5 7

1   2   3   4
5   6   7   8
9   3   5   7
```

Explanation

The class matrix is defined with a pointer to pointer to `int` type **a** and two plain `int` members **r** and **c.** The member **a** represents the two-dimensional array being created and **r** and **c** represent the number of rows and the number of columns respectively. The class consists of two overloaded constructors. One of them does not take any arguments and even the body of the function is empty. This is required to declare objects of the class without arguments. The second constructor forms the core part of the program since it is in this function memory for the matrix is allocated dynamically. It takes two arguments **r1** and **c1**, which are to set the member data **r** and **c** of the class. The statement `a = new int*[r];` when executed allocates contiguous space for **r** pointers to `int` type and the starting address of the block is assigned to **a**.

Suppose `r = 5`, memory gets allocated as follows:

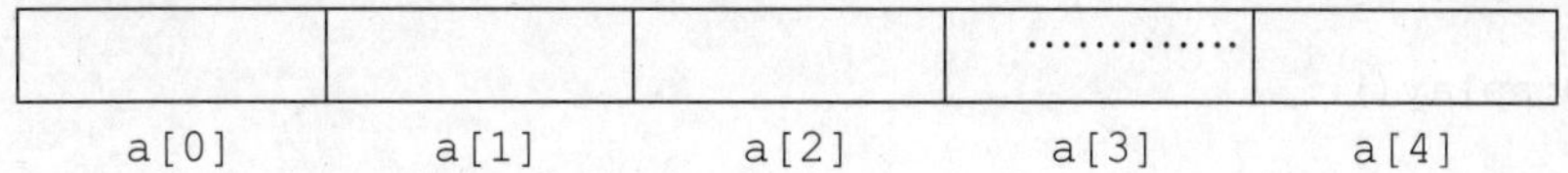

Here note that each **a[i]** is a pointer to `int` type and thus can represent a one-dimensional array. Now consider the segment,

```
for(i = 0; i < r; i++)
    a[i] = new int[c];
```

Here, when **i** takes 0, memory for the first one-dimensional array with **c** elements (first row) is allocated. Similarly when **i** takes 1, memory for the second one-dimensional array with **c** elements gets allocated and so on. When the loop completes, memory for the entire two-dimensional array is made available with **a[i][j]** representing the location in the **i**th row and **j**th column.

The member functions `read()` and `display()` do the job of accepting and displaying the matrix elements.

In the `main()`, the values of rows and columns are accepted and they are dynamically set to the member data **r** and **c** of the object **m** with the statement `m = matrix(rows, cols);`. Note that the constructor is called explicitly. After the execution of the constructor, the two-dimensional array with the given number of rows and columns has been created. The statements `m.get();` and `m.display();` accept and display the matrix elements respectively.

13.4 MULTIPLE CONSTRUCTORS IN A CLASS

A class can have more than one constructor. When used, a proper constructor will be invoked depending on the signature of the constructor. Programs 13.7 and 13.8 illustrate the inclusion of default constructor, parameterized constructor and copy constructor in a single class.

Program 13.7 To Illustrate Multiple Constructors

```
#include <iostream.h>

class integer
{
   private:
        int x;

   public:
        integer()
        {
             x = 10;
        }
        integer(int y)
        {
             x = y;
        }
        integer(integer& b)
```

```
    {
        x = b.x;
    }
    void display()
    {
        cout << x << "\n";
    }
};


int main(void)
{
    integer a, b(15), c(b);

    cout << "Member data of a = " ;
    a.display();
    cout << "Member data of b = " ;
    b.display();
    cout << "Member data of c = " ;
    c.display();

    return 0;
}
```

Input-Output:

```
Member data of a = 10
Member data of b = 15
Member data of c = 15
```

Explanation

The objects **a**, **b** and **c** are initialized with the help of default constructor, parameterized constructor and copy constructor respectively. The member data of the object **a** is displayed to be 10. The member data of both **b** and **c** are displayed to be 15. Note that the object **c** is a duplicate of **b**.

Program 13.8 To Illustrate Multiple Constructors

```
#include <iostream.h>

class measure
{
    private:
        int feet;
        float inches;
    public:
        measure()
        {
            feet = 5;
            inches = 5.25;
        }
        measure(int f, float i)
```

```
        {
            feet = f;
            inches = i;
        }
        measure(measure& m)
        {
            feet = m.feet;
            inches = m.inches;
        }
        void display()
        {
            cout << feet << "-" << inches << "\n";
        }
};

int main(void)
{
    measure m1, m2(10, 5.6), m3(m2);

    cout << "m1 = ";
    m1.display();
    cout << "m2 = ";
    m2.display();
    cout << "m3 = ";
    m3.display();

    return 0;
}
```

Input-Output:

```
m1 = 5-5.25
m2 = 10-5.6
m3 = 10-5.6
```

Explanation

The objects **m1**, **m2** and **m3** are initialized with the help of default constructor, parameterized constructor and copy constructor respectively. The member data of the object **m1** is displayed to be `5 (feet)` and `5.25 (inches)`. The member data of both **m2** and **m3** are displayed to be `10 (feet)` and `5.6 (inches)`. Note that the object **m3** is a duplicate of **m2.**

13.5 USING A CONSTRUCTOR TO RETURN AN OBJECT

A constructor can be employed to return an object from a function without using a temporary object within the function. Let us now understand this with the following programs.

Program 13.9 To Return an Object Using a Constructor

```
#include <iostream.h>

class integer
```

```
{
   private:
      int x;
   public:
      integer();
      integer(int);
      void get();
      void display();
      integer sum(integer&);

};

integer:: integer()
{
   x = 0;
}

integer :: integer(int y)
{
   x = y;
}

void integer :: get()
{
   cin >> x;
}

void integer :: display()
{
   cout << x << "\n";
}

integer integer :: sum(integer& b)
{

   x += b.x;
   return integer(x);
}

int main(void)
{
   integer a, b, c;

   cout << "Enter the value of a \n";
   a.get();
   cout << "Enter the value of b \n";
   b.get();
   cout << "The value of a =";
   a.display();
   cout << "The value of b =";
   b.display();
```

```
    c = a.sum(b);

    cout << "The sum of a and b = ";
    c.display();

    return 0;
}
```

Input-Output:

```
Enter the value of a
4

Enter the value of b
8

The value of a = 4

The value of b = 8

The sum of a and b = 12
```

Explanation

The member function `sum()` is to find the sum of two objects of the class integer. After adding the member data of the object, which is passed as the argument, to the member data **x** in the function, we have used the expression `integer(x)` as part of the return statement. Here an object is constructed with the member data value **x** and it is returned to the calling program.

In the `main()`, the statement `c = a.sum(b);` invokes the `sum()` member function of the class, in which the sum of **a** and **b** is found out. The new object created by the function is collected by the object **c**.

Program 13.10 To Return an Object Using a Constructor

```
#include <iostream.h>

class measure
{
    private:
        int feet;
        float inches;
    public:
        measure();
        measure(int, float);
        void get();
        void display();
        measure sum(measure&);
};

measure :: measure()
{
    feet = inches = 0;
}
```

```
measure :: measure(int f, float i)
{
    feet = f;
    inches = i;
}

void measure :: get()
{
    cin >> feet >> inches;
}
void measure :: display()
{
    cout << feet << "-" << inches << "\n";
}

measure measure :: sum(measure& m)
{
    feet += m.feet;
    inches += m.inches;
    if (inches >= 12)
    {
        feet++;
        inches -= 12;
    }
    return measure(feet, inches);
}

int main(void)
{
    measure m1, m2;

    cout << "Enter feet and inches of m1 \n";
    m1.get();
    cout << "Enter feet and inches of m2 \n";
    m2.get();

    measure m3 = m1.sum(m2);
    cout << "Sum =";
    m3.display();

    return 0;
}
```

Input-Output:

```
Enter feet and inches of m1
4
5
Enter feet and inches of m2
6
5
Sum = 10-10
```

Explanation

The member function `sum()` is to find the sum of two objects of the class measure. Within the body of the function, the two measurements are added. The sum is collected by the member data of the object with which the function is invoked. We have used the expression `measure(feet, inches)` as part of the return statement. Here an object is constructed with the member data value **feet** and **inches** and it is returned to the calling program.

In the `main()`, the statement `m3 = m1.sum(m2);` invokes the `sum()` member function of the class, in which the sum of **m1** and **m2** is found out. The new object created by the function is collected by the object **m3**.

13.6 DESTRUCTOR AND ITS CHARACTERISTICS

A destructor is defined to be another special member function of a class, which helps in releasing the memory occupied by an object when it goes out of scope.

The following are the characteristics of a destructor:

- It should be a public member.
- The name of the destructor should be as that of the class name and it is preceded by the tilde symbol ~.
- It can not take arguments and does not return any value.
- No return type should be specified including void .
- **Delete** operator is to be used to deallocate the memory allocated by **new** operator in the constructors.

Program 13.11 To Illustrate Destructor

```
#include <iostream.h>

int count = 0;
class integer
{
   private:
       int x;
   public:
       integer(int y)
       {
           count++;
           cout << "Object-" << count << " created" << "\n";
           x = y;
       }
       ~integer()
       {
           cout << "object-" << count << " destroyed" << "\n";
           count--;
       }
};

int main(void)
```

```
{
    integer a(10), b(20);
    return 0;
}
```

Input-Output:

```
Object-1 created
Object-2 created
Object-2 destroyed
Object-1 destroyed
```

Explanation

The class integer has a constructor with one argument and it also has destructor. A global variable count with initial value zero is used to assign a number to each object while it is created. Within the constructor the variable is incremented with the statement `count++;`.

Program 13.12 To Illustrate Destructor

```
#include <iostream.h>

class vector
{
    private:
        int *a;
        int n;
    public:
        vector(int m)
        {
            n = m;
            a = new int[n];
        }
        void display()
        {
            int i;
            for(i = 0; i < n; i++)
            cout << a[i] << "\n";
        }
        void accept()
        {
            int i;
            for(i = 0; i < n; i++)
            cin >> a[i];
        }
        ~vector()
        {
            delete a;
        }
};
```

```
int main(void)
{
    vector v(5);

    cout << "Enter 5 values \n";
    v.accept();
    cout << "The values of v are \n";
    v.display();

    return 0;
}
```

Input-Output:

```
Enter 5 values
3 4 6 8 9
The values of v are
3
4
6
8
9
```

Explanation

The class `vector` has a pointer to `int` type **a**, and an `int` member **n** as its member data. An object of vector type can represent an array of `int` type. The class `vector` employs a dynamic constructor with an argument **m** of `int` type as its argument. Within the function the argument **m** is assigned to the member **n** and it allocates memory for the array of **n** elements in the memory heap. Once the dynamic array is allocated, the address of the first element in the array is assigned to the pointer **a**.

The dynamically allocated memory for the vector is not released even after the vector goes out of scope. Only the memory allocated for **a** and **n** are released (they are allocated memory in the stack). Whereas the memory occupied by the dynamic array remains intact. It is released explicitly with the help of the destructor.

```
~vector()
{
    delete a;
}
```

REVIEW QUESTIONS

13.1 What is a constructor? Why do we need it?

13.2 What is a default constructor? Give an example.

13.3 What is a parameterized constructor? Exemplify.

13.4 What is a copy constructor?

13.5 Define dynamic constructor.

13.6 What is destructor? Why is it required?

13.7 How can we return an object from a function using a constructor? Explain.

True/False Questions

T13.1 Constructors are used to initialize objects while they are declared.

T13.2 Constructors can be overloaded.

T13.3 In each class it is mandatory to have a constructor.

T13.4 We can have multiple constructors in a class.

T13.5 Destructor can take arguments.

T13.6 If new operator is used in constructor delete operator should be used in the destructor.

T13.7 Copy constructor takes a reference to the same class object as the argument.

T13.8 The order of destruction of objects is same as their order of construction.

T13.9 A constructor can be called explicitly.

T13.10 Constructors and destructor should be public members.

T13.11 Arguments to constructors can take default values.

PROGRAMMING EXERCISES

P13.1 Provide constructors for the class complex.

P13.2 Provide copy constructor for the vector class and the matrix class.

P13.3 Create a class by name student with the member data roll_number, name, percentage of marks. Provide constructors for the class. Check to see whether all of them work.

P13.4 Create a class by name circle with radius as its member data. Provide constructors to initialize the objects of the class and find the area and circumference of a circle.

Area = 3.14 * radius *radius Circumference = 2 * 3.14 * radius

P13.5 Create a class by name rectangle with length and breadth as its member data. Provide constructors to initialize the objects of the class and find the area and the perimeter of a rectangle.

Area = length * breadth Perimeter = 2 * (length + breadth)

Chapter 14

Operator Overloading and Type Conversion

14.1 INTRODUCTION

Suppose **i**, **j** and **k** are variables of `int` type. The statement `k = i + j;` is valid and it is intended to collect the sum of **i** and **j** in the variable **k**. Suppose **a**, **b** and **c** are objects of type `integer` class and if we want to collect the sum of the member data of the objects **a** and **b** in the object **c**, can we write the assignment statement `c = a + b;` ? It is not possible simply because the operator + is not aware of the objects **a** and **b** of `integer` type and the expression `a + b` does not evaluate to what we expect. In order to find the sum of two objects of integer class and assign it to another object in the classes and objects chapter, we had defined a member function `sum()` as part of the integer class and the statement `c = a.sum(b);` accomplished the job.

The statement `c = a + b;` is more comprehensible than the statement `c = a.sum(b);`. To be able to use the operator + with the objects of integer type it should be made aware of the class type and should be assigned the job of summing up of two objects. This is where the concept of operator overloading comes into picture.

Operator overloading is one of the important features of C++ language. It assigns additional functionality to the existing operators so that they also operate over operands of derived types. By providing the ability for the operators to perform operations over the operands of derived types, it brings derived type operands close to the operands of built-in type like int, float, etc. This is in line with the philosophy of the object oriented programming paradigm.

14.2 SYNTAX OF OPERATOR OVERLOADING FUNCTION

Overloading an operator in a class is accomplished with the help of a special member function of the class. The general form of the function is as follows:

```
type operator operator_to_ be_overloaded(Formal Arguments)
{
```

```
    local variables

    statements
    return (expression);
}
```

`type` specifies the type of the value being returned by the function. *Operator* is the keyword in C++. `operator_to_ be_overloaded` is an operator being overloaded in the class. It can be +, ++, *, etc. As can be seen the syntax looks similar to that of a normal function except the fact that the keyword *operator* followed by the operator to be overloaded replaces the function name. If the return type is **void,** the statement `return (expression);` will be absent.

14.3 OVERLOADING UNARY OPERATORS

We know that a unary operator is one, which is defined over a single operand. Examples of unary operators include unary -, unary +, ++ and --.

The general form of the member function for overloading a unary operator is as follows:

```
type operator operator_to_ be_overloaded()
{
    local variables

    statements
    return (expression);
}
```

Note that the special member function used for overloading a unary operator does not require any arguments. This is because the operator can operate on only one object of the class involved and that object is the one with which the operator is used. For example, if `unary -` is overloaded in `integer` class then `-a`, where **a** is an object of `integer` class, becomes a valid expression. The operator `unary -` to the left of the object **a** invokes the overloading function.

Program 14.1 To Overload Unary—in Integer Class

```
#include <iostream.h>

class integer
{
    private:
        int x;
    public:
        integer(int y =0)
        {
            x = y;
        }
        integer operator -()
        {
            integer t;
```

```
        t.x = - x;
        return t;
    }
    void display()
    {
        cout << "x =" << x << "\n";
    }
};

int main(void)
{
    integer a, b(5), c(-7);

    cout << "b = ";
    b.display();
    a = -b;
    cout << "-a = ";
    a.display();

    cout << "c = ";
    c.display();
    a = -c;
    cout << "a = ";
    a.display();

    return 0;
}
```

Input-Output:

```
b = 5
-b = -5
c = -7
-c = 7
```

Explanation

The member function, which does the job of overloading the unary – in the integer class, is:

```
integer operator -()
{
    integer t;

    t.x = - x;
    return t;
}
```

Note that the function does not require any argument and it operates on the member data of the object with which it is invoked. Within the body of the function **t** is declared to be an object of `integer` type. The statement `t.x = -x;` assigns the negated value of **x**, the member data of the object with which the `unary -` operator is associated, to **t.x**. The object **t** is then returned from the function.

In the `main()`, **a, b** and **c** are declared to be objects of `integer` type. The objects **b** and **c** are initialized with the values `5` and `-7` respectively. Consider the statement `a = -b;`. Here the `unary`

- operator is used with the object **b** and it invokes the overloading function which, when executed, assigns the negated value of **b**, i.e., `-5` to the object **a**. The new value of **a** is then displayed. Similarly, the statement `a = -c;` also invokes the overloading function. After the execution of the function the negated value of **c**, i.e., `7` is assigned to the object **a**. The value of **a** is redisplayed to be `7`.

Program 14.2 To Overload Unary—in Point Class

```
#include <iostream.h>

class point
{
    private:
        int x, y;

    public:
        point(int x1 = 0, int y1 = 0)
        {
            x = x1;
            y = y1;
        }

        void display()
        {
            cout << "x = " << x << "y = " << y << "\n";
        }

        point operator -()
        {

            point temp;

            temp.x = -x;
            temp.y = -y;

            return (temp);

        }
};

int main(void)
{
    point p1(4, -5), p2 ;

    cout << "p1: ";
    p1.display();
    p2 = -p1;
    cout << "-p1: ";
    p2.display();
    return 0;
}
```

Input-Output:

```
P1: x = 4 y = -5
-P1: x = -4 y = 5
```

Explanation

The class `point` is defined with two member data **x** and **y** of `int` type. Any object of `point` type represents the *x* and *y* co-ordinate positions of a point in a *XY* plane. A constructor with two arguments is used to initialize the objects while they are declared. The member function `display()` serves the job of displaying the co-ordinates of a point. The unary – operator is overloaded in the point class with the following function:

```
point operator -()
{

    point temp;

    temp.x = -x;
    temp.y = -y;

    return (temp);
```

Within the function the negated values of **x** and **y**, the member data of the object of `point` type with which the unary – operator is associated, are assigned to **temp.x** and **temp.y** respectively. The object **temp** is then returned from the function.

In the `main()` **p1** and **p2** are declared to be objects of `point` type. The object **p1** is initialized with the values `4` and `-5,` and they are displayed with the statement `p1.display();`. Now consider the statement `p2 = -p1;` Here the unary – operator is used with the object **p1** and it invokes the overloading function. The function on its execution negates the **x** and **y** values of the object; assigns the new values to the corresponding members of the object **temp** and returns the object **temp** which is assigned to the object **p2**. The members of **p2** would thus be `-4` and `5` respectively and they are displayed.

Program 14.3 To Overload ++ Operator in Integer Class

```
#include <iostream.h>

class integer
{
    private:
        int x;
    public:
        integer(int y = 0)
        {
            x = y;
        }

    void operator ++()

    {
        ++x;
```

```
    }

    void operator ++(int)
    {
        x++;
    }
    void display()
    {
        cout << x << "\n";
    }
};

int main(void)
{
    integer a(5);

    cout << "a = ";
    a.display();
    ++a;
    cout << "After ++a;, a = ";
    a.display();
    a++;
    cout << "After a++;, a = ";
    a.display();

    return 0;
}
```

Input-Output:

```
a = 5
After ++a;, a = 6
After a++;, a = 7
```

Explanation

The program enables us to use the increment operator ++ with the objects of `integer` type. Since the operator can either be prefixed or suffixed to a variable, the class is provided with two overloading functions. The member function responsible for prefixing ++ operator with an object of `integer` type is as follows:

```
void operator ++()

{
    ++x;
}
```

As we discussed earlier the function does not require any argument. It increments the member data of the object with which the ++ is associated.

The member function responsible for suffixing ++ operator with an object of integer type is:

```
void operator ++(int)
{
    ++x;
}
```

Note that the keyword `int` has been used within the parentheses in the header. It is not to mean that the function requires an argument of `int` type (A function which overloads unary operator does not require any argument). It is to merely tell the compiler that the function be invoked whenever the ++ operator is suffixed with an object of `integer` type.

Since the return type of the above functions is **void**, `++a` and `a++` can be used only as independent statements as `++a;` and `a++;` where **a** is an object of `integer` type. They can not be used as parts of an assignment statement. The following functions enable the same:

```
integer operator ++()

{
    ++x;
    return (integer(x));
}
```

```
b = ++a;
```

is now a valid statement.

```
integer operator ++(int)
{
    x++;
    return (integer(x));
}
```

```
b = a++;
```

is now a valid statement.

Note that both the functions return an object of `integer` type and thus facilitates the use of `++a` and `a++` as rvalues (parts of expressions).

14.4 OVERLOADING BINARY OPERATORS

We know that a binary operator is one, which is defined over two operands. Examples of binary operators include +, -, *, / , <, >=, etc.

The general form of the member function for overloading a binary operator is as follows:

```
type operator operator_to_ be_overloaded(formal argument)
{
    local variables

    statements
    return (expression);
}
```

Note that the special member function used for overloading a binary operator requires one argument of the class type. This is because the operator can operate on two objects of the class involved. One object is written to the left of the operator and the other is written to the right of the operator. For example, if + is overloaded in integer class `a + b` becomes the valid expression. Here the object **a** invokes the overloading member function and the object **b** is passed as the actual argument to the function.

Program 14.4 To Overload + Operator in Measure Class

```
#include <iostream.h>

class measure
{
  private:
     int feet;
     float inches;

  public:
     measure(int f = 0, float i = 0)
     {
        feet = f;
        inches = i;
     }

     measure operator +(measure& m)
     {

        measure t;

        t.feet = feet + m.feet;
        t.inches + inches + m.inches;
        if (t.inches >= 12)
        {
           t.feet++;
           t.inches -= 12;
        }

        return (t);
     }
  void display()
  {
     cout << feet << "-" << inches << "\n";
  }
};

int main(void)
{
  measure m1(2, 3), m2(4, 10), m3;
```

```
    cout << "m1: ";
    m1.display();
    cout << "m2: ";
    m2.display();

    m3 = m1 + m2;

    cout << "Sum =" ;
    m3.display();
    return 0;
}
```

Input-Output:

```
m1: 2 - 3
m2: 4 - 10
Sum = 7 - 1
```

Explanation

The program overloads the + operator in measure class so that it can be used with two objects of type measure to find the sum of the measurements. The special member function responsible for overloading the operator is reproduced as follows:

```
measure operator +(measure& m)
{

    measure t;

    t.feet = feet + m.feet;
    t.inches = inches + m.inches;
    if (t.inches >= 12)
    {
        t.feet++;
        t.inches -= 12;
    }

    return (t);
}
```

Note that an object **m** of type measure is provided with the function as a formal argument. This is because the + operator being a binary operator requires two operands. In this case it requires two objects of `measure` type. One object is represented by **m**, the formal argument and the other object is the one, which invokes the overloading function. Within the function the summation is done as follows:

The sum of the feet parts of the two measurements is assigned to **t.feet**. (**t** is a local object of `measure` type.) and the sum of the inches parts of the two measurements is assigned to **t.inches**. Now, there is a possibility of **t.inches** being equal to 12 or exceeding 12. That is why if **t.inches** is greater than or equal to 12 then **t.feet** is incremented by one and **t.inches** is decremented by 12. This is because one foot is equal to 12 inches. The object **t**, which collects the sum, is then returned from the function.

Program 14.5 To Overload < Operator in Measure Class

```
#include <iostream.h>

class measure
{
   private:
      int feet;
      float inches;
   public:
      measure(int f, float i)
      {
         feet = f;
         inches = i;
      }

      void display()
      {
         cout << feet << "-" << inches << "\n";
      }

      int operator < (measure m)
      {
         float f1, f2;

         f1 = feet + inches / 12;
         f2 = m.feet + m.inches /12;

         return (f1 < f2);
      }

};

int main(void)
{
   measure m1(3,4.5), m2(4, 5.6);

   if (m1 < m2)
   {
      m1.display();
      cout << "is less than ";
      m2.display();
   }
   else
   {
      m1.display();
      cout << "is not less than ";
      m2.display();

   }
```

```
    return 0;
}
```

Input-Output:

```
3-4.5 is less than 4-5.6
```

Explanation

Program 14.5 overloads the relational operator < in the measure class so that the operator can be used with objects of measure type. The member function responsible for overloading the < operator in the class is reproduced as follows:

```
int operator < (measure m)
{
        float f1, f2;

        f1 = feet + inches / 12;
        f2 = m.feet + m.inches /12;

        return (f1 < f2);
}
```

Since the < operator is also a binary operator, one argument of `measure` type is passed to the function. We know that the value of a relational expression is either `0` or `1` the function is made to return the value (`int`). Within the function the variable **f1** collects only feet equivalent of one measurement and **f2** collects only feet equivalent of the other measurement and the value of `f1 < f2`, which is 1 if **f1** is less than **f2**, 0 otherwise, is then returned by the function.

In the `main()`, **m1** and **m2** are declared to be objects of type `measure` and both are initialized with values while they are declared. Because the < operator has been overloaded in the class, we could use the test-expression `m1 < m2` in the if statement.

Program 14.6 To Overload += Operator to Concatenate Two Strings

```
#include <iostream.h>
#include <string.h>

class string
{
    private:
        char str[20];
    public:
        string(char s[])
        {
            strcpy(str, s);
        }

        void operator += (string& s)
        {
            strcat(str, s.str);
        }
```

```
    void display()
    {
        cout << str << "\n";
    }
};

int main(void)
{
    string s1("abc"), s2("xyz");

    cout << "s1 = ";
    s1.display();
    cout << "s2 = ";
    s2.display();
    s1 += s2;
    cout << "After concatenation \n";
    s1.display();

    return 0;
}
```

Input-Output:

```
s1 = abc
s2 = xyz
After concatenation
abcxyz
```

Explanation

The class string is defined with a member data **str**, an array of `char` type. An object of string type can thus represent a string. We know how the built-in function `strcat()` works. It appends one string at the end of another string. The program overloads += operator to concatenate two strings with the following function:

```
void operator += (string& s)
{
        strcat(str, s.str);
}
```

The function requires an object of string type as its argument. Within the body of the function `strcat()` is invoked to append the string **s.str** where **s**, an object of string type is the formal argument to the function, to the end of **str**.

14.5 OVERLOADING >> AND << OPERATORS

Suppose **a** is a variable of basic type, the statement `cin >> a;` enables us to accept a value into the variable and the statement `cout << a;` displays the value of the variable. Suppose **b** is an object of some derived type. Can we use the statement `cin >> b;` to accept the members of the object? And can we use the statement `cout << b;` to display the members of the object? The answer is No. It is because the operators do not know about the derived type. However, if the operators are overloaded in the class we can use the statements.

The operators are overloaded using friend functions. The friend function which overloads >> operator takes a reference to **istream** object and a reference to derived type object and returns the reference to the **istream** object. The friend function which overloads << operator takes a reference to **ostream** object and a reference to derived type object and returns the reference to the **ostream** object.

Program 14.7 To Overload >> and << Operators

```
#include <iostream.h>

class date
{
    private:
        int d, m , y;


    public:
        friend istream& operator >> (istream& is, date& dt)
        {
            is >> dt.d >> dt.m >> dt.y;

            return is;
        }

        friend ostream& operator << (ostream& os, date& dt)
        {
            os << dt.d << "/" << dt.m << "/" << dt.y;

            return os;
        }

};

int main(void)
{
    date dt;

    cout << "Enter a date \n";
    cin >> dt;
    cout << "The date entered is \n";
    cout << dt;

    return 0;
}
```

Input-Output:

```
Enter a date
12
3
1998
The date entered is 12/3/1998
```

The class date is defined with three members **d**, **m** and **y** of int type. An object of type date is to store day, month and year of a date. In the class both the insertion operator >> and the extraction operator are overloaded so that they can be used with an object of date type to accept and display a date. Note that both the functions are friends of the class date.

14.6 OVERLOADING ARRAY SUBSCRIPT OPERATOR [ ]

So far we have used the [ ] operator with arrays to access the individual elements of the arrays. For example, a[5] denotes the 6th element in the one-dimensional array. We are also aware of the fact that the value within the pair of square brackets should be an integer. C++ allows us to overload this operator so that a non-integer can also be specified within the square brackets as subscripts. Since the overloaded [] operator is restricted to being considered as a binary operator, it can take only one argument.

Program 14.8 To Overload [] Operator

```
#include <iostream.h>
#include <string.h>

struct emp
{
   int empno;
   char name[20];
};

class emp_list
{
   private:
       emp *e;
       int n;

   public:

       emp_list(int);
       void get();
       void display();
       char* operator [] (int);
       int operator [] (char* ename);
};

   emp_list :: emp_list(int m)
   {
       n = m;
       e = new emp[n];
   }

   void emp_list ::get()
   {
```

```
    int i;
    for(i = 0; i < n; i++)
        cin >> e[i].empno >> e[i].name;
}

void emp_list ::display()
{
    int i;
    for(i = 0; i < n; i++)
        cout << e[i].empno << "   " << e[i].name << "\n";
}

char* emp_list :: operator [] (int eno)
{
    int i;

    for(i = 0; i < n; i++)
        if (eno == e[i].empno)
            return e[i].name;
}

int emp_list :: operator [] (char* ename)
{
    int i;

    for(i = 0; i < n; i++)
        if (strcmp(e[i].name, ename) == 0)
            return e[i].empno;
}

int main(void)
{
    emp_list el(5);

    cout << "Enter empno and name of five employees \n";
    el.get();
    el.display();

    int eno;
    eno = el["Nishu"];
    cout << "empno of Nishu = " << eno;
    char *ename;
    ename = el[123];
    cout << "Name of employee with empno 123 " << ename << "\n";

    return 0;
}
```

Input-Output:

```
Enter empno and name of five employees

121  Nishu
122  Harsha
123  Raghu
124  Leela
125  Dev

empno of Nishu = 121
Name of employee with empno 123 Raghu
```

Explanation

The structure emp is defined with the members empno and name of type int and array of char type respectively.

The class emp_list is defined with a pointer to emp type **e** and an integer member **n**. The constructor in the emp_list class takes an argument **m** of int type; sets **m** to the member **n**; allocates memory for *n* employees' details. The member functions get() and display() accept and display the details of *n* employees. The following two member functions overload the [ ] operator:

```
char* operator [] (int eno)
{
        int i;
        for(i = 0; i < n; i++)
                if (eno == e[i].empno)
                        return e[i].name;
}
```

The above function takes **eno** of int type as its argument. Within the function a loop is set up to find a matching **empno** in the list of employees. On finding a match the name of the employee is returned by the function. Note that now a variable of emp_list can now be associated with the [] operator with the value of empno specified within the square brackets and it produces the name of the corresponding employee.

```
int operator [] (char* ename)
{
        int i;
        for(i = 0; i < n; i++)
                if (strcmp(e[i].name, ename) == 0)
                        return e[i].empno;
}
```

The above function takes **ename,** a pointer to char type**,** as its argument. Within the function a loop is set up to find a matching name in the list of employees. On finding a match the empno of the employee is returned by the function. Note that now a variable of emp_list can now be associated with the [] operator with name of an employee in the list specified within the square brackets and it produces the empno of the corresponding employee.

14.7 OVERLOADING FUNCTION CALL OPERATOR ()

The function call operator () is rather unusual and infrequently overloaded. The most distinguishing feature of this operator is that it is "*n*-ary" operator and it can be applied to multiple arguments. The function call operator is the only operator that can have more than one argument. Program 14.9 illustrates overloading the operator.

Program 14.9 To Overload Function Call Operator ()

```
#include <iostream.h>
#include <iomanip.h>

class matrix
{
   private:
      int a[3][3];

   public:
      int& operator ()(int, int);
};

int& matrix :: operator ()(int i, int j)
{
   return a[i][j];
}

int main(void)
{
   matrix m;
   int i, j;

   cout << "Enter the matrix elements \n";
   for(i = 0; i < 3; i++)
   for(j = 0; j < 3; j++)
      cin >> m(i, j);

   cout << "The matrix m is \n";
   for(i = 0; i < 3; i++)
   {
      for(j = 0; j < 3; j++)
         cout << setw(4) << m(i, j);
      cout << "\n";
   }

   return 0;
}
```

Input-Output:

```
Enter the matrix elements 3*3
1 2 3 4 5 6 7 8 9
```

```
The matrix m is
1  2  3
4  5  6
7  8  9
```

Explanation

The class `matrix` is defined with an array **a** of two dimensions as its member data. The line of code `int& operator ()(int, int);` within the class is the prototype of the function, which overloads the function call operator (). The function takes arguments of `int` type and it returns a reference to `int` type. The purpose of the function is to return a reference to a matrix element identified by the row subscript and the column subscript passed as the arguments. So an expression `m(i, j)` where **m** is an object of `matrix` class turns out to be a reference to the element in the **i**th row and the **j**th column of the matrix.

In the `main()`, **m** is declared to be an object of `matrix` type. The elements of the two-dimensional array, the member data of the object **m**, are accepted and displayed using overloaded function call operator.

14.8 OVERLOADING NEW AND DELETE OPERATORS

We know that the new and the delete operators enable us to allocate and deallocate memory during runtime of a program. The C++ language further enhances their ability to deal with customized allocation and deallocation thereby enabling us to take full control over memory allocation and deallocation.

Program 14.10 To Overload New and Delete Operators

```
#include <stddef.h>
#include <iostream.h>
#include <iomanip.h>
#define SIZE 10

class vector
{
   private:
      int *a;

   public:
      void* operator new(size_t);
      void get();
      void display();
      void operator delete(void*);
};

   void* vector :: operator new(size_t m)
   {
      return new int* [SIZE];
   }

   void vector :: get()
   {
```

```
        int i;
        cout << "Enter" << SIZE << "numbers" << "\n";
        for(i = 0; i < SIZE; i++)
            cin >> a[i];
    }

    void vector :: display()
    {
        int i;
        cout << "The numbers are \n";
        for(i = 0; i < SIZE ;i++)
            cout << setw(4) << a[i];
    }

    void vector :: operator delete(void* p)
    {
        delete p;
    }

    int main(void)
    {
        vector* v = new vector;

        v -> get();
        v -> display();

        delete v;
        return 0;
    }
```

Input-Output:

```
Enter 10 numbers
10 21 23 54 65 78 43 87 56 54
The numbers are
10 21 23 54 65 78 43 87 56 54
```

Explanation

The class `vector` is defined with a pointer to `int` type **a** as its member data. The line of code `void* operator new(size_t);` is the prototype for the new operator overloading function. It indicates that the function takes an argument of `size_int` type and returns a pointer to void type. The line of code void operator `delete(void*);` is the prototype of the delete operator overloading function.The function requires a pointer to void type as the argument.
Now, we will have a look at the definition of the functions.

```
void* vector :: operator new(size_t m)
{
        return new int* [SIZE];
}
```

The function allocates memory for SIZE values of `int` type and pointer to it is returned by the function.

Because of the presence of the above function as part of the class, the statement `vector* v = new vector;` causes memory to be allocated for SIZE values of `int` type. Note that in the absence of the function the statement causes memory for a pointer to an integer only.

The delete operator overloading function requires a pointer to void type as its argument and within its body it uses the operator delete with the pointer to deallocate the memory.

14.9 OVERLOADING OPERATORS USING FRIEND FUNCTIONS

Suppose **a** is an object of `integer` class and **i** is a variable of `int` type. The statement `b = a * i;` will be a valid statement if the operator * is overloaded in the class. The member function for the purpose would be as follows:

```
integer integer :: operator *(int i)
{
    integer t;

    t. x   = x * i;
    return t;
}
```

Note that the function is a member of the class and this requires the object of `integer` type to the left of the * operator and a value of `int` type to its right as in the expression `a * i`. Here the expression `i * a` is intuitively expected to produce the same value. It can not be used simply because of the requirement that an object of `integer` type should be to the left of the operator *. By using a friend function to overload the operator, we can have `i * a` also as a valid expression, i.e., we can use a value of `int` type to the left of the * operator.

The definition of the friend function would be as follows:

```
integer operator *  (int i, integer& a)
{
    integer t;

    t.x = a.x * i;

    return t;
}
```

Now, the statement `b = i * a;` would also be permissible.

Program 14.11 To Illustrate the Use of a Friend Function in Overloading Operators

```
#include <iostream.h>

class vector
{
    private:
        int a[5];
    public:
        void get();
        void display();
```

```
        vector operator * (int);
        friend vector operator *(int, vector&);

};

void vector :: get()
{
    int i;

    for(i = 0; i < 5; i++)
        cin >> a[i];
}

void vector :: display()
{
    int i;

    for(i = 0; i < 5; i++)
        cout << a[i] << "\n";
}

vector vector :: operator * (int x)
{
    vector v;
    int i;

    for(i = 0; i < 5; i++)
        v.a[i] = a[i] * x;
    return v;
}

vector  operator * (int x, vector& v)
{
    int i;
    vector t;
    for(i = 0; i < 5; i++)
        t.a[i]  = v. a[i] * x;
    return t;
}

int main(void)
{
    vector v1;

    cout << "Enter five numbers for vector v1 \n";

    v1.get();
    cout << "vector v1: \n";
    v1.display();
```

```
    vector v2;
    v2 = v1 * 5;
    cout << "vector v2: \n";
    v2.display();
    vector v3 = 4 * v1;
    cout << "vector v3: \n";
    v3.display();

    return 0;
}
```

Input-Output:

```
Enter five numbers for vector v1
1 2 3 4 5
vector v1:
1
2
3
4
5
vector v2:
5
10
15
20
25
vector v3:
4
8
12
16
20
```

Explanation

The class `vector` is defined with an array **a** of one dimension of `int` type and of size 5. The member functions `get()` and `display()` are as usual to accept and display the member data of an object the class. The operator * is overloaded in the class so that an object of `vector` type can be multiplied by an integer value. There are two functions, which are entrusted with the responsibility. One is the member function and the other is the friend function of the class.

Following is the definition of the overloading member function:

```
vector vector :: operator * (int x)
{
    vector v;
    int i;

    for(i = 0; i < 5; i++)
        v.a[i] = a[i] * x;
    return v;
}
```

Note that the function takes a formal argument of `int` type, the value of which is multiplied with each element of the array. The vector object **v**, which collects the resultant values, is then returned by the function. Because of the presence of the function we can use an expression of the form `v * n`, where **v** is an object of `int` type and **n** is an `integer` variable or `integer` constant.

Following is the definition of the overloading friend function:

```
vector operator *  (int x, vector& v)
{
    vector t
    int i;

    for(i = 0; i < 5; i++)
        t.a[i] = v.a[i] * x;
    return t;
}
```

Note that the function takes two formal arguments **x** and **v** of type `int` and `vector` respectively. The value of **x** is multiplied with each element of the array of **v**. The vector object **t**, which collects the resultant values, is then returned by the function. Because of the presence of the function we can use an expression of the form `n * v`, where **n** is an `integer` variable or `integer` constant and **v** is an object of `vector` type.

14.10 TYPECASTING

Typecasting is the forcible conversion from one type to another type. As far as the basic types are concerned the compiler is provided with the required conversion routines. For example, consider an expression `5/2`. The value of the expression would be 2. In order to get the correct result we use the typecasting operator `(float)`. The new expression would thus be `(float) 5/2`. Here the typecasting operator `(float)` forcibly converts 5 to 5.0 a float value and the result of the expression would be 2.5. What if one of the operands is of derived type or both are of derived types? In this case the programmer should provide the required conversion routine to do the required conversion.

14.10.1 Conversion from Basic Type to Derived Type and Vice-versa

Suppose **A** is a class and **a** is an object of the class. Let **B** be basic type and **b** be a variable of the type. Even if the conversion from the basic type to the derived type **A** is meaningful we can not use the statement `a = b;`. Similarly even if the conversion from the derived type **A** to basic type **B** is meaningful we can not use the statement `b = a;`. To be able to use the above statements we should provide the appropriate conversion member functions in the class.

A constructor in class **A** with an argument of type **B** with the statements responsible for obtaining the member data of the class by means of the argument serves the purpose of converting from the basic type to derived type. It appears as follows:

```
A(B b)
{
    Statements to obtain members of A through b
}
```

To be able to convert from the derived type **A** to the basic type **B** we should define a function in class **A**, which overloads the type **B** itself. The statements within the function should be responsible for obtaining a value of **B** type by means of the member data of class **A** and the function should return the value.

The member function definition in class **A** appears as follows:

```
operator  B()
{
        statements to obtain a value of B type by means of member data of A
        return (expression)
}
```

Program 14.12 To Convert from Basic Type to Derived Type and Vice-versa

```
#include <iostream.h>

class measure
{
   private:
        int feet;
        float inches;

   public:
        measure(int f = 0, float i = 0)
        {
            feet = f;
            inches = i;
        }

        measure(double metres)
        {
            float f1;

            f1 = metres * 3.28;
            feet = f1;
            inches = (f1 - feet) * 12;
        }

        operator float()
        {
            float f;

            f = feet + inches /12;
            return (f / 3.28);
        }

        void display()
        {
            cout << feet << "-" << inches << "\n";
        }
};
```

```
int main(void)
{
    measure m1(4, 5);
    float f1;
    cout << "m1: ";
    m1.display();
    f1 = m1;    // could be written as f1 = (float) m1; as well
    cout << "metres equivalent of m1 = " << f1 << "\n";

    measure m2(5.6);
    cout << "5.6 metres in terms of feet and inches ";
    m2.display();

    return 0;
}
```

Input-Output:

```
m1: 4-5
metres equivalent of m1 = 1.346545
5.6 metres in terms of feet and inches = 18-4.416
```

Explanation

Program 14.12 demonstrates the conversion from float type to measure type and vice-versa. We know that one metre is equal to 3.28 feet. Given a measurement in terms of metres, conversion of the measurement into feet and inches equivalent is meaningful. As we stated earlier the conversion is accomplished with the help of the following constructor:

```
measure(float metres)
{
        float f1;

        f1 = metres * 3.28;
        feet = f1;
        inches = (f1 - feet) * 12;
}
```

The local variable **f1** collects the feet equivalent of **metres**. The integral part of **f1** is assigned to **feet** and the value of `(f1-feet)*12` is assigned to inches. Here `f1 - feet` gives a fraction of a foot when multiplied by 12 gives inches equivalent of the fraction. Thus, the member data of `measure` type are obtained.

The following member function converts from measure type to float type:

```
operator float()
{
        float f;

        f = feet + inches /12;
        return (f / 3.28);
}
```

Here the typecasting operator float is overloaded in the measure class. The metres equivalent of the feet and inches is found out and it is returned by the function.

In the `main()`, **m1** is declared as an object of `measure` type with two values 4 (feet) and 5 (inches) as the initial values. The measurement is displayed with the statement `m1.display();`. The statement `f1 = m1;` invokes the overloaded `float` operator function and which when executed produces the metres equivalent of `feet` and `inches` of **m1** and returns a float value. The float value is collected by the variable **f1** and it is displayed. One more object **m2** is declared with an initial value 5.6. During the creation of the object, the constructor in the class with a float value as the argument gets executed. We know that the constructor is to convert from `float` (metres) to `measure` type. Accordingly the values of `feet` and `inches` of **m2** are obtained by the function. The statement `m2.display();` displays 5.6 metres in terms of `feet` and `inches`.

Program 14.13 To Convert from Derived Type to Basic Type

```
#include <iostream.h>

class vector
{
    private:
        int a[5];
    public:
        void get();
        void display();
        operator int();
};

void vector :: get()
{
    int i;

    for(i = 0; i < 5; i++)
        cin >> a[i];
}

void vector :: display()
{
    int i;

    for(i=0; i < 5; i++)
        cout << a[i] << "\n";
}

vector :: operator int()
{
    int i, s = 0;

    for(i=0;i < 5; i++)
        s += a[i];

    return s;
}
```

```
int main(void)
{
   vector v;
   int s;

   cout << "Enter five numbers \n";
   v.get();
   cout << "vector v:\n";
   v.display();

   s = v; // could be written as s = (int) v; as well

   cout << "sum of the vector elements = " << s;

   return 0;
}
```

Input-Output:

```
Enter five numbers
2 3 4 5 7
The vector v:
2
3
4
5
7
sum of the vector elements = 21
```

Explanation

The class `vector` contains an array of `int` type and of size 5 as its member data. Any object of `vector` type thus comes packaged with the array. The `get()` and `display()` member functions are to accept and display the elements of the member data (array) of an object. Here we need to find the sum of the elements of a vector and we intend to use a statement like `s = v;` where **s** is a variable of `int` type and **v** is an object of `vector` type. After the execution of the statement the variable **s** is expected to collect the sum of the elements in the vector **v**. This job has to be accomplished by means of a member function of the `vector` class and the function has to be a converter from `vector` to `int` type. No doubt, the function should overload the typecasting operator (`int`) in the `vector` class. The definition of the function is as follows:

```
vector :: operator int()
{
   int i, s = 0;

   for(i = 0; i < 5; i++)
       s += a[i];

   return s;
}
```

The variable **s** within the member function would collect the sum of all the elements of the vector and it is returned by the function.

In the `main()`, **v** is declared to be an object of `vector` type and **s** is declared to be a variable of `int` type. The elements of the vector **v** are accepted with the statement `v.get();` and are displayed with the statement `v.display();`. The core part of the `main()` is the statement `s = v;`. Because this is the statement which causes the above overloading function to get executed. On its execution, the function returns the sum of the elements in the vector **v**, which is collected by the variable **s**. The value of the variable **s** is then displayed.

14.10.2 Conversion from One Derived Type to Another Derived Type and Vice-versa

Suppose **A** is a class and **a** is an object of the class. Let **B** be another class and **b** be an object of the class type. Even if the member data of the objects **a** and **b** are interconvertible we can not use the statement `a = b;` to convert from **b** to **a**. Similarly, we can not use the statement `b = a;` to convert from **a** to **b**. To be able to use the above statements we should provide the appropriate conversion member functions in either of the classes.

Let us consider the case of conversion from **B** to **A** type, i.e., to have the statement `a = b;` Here class **A** is the destination class and **B** is the source class. The required conversion function can either be written in the destination class **A** or in the source class **B**. Hence there are two approaches to solve this problem.

Conversion function in destination class: A constructor in the class **A** with an argument of type **B** with the statements responsible for obtaining the member data of the class **A** by means of the member data of the argument serves the purpose of converting from the **B** type to **A** type. Which appears as follows:

```
A(B b)
{
    Statements to obtain members of A through the members of b

}
```

Conversion function in source class: The conversion function in the source class **B** should overload the typecasting operator **A** and the statements within the function should obtain the members of **A** type by means of the members of **B**. An object of **A** type constructed within the function should then be returned. The function appears as follows:

```
operator A()
{
    Statements to obtain the members of A type by means of the members of B
    return A(members of A delimited by commas);
}
```

We will now write some programs, which involve conversion from one derived type to another derived type.

Program 14.14 To Convert from One Derived Type to Another Derived Type

```
#include <iostream.h>

class item1
{
   private:
      int itemcode;
      int noi;
      float unitprice;
   public:
      item1(int i, int n, int u)
      {
         itemcode = i;
         noi = n;
         unitprice = u;
      }

      int get_itemcode()
      {
         return itemcode;
      }

      int get_noi()
      {
         return noi;
      }

      float get_unitprice()
      {
         return unitprice;
      }

      void display()
      {
         cout << " Item Code = " << itemcode << "\n";
         cout << "No. of Items = " << noi << "\n";
         cout << "Unit Price = " << unitprice << "\n";
      }
};

class item2
{
   private:
      int itemcode;
      float totprice;

   public:
      item2(int i = 0, float t = 0)
      {
         itemcode = i;
```

```
        totprice = t;
    }

    item2(item1 t)
    {
        itemcode = t.get_itemcode();
        totprice = t.get_noi() * t.get_unitprice();

    }

  void display()
  {
    cout << "Item Code " << itemcode << "\n";
    cout << "Total Price = " << totprice << "\n";
  }
};


int main(void)
{
  item1 t1(121, 8, 23.45);
  item2 t2;

  cout << "t1: \n";
  t1.display();
  t2  = t1;
  cout << "t2: \n";
  t2.display();

  return 0;
}
```

Input-Output:

```
t1:
Item Code = 121
No. of Items = 8
Unit Price = 23

t2:
Item Code 121
Total Price = 184
```

Explanation

The class `item1` is defined with the member data **itemcode**, **noi** (numer of items) and **unitprice** of type `int`, `int` and `float` respectively. Any object of `item1` type would thus come packaged with the three member data. If **t1** is an object of `item1` type **t1.itemcode**, **t1.noi**, **t1.unitprice** are the member data of **t1**. The class `item2` is defined with the member data **itemcode** and **totprice**. Here we intend to obtain an object of type `item2` by means of an object of `item1` class. This is to be done by assigning the **itemcode** of `item1` to **itemcode** member of `item2` and assigning the product of **noi** (number of items) and **unitprice** to **totprice** of `item2`.

Item2		**Item1**
itemcode	⟵	itemcode
totprice	⟵	noi * unitprice

This calls for a conversion function, which is defined in the destination class `item2`. The function turns out to be a constructor with an object of type `item1` as its argument. The definition of which is as follows:

```
item2(item1 t)
{
    itemcode = t.get_itemcode();
    totprice = t.get_noi() * t.get_unitprice();

}
```

Note that `get_itemcode()`, `get_noi()` and `get_unitprice()` are the member functions of `item1` class and are used with the object **t** in the constructor to access the corresponding members of the `item1` class.

In the main **t1** is declared to be an object of `item1` class and it is also initialized with values for its three members. **t2** is declared to be an object of type `item2` class. The statement `t2 = t1;` invokes the constructor (with the argument of type `item1`) in the `item2` class gets executed, which when executed the object **t2** gets created.

Let us now consider another example of conversion from one derived type to another and vice-versa. A point in a *XY* plane can be represented by two types of co-ordinates: (a) Rectangualr co-ordinates (b) Polar co-ordinates.

Rectangular co-ordinates are denoted by (x, y) where x is the distance of the point from the origin along the *X*-axis and y is the distance of the point from the origin along the *Y* axis. The polar co-ordinates are denoted by (r, a), where r is the length of the line joining the origin and the point $p(x, y)$ and a is the angle made by the line with the *X* axis.

We have the following conversion formulae:

```
x = r*cos a          r = sqrt(x*x + y*y)
y = r * sin a        a = atan(y/x)
```

So when one kind of co-ordinates are given the other kind of arguments can be obtained using the conversion formulae.

Program 14.15 To Convert from One Derived Type to Another Derived Type and Vice-versa

```
#include <iostream.h>
#include <math.h>

class polar;

class rect
{
    private:
        float x, y;

    public:
```

```
        rect(float x1 = 0, float y1 = 0)
        {
            x = x1;
            y = y1;
        }

        void display()
        {
            cout << x << "," << y << "\n";
        }

        float get_x()
        {
            return x;
        }
        float get_y()
        {
            return y;
        }
};

class polar
{
    private:
        float r, a;
    public:
        polar(float r1 = 0, float a1 = 0)
        {
            r = r1;
            a = a1;
        }

        polar(rect p)
        {
            float sqr_x, sqr_y;

            sqr_x =  p.get_x() * p.get_x();
            sqr_y =  p.get_y() * p.get_y();

            r = sqrt(sqr_x + sqr_y);
            a = atan(p.get_y() / p.get_x());
        }

        void display()
        {
            cout << r << "," << a << "\n";
        }

        operator rect()
```

```
        {
            float x, y;

            x = r * cos(a);
            y = r * sin(a);
            return (rect(x, y));
        }

};

int main(void)
{
    rect rc1(5.0897, 4.0710), rc2;
    polar pc1, pc2(6, 0.785398);

    cout << "rc1 =";
    rc1.display();
    pc1 = rc1;     // Invokes polar(rect p) constructor
    cout << "pc1 =";
    pc1.display();

    cout << "pc2 =";
    pc2.display();
    rc2 = pc2;     // Invokes operator rect() function
    cout << "rc2 =";
    rc2.display();

    return 0;
}
```

Input-Output:

```
rc1 =5.0897,4.071
pc1 =6.517522,0.67465

pc2 =6,0.785398
rc2 =4.242641,4.24264
```

Explanation

The following constructor in the polar class converts from rect to polar and enables us to use the statement `p = r;` where **p** is an object of polar type and **r**, an object of rect type.

```
        polar(rect p)
        {
            float sqr_x, sqr_y;

            sqr_x =  p.get_x() * p.get_x();
            sqr_y =  p.get_y() * p.get_y();

            r = sqrt(sqr_x + sqr_y);
            a = atan(p.get_y() / p.get_x());
        }
```

Note that the conversion function is defined in the destination class.

The following function converts from polar to rect type and enables us to use the statement `r = p;` where **r** is an object of rect type and **p**, an object of polar type.

```
operator rect()
{
        float x, y;

        x = r * cos(a);
        y = r * sin(a);
        return (rect(x, y));
}
```

Note that the conversion function is defined in the source class.

14.11 SOME GUIDELINES

Operator overloading enables us to invent a new language itself by permitting the usage of the operators with user defined types. The program listings with the operators overloaded are no doubt more intuitive and readable. If not used in a proper manner, the programs may turn out to be obscure and hard to understand. Here are some guidelines to be followed.

Use similar meanings: While overloading an operator it is important to keep in mind that the overloaded operator does the same operation that is similar to that performed on basic types. We could overload + operator to perform subtraction operation on the derived types. But it would hardly make the program listing more comprehensible.

Use similar syntax: It is important that the same syntax is retained when an operator is overloaded to be used with derived types. For example, if + is overloaded in measure class we should be able to use the statement `m3 = m1 + m2` where **m1**, **m2** and **m3** are objects of measure type. This is in conformity with the usage of the operator with basic types like int, float, etc.

Use overloaded operators sparingly: The ability to add functionality to operators is a blessing in that it makes programs more intuitive and readable, but at the same time it can also have opposite effect if the number of overloaded operators grows too large. That is why we need to think of overloading operators in obvious situations only. When in doubt, we better use functions to do the job.

Avoid ambiguity: There are a number of situations where we have more than one way of achieving the same job. For example, to convert from a basic type to derived type, we can overload the assignment operator with an argument of basic type in the class or we can use a constructor with an argument of basic type in the class. We have to define one of them. If both the functions are made available as part of the class, the compiler gets confused as to which to select.

14.12 OPERATORS WHICH CAN NOT BE OVERLOADED

Not all operators can be overloaded. Following are the operators, which can not be overloaded. This is to prevent undesirable interactions with the C++ language itself.

The dot operator (**.**)
The scope resolution operator (**::**)
The conditional operator (**?:**)
The pointer to member operator (**.***)

REVIEW QUESTIONS

14.1 What is operator overloading? Why do we need it?

14.2 Write the general form of an operator overloading function.

14.3 Mention the difference between overloading a unary operator and a binary operator.

14.4 Can we overload the array subscription operator? Give an example.

14.5 Can we overload the function call operator ()? Give an example.

14.6 Why do we need to overload new and delete operators? Explain.

14.7 When do we require friend functions in operator overloading? Give an example situation.

14.8 Write the syntax of the overloading functions for the insertion operator (>>) and extraction operator (<<).

14.9 What is typecasting?

14.10 How do you convert from basic type to derived type and vice-versa. Explain.

14.11 How do you convert from one derived type to another derived type and vice-versa. Explain.

14.12 List the operators, which can not be overloaded.

True/False Questions

T14.1 New operators can not be created through overloading, only existing operators can be overloaded.

T14.2 A unary operator overloading function requires one argument.

T14.3 A binary operator overloading function requires two arguments.

T14.4 Overloading functions should be member functions of classes.

T14.5 We do not require friend functions in operator overloading at all.

T14.6 + operator can be overloaded in a class to perform subtraction.

T14.7 Conversion from basic type to derived type is done with the help of a constructor with the basic type as its argument.

T14.8 Conversion from basic type to derived type can be done by overloading = in the class.

T14.9 Overloading the basic type casting operator does conversion from derived type to basic type.

T14.10 All the operators can be overloaded.

PROGRAMMING EXERCISES

P14.1 Modify the integer class to perform the following:

(a) Overload + to add two integers

(b) Overload – to subtract one integer from another integer

(c) Overload * to multiply two integers

(d) Overload / to divide one integer by the other integer

(e) Overload % to obtain the remainder after division of an integer by another integer

Write a menu driven program with the five options to selectively add, subtract, multiply, divide and obtain the remainder.

P14.2 Modify the measure class to perform the following:
(a) To overload >= operator
(b) To overload == operator

P14.3 Create a class by name string with a member data, an array of char type. Overload < operator in the class to find whether one string is lexicographically less than the other. Use the function to sort a list of strings in the decreasing order alphabetically.

P14.4 Overload +=, –=, *=, /= and %= in the vector class.

P14.5 Modify the class matrix to perform the following:
(a) To overload + to add two matrices
(b) To overload – to subtract one matrix from another
(c) To overload * to multiply two matrices

P14.6 Design a class for storing a complex number, which is of the form $x + iy$, where x is the real part and y is the imaginary part. Perform the following:
(a) Overload + to add two complex numbers
(b) Overload – to subtract one complex number from the other
(c) Overload * to multiply two complex numbers
(d) Overload / to divide one complex number by the other

P14.7 Create a class by name date with the member data day, month and year. Perform the following:
(a) Overload all relational operators < , <=, >, >=, ==, !=
(b) Overload ++ operator to increment a date by one day
(c) Overload + to add given number of days to find the next date
(d) Provide the necessary function to use the statement like `days = dt`; where days is an int variable and **dt** is an object of date class. The statement is intended to assign the number of days elapsed in the current year of the date to the variable days. Note that this is a case of conversion from derived type to basic type.

P14.8 Create a class by name distance with member data metres and centimetres. Provide conversion functions to convert from distance type to measure type (feet, inches) and vice-versa.

P14.9 Create a class by name date with data members day, month and year. Create another class by name customdate with data members day and year. Provide the required conversion function to convert from date type to custmdate type. (Note that day part of customdate will have the number of days elapsed in the year). Test it with a complete program.

P14.10 Create two classes by name Fahrenheit and Celsius both having temperature as their member data. Write conversion functions to convert from Fahrenheit to Celsius type and vice-versa.

Chapter 15

Inheritance

15.1 INTRODUCTION

Inheritance is another important feature of C++. The concept of inheritance enables us to reuse the existing code. It is implemented through classes. Here we start with a foundation class and keep extending it depending on the requirement. Because of this reason, the concept of inheritance is said to support bottom-up approach of programming, which in turn facilitates hierarchical growth of a program.

Suppose **A** is a class already defined and we need to define another class **B**, which should provide some or all the facilities provided by the class **A** in addition to its own. Here the direct option available at our disposal is defining the class **B** from scratch including the facilities provided by **A** in addition to its own. The problems with this option are the following:

1. Code written in **A** gets repeated in **B** leading to unnecessary consumption of more memory space.
2. The code in **B** (Even the repeated code of **A**) needs to be tested to perfection. If the class **A** had already been tested to perfection, the testing also becomes cumbersome.

The above problems can be eliminated if we can reuse the code of **A** even in **B** (without rewriting it in **B**). It is possible through inheritance. Here the class **B** is made to inherit the properties of **A**. The class **A** is called the **base class** and the class **B** is called the **derived class**. Symbolically it is denoted as:

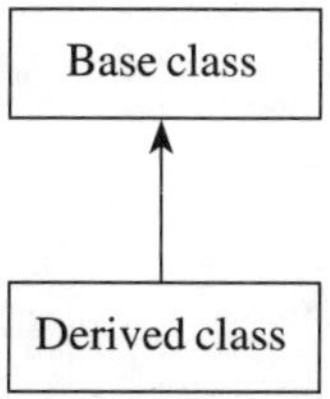

Programmatically, the derivation of **B** from **A** is done with the following class definition of **B**:

```
class B : public A
{

};
```

15.2 SINGLE LEVEL INHERITANCE

If only two classes are involved in the derivation then it is called **single level inheritance.** The following programs illustrate single level inheritance.

Program 15.1 To Illustrate Inheritance

```
#include <iostream.h>

class integer
{
   protected:
      int x;
   public:
      void get();
      void display();
      void increment();
};

void integer :: get()
{
   cin >> x;
}

void integer :: display()
{
   cout << x << "\n";
}

void integer :: increment()
{
   x++;
}


class d_integer : public integer
{

   public:

      void decrement();
};

void d_integer :: decrement()
```

```
{
    x--;
}

int main(void)
{
    d_integer d;

    cout << "Enter a value for d \n";
    d.get();
    cout << "The value of d =";
    d.display();
    d.increment();
    cout << "the value of d after incrementing \n";
    d.display();
    d.decrement();
    cout << "The value of d after decrementing \n";
    d.display();
    return 0;
}
```

Input-Output:

```
Enter a value for d
5
The value of d =5
the value of d after incrementing
6
The value of d after decrementing
5
```

Explanation

The class `integer` is defined with a member data **x** of `int` type with the access specifier **protected**. The `get()`, `display()` and `increment()` are the member functions of the class. The member functions `get()` and `display()` are to accept the member data of an object and display it respectively. The member function `increment()` is to increment the member data of an object with which the function is called. Note the presence of the statement `x++;` within the body of the function.

The class `d_integer` is derived from the class `integer` and the derived class has the member function `decrement()`, the purpose of which is to decrement the member data of an object with which the function is called by one. Note the statement `x–;` within the body of the function. The **protected** access specifier used while declaring the member data **x** within the base class `integer` extends the accessibility even to the member functions of `d_integer`, the derived class.

In the `main()`, **d** is declared to be an object of class `d_integer`. The statements `d.get()` and `d.display()` accept and display the member data of the object **d** respectively. `d.increment()` increments the member data of the object **d** and `d.decrement()` decrements the member data of the object **d** respectively. Note that an object of derived class (`d_integer` in this case) can access all the public members of the base class (`integer` in this case).

Program 15.2 To Illustrate Inheritance

```
#include <iostream.h>

class date
{
   protected:

      int d, m, y;
   public:

      void get();
      void display();
};

void date :: get()
{
   cout << "Enter d, m and y \n";
   cin >> d >> m >> y;
}

void date :: display()
{
   cout << d << "/" << m << "/" << y << "\n";
}


class datetime : public date
{
   private:
      int h, m, s;

   public:
      void get();
      void display();
};


void datetime :: get()
{
   date :: get();
   cout << "Enter h, m and s \n";
   cin >> h >> m >> s;
}

void datetime :: display()
{
   date :: display();
   cout << h << ":" << m << ":" << s << "|n";
}
```

```
int main(void)
{
    datetime dt;

    dt.get();
    dt.display();

    return 0;
}
```

Input-Output:

```
Enter d, m and y
12 3 1998
Enter h, m and s
3 25 54

12/3/1998
3:25:54
```

Explanation

The class `date` is defined with three member data **d**, **m** and **y** all of `int` type. Any object of `date` type would thus represent a date (day, month, year). The member functions `get()` and `display()` within the class are to accept and display the values of the member data of an object of type `date`. Note that the member data are declared under the access specifier **protected.**

The class `datetime` is derived from the class `date`. The protected members **d**, **m** and **y** of the date class are thus available even within the class `datetime`. In addition to these, the class `datetime` has its own members **h**, **m** and **s** all of `int` type representing hours, minutes and seconds respectively. Any object of type `datetime` would thus represent both date and time of an event.

The member functions `get()` and `display()` within the class are to accept and display both date and time. Note the definition of the `get()` in the datetime which is as follows:

```
void datetime :: get()
{
    date :: get();
    cout << "Enter h, m and s \n";
    cin >> h >> m >> s;
}
```

The statement `date::get();` is embedded within the body of the function `get()` of datetime class. It is for accepting the date values (`d,m,y`). `date::` is for indicating that the function `get()` is from the class `date`, the base class. After the date values are accepted, the values of **h**, **m** and **s** are accepted. This is true even in the case of `display()` member function of datetime class.

In the `main()`, **dt** is declared to be an object of `datetime` class and it can represent both date and time. The statement `dt.get();` enables us to accept both date and time and the statement `dt.display();` enables us to display both date and time represented by the object **dt**.

Through the Program 15.1 we learnt that an object of derived class can access the public members of the base class with the use of the dot operator. Even then the statement `dt.get();` invokes the `get()` of `datetime` class ignoring the `get()` of `date` class, the base class. Here the same named get() in the derived class datetime is given priority and it gets executed. Similarly, the statement dt.display(); invokes the display() of the datetime class ignoring the display() of date class.

The phenomenon of ignoring the same named functions in the base class and invoking the same named functions of the derived class whenever an object of the derived class accesses the functions is called **Function overriding.**

In the Program 15.2 the signatures of the same named functions were incidentally same. (Signature of a function is the number of arguments, their type and the order of their presence). Even the difference in the signatures of the functions in the base class and the derived class can not prevent overriding. Consider the following code:

```
#include <iostream.h>

class A
{
    public:
        void f(int i, double d)
        {
            cout << "i=" << i<< "d=" << d << "\n";
        }
};

class B : public A
{
    public:
        void f()
        {
            cout << "B";
        }
};

int main(void)
{
    B b;
    b.f(10, 5.6); // Compile-time error
    return 0;
}
```

The member function f() in **A** has two arguments and that in **B** has no argument. An attempt to invoke the function f() of the base class **A** with the statement b.f(10, 5.6); fails, where **b** is an object of **B** type. This is because the object **b** invokes f() of its class and it does not require any argument but it is provided with arguments.

15.3 MULTIPLE INHERITANCE

Suppose **A**, **B** and **C** are three classes and if the class **C** is derived from both **A** and **B** then it is said to exhibit multiple inheritance. It is symbolically denoted as follows:

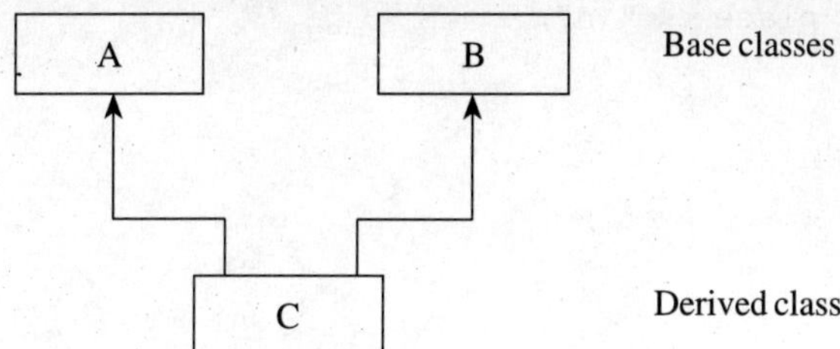

In general, in multiple inheritance there can be more than two base classes also:

EXAMPLE

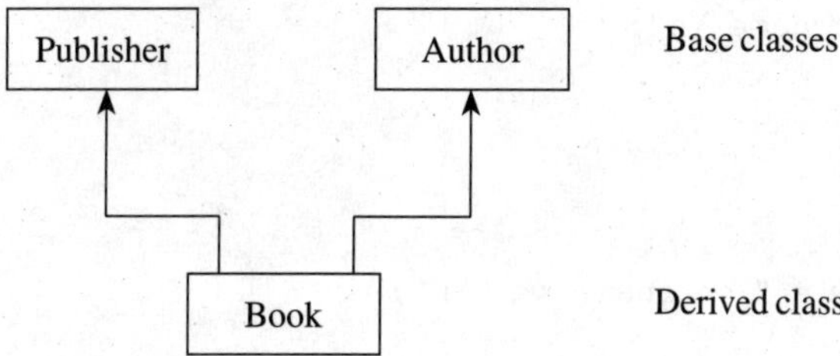

Here the class book is inherited from both publisher and author classes.

Program 15.3 To Illustrate Multiple Inheritance

```
#include <iostream.h>
#include <stdio.h>

class publisher
{
   protected:
      char pname[40];
      char place[20];
   public:
      void get();
      void display();
};

void publisher :: get()
{
   cout << "Enter publisher name and place \n";
   cin >> pname >> place;
}

void publisher :: display()
{
   cout << "Publisher's Name = " << pname << "\n";
```

```
    cout << "Place = " << place << "\n";
}

class author
{
    protected:
        char aname[20];

        void get();
        void display();
};

void author :: get()
{
    cout << "Enter author name \n";
    cin >> aname;
}

void author :: display()
{
    cout << "Author' Name = " << aname << "\n";
}

class book : public publisher, public author
{
    private:
        char title[20];
        float price;
        int pages;

    public:
        void get();
        void display();

};

void book :: get()
{
    publisher :: get();
    author :: get();
    cout << "Enter title, pages and price \n";
    cin >> title;
    cin >> pages >> price;
}

void book :: display()
{
    publisher :: display();
    author :: display();
    cout << "Title = " << title << "\n";
    cout << "Pages =" << pages << "\n";
```

```
    cout << "Price = " << price;
}
int main(void)
{
    book b;

    b.get();
    b.display();
    return 0;
}
```

Input-Output:

```
Enter publisher name and place
PHI
Delhi
Enter author name
Somashekara

Enter title, pages and price
Programming-in-C
324
225

Publisher's Name = PHI
Place = Delhi
Author' Name = Somashekara
Title = Programming-in-C
Pages = 324
Price = 225
```

Explanation

The class `publisher` is defined with the **protected** member data **pname** and **place** both of type array of `char` type representing the publisher name and the place of publishing. The member functions `get()` and `display()` are to accept and display the member data of the class.

The class `author` is defined with the **protected** member data **aname** and **institution** both of type array of `char` type representing the author name and the institution of the author. The member functions `get()` and `display()` are to accept and display the member data of the class.

The class `book` is derived from both `publisher` and `author` classes. Note that for the derived class book, there are two base classes. The class book has title, price and pages as its own member data. As a result any object of book type can collect pname, place, aname, institution, title, price and pages of a book.

Note the definition of `get()` of book class which is as follows:

```
void book :: get()
{
    publisher :: get();
    author :: get();
    cout << "Enter title, pages and price \n";
    cin >> title;
        cin >> pages >> price;
        }
```

The `get()` belonging to the class book contains the `get()` functions of both `publisher` and `author` and they are called with the statements `publisher :: get();` and `author :: get();` so that the publisher details and the author details can be accepted. Similarly, the `display()` of book class is defined.

In the `main()`, **b** is declared to be an object of `book` type. `b.get();` and `b.display()` are responsible for accepting the details of a book and display them.

15.4 MULTILEVEL INHERITANCE

Suppose **A**, **B** and **C** are three classes, if the class **B** is derived from **A** and in turn **C** is derived from the class **B**, it is said to exhibit multilevel inheritance. It is symbolically denoted as follows:

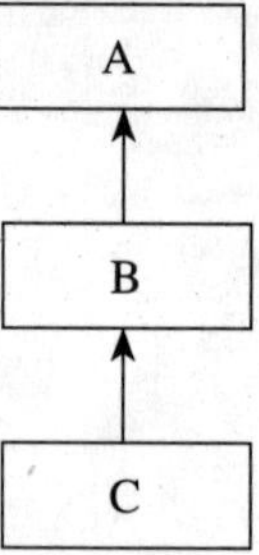

In general, in multilevel inheritance there can be number of levels of inheritance, i.e., if need be, another class **D** can be derived from the class **C** and another class **E** can be derived from the class **D** and so on.

EXAMPLE

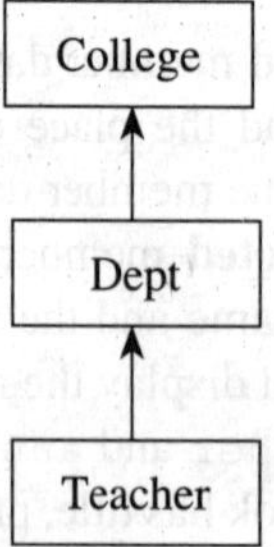

The class dept is derived from the class college and the class teacher is derived from dept class.

Program 15.4 To Illustrate Multilevel Inheritance

```
#include <iostream.h>

class college
{
   protected:
        char cname[20];
        char city[20];
```

```
    public:
        void get()
        {
            cout << "Enter college name and city \n";
            cin >> cname;
            cin >> city;
        }
        void display()
        {
            cout << "College = " << cname << "\n";
            cout << "City  = " << city << "\n";
        }

};

class dept : public college
{
    protected:
        char dname[20];
    public:
        void get()
        {
            college :: get();
            cout << "Enter Dept name \n";
            cin >> dname;
        }
        void display()
        {
            college::display();
            cout << "Department = " << dname << "\n";
        }

};

class teacher : public dept
{
    private:
        char tname[20];
        char qualification[20];
    public:
        void get()
        {
            dept :: get();
            cout << "Enter tname and qualification \n";
            cin >> tname;
            cin >> qualification;
        }

        void display()
        {
            dept :: display();
```

```
        cout << "Teacher = " << tname << "\n";
        cout << "Qualification = " << qualification;
    }

};

int main(void)
{
    teacher t;

    t.get();
    t.display();

    return 0;
}
```

Input-Output:

```
Enter college name and city
Maharani's-College
Bangalore

Enter Dept name
Computer-Science

Enter tname and qualification
Manjunath
M.Sc.

College = Maharani's-College
City  = Bangalore
Department = Computer-Science
Teacher = Manjunath
Qualification = M.Sc.
```

Explanation

The class `college` is defined with the **protected** members `cname` and `city` of string type. The member data represent the college name and the city in which the college is situated. The `get()` and `display()` are the input and output functions for the class.

The class `dept` is derived from the class `college`. `dname` and `nof` are the **protected** member data of the `dept` class representing the department name and the number of faculties in the department. The `get()` and `display()` are the input and output functions for the `dept` class.

```
void get()
{
        college :: get();
        cout << "Enter dname \n";
        cin >> dname;
}
```

The statement `college::get();` is to accept the college name and the city of the college. Note that the member function `get()` of `college` class (Base class) is accessible in `dept` class (Derived class). The statement `cin >> dname;` accepts the department name.

Note the definition of `display()` in `dept` class which is given as:

```
void display()
{
        college::display();
        cout << "Department = " << dname << "\n";
}
```

The statement `college::display();` is to display the college name and the city of the college. The statement `cout << dname;` displays the department name.

The class `teacher` is derived from the class `dept`. **tname** and **qualification** are the member data of the `teacher` class representing teacher name and the qualification of the teacher. The `get()` and `display()` are the input and output functions for the class.

```
void get()
{
        dept :: get();
        cout << "Enter tname and qualification\n";
        cin >> tname;
        cin >> qualification;
}
```

The statement `dept::get();` is to accept the cname, city, dname and nof values . The statements

```
cin >> tname;
Cin >> qualification;
```

accept the tname and qualification.

Note the definition of `display()` in `teacher` class which is given as:

```
void display()
{
        dept :: display();
        cout << "Teacher = " << tname << "\n";
        cout << "Qualification = " << qualification;
}
```

The statement `dept :: display();` is to display the cname, city, dname. The statements

```
cout << "Teacher = " << tname << "\n";
cout << "Qualification = " << qualification;
```

display the tname and qualification.

In the `main()`, **t** is declared to be an object of `teacher` class. Because of the multilevel inheritance the object **t** comes packaged with the member data `cname`, `city`, `dname`, `nof`, `tname` and `qualification`. The statement `t.get();` thus accepts the values of the member data and the statement `t.display();` displays the values of all the member data.

15.5 HIERARCHICAL INHERITANCE

Suppose **A**, **B** and **C** are three classes and the classes **B** and **C** are derived from the class **A**. It is said to exhibit hierarchical inheritance. In hierarchical inheritance, there is only one base class and more than one derived class. In essence hierarchical inheritance is the reverse of multiple inheritance. Symbolically, it is denoted as follows:

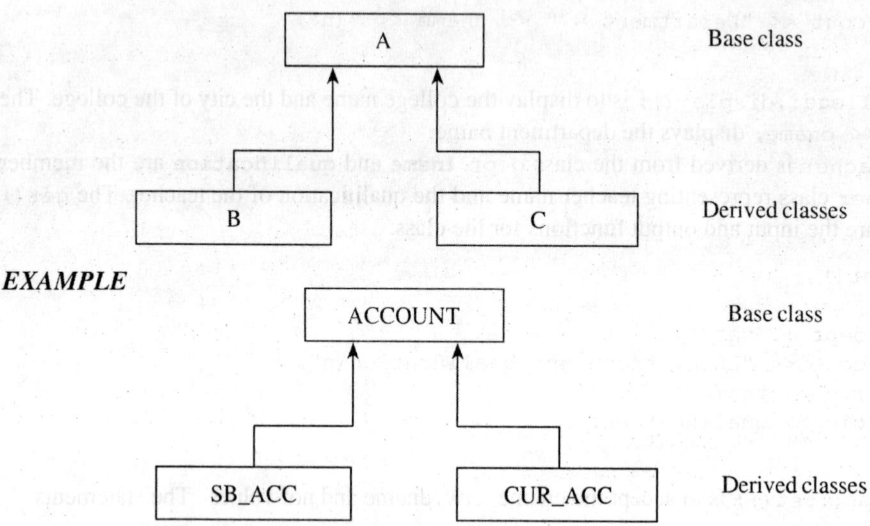

EXAMPLE

The class account is the base class for both SB_ACC and CUR_ACC classes.

Program 15.5 To Illustrate Hierarchical Inheritance

```
#include <iostream.h>
class account
{
    protected:
        int accno;
        char name[20];
    public:
        void get()
        {
            cout << "Enter accno and name \n";
            cin >> accno >> name;
        }
        void display()
        {
            cout << accno << name;
        }
};

class sb_acc : public account
{
    private:
        float roi;
    public:
        void get()
```

```
    {
        account :: get();
        cout << "Enter roi \n";
        cin >> roi;
    }

    void display()
    {
        account :: display();
        cout << roi << "\n";
    }

};

class cur_acc : public account
{
    private:
        float odlimit;
    public:
        void get()
        {
            account :: get();
            cout << "Enter odlimit \n";
            cin >> odlimit;
        }

        void display()
        {
            account :: display();
            cout << odlimit << "\n";
        }
};

int main(void)
{

    sb_acc s;
    cur_acc c;

    s.get();
    s.display();
    c.get();
    c.display();

    return 0;
}
```

Input-Output:

```
Enter accno and name
13456 Nitin
Enter roi
```

```
6
Account Number = 13456
Name = Nitin
Rate of Interest = 6%

Enter accno and name
13765 Nishanth
Enter odlimit
25000

Account Number = 13765
Name = Nishanth
Overdraft Limit = 25000
```

Explanation

The class `account` is defined with the protected member data **accno** and **name** of type `int` and array of `char` respectively. The `get()` and `display()` member functions are the input and output interfaces to the class.

The class `sb_acc` is derived from the class `account` and **roi** (Rate of interest) is its own member data. So, an object of type **sb_acc** has access to the member data **accno** and **name** of the `account` class in addition to its own member data **roi**. The member functions `get()` and `display()` within **sb_acc** are to accept the details of an **sb_acc** object and display them.

The class `cur_acc` is also derived from the class `account` and **odlimit** (Overdraft limit) is its own member data. So, an object of type **cur_acc** has access to the member data **accno** and **name** of the `account` class in addition to its own member data **odlimit**. The member functions `get()` and `display()` within **cur_acc** are to accept the details of a **cur_acc** object and display them.

Within `main()` **s** and **c** are declared to be objects of type **sb_acc** and **cur_acc** respectively. The details of SB A/C and CUR A/C are accepted and displayed.

15.6 HYBRID INHERITANCE

So far we have discussed about different types of inheritance separately. There arise some situations where we need to combine two or more types of inheritance to satisfy the requirements. The combination of two or more types of inheritance leads to what is known as **hybrid inheritance**.

Suppose **A**, **B**, **C** and **D** are the classes where class **B** is derived from **A**, class **C** is derived from both **B** and **D**. Symbolically which is depicted as follows:

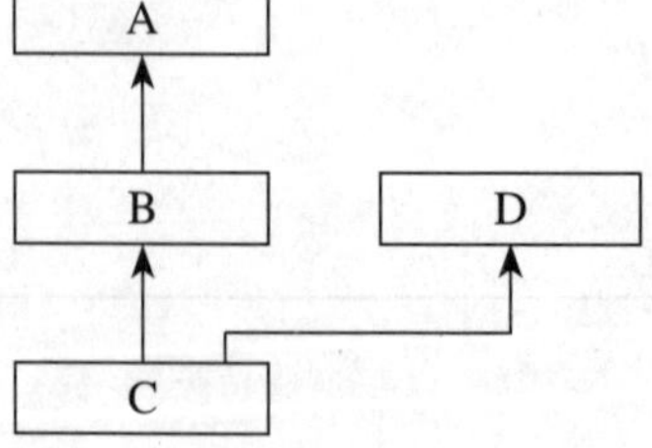

EXAMPLE

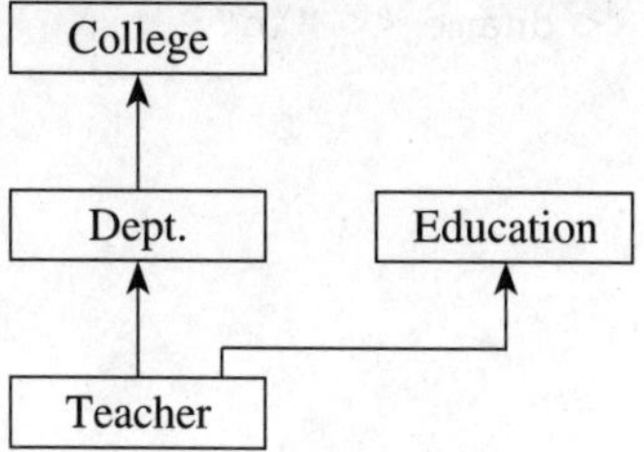

It can be seen that the resulting inheritance is the combination of both multilevel inheritance and multiple inheritance

Program 15.6 To Illustrate Hybrid Inheritance

```
#include <iostream.h>
class college
{
   protected:
      char cname[20];
      char city[20];
   public:
      void get()
      {
         cout << "Enter cname and city \n";
         cin >> cname;
         cin >> city;
      }
      void display()
      {
         cout << "College = " << cname << "\n";
         cout << "City = " << city  << "\n";
      }

};

class dept : public college
{
   protected:
      char dname[20];
   public:
      void get()
      {
         college :: get();
         cout << "Enter dname \n";
         cin >> dname;
      }
      void display()
```

```
        {
            college::display();
            cout << "Department = " << dname << "\n";
        }

};

class education
{
    protected:
        char degree[20];
        char university[20];
    public:
        void get()
        {
            cout << "Enter degree and university \n";
            cin >> degree;
            cin >> university;
        }
        void display()
        {
            cout << "Degree = " << degree << "\n";
            cout << "University = " << university << "\n";
        }

};

class teacher : public dept, public education
{
    private:
        char tname[20];
    public:
        void get()
        {
            dept :: get();
            cout << "Enter tname \n";
            cin >> tname;
        }

        void display()
        {
            dept :: display();
            cout << "Teacher = " << tname ;
        }

};

int main(void)
{
    teacher t;
```

```
    t.get();
    t.display();
    return 0;
}
```

Input-Output:

```
Enter cname and city
Yuvaraja's-College
Mysore
Enter dname
Computer-Science
Enter tname
Mukund

College = Yuvaraja's-College
City = Mysore
Department = Computer-Science
Teacher = Mukund
```

Explanation

In Program 15.6, the classes `college`, `dept` and `teacher` are involved in the multilevel inheritance and the classes `dept`, `education` and `teacher` are involved in the multiple inheritance. So the combination of multilevel and multiple inheritance is exhibited by the class hierarchy. An object of `teacher` class would thus represent the details of a teacher, which include cname, city, dname, degree, university and tname of the teacher.

In the `main()`, **t** is declared to be an object of `teacher` class. The statement `t.get();` accepts all the details of a teacher and the statement `t.display();` displays them.

15.7 VIRTUAL BASE CLASS

Consider a situation wherein there are four classes **A**, **B**, **C** and **D**. The classes **B** and **C** are derived from the class **A** and in turn both **B** and **C** are the base classes for the class **D**. Symbolically the inheritance relationship can be represented by the following graphical notation. Here, as can be seen there are two paths through which the members of **A** are accessed to the class **D** and thus gives rise to ambiguity. The problem of ambiguity is eliminated by ensuring that the member data of **A** are accessed through only one path. This can be done by using the keyword virtual with the class name **A** while deriving both **B** and **C** as shown hereinafter.

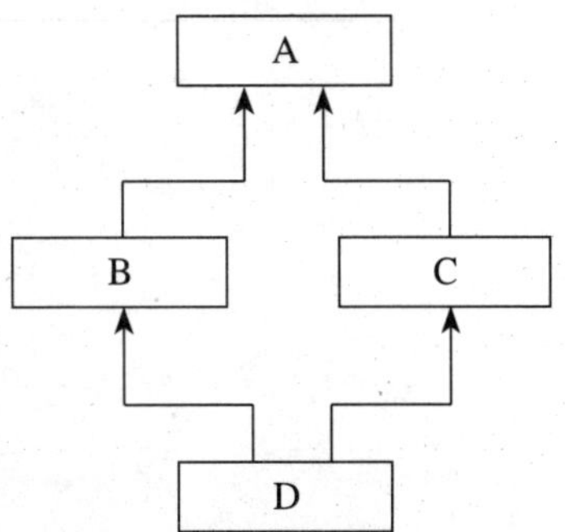

```
class B : virtual public A
{

};

class C : public virtual  A
{

};
```

Note that the keywords *virtual* and *public* can be interchanged.

```
class D : public B, public C
{

};
```

EXAMPLE

Consider the following situation. The class `publisher` is the base class for the classes `distributor` and `author`. In turn the classes `distributor` and `author` are the base classes for the class `book`.

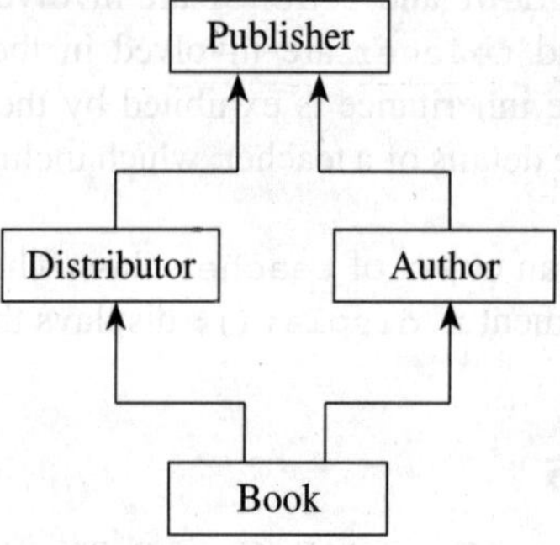

This is a perfect example, which calls for virtual base classes concept since there are two paths for the `book` class to inherit the members of `publisher` class, i.e., through `distributor` and `author` classes thereby giving rise to ambiguity error. Making the class `publisher` as the virtual base class for the `book` class eliminates the ambiguity problem.

Program 15.7 To Illustrate Virtual Base Class

```
#include <iostream.h>

class publisher
{
protected:
    char pname[20];
public:
    void get();
    void display();
};
```

```
void publisher :: get()
{
   cout << "Enter Publisher's Name \n";
   cin >> pname;
}

void publisher :: display()
{
   cout << "Publisher's Name = " << pname << "\n";
}

class distributor :  virtual public publisher
{
protected:
   char dname[20];
public:
   void get();
   void display();
};

void distributor :: get()
{
   cout << "Enter Distributor's Name \n";
   cin >> dname;
}

void distributor :: display()
{
   cout << "Distributor's Name = " << dname << "\n";
}

class author : virtual public publisher
{
protected:
   char aname[20];

public:
   void get();
   void display();
};

void author :: get()
{
   cout << "Enter Author's Name \n";
   cin >> aname;
}

void author :: display()
{
   cout << "Author's Name = " << aname << "\n";
}
```

```
class book : public distributor, public author
{
    private:
        char title[20];

    public:
        void get();
        void display();
};

void book :: get()
{
    publisher :: get();
    distributor :: get();
    author :: get();
    cout << "Enter Title \n";
    cin >> title;
}

void book :: display()
{
    publisher :: display();
    distributor :: display();
    author :: display();
    cout << "Title = " << title ;
}

int main(void)
{
    book b;

    b.get();
    b.display();

    return 0;
}
```

Input-Output:

```
Enter Publisher's Name
PHI
Enter Distributor's Name
UBS
Enter Author's Name
Somashekara
Enter Title
Programming-in-C

Publisher's Name = PHI
Distributor's Name = UBS
Author's Name = Somashekara
Title = Programming-in-C
```

15.8 POINTERS TO OBJECTS

We can even have pointers to objects and access the members of them indirectly with the help of pointer to member operator ->. Program 15.8 illustrates the concept.

Program 15.8 To Illustrate Pointers to Objects

```
#include <iostream.h>

class emp
{
    private:
        int empno;
        char name[20];
        float salary;

    public:
        void get();
        void display();
};

void emp :: get()
{
    cout << "Enter empno, Name and Salary \n";
    cin >> empno >> name >> salary;
}

void emp :: display()
{
    cout << "Empno = " << empno << "\n";
    cout << "Name = " << name << "\n";
    cout << "salary = " << salary;
}

int main(void)
{
    emp e, *ep;

    ep = &e;
    ep -> get();
    ep -> display();

    return 0;
}
```

Input-Output:

```
Enter empno, Name and Salary
123 Pooja 34000

Empno = 123
Name = Pooja
salary = 34000
```

Explanation

In Program 15.8, **e** and **ep** are declared to be an object of **emp** type and a pointer to **emp** type respectively. The address of the object **e** is retrieved and assigned to the pointer **ep** with the statement `ep = &e;`. The member data of **e** are accepted and displayed through the statements `ep -> get();` and `ep -> display();` respectively.

We could have even created an object dynamically with the statement `ep = new emp;`.

Dynamic array of objects: Similar to the way we create dynamic arrays of basic types we can even create arrays of objects dynamically. The syntax of creating a dynamic array of objects is as follows:

```
ptr = new class-type[size];
```

where `ptr` is a pointer to `class-type`. **new** is the operator for memory allocation. `class-type` is the tagname of the class under consideration. `size` is the number of objects to be created.

Program 15.9 To Illustrate Dynamic Array of Objects

```
#include <iostream.h>
#include <iomanip.h>
class emp
{
    private:
        int empno;
        char name[20];
        float salary;

    public:
        void get();
        void display();
};

void emp :: get()
{
    cin >> empno >> name >> salary;
}

void emp :: display()
{
    cout << setw(6) << empno << setw(12) << name
         << setw(9) << salary << "\n";
}

int main(void)
{
    emp *ep;
    int n;

    cout << "Enter the number of employees \n";
    cin >> n;

    ep = new emp[n];
```

```
    cout << "Enter" << n << "Employees's Details\n";
    for(int i = 0; i < n; i++)
        ep[i].get();

    cout << "Employees's Details \n";
    for(i = 0; i < n; i++)
        ep[i].display();

    delete ep;
    return 0;
}
```

Input-Output:

```
Enter the number of employees
2
Enter2Employees's Details
124     Nishu    3400
125     Harsha   3500
Employees's Details
124     Nishu    3400
125     Harsha   3500
```

Explanation

ep is declared to be a pointer to **emp** type. After accepting the number of objects to be created into the variable **n**, memory for the objects is allocated with the statement `ep = new emp[n];`

The pointer **ep** points to the first object in the dynamically allocated array. `ep + 1` points to the second object and so on. `ep[0]`, `ep[1]`, ..., `ep[n-1]` would thus denote the objects themselves.

The member data of the objects are accepted through the statements:

```
    for(int i = 0; i < n; i++)
        ep[i].get();
```

and they are displayed with the statements:

```
    for(int i = 0; i < n; i++)
        ep[i].display();
```

15.9 POINTERS TO DERIVED CLASSES AND VIRTUAL FUNCTIONS

Suppose **A** is the base class for the class **B**. Any pointer to **A** type (base class) can be assigned the address of an object of the class **B** (Derived class). In addition to the address of an object of its own class, i.e., pointers to objects of base class are type-compatible with pointers to objects of derived class.

```
A a, *ap;
ap = &a;
```

The pointer **ap** is made to point to **a**, an object **A** type. This is quite obvious. All the public members of the class can be accessed through **ap** with the help of -> operator. If `display()` is a member function of the class, `ap -> display();` is a valid statement.

```
B b;
```

The C++ language permits the pointer **ap** to be able to point to **b** also using the assignment `ap = &b;`. Even though this is possible the public members of the class **B** can not be accessed through **ap**. Suppose the class **B** also has the member function by name `display()`, even then `ap -> display();` refers to the function in the base class **A** itself. Selection of the public members through the pointer **ap** depends on the type of the pointer rather than the content of the pointer.

How do we use a pointer to base type to access the public members of the base class when it is made to point to an object of the base type, and to access the public members of the derived class when it is made to point to an object of the derived type? This is where the concept of virtual functions comes into picture.

The objective is achieved by using the keyword *virtual* in the header of the base class functions. Program 15.10 illustrates this.

Program 15.10 To Illustrate Virtual Functions

```
#include <iostream.h>

class alpha
{
   protected:
      int a;
   public:
      alpha(int i = 0)
      {
         a = i;
      }

      virtual void display()
      {

      cout << "a = " << a << "\n";
      }
};

class beta : public alpha
{

   private:
      int b;
   public:
      beta(int j= 0)
      {
         b = j;
      }


      void display()
      {
         cout << "b =" << b << "\n";

      }
   };
```

```
int main(void)
{
    alpha a1(10), *ap;
    beta b1(20);

    ap = &a1;
    ap -> display();

    ap = &b1;
    ap -> display();

    return 0;
}
```

Input-Output:

```
a = 10
b = 20
```

Explanation

In Program 15.10, `alpha` is the base class and `beta` is its derived class. The member function `display()` in `alpha` is made virtual and the same named function is defined even within the derived class `beta`. The pointer to base type (**`alpha`**) **ap** is made to point to **a1**, an object of alpha type, `ap->display();` is then invoked to display the member data of **a1**. The `display()` is from the base class `alpha`. The same pointer is assigned the address of the object **b1**, an object of `beta` type, and `ap ->display();` is invoked to display the member data of the object **b1**. The `display()` is from the derived class `beta`. This has been made possible because the same named function in the base class `alpha` has been made virtual.

As can be observed from Program 15.10, the member function selected for execution depends on the content of the pointer rather than the type of the pointer. The function calls are resolved during the runtime of the program and hence the phenomenon is called **runtime polymorphism** or **late binding** or **dynamic binding**.

15.10 PURE VIRTUAL FUNCTIONS AND ABSTRACT CLASS

We just learnt that the runtime polymorphism is implemented with the use of virtual functions in the base class and redefining the same named functions in the derived classes. Many a time, the virtual functions in the base class hardly accomplish anything but they should be included in the base class and the same named functions in the derived classes are defined to perform the required tasks. In this situation we embed only the prototype of the virtual functions in the base class followed by `"=0"`. These functions are called **pure virtual functions**. The pure virtual functions are also called **"do-nothing"** functions. Program 15.11 illustrates the usage of pure virtual functions.

Program 15.11 To Illustrate Pure Virtual Functions

```
#include <iostream.h>
class account
{
```

```
    protected:
        int accno;
        char name[20];
    public:
        virtual void get() = 0;
        virtual void display() = 0;

};

class sb_acc : public account
{
    private:
        float roi;
    public:
        void get()
{
    cout << "Enter accno, name and roi \n";
    cin >> accno >> name >> roi;
}

void display()
{
    cout << "Account Number = " << accno << "\n";
    cout << "name = " << name << "\n";
    cout << "Rate of Interest = " << roi << "\n";
}

};

class cur_acc : public account
{
    private:
        float odlimit;
    public:
        void get()
{
    cout << "Enter accno, name and odlimit \n";
    cin >> accno >> name >> odlimit;
}

void display()
{
    cout << "Account Number = " << accno << "\n";
    cout << "name = " << name << "\n";
    cout << "OD Limit = " << odlimit << "\n";
}

};

int main(void)
```

```
{
    account *ap;
    sb_acc s;
    cur_acc c;

    ap = &s;
    ap -> get();
    ap -> display();

    ap = &c;
    ap -> get();
    ap -> display();

    return 0;
}
```

Input-Output:

```
Enter accno, name and roi
12343 John 7

Account Number = 12343
name = John
Rate of Interest = 7

Enter accno, name and odlimit
12876 Jacob 25000

Account Number = 12876
name = Jacob
OD Limit = 25000
```

Explanation

The class `account` is defined with the member data **accno** and **name** to be inherited by the derived classes. The member functions `get()` and `display()` are declared to be pure virtual functions. Note that they do not have definitions. The class `sb_acc` is derived from `account` class and it has **roi** as its own member data. The member functions `get()` and `display()` are to accept and display the **accno**, **name** and **roi** of an object of class `sb_acc`. The class `cur_acc` is derived from `account` class and it has **odlimit** as its own member data. The member functions `get()` and `display()` are to accept and display the **accno, name** and **odlimit** of an object of class `cur_acc`.

In the `main()`, **ap** is declared to be pointer to **account** type (Base type). **s** and **c** are declared to be objects of **sb_acc** and **cur_acc** type respectively. Initially the address of **s** is assigned to **ap**. The member data of **s** (inherited member data from account and its own) are accepted through the statement `ap -> get();` and they are displayed with the statement `ap ->display();`. Note that the `get()` and the `display()` are from the `sb_acc` class. This is because the same named functions in the base class account are made virtual functions. Similar arguments hold good for the object **c** also.

Points to remember:

1. The signatures of the same named functions in both the base class and the derived classes should be same for the member functions in the base class to be made virtual.

2. The virtual functions, which do not have definition, are called **pure virtual functions**. The prototypes of the pure virtual functions are ended with "=0".
3. A class, which contains pure virtual functions, is called an **abstract class** and it can not be instantiated.

15.11 CONSTRUCTORS AND DESTRUCTORS IN DERIVED CLASSES

Suppose **A** is the base class for the class **B**. If the class **A** contains constructor without any arguments only. It is optional to have the constructor without any arguments in the derived class. If an object of derived class is declared the constructor in the base class itself only gets executed. But if the class **A** contains constructors with arguments and if we wish to declare an object of derived class with initial values we do not succeed in doing so unless we provide the corresponding constructors in the derived class as well.

The general form of the constructors with arguments in the derived class **B** is as follows:

```
B(ArgList1, ArgList2) : A(ArgList1)
{
// Statements for assigning the values in the ArgList2 to the members in B.

}
```

`ArgList1` is the arguments required by the constructor in the base class and `ArgList2` is the arguments required by the derived class if any. Note that the header of the derived class constructor is followed by a colon and the base class name followed by the arguments enclosed within parentheses.

As far as the destructors are concerned, this problem does not arise since they do not take arguments.

Program 15.12 To Illustrate Constructors and Destructors in Derived Classes

```
#include <iostream.h>
#include <conio.h>

class date
{
   protected:
       int d, m, y;
   public:
      date()
      {
          d = m = y = 0;
          cout << "date constructed \n";
      }

      date(int d1, int m1, int y1)
      {
          d = d1;
          m = m1;
          y = y1;
      }
```

```
        ~date()
        {
            cout << "date destroyed" << "\n";
        }

        void display()
        {
            cout << d << "/" << m << "/" << y << "    ";
        }
};

class datetime : public date
{
    private:
        int h, m, s;
    public:
        datetime():date()
        {
            h = m = s = 0;
            cout << "datetime constructed\n";
        }

        datetime(int d1, int mo1, int y1, int h1, int m1, int s1)
              : date(d1, mo1, y1)
        {
            h = h1;
            m = m1;
            s = s1;
        }

        ~datetime()
        {
            cout << "datetime destroyed" << "\n";
        }

        void display()
        {
            date:: display();
            cout << h << ":" << m << ":" << s << "\n";

        }

};

int main(void)
{
    datetime dt1, dt2(12, 3, 2000, 2, 34, 56);

    dt1.display();
    dt2.display();
    return 0;
}
```

Input-Output:

```
date constructed
datetime constructed
0/0/0   0:0:0
12/3/2000   2:34:56
datetime destroyed
date destroyed
datetime destroyed
date destroyed
```

Explanation

In Program 15.12, **dt1** is declared to be an object of **datetime** without any initial values. As a result, the constructors in the classes without any arguments get executed. The other object **dt2** is provided with the initial values for the member data of both the classes. As a result, the constructors with arguments in both the base class and the derived class get executed. The important thing to notice here is that the constructor in the base class (**date**) gets executed first and then the constructor in the derived class (**datetime**). But in the case of destructors the order is reverse, i.e., the destructor in the derived class (**datetime**) gets executed first and then the destructor in the base class (**date**).

15.12 CONSTRUCTORS AND DESTRUCTORS IN MULTIPLE INHERITANCE

If the class **C** is derived from the classes **A** and **B** with the definition:

```
class C : public A, public B
{

};
```

When an object of type **C** is created, the constructor in **A** gets executed first, followed by the constructor in **B**, which is then followed by the constructor in **C**. Whereas the destructors in the classes get executed in the reverse order.

Program 15.13 To Illustrate Constructors and Destructors in Multiple Inheritance

```
#include <iostream.h>

class A
{
    public:
        A()
        {
            cout << "Constructor of A\n";
        }
        ~A()
        {
            cout << "Destructor of A\n";
        }

};
```

```
class B
{

    public:
        B()
        {
            cout << "Constructor of B\n";
        }
        ~B()
        {
            cout << "Destructor of B\n";
        }
};

class C : public A, public B
{
    public:
        C()
        {
            cout << "Constructor of C\n";
        }
        ~C()
        {
            cout << "Destructor of C\n";
        }

};

int main(void)
{
    C c;

    return 0;
}
```

Input-Output:

```
Constructor of A
Constructor of B
Constructor of C
Destructor of C
Destructor of B
Destructor of A
```

Explanation

If the derivation of **C** is:

```
class C : public A, virtual public B
{

};
```

The order of the execution of the constructors is as follows:

The constructor of virtual base class **B** followed by the constructor of **A** and then the constructor of the derived class **C**.

15. 13 VIRTUAL DESTRUCTOR

In the inheritance relationship, we are now aware of the fact that during the process of destruction, the destructor in derived class executes first and then the destructor in the base class. This is how it should be.

Let us consider a situation, which violates this normal rule. We know that a pointer to base type can point to an object of derived class type also. Suppose we dynamically allocate space for derived type object and assign it to the base pointer and after using the object if deallocate the space by the use of delete operator, the destructor in the base class only gets executed. The normal rule of the order of execution of destructors can be reinforced with what is known as **virtual destructor**. The destructor in the base class is made virtual by preceding its header with the keyword virtual. Take a closer look at Program 15.14.

Program 15.14 To Illustrate Virtual Destructor

```
#include <iostream.h>

class A
{
    public:
        A()
        {
            cout << "A constructed \n";
        }

     virtual ~A()
        {
            cout << "A destructed \n";
        }
};

class B  : public A
{
    public:
        B()
        {
            cout << "B constructed \n";
        }

        ~B()
        {
            cout << "B destructed \n";
        }

};
```

```
int main(void)
{
    A *ap;

    ap = new B;

    delete ap;

    return 0;
}
```

Input-Output:

```
Constructor of A
Constructor of B
Destructor of B
Destructor of A
```

15.14 PRIVATE INHERITANCE

When class **B** is derived from the class **A** publicly (i.e., with the line `class B : public A` in the definition of **B**), we know that the protected and the public members of the class **A** are accessible in the class **B** and also an object of derived class **B** can access all the public members of the base class **A** outside the class.

Consider the following class definition:

```
class B : private A
{

};
```

Here the class **B** is said to be privately derived from the class **A**. All the protected and public members of the base class **A** are accessible in the derived class **B**. But an object of the class **B** can not access even the public members of the base class **A** also. The protected and public members of the base class will become the private members of the derived class. The functionality of the base class **A** is hidden in the derived class **B**. But there is a way out for making only some pubic member functions of the base class accessible to objects of derived class, i.e., by using the base class name followed by :: followed by the function name in the public section of the derived class.

Consider the following code:

```
class alpha
{
    protected:
        int j;
    public:
        int k;

};
class beta : private alpha
```

```
{
    public:
        void set()
        {
            j = 20;
            k = 30;
        }
        void display()
        {
            cout << "within display() of beta \n";
            cout << "j = " << j;
            cout << "k = " << k;
        }
};

class gama : private beta
{
    public:
        void show()
        {
            cout << "within show() of gama \n";
            cout << "j = " << j; // error
            cout << "k = "<< k; //error
        }

};
```

The class `alpha` has a protected member **i** and a public member **j** of `int` type. The class `beta` is privately derived from the class `alpha`. As a result, both **i** and **j** of `alpha` class become private members of `beta` class. Within the `beta` class, the member function `set()` assigns values to both **i** and **j**, and the member function `display()` displays the values of both **i** and **j**.

The class `gama` is derived from beta. Within `gama` the members **i** and **j** can not be accessed. An attempt to display them through `show()` of `gama` class would thus fail.

The line of code `beta :: display;` in the public section of `gama` makes the `display()` of `beta` be accessible with an object of `gama` class. If **g** is an object of `gama` class then `g.display();` would be a valid function call.

15.15 PROTECTED INHERITANCE

Now, consider the following definition:

```
class B : protected A
{

};
```

Here the class **B** is said to be protectedly derived from the class **A**. All the protected and public members of the base class **A** would now become protected members of the derived class **B** and hence they can be accessed within the class **B** and in any other class which is derived from **B**. No members of the class **A** can be accessed by an object of class **B**.

Consider the following code:

```
class alpha
{
    protected:
        int j;
    public:
        int k;

};

class beta : protected alpha
{
    public:
        void set()
        {
            j = 20;
            k = 30;
        }
        void display()
        {
            cout << "within display() of beta \n";
            cout << "j = " << j;
            cout << "k = " << k;
        }
};

class gama : protected beta
{
    public:
        void show()
        {
            cout << "within show() of gama \n";
            cout << "j = " << j;
            cout << "k = " << k;
        }
};
```

The class `alpha` has a protected member **i** and a public member **j** of `int` type. The class `beta` is protectedly derived from the class `alpha`. As a result, both **i** and **j** of `alpha` class become protected members of `beta` class. Within the `beta` class, the member function `set()` assigns values to both **i** and **j**, and the member function `display()` displays the values of both **i** and **j**.

The class `gama` is derived from `beta`. Within `gama` the members **i** and **j** can still be accessed. The member function `show()` of `gama` display both the values.

15.16 CONTAINERSHIP

The containership is another way of reusing existing code. In this case objects of one class are made the members of another class. Suppose **A** is a class and **a** is an object of the class. In another class, say **B**, the object **a** can be made a member. As a result of this, the code in the class **A** is reused in the class **B** as well. Since the class **B** contains an instance of class **A**, it is said to exhibit “Has a Relationship”.

Program 15.15 To Illustrate Containership

```
#include <iostream.h>

class time
{
   private:
      int h, m, s;

   public:
      void get();
      void display();
};


void time :: get()
{
   cout << "Enter hours, minutes and seconds \n";
   cin >> h >> m >> s;
}

void time :: display()
{
   cout << h << ":" << m << ":" << s << "\n";
}

class date
{
   private:

      int d, m, y;
      time t;
   public:

      void get();
      void display();
};
void date :: get()
{
   cout << "Enter day, month and year \n";
   cin >> d >> m >> y;
   t.get();
}

void date :: display()
{
   cout << d << "/" << m << "/" << y << "\n";
   t.display();
}
```

```
int main(void)
{
    date dt;

    dt.get();
    dt.display();

    return 0;
}
```

Input-Output:

```
Enter day, month and year
12 4 2000
Enter hours, minutes and seconds
11 34 25

12/4/2000
11:34:25
```

Explanation

In Program 15.15, an object of time is made a member of the class date thereby making the code of time class reusable in the date class. An object of date type comes packaged with member data of both time and date classes.

The member data of the date class and those of the object **t** of time type are accepted through the function:

```
void date :: get()
{
    cout << "Enter day, month and year \n";
    cin >> d >> m >> y;
    t.get();
}
```

The member data of the date class and those of the object **t** of time type are displayed through the function:

```
void date :: display()
{
    cout << d << "/" << m << "/" << y << "\n";
    t.display();
}
```

15.17 WHEN TO INHERIT

Anytime we build a new class, we should determine whether we can use the preexisting class as a base class. Many a time, we find classes that provide almost the right behaviour. These are the candidate classes to inherit from. We can inherit all the desired features and disable the unwanted ones. Disabling the unwanted functions in the base class is done using function overriding. We try to inherit as many features as possible from the already existing classes. This reduces both the size of the program code and the time required for debugging.

15.18 WHAT CAN'T BE INHERITED?

As in real life, even in C++ also not everything can be passed on through inheritance. The following can not be inherited:

- Constructors
- Destructor
- User-defined new operators
- User-defined assignment operators
- Friend relationships.

REVIEW QUESTIONS

15.1 What is inheritance?

15.2 What are the advantages offered by inheritance?

15.3 What is the use of protected access specifier?

15.4 Define single level inheritance. Give an example.

15.5 Define multiple inheritance. Give an example.

15.6 What is function overriding?

15.7 What is multilevel inheritance? Give an example.

15.8 What is hybrid inheritance? Give an example.

15.9 In inheritance relationship, what is the order of construction and destruction?

15.10 What is private inheritance?

15.11 What is public inheritance?

15.12 What is protected inheritance?

15.13 Why do we need virtual destructor?

15.14 What is a virtual function? Why do we need it?

15.15 What is a pure virtual function?

15.16 What is containership?

15.17 When do we need to inherit?

15.18 Mention the members of base classes, which can not be inherited.

True/False Questions

T15.1 Inheritance facilitates reusability of existing code.

T15.2 Even private members of a base class can be inherited in derived class.

T15.3 In public derivation, an object of the derived class can access the public members of the base class.

T15.4 There is no difference between function overriding and function overloading.

T15.5 In protected derivation, protected and public members of the base class become private members of the derived class.

T15.6 The private members of a base class can be inherited in the derived class by privately derivation.

T15.7 A pointer to base type can not point to an object of derived type.

T15.8 Abstract class can be instantiated.

T15.9 Constructors and destructor can be inherited.

T15.10 A pure virtual function can have statements in its body.

PROGRAMMING EXERCISES

P15.1 Design a class by name **matrix** with a two-dimensional array as its member data. Include the member functions for addition and multiplication of two matrices. Derive a new class **new_matrix** from the class **matrix** and include the functions for checking compatibility of the matrices for addition and multiplication.

(If **m1** and **m2** are two matrices, they are said to be compatible for addition if the number of rows of **m1** is equal to that **m2**. And similarly with regard to columns. They are said to be compatible for multiplication if the number of columns of **m1** is equal to the number of rows of **m2**.)

P15.2 Implement the following class hierarchy:

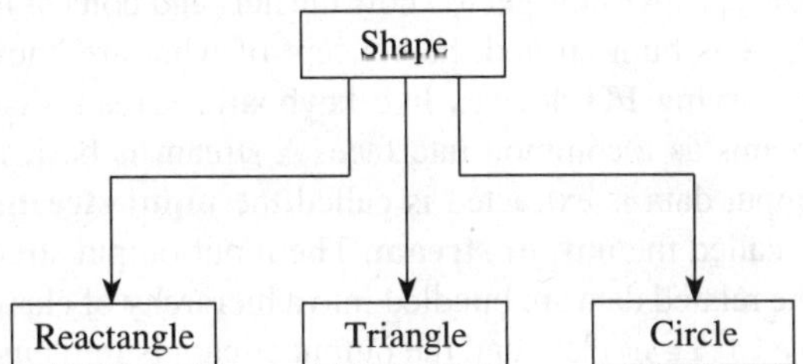

Chapter 16

I/O Streams

16.1 INTRODUCTION

So far, we used the **cin** and **cout** to perform I/O operations. Not much was discussed about these except the fact that they are used to accept inputs through keyboard and display outputs on the screen. In fact, this was intentional since detailed discussion about these and the power of the I/O facility provided by C++ required the concepts like classes, operator overloading and inheritance. Having gained sufficient knowledge about these concepts, we now get to know the nuts and bolts of I/O facility in C++.

The I/O system in C++ is built around the concept of what are known as **streams.** The system is tailored to work with varying I/O devices like keyboard, screen, disks and tape drives with no differences using the streams as a common interface. A stream is basically a sequence of bytes. A stream from which the input data is extracted is called the **input stream** and a stream to which the output data is inserted is called the **output stream**. The input-output streams are shown in Fig. 16.1. The I/O operations and the related data are bundled into a hierarchy of classes shown in Fig. 16.2. Input stream is implemented by `istream` class and the output stream is implemented by `ostream` class.

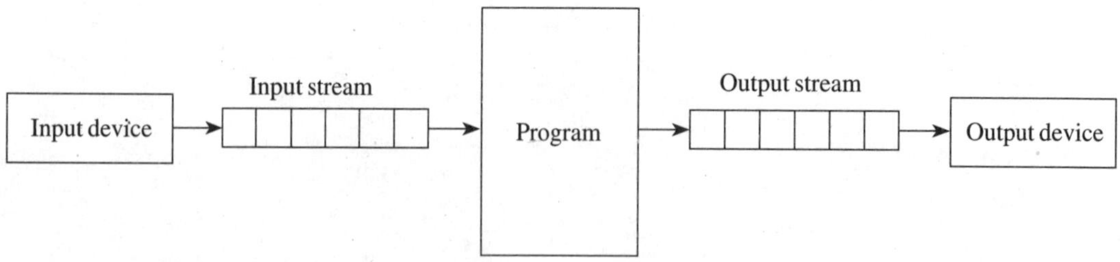

Fig. 16.1 Input-output streams.

16.2 BUILT-IN CLASSES SUPPORTING I/O

A number of classes help facilitate I/O operations. The class hierarchy is exhibited in Fig. 16.2.

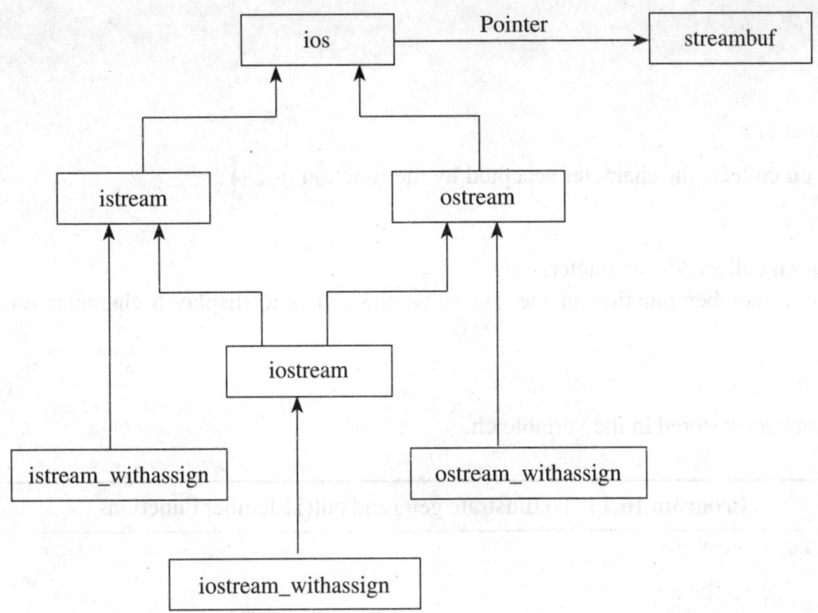

Fig. 16.2 Class hierarchy for I/O operations.

In the class hierarchy, the class `ios` provides the basic supportive facility for I/O operations and is the base class for both istream and ostream classes. It also contains a pointer to **streambuf** type. The class `streambuf` provides the facility for buffering and interaction with the I/O devices. The class **iostream** is derived from both `istream` and `ostream` classes through multiple inheritance. Note that the class `ios` has been made a virtual base class to ensure that only one copy its members are accessed in the class `iostream`. The classes `istream_withassign`, `ostream_withassign` and `iostream_withassign` are derived from `istream`, `ostream` and `iostream` respectively.

16.3 UNFORMATTED I/O OPERATIONS

In addition to the basic I/O facilities provided by the `ios` class, the `istream` class provides `get()`, `getline()` and `read()` member functions and the overloaded extraction operator >> to enable input operations and the class `ostream` provides `put()`, `write()` member functions and the overloaded insertion operator << to enable output operations. The class `iostream` having been derived from both `istream` and `ostream` provides all the facilities that are available in its base classes. Since all these classes are defined in the header file **`iostream.h`**, the header file should be included as part of all the C++ programs, which require console I/O, with the preprocessor directive `#include <iostream.h>`.

The get() and put() member functions: The `get()` is the member function of `istream` class. It is to accept a character from the input device. The characters include even the non-printable characters like blank space, tab space and new line character. There are two versions of `get()`. The prototypes of the functions are:

1. `istream& get(char&)`
2. `int get(void)`

EXAMPLE

```
char ch;

ch = cin.get();
```

The variable **ch** collects the character accepted by the function `get()`.

```
cin.get(ch);
```

The argument **ch** collects the character.
The `put()` is a member function of the `ostream` class. It is to display a character on the output device.

```
cout.put(ch);
```

displays the character stored in the variable **ch**.

Program 16.1 To Illustrate get() and put() Member Functions

```
#include <iostream.h>

int main(void)
{
    char ch;

    cout << "Enter a line of text \n";
    cin.get(ch);
    while (ch != '\n')
    {
        cout.put(ch);
        cin.get(ch);
    }

    return 0;
}
```

Input-Output:

```
Enter a line of text
C++ Programming is funny
C++ Programming is funny
```

The getline() and write() member functions: The member function `getline()` enables us to accept a string up to a new line character. Even the white spaces can be part of the input string.

EXAMPLE

```
char str[30];
cin.getline(str, 30);
```

accepts a line of text into the string variable **str**.

The `write()` is another member function of `ostream` class and it displays the specified number of characters in a string.

EXAMPLE

```
char str[5] = "abcd";
cout.write(str, 4);
```

displays the string "abcd".

If the number of characters, the second argument, is greater than the actual number of characters in the string , the function continues to display beyond the string.

Program 16.2 To Illustrate getline() and write() Member Functions

```
#include <iostream.h>
#include <string.h>

const int size = 50;

int main(void)
{
    char line_of_text[size];
    cout << "Enter a line of text \n";
    cin.getline(line_of_text, size);
    cout << line_of_text << "\n";

    cout << "Enter another line of text \n";
    cin.getline(line_of_text, size);
    cout << line_of_text << "\n";

    cout.write(line_of_text, strlen(line_of_text));

    return 0;
}
```

Input-Output:

```
Enter a line of text
Bangalore is the capital city of Karnataka

Bangalore is the capital city of Karnataka

Enter another line of text
Mumbai is the capital city of Maharastra

Mumbai is the capital city of Maharastra
```

16.4 FORMATTING OF OUTPUTS

Formatting of outputs is nothing but displaying the outputs in more readable and comprehensible manner. It is a way of dressing up of the outputs for better appearance. Formatting of outputs can be achieved in two ways. One, Using `ios` class functions and flags. Two, using manipulators.

16.4.1 ios Class Functions and Flags

The `ios` class includes a number of member functions and flags, which are used to display the outputs in desirable fashion. The member functions should be invoked with an object of the `ostream` class. We use the object **cout** to invoke these functions. We will now discuss them in detail and put them to use in the example programs.

The member function `width()` is used to specify the width in which a value has to be displayed. The syntax of its usage is as follows:

```
cout.width(w);
```

where **w** is the width, the number of spaces, within which a value has to be displayed.

```
int a = 234;
cout.width(6);
cout << a;
```

displays the value of **a** within the specified width as shown. Note that the value occupies the right portion of the specified width. Here, we say that the value is right justified.

			2	3	4

The `width()` can be used to specify the width of only one data item, which is displayed immediately after the function call. Consider the following example:

```
int a = 234, b = 769;

cout.width(6);
cout << a ;
cout << b;
```

			2	3	4	7	6	9

Here, six columns are allocated for the display of the value of the variable **a**. But, the value of **b** is displayed as usual. No width is allocated for the variable **b**.

Specifying the widths separately for both **a** and **b** allocates the required width for both the values and the values are displayed as follows:

```
cout.width(6);
cout << a;
cout.width(6);
cout << b;
```

			2	3	4				7	6	9

If the width specified is less than the number of digits of a number being displayed, C++ simply ignores the specified width and displays the value by using the default. Formatting does not tamper with the value being displayed.

```
int a = 234;

cout.width(2);
cout << a;
```

2	3	4

Here, the width is less than the number of digits in the number **a**. C++ displays the complete value of the variable by ignoring the specified width.

The member function `precision()` is used to set the number of digits after the decimal point. By default, float values are displayed with six digits after the decimal point. The member function `precision()` enables us to have a say in displaying floating point numbers with the required numbers after the decimal point.

```
float f = 34.78986547;
cout << f;
```

3	4	.	7	8	9	8	6	5

```
cout.precision(2);
cout << f;
```

3	4	.	7	9

Only two digits are displayed after the decimal point. Note that the number if rounded off to the second digit after the decimal point. Unlike the `width()`, the `precision()` affects all the floating point values that are displayed after its call. However, we can set different precision for different values by explicitly calling the function. Consider the following segment of code:

```
float f = 12.4567,  g = 67.6544;


cout.precision(2);
cout << f << "\n";
cout.precision(3);
cout << g << "\n";
```

The value of **f** is displayed with two digits after the decimal point as 12.46 and the value of **g** is displayed with three digits after the decimal point as 67.654.

```
float f = 2376.00;
cout << f;
```

displays 2376 with the zeros after the decimal point truncated.

```
cout.precision(2);
cout << f;
```

In spite of the precision setting, here also, the value is displayed as 2376 with the zeros after the decimal point truncated. Later, we will learn to display the decimal point and the trailing zeros.

The member function `fill()` is used to pad the unused positions in the specified width for values with a desired character. This is normally used while printing amount in figures on cheques and demand drafts to prevent malicious tampering with the amounts.

```
int a = 2345;

cout.width(8);
cout.fill('*');
cout << a;
```

would display as:

*	*	*	*	2	3	4	5

Similar to the `precision()`, the `fill()` also affects all the values, which are displayed after its call.

When we display a value within a specified width, which is greater than the number of digits or characters of the value, irrespective of whether it is numeric or non-numeric, it occupies the right portion of the width. Normally we would prefer to display the numeric data to the right of the specified width (right justification) and strings to the left of the specified width (left justification) for better appealing of the outputs. When we need to display very small and very big floating point values, we prefer to use the exponential notation. These and many other formatting features are added to the display of outputs with the help of the flags defined in the class `ios`.

The member function `setf()` is to set various flags, each of which will play a role in formatting the outputs. Since they are defined in the `ios` class, they are preceded by `ios::`. The list of them and their purpose are depicted in Table 16.1.

EXAMPLE

```
cout.setf(ios::left);
```

enforces left justification.

```
cout.setf(ios::showpoint);
```

enforces the display of the decimal point in the case of floating values.

```
cout.setf(ios::showpos);
```

enforces the display of + sign before a positive number.

Table 16.1 ios Flags

Flags	*Purpose*
ios::left	Left-justify output
ios::right	Right-justify output
ios::internal	Padding after base indicator or sign
ios::fixed	Floating point notation (3487.567)
ios::scientific	Scientific notation (3.487567E3)
ios::dec	Decimal base
ios::oct	Octal base
ios::hex	Hexadecimal base
ios::showbase	Use base indicator on output
ios::showpoint	Use decimal point in floating-point output
ios::showpos	Prefix positive numbers with '+'
ios::uppercase	Use uppercase letters for hexadecimal output
ios::unitbuf	Flush al streams after insertion
ios::stdio	Flush stdout and stderr after insertion
ios::skipws	Skip white space on input

The member function `unsetf()` is the counterpart of the `setf()`. It is used to unset the flags which were set by the `setf()` member function.

EXAMPLE

```
cout.unsetf(ios::left);
```

clears the flag **ios::left** and forces default justification.

```
cout.unsetf(ios::showpoint);
```

clears the flag **ios::showpoint** and as a result, suppresses the display of the decimal point in the case of floating point numbers with zeros after the decimal point.

Program 16.3 To Illustrate Formatting Using ios Functions and Flags

```
#include <iostream.h>

struct emp
{
   int empno;
   char name[20];
   float salary;
};

int main(void)
{
   emp e[3] = {{121, "Nishu", 32300.00},
               {122, "Prashanth", 9450.98},
               {123, "Shyam", 14500.76}};
   cout << "      List of Employees      \n\n";
   cout << "Empno    Name       Salary" << "\n\n";
```

```
    for(int i = 0; i < 2; i++)
    {
        cout.width(10);
        cout.setf(ios::left);
        cout << e[i].empno;
        cout.width(10);
        cout.setf(ios::left);
        cout << e[i].name;
        cout.width(10);
        cout.setf(ios::right);
        cout.precision(2);
        cout.setf(ios::fixed);
        cout.setf(ios::showpoint);
        cout << e[i].salary << "\n";
    }
    return 0;
}
```

Input-Output:

```
List of Employees

Empno     Name      Salary

121       Nishu     32300.00
122       Prashanth 9450.98
123       Shyam     14500.76
```

Explanation

empno is left justified within the specified space of 10 columns. **name** is also left justified within the specified space of 10 columns. **salary** is right justified within the specified space of 10 columns and it is displayed in fixed notation with the number of digits after the decimal point specified as two and also the display of the decimal point is made mandatory even if it is not required with the help of the flag **ios::showpoint**. Note that salary of the employee Nishu is 32300.00 if the flag is not used, the salary would be displayed as 32300.

16.4.2 Manipulators

Manipulators offer much easier formatting facility. They provide all the features supported by the `ios` class functions but with increased degree of convenience. Unlike the `ios` class functions, the manipulators can be directly inserted into the stream. For this reason, the manipulators are preferred over the `ios` class functions especially while displaying columnar data.

The syntax of the usage of the manipulators is as follows:

```
cout << manipulator << data;
```

We can even have more than one manipulator to format a data item with the following general form:

```
cout << manipulator1 << manipulator2 << data;
```

Built-in manipulators: Following are the most frequently used built-in manipulators while formatting outputs. Since they are defined in the header file **iomanip.h**, the file has to be included as part of the program, which uses these, with the help of the preprocessor directive `#include`.
The manipulator `setw()` is used to specify the width in which a value is to be displayed.
The syntax of its usage:

```
cout << setw(w) << data;
```

where **w** is the width in which data has to be displayed.

EXAMPLE

```
int a = 1234;
cout << setw(6) << a << "\n";
```

The value of **a** is displayed in the specified width of six columns left justified. Note that the manipulator `setw()` is equivalent to the member function `width()` of `ios` class.

The manipulator `setprecision()` is used to specify the number of digits after the decimal point in the case of floating point numbers. The syntax of its usage is as follows:

```
cout << setprecision(d) << float_data;
```

where **d** is the number of digits to be displayed after the decimal point for the value float_data.

EXAMPLE

```
float f = 34.5678;
cout << setprecision(2) << f << "\n";
```

The value of **f** is displayed with two digits after the decimal point.

Note that the manipulator `setprecision()` is equivalent to the member function `precision()` of `ios` class.

The manipulator `setfill()` is used to fill the unused positions of data item in the specified width with a character. The syntax of its usage is as follows:

```
cout << setw(w) << setfill(c) << data;
```

where **w** is the width in which the value **data** is displayed and the character **c** is used to fill the unused positions for the value **data**.

EXAMPLE

```
int a = 5674;
cout << setw(6) << setfill('*') << a << "\n";
```

displays the value of **a** in six columns right justified with the two leading unused positions filled with the character *.

Note that the manipulator `setfill()` is equivalent to the member function `fill()` of `ios` class.

The manipulator `setiosflags()` is used to set various flags defined in the class `ios`. Each of which plays a role in formatting the outputs in different manner. We have already discussed them earlier. The syntax of its usage is as follows:

```
cout << setiosflags(iosflag) << data;
```

iosflag can be any flag defined in the class `ios`. It affects the display of the value data as per its definition.

EXAMPLE

```
float f = 456.78;
cout << setiosflags(ios::scientific) << f << "\n";
```

displays the value of f in scientific notation.

Note that the manipulator `setiosflags()` equivalent to the member function `setf()` of `ios` class.

The manipulator `resetiosflags()` is used to clear the flags which were set by the `setiosflags()` manipulator earlier. The syntax of its usage is similar to that of the `setiosflags()` mainipulator.

```
cout << resetiosflags(iosflags) << data;
```

iosflags is any flag defined in the class `ios`.

EXAMPLE

```
float f = 34.567;
cout << resetiosflags(ios::scientific) << f << "\n";
```

reverts back to the fixed notation for floating point values.

Note that the manipulator `resetiosflags()` equivalent to the member function `unsetf()` of `ios` class.

Program 16.4 To Illustrate Formatting Using Manipulators

```
#include <iostream.h>
#include <iomanip.h>

struct emp
{
    int empno;
    char name[20];
    float salary;
};

int main(void)
{
    emp e[3] = {{121, "Nishu", 32300.67},
                {122, "Prashanth", 9450.98},
                {123, "Shyam", 14500.76}};

    cout << "      List of Employees      \n\n";
    cout << "Empno    Name       Salary" << "\n\n";
    for(int i = 0; i < 3; i++)
      cout << setw(10) << setiosflags(ios::left) << e[i].empno
           << setw(10) << setiosflags(ios::left) << e[i].name
           << setw(10) << setiosflags(ios::right)
           << setprecision(2)<< setiosflags(ios::fixed)
           << e[i].salary << "\n";

    return 0;
}
```

Input-Output:

```
List of Employees

Empno     Name       Salary
121       Nishu      32300.67
122       Prashanth   9450.98
123       Shyam      14500.76
```

Explanation

empno is left justified within the specified space of 10 columns. **name** is also left justified within the specified space of 10 columns. **salary** is right justified within the specified space of 10 columns and it is displayed in fixed notation with the number of digits after the decimal point specified as two.

16.4.3 User-defined Manipulators

We can define our own manipulators depending on requirements. Creation of a manipulator requires a function to be defined. The general form of the function for a manipulator without arguments is as follows:

```
ostream& manipulator_name(ostream& os)
{
    statements
    return os;
}
```

Here, manipulator_name is the name of the manipulator being created and it should be a valid C++ identifier. The manipulator function takes a reference to ostream type and returns the reference to ostream after the required manipulation.

```
ostream& currency(ostream& os)
{
    os << "$";
    return os;
}
```

Now, the statement:

```
cout << currency << 3456;
```

produces the following output

```
$3456
```

Program 16.5 To Illustrate User-defined Manipulators

```
#include <iostream.h>
#include <iomanip.h>
ostream& km(ostream& os)
{
    os << " Kilometres";
```

```
    return os;
}

int main(void)
{

    cout << "The Distance between Bangalore and Mysore is "
          << 158 << km;

    return 0;
}
```

Input-Output:

```
The Distance between Bangalore and Mysore is 158 Kilometres
```

Here, the manipulator **km,** inserted into the output stream after the integer value 158, displays the string kilometres.

One or more manipulators can be combined together to create a new manipulator. The new manipulator will then do all the operations of all manipulators in the group.

EXAMPLE

```
ostream& combine(ostream& os)
{
    os << setw(6) << setiosflags(ios::right) << setprecision(2);
    return os;
}
```

Here, the manipulator **combine** performs the job of three manipulators `setw()`, `setiosflags()` and `setprecision()`.

```
cout << combine << 345.678;
```

is equivalent to

```
cout << setw(6) << setiosflags(ios::right) << setprecision(2)
        << 345.678;
```

Program 16.6 To Illustrate User-defined Manipulators

```
#include <iostream.h>
#include <iomanip.h>

ostream& format_empno(ostream& out)
{
    out << setw(10) << setiosflags(ios::left);
    return out;
}

ostream& format_name(ostream& out)
{
    out << setw(15) << setiosflags(ios::left);
```

```
    return out;
}
ostream& format_salary(ostream& out)
{
    out << setw(10) << setiosflags(ios::right)
        << setiosflags(ios::fixed) << setprecision(2);
    return out;
}

struct emp
{
    int empno;
    char name[20];
    float salary;
};

int main(void)
{
    emp e[3] = {{121, "Nishu", 32300.67},
                {122, "Prashanth", 9450.98},
                {123, "Shyam", 14500.76}};
    cout << "     List of Employees       \n\n";
    cout << "Empno    Name             Salary" << "\n\n";
    for(int i = 0; i < 3; i++)

        cout << format_empno << e[i].empno
             << format_name << e[i].name
             << format_salary << e[i].salary << "\n";

    return 0;
}
```

Input-Output:

```
List of Employees

Empno     Name          Salary
121      Nishu           32300.67
122      Prashanth        9450.98
123      Shyam           14500.76
```

User-defined manipulators with arguments: We can even define manipulators with arguments. The manipulators are implemented with the use of a class definition. In the class, the insertion operator << is overloaded with the help of a friend function with a reference to ostream type and a reference to the class type.

The general form of the class and the friend function are as follows:

```
class class_name
{
    private:
        member data
    public:
```

```
        constructors
        friend ostream& operator << (ostream&, class_name&);
};
```

Definition of the friend function:

```
ostream& operator << (ostream& os, class_type& object)

{
    statements

    return os;
}
```

The syntax of invoking the manipulator with argument is as follows:

```
cout << class_type(argument);
```

`class_type(argument)` constructs an object of type `class_type` and the << overloading function is invoked, which when executed produces the expected result.

Using a manipulator to convert from decimal to octal:

Program 16.7 To Illustrate User-defined Manipulator with Argument

```
#include <iostream.h>

class octal
{
    private:
        int n;
    public:
        octal(int x = 0)
        {
            n = x;
        }

        friend ostream& operator <<(ostream&, octal&);
};

ostream& operator << (ostream& os, octal& oc)
{
    int rem, oct=0, pos = 1;

    while(oc.n > 0)
    {
        rem = oc.n % 8;
        oct = oct + pos * rem;
        oc.n /= 8;
        pos *= 10;
    }
```

```
    os << oct;
    return os;
}

int main(void)
{

    int dec_num;

    cout << "Enter a Decimal Number \n";
    cin >> dec_num;
    cout << "The Octal Equivalent of " << dec_num << " = "
         << octal(dec_num);

    return 0;
}
```

Input-Output:

```
Enter a Decimal Number
456

The Octal Equivalent of 456 = 710
```

The class **octal** is defined with a member data **n** of integer type. The constructor with a default argument is included in the class for constructing an object of **octal** type. A friend function is employed to overload the insertion operator <<, which takes a reference to **ostream** type and a reference to **octal** type as its arguments. Within the friend function the member data of **octal** type is converted into its octal equivalent and the octal equivalent number is inserted into the output stream **os**. The reference to **os** is then returned by the function.

In the `main()`, we accept a decimal number into the variable **dec_num** and explicitly call the constructor with the decimal number as its argument to create an object of octal type which is then passed as the argument to the overloaded << operator friend function, the other argument being a reference to ostream type, which appears to the left of the operator in the statement:

```
cout << "The Octal Equivalent of " << dec_num  << " = "
               << octal(dec_num);
```

Note that the code, `cout << "The Octal Equivalent of " << dec_num << " = "` evaluates to a reference to **ostream** type.

REVIEW QUESTIONS

16.1 What is a stream?

16.2 Distinguish between input stream and output stream.

16.3 Give an account of built-in classes, which support I/O operations in C++.

16.4 Explain the syntax and working of put() and get() member functions.

16.5 Explain the syntax and working of getline() member function.

16.6 Explain the syntax and working of write() member function.

16.7 Give an account of formatting facility provided through ios functions.

16.8 Explain width(), precision(), fill() member functions.

16.9 Explain setw(), setprecision() and setfill() manipulators.

16.10 Explain the significance of various flags supported by ios class.

True/False Questions

T16.1 The inclusion of iostream.h in a program is optional.

T16.2 The class ios is the base class for the classes istream and ostream.

T16.3 The ios flags can be set or unset using the member functions only.

T16.4 cin is the object of istream class and cout is the object of ostream class.

T16.5 Manipulators and ios member functions can be used interchangeably.

T16.6 The get() function can be used to accept a line of text.

T16.7 We can not create manipulators of our own.

T16.8 Manipulators with arguments should be created with the help of classes and friend functions.

T16.9 The header file iomanip.h should be included as part of each program.

T16.10 The following segment of code:

```
int i = 12345;
cout << setw(2) << i;
```

produces an error since the number of digits in the number **i** is more than the specified width.

T16.11 The number of digits displayed after the decimal point for a float number is eight by default.

T16.12 The member function fill() and the manipulator setfill() do the same operation.

PROGRAMMING EXERCISES

P16.1 Write a program to accept words that form a sentence and display them in a sentence with a full stop at the end.

P16.2 Write a program to accept five words possibly with spaces and display them.

P16.3 Write a program to accept the details of five students like regno, name, percentage of marks and display them in tabular format.

P16.4 Create a user-defined manipulator of your own.

P16.5 Create a manipulator of your own with arguments.

Chapter 17

File Handling

17.1 INTRODUCTION

Each program revolves around some data. It requires some inputs; performs manipulations over them; produces required outputs. So far, in all our earlier programs, the inputs originated from the standard input device, keyboard, with the help of `cin`, `getchar()` and `gets()`. We displayed the outputs produced, through the standard output device, screen, by the use of library facilities `cout`, `putchar()` and `puts()`. This scheme of I/O operations suffers from the following drawbacks:

Firstly, the data involved in the I/O operations are lost when the program is exited or when the power goes off.

Secondly, this scheme is definitely not ideal for programs, which involve voluminous data.

But, many real life programming circumstances require to deal with large amount of data and require the data to be permanently available even when the program is exited or when the power goes off. This is where the concept of files comes into picture.

A file is defined to be a collection of related data stored on secondary storage device like disk. It is a named storage on secondary storage devices. The concept of files enables us to store large amount of data permanently on the secondary storage devices. The ability to store large amount of data and the ability to store them permanently are attributed to the physical characteristics of the devices.

The beauty of the C++ language is that even file handling also is brought under the umbrella of OOPs concept. The files and the operations over them are bundled into objects. We will now learn the built-in classes, which support file handling and put them to use.

17.2 BUILT-IN CLASSES FOR FILE I/O OPERATIONS

The class `fstreambase` is derived from the basic class `ios`. The class `ifstream` is derived from both `istream` and `fstreambase` and similarly, the class `ofstream` is derived from both the `ostream` and `fstreambase`. Both `ifstream` and `ofstream` act as base classes for `fstream` class. The class `filebuf` is derived from the class `streambuf`. The complete class hierarchy is shown in Fig. 17.1. Central to

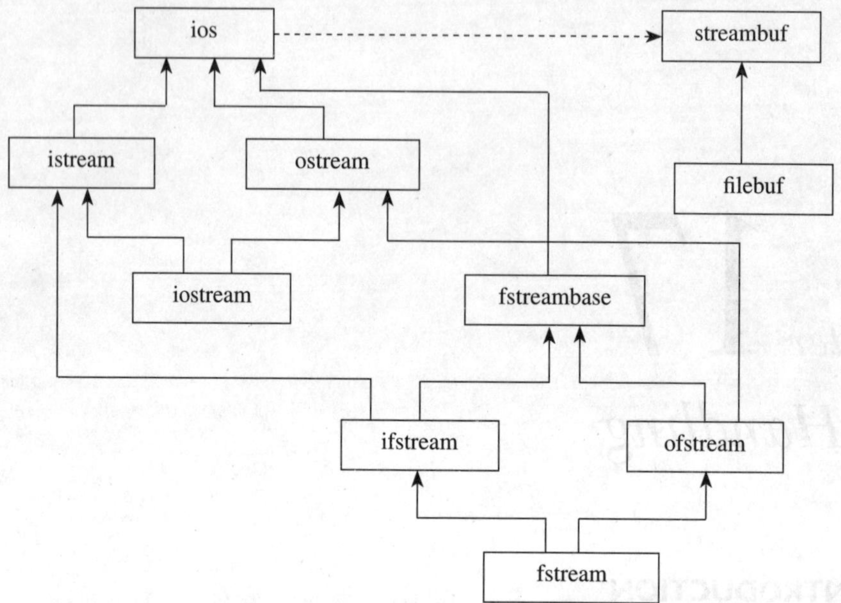

Fig. 17.1 Class hierarchy for file operations.

file handling are three classes. They are **`ifstream`**, **`ofstream`** and **`fstream`**. Since all these classes are defined in the header file **fstream.h**, the header file should be included as part of all the programs, which deal with files, with the preprocessor directive `#include <fstream.h>`. Once the header file **fstream.h** is included, we don't require to include the file **iostream.h** since the preprocessor directive `#include <iostream.h>` is embedded in the file **fstream.h** itself.

The facility provided by each file-related class is given in Table 17.1.

Table 17.1 File Related Classes and Their Purpose

Class	*Purpose*
filebuf	It deals with the file buffers during reading and writing operations. It is derived from `streambuf` class.
fstreambase	It provides the facilities for file operations and consists of `open()` and `close()` member functions. It serves as a base class for both `ifstream` and `ofstream` and a virtual base class for `fstream` class.
ofstream	It provides file output facility and contains `open()` with default output mode. Inherits the member functions `put()`, `write()`, overloaded insertion operator <<, `seekp()` and `tellp()` from the class `ostream`.
ifstream	It provides file input facility and contains `open()` with default input mode. Inherits the member functions `get()`, `getline()`, `read()`, overloaded extraction operator >>, `seekg()` and `tellg()` from the class `istream`.
fstream	It provides both input and output facility. It is derived from both `ifstream` and `ofstream` classes.

17.3 TYPES OF DATA FILES (TEXT FILES AND BINARY FILES)

Depending on how data are stored and retrieved, the files are classified into two types: (a) Text files, (b) Binary files. In a text file, data are stored as ASCII values. Strings and characters are stored as ASCII values. Even the numeric data also are stored as ASCII values only, each digit occupying one byte of memory space. For example, the value 23456 is stored in five bytes of memory space. Data in a text file is organized into lines with new-line characters as the terminators. Any text editor can be used to see the contents of the file.

Whereas in a binary file exact copies of the memory contents are stored. Strings and characters are stored as binary data (eight-bit values) with no special meaning attached to any character including the null character '\0', the string terminator. The numeric data are also stored as their binary equivalent. For example, the value 23456 occupies only two bytes of memory since its binary equivalent is stored. So a binary file is essentially a replica of the memory contents stored on the secondary storage devices.

17.4 OPENING AND CLOSING A TEXT FILE

An object of **ofstream** represents output file stream and it can be attached to a file to be opened for output (writing) purpose only. An object of **ifstream** represents input file stream and it can be attached to a file to be opened for input (reading) purpose only. Whereas an object of `fstream` class can be attached to a file to be opened for both input and output purposes.

Opening a file, irrespective of the purpose, basically establishes the linkage between a file stream object and the name of a file (to be remembered by the underlying operating system). Once the linkage is established, we can use the object to manipulate the contents of the file.

Opening a file can be accomplished in two ways: (a) By using the constructor (b) By using the `open()` member function.

By using the constructor: The syntax of opening a file for output purpose only using an object of `ofstream` class and the constructor is as follows:

```
ofstream ofstream_object("filename");
```

ofstream_object is an object of type **ofstream** and "**filename**" is any valid name of a file to be opened for output purpose only.

EXAMPLE

```
ofstream fout("text.dat");
```

fout is declared to be an object of `ofstream` type and it is made to represent the file **text.dat** opened for output purpose only.

The syntax of opening a file for input purpose only using an object of type `ifstream` class and the constructor is as follows:

```
ifstream ifstream_object("filename");
```

ifstream_object is an object of type **ifstream** and "**filename**" is any valid name of a file to be opened for input purpose only.

EXAMPLE

```
ifstream fin("text.dat");
```

fin is declared to be an object of **ifstream** type and it is made to represent the file **text.dat** opened for input purpose only.

By using the open member function: The syntax of opening a file for output purpose only using an object of `ofstream` class and `open()` member function is as follows:

```
ofstream_object.open("filename");
```

ofstream_object is an object of type **ofstream** and **"filename"** is any valid name of a file to be opened for output purpose only.

EXAMPLE

```
Ofstream fout;

fout.open("text.dat");
```

fout is declared to be an object of **ofstream** type and it is made to represent the file **text.dat** opened for output purpose only.

The syntax of opening a file for input purpose only using an object of type `ifstream` class and the `open()` member function is as follows:

```
ifstream_object.open("filename");
```

ifstream_object is an object of type **ifstream** and **"filename"** is any valid name of a file to be opened for input purpose only.

EXAMPLE

```
ifstream fin;

fin.open("text.dat");
```

fin is declared to be an object of **ifstream** type and it is made to represent the file **text.dat** opened for input purpose only.

If we have to open a file for both input and output operations, we use objects of `fstream` class. We know that the class `fstream` is derived from both `ifstream` and `ofstream`. As a result, objects of the class can invoke all the member functions of its base classes.

The syntax of opening a file an object of type `fstream` class and the **constructor** is as follows:

```
fstream fstream_object("filename", mode_of_opening);
```

The syntax of opening a file an object of type `fstream` class and the `open()` member function is as follows:

```
fstream_object.open("filename", mode_of_opening);
```

Note that here we need to provide one more argument, i.e., `mode_of_opening`. The list of all the modes of opening a file are provided in Table 17.2.

Table 17.2 Modes of Opening a File

Mode	*Purpose*
ios::out	Open file for creating (writing)
ios::in	Open file for reading only
ios::app	Open file for appending data to the file
ios::ate	Open file for updation and move the file pointer to the end of the file
ios::noreplace	Turn down opening if the file already exists
ios::nocreate	Turn down opening if the file does not exist
ios::trunc	On opening, delete the contents of the file
ios::binary	Open a binary file

EXAMPLE

```
fstream fout("text.dat", ios::out);
```

opens **text.dat** in output mode.

```
fstream fin("text.dat", ios::in);
```

opens **text.dat** in input mode.

```
fstream file("text.dat", ios::out | ios::in);
```

opens **text.dat** both in input and output mode.

Note that we can specify more than one mode while opening a file. In this case they are to be bitwise ORed with the operator bitwise OR operator |.

Points to remember: Opening a file in **ios::out** mode creates a new file. If the file already exists, the contents of the file are deleted.

Opening a file in **ios::in** opens the file in input mode. The file being opened should exist for the operation to be successful. Otherwise it fails.

Opening a file in **ios::app** mode opens the file in append mode and the file pointer is positioned at the end of the file so that any subsequent write operation proceeds from the end of the file. If the file does not exist, it is created newly.

Opening a file in **ios::ate** mode opens the file and the file pointer is moved to the end of the file so that we can append data to the file. It also permits us to modify the existing contents of the file.

Which method of opening to use and when? (Whether constructor or open()): When we use a stream object to represent a single file throughout the program, we can use either of the methods to open the file. But when we need the same object to refer to different files in different parts of a program, of course, closing one file before opening another, we should use the `open()` member function.

Closing a file: We learnt that opening a file establishes the linkage between a stream object and an operating system file. After the intended operations are done with the file, the file should be safely saved on the secondary storage for later retrieval. This is done by the member function `close()`. The function on its execution removes the linkage between the file and the stream object. The syntax of its usage is as follows:

```
stream_object.close();
```

`stream_object` can be either of **ifstream** or **ofstream** or **fstream** type. The function does not require any argument.

EXAMPLE

```
ifstream fin("text.dat");
fin.close();
```

closes the file **text.dat** represented by the stream object **fin**.

```
ofstream fout("text.dat");
fout.close();
```

closes the file **text.dat** represented by the stream object **fout**.

17.5 DETECTING END OF A FILE

While reading the contents of a file, care has to be taken to see to it that the operation does not cross the end of the file. The `ios` class provides a member function by name `eof()`, which helps in detecting the end of a file. Once the end of a file is detected with the use of the `eof()` member function, we can stop reading further. The prototype of the function is as follows:

```
int eof();
```

The function returns a non-zero value on reaching the end of the file. Otherwise, it returns zero.

Since it is a member function, it should be invoked with an object of the input file stream classes (`ifstream` or `fstream`). Since the function returns true or false kind of values, the function call would be in the form of a test-expression. The syntax of its usage is as follows:

```
if (fin.eof())
{
    statements
}
```

This is to execute the block of statements on reaching the end of the file represented by the object **fin**.

or

```
while(!fin.eof())
{
    statements
}
```

This is to execute the statements in the body of the loop as long as the end of the file represented by the object **fin** is not reached. On reaching the end of the file, the loop is terminated and the control is transferred to the statement, which follows the closing brace of the loop. This is used normally while reading the contents of a file.

We can even use the file stream object alone as a test-expression. The object evaluates to zero on reaching the end of the file. Otherwise it evaluates to a non-zero value. This property can also be used to check the end of a file.

```
if(fin)
{
    statements
}
```

is equivalent to

```
if (!fin.eof())
{
    statements
}
```

and

```
while(fin)
{
    statements
}
```

is equivalent to

```
while (!fin.eof())
{
    statements
}
```

17.6 TEXT FILES

We know that a text file consists of a group of ASCII values. The data in a text file are organized into lines with new-line characters as the terminators. We will now discuss input and output operations facility for text files.

17.6.1 Character I/O - put(), get() Member Functions

The `put()` member function belongs to the class ofstream and it is to write a character onto a text file. The syntax of its usage is as follows:

```
ofstream_object.put(ch);
```

ch is a character constant or `char` variable. The function writes **ch** onto the file represented by **ofstream_object**.

```
char ch = 'a';
ofstream fout("text.dat");

fout.put(ch);
```

writes the character stored in **ch** onto the file represented by the object **fout**, i.e., **text.dat**.

The `get()` member function belongs to the class `ifstream` and it is to read a character from a file into a **char** variable. The syntax of its usage is as follows:

```
ifstream_object.get(ch);
```

ch is a variable of `char` type. The function reads a character from the file represented by the **ifstream_object** into the variable **ch**.

```
char ch;
ifstream fin("text.dat");

fin.get(ch);
```

reads a character into the variable **ch** at the current byte position from the file represented by the object **fin,** i.e., **text.dat**.

Program 17.1 To Create a File of Characters and Read the Characters from the File

```
#include <fstream.h>

int main(void)
{
    ofstream fout;
    char ch;

    fout.open("text.dat");

    cout << "Enter a character and type 'q' to terminate \n";
    cin >> ch;
    while (ch != 'q')
    {
        fout.put(ch);
      cin >> ch;
    }

    fout.close();
    cout << "The contents of the file text" << "\n";

    ifstream fin;
    fin.open("text.dat");
    while (!fin.eof())
    {
        fin.get(ch);
        cout << ch;
    }
    fin.close();

    return 0;
}
```

Input-Output:

```
Enter a character and type 'q' to terminate
abcdseryuooppq
The contents of the file text
abcdseryuoopp
```

Explanation

fout is declared to be an object of **ofstream** type and it is to represent the file **text.dat** to be opened in output mode. The char variable **ch** is to accept a character one at a time, the content of which is written onto the file. The statement `fout.open("text.dat");` opens the file **text.dat** in output mode and now, the object **fout** represents the file and it is used to write characters that are accepted onto the file.

The following segment of code keeps accepting characters and write them onto the file till we type the character 'q':

```
cin >> ch;
while (ch != 'q')
```

```
    {
        fout.put(ch);
        cin >> ch;
    }
```

Once the character 'q' is typed, since the condition `(ch!='q')` evaluates to false, the loop is exited. Now, the file contains all the characters that are typed before 'q' is typed. The file is then closed with the statement `fout.close();`. The file should be closed since we reopen the same file in input mode in the code to follow.

fin is declared to be an object of **ifstream** type and the file **text.dat**, which was just created, is opened in input mode with the statement `fin.open("text.dat");`. Now, the object **fin** represents the file and it is used while reading the contents of the file.

The segment of code responsible for reading the contents of the file and displaying them on the screen is:

```
while (!fin.eof())
{
    fin.get(ch);
    cout << ch;
}
```

As long as the end of the file is not reached, each character in the file is read into the variable **ch** and it is displayed on the screen.

The file is then closed with the statement `fin.close();`. Here closing the file explicitly with the use of `close()` is not mandatory. This is because the object **fin** goes out of scope after the `main()` is exited and it gets destroyed since the destructor of the class `ifstream`, of which **fin** is an object, gets executed. Once the destructor gets executed, the file represented by the object would also be closed.

17.6.2 String I/O – The << Operator and the getline() Member Function

The insertion operator << has been overloaded to write built-in type data onto file streams. We can write values of `int` type, `float` type and even strings also. All of these appear to the right of the operator and the file stream object appears to the left of it. We write strings onto a file using the insertion operator in this program:

```
fout << "Object Oriented Programming\n";
```

where **fout** is an object of `ofstream` class and represents a output file stream. The statement on its execution writes the string within double quotes to the file.

The `getline()` member function belongs to the class `ifstream` and it is to read a string from a file into buffer. The syntax of its usage is as follows:

```
fin.getline(buffer, size);
```

reads **size** characters from the file represented by the object **fin** or till the new line char is encountered, whichever comes first, into the buffer.

Program 17.2 To Create a File Consisting of Strings and Read the Strings from the File

```
#include <fstream.h>
int main(void)
```

```
{
    ofstream fout;

    fout.open("strings.dat");

    fout << "Data Encapsulation\n";
    fout << "Polymorphism\n";
    fout << "Inheritance\n";

    fout.close();
    ifstream fin;
    char str[20];

    fin.open("strings.dat");
    cout << "The contents of the file strings.dat \n";
    while(!fin.eof())
    {
        fin.getline(str, 20);
        cout << str << "\n";
    }
    fin.close();

    return 0;
}
```

Input-Output:

```
The contents of the file strings.dat
Data Encapsulation
Polymorphism
Inheritance
```

Explanation

fout is declared to be an object of **ofstream** type and it is to represent the file **strings.dat** to be created. The statement `fout.open("strings.dat");` opens the file **strings.dat** in output mode. Now, the object **fout** represents the file and it is used to write strings onto the file. The following statements write three strings onto the file:

```
fout << "Data Encapsulation\n";
fout << "Polymorphism\n";
fout << "Inheritance\n";
```

The file is then closed with the statement `fout.close();` since we need to reopen the file for reading purpose.

fin is declared to be an object of **ifstream** type and **str** is declared to be an array of `char` type and of size 20. We open the file **strings.dat** in input mode with the statement `fin.open("strings.dat");`. Now, the object **fin** represents the file **strings.dat** and it is used to read the strings contained in it. The following segment of code is responsible for reading each string from the file and displaying on the screen:

```
    while(!fin.eof())
    {
        fin.getline(str, 20);
        cout << str << "\n";
    }
```

As long as the end of the file is not reached, each string from the file is read into the char array **str** and it is displayed on the screen. The file **strings.dat** is then closed with the statement `fin.close();`. Note once again that closing the file explicitly with the use of `close()` is not mandatory. This is because the object **fin** goes out of scope after the `main()` is exited and it gets destroyed since the destructor of the class `ifstream`, of which **fin** is an object, gets executed. Once the destructor gets executed, the file represented by the object would also be closed.

17.6.3 Mixed Data I/O—The Overloaded Insertion Operator (<<) and Extraction Operator (>>)

The insertion operator << has been overloaded to write built-in type (`int`, `char`, `float`, etc.) data onto files.

```
fout << 125 << "\n";
fout << 's' << "\n";
fout << 123.56 << "\n";
```

where **fout** is an object of **ofstream** type, are all valid statements and they write the values to the right of the extraction operator << onto the file represented by the stream object **fout**. It is important to note that the new line character delimits each data item in the file. It is required because a text file is organized into lines of text and this property is used while reading the data items from the file.

Similarly, the extraction operator >> has also been overloaded to read built-in type (`int`, `char`, `float`, etc.) data from files.

```
fin >> i;
fin >> c;
fin >> f;
```

where **fin** is an object of **ifstream** type, are all valid statements and they read the values delimited by the new line character from the file represented by the object **fin** into the variables **i**, **f** and **c**.

Program 17.3 Creating a File Consisting of Mixed Types of Data and Read the Data from the File

```
#include <fstream.h>

int main(void)
{

    ofstream fout;
    int i = 12345;
    float f = 315.25;
    char c = 'a';

    fout.open("mixed.dat");
```

```
    fout << i << "\n";
    fout << f << "\n";
    fout << c << "\n";

    fout.close();

    cout << "The contents of the file mixed.dat \n";
    ifstream fin;
    fin.open("mixed.dat");

        fin >> i;
        cout << i << "\n";
        fin >> f;
        cout << f << "\n";
        fin >> c;
        cout << c << "\n";

    fin.close();

    return 0;
}
```

Input-Output:

```
The contents of the file mixed.dat
12345
315.25
a
```

Explanation

The working of this program is similar to the earlier two programs except the fact that the file **mixed.dat** created in this program stores mixed types of data and they are read and displayed on the screen.

17.7 BINARY FILES

The binary files are of very much use when we have to deal with databases consisting of records. Since the records usually comprise heterogeneous data types, the binary files help optimize storage space and file I/O would be faster when compared to text files.

17.7.1 Objects I/O–write() and read() Member Functions

The **ofstream** provides the member function `write()`, which is used to write binary data to a file. The syntax of its usage is as follows:

```
fout.write((char*) &variable, sizeof(variable));
```

fout is an object of type **ofstream**. The function requires two arguments. The first argument is the address of the variable, the contents of which are written to the file and the second argument is the size of the variable. Note that the address of the variable is typecasted to pointer to char type. It is because, the write function does not bother to know the type of the variable. It requires data in terms of only bytes. The function writes the content of **variable** to the file represented by the object **fout**.

EXAMPLE

```
emp e;
ofstream fout("emp.dat", ios::binary);

fout.write((char*) & e, sizeof(e));
```

writes the contents of the object **e** to the file **emp.dat**.

The **ifstream** provides the member function `read()`, which is used to read binary data from a file. The syntax of its usage is as follows:

```
fin.read((char*) &variable, sizeof(variable));
```

fin is an object of **ifstream** type. The function reads a record from the file represented by the object **fin** to the object **e**.

EXAMPLE

```
emp e;
ifstream fin("emp.dat", ios::binary);

fin.read((char*) & e, sizeof(e));
```

reads an employee record from the file **emp.dat** into the object **e**.

Program 17.4 To Create a File Consisting of Employees' Details and Display its Contents

```
#include <fstream.h>
#include <iomanip.h>

class emp
{
    private:
            int empno;
            char name[20];
            float salary;
        public:
            void get()
            {
                cout << "Enter empno, name and salary \n";
                cin >> empno >> name >> salary;
            }

            void display()
            {
                cout << setw(6) << empno << setw(12) << name
                     << setw(8) << salary << "\n";
            }

    };

int main(void)
```

```
{
    ofstream fout;
    emp e;
    int i, n;

    fout.open("emp.dat", ios::binary);

    cout << "Enter the number of employees \n";
    cin >> n;
    cout << "Enter" << n << "Employees details \n";
    for(i = 1; i <= n; i++)
    {
        e.get();
        fout.write((char*) &e, sizeof(e));
    }

    fout.close();

    ifstream fin;
    fin.open("emp.dat", ios::binary);
    fin.read((char*)&e, sizeof(e));
    while (!fin.eof())
    {
        e.display();
        fin.read((char*)&e, sizeof(e));
    }

    fin.close();

    return 0;
}
```

Input-Output:

```
Enter the number of employees
2
Enter 2 Employees details

Enter empno, name and salary
121 Nishu 2300
Enter empno, name and salary
122 Harsha 4500

The contents of the file emp.dat
121     Nishu   2300
122     Harsha    4500
```

Explanation

The class emp is defined with three member data empno of type `int`, name of type array of `char` and salary of type `float`. The member functions of the class `get()` and `display()` are to accept the details of an employee and display them.

In the `main()`, **fout** is declared to be an object of **ofstream** type and it is to represent the file **emp.dat** being created in the program. The statement `fout.open("emp.dat", ios::binary);` opens the file **`emp.dat`** in binary output mode and the object **fout** will now represent the file. The object **fout** is used to write employees' details onto the file. The following segment of code is responsible for accepting *n* employees' details and writing them onto the file:

```
for(i = 1; i <= n; i++)
{
    e.get();
    fout.write((char*) &e, sizeof(e));
}
```

Note that **e** is an object of the class `emp` type and `e.get();` accepts the details of an employee and the statement `fout.write((char*)&e, sizeof(e));` writes the contents of the object **e** onto the file represented by the object **fout**. Once the loop completes, *n* employees' details are written into the file. The file is then closed with the statement `fout.close();`.

fin is declared to be an object of **ifstream** type and it is made to represent the file **emp.dat**, which was just created, opened in input mode with the statement `fin.open("emp.dat", ios::binary);`. We then read the file and display the employee records in the file with the following segment:

```
fin.read((char*)&e, sizeof(e));
while (!fin.eof())
{
    e.display();
    fin.read((char*)&e, sizeof(e));
}
```

Once all the records are read and displayed, the file is closed with the statement `fin.close();`.

Searching for required data in a binary file: Program 17.5 searches for an employee in the employee file **emp.dat** created in the earlier program.

Program 17.5 To Search for an Employee in `emp.dat`

```
#include <fstream.h>
#include <iomanip.h>

class emp
{
    private:
        int empno;
    char name[20];
        float salary;
    public:
        void get()
        {
            cout << "Enter empno, name and salary \n";
            cin >> empno >> name >> salary;
        }

        void display()
```

```
        {
            cout << setw(6) << empno << setw(12) << name
                 << setw(8) << salary << "\n";
        }

        int is_empno_equal(int eno)
        {
            return empno == eno;
        }
};

int main(void)
{
    ifstream fin("emp.dat", ios::binary);
    int eno, flag = 0;
    emp e;

    cout << "Enter eno \n";
    cin >> eno;

    while(fin.read((char*)&e, sizeof(e)))
    {
        if (e.is_empno_equal(eno))
        {
            flag = 1;
            break;
        }
    }

    if (flag)
        cout << "Employee with empno" << eno << "is found";
    else
        cout << "Employee with empno" << eno << "is not found";

    return 0;
}
```

Input-Output:

```
Enter eno
121
Employee with empno 121 is found
```

Explanation

The class `emp` is provided with a new member function `is_empno_equal()`. The purpose of the function is to check whether **eno** passed as the argument to the function matches with the **empno** of the object with which it is called. The function returns one (true) if they match. Otherwise zero (false). The function is called during the searching operation.

The file **emp.dat** is opened in read mode with the statement ifstream `fin("emp.dat", ios::binary);`. We assume that **empno's** in the file are distinct and search for an employee by means of **empno**. **eno** and **flag** are declared to be variables of `int` type. The variable **eno** is to accept the empno of the employee to be searched and the variable **flag** is to determine whether the required employee is found in the file or not. We start with the assumption that the employee is not available in the file by initializing it with zero (false). The empno of the employee to be searched is accepted into the integer variable **eno**. The segment of code responsible for searching is:

```
while(fin.read((char*)&e, sizeof(e)))
{
        if (e.is_empno_equal(eno))
        {
                flag = 1;
                break;
        }
}
```

The segment of code starts reading each record in the file and the empno value in the record is checked for equality with **eno**. If they are equal, it assigns the value one (true) to the variable **flag** and the loop is terminated. Once the loop is exited, we check the value of flag. If it is found to be one, we display that the required employee is found in the file. Otherwise, we display that the employee is not found.

Note that the statement `fin.read((char*)&e, sizeof(e))` is used as a test-expression. It is perfectly valid since the member function `read()` of `istream` class returns a reference to `istream` type on success. Zero on failure, i.e., when the end of the file is reached.

17.7.2 Random Accessing of a Binary File (seekg() and seekp() Member Functions)

All the programs, which have been written so far, for reading the contents of files, employed sequential access mode. That is, the contents were read from the beginning of the files till their end is reached in a serial manner. In majority of the programming situations, we need to access the contents at particular positions in the files directly. This is referred to as random accessing of files. The stream classes provide the following member functions support this.

Associated with each file are two pointers. One is known as **get pointer** and the other is known as **put pointer**. The get pointer is used to keep track of the byte position in an input file where the read operation has to start from, and the put pointer is used to keep track of the byte position in an output file where the write operation has to start from.

When a file is opened for input purpose, the get pointer for the file is positioned automatically at the first byte (zeroth byte) of the file, which is shown pictorially below. Note that the numbering starts from zero and ends with `n - 1` for a file of size ***n*** bytes.

Input file "text.dat"

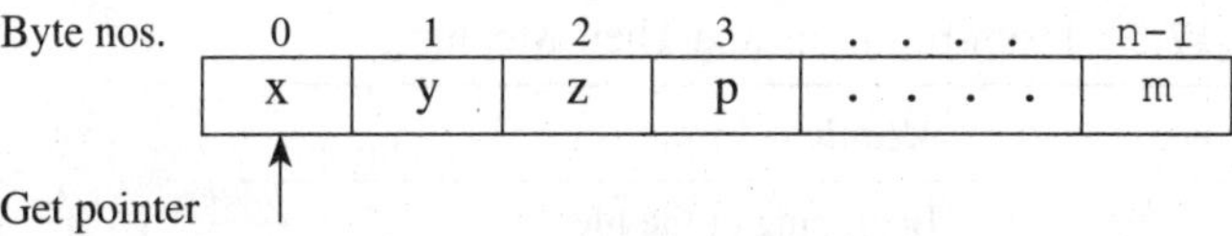

Similarly, when a file is opened for output purpose, the put pointer for the file is positioned automatically at the first byte (zeroth byte) of the file.

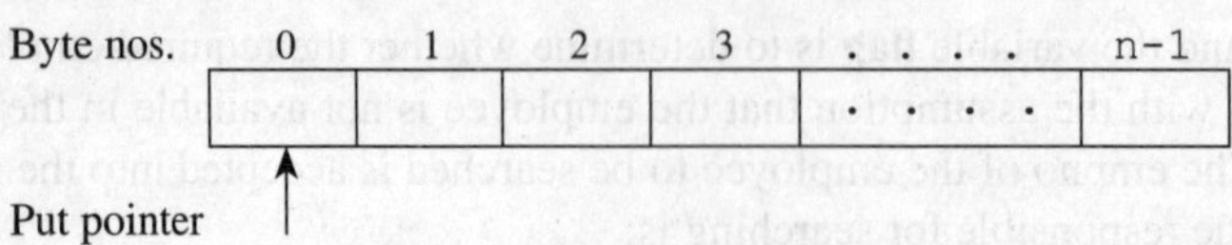

When a file is opened for appending purpose, the put pointer for the file is positioned automatically at the end of the file since the next write operation has to proceed from the end of the file.
File to append to : "text.dat"

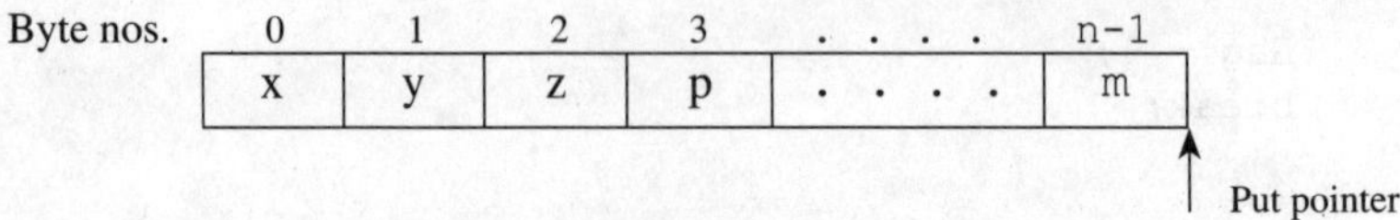

Random accessing of a file requires movement of the appropriate pointer (either the get pointer or the put pointer to read or write from the required byte position) to the required byte position before the intended operation is performed. For this purpose the `ifstream` and the `ofstream` classes provide the member functions `seekg()` and `seekp()` respectively. The member function `seekg()` is to move the get pointer to the required byte position in an input file and the member function `seekp()` is to move the put pointer to the required byte position in an output file. The syntax and working of both of these functions are same. We discuss below the syntax and working of the `seekg()`, which manipulates get pointer. They hold good even for the `seekp()` also. Only difference is `seekp()` manipulates the put pointer.

The member function `seekg()` has two variations:
The general form of first variation of the function is as follows:

```
fin.seekg(long);
```

where **fin** is the input file stream object and the argument of **long** type specifies the byte number to which the get pointer has to be moved.

EXAMPLE

```
fin.seekg(30);
```

moves the get pointer to the 30th byte in the file represented by the object **fin**.
The general form of the second variation is as follows:

```
fin.seekg(offset, from_position)
```

It takes two arguments: **offset** and **from_ position.** The function moves the get pointer to **offset**th byte from the specified **from_position**. Offset can be any `long` integer value. The values that from_position can take and their meanings are tabulated in Table 17.3.

Table 17.3 From-positions and Their Meaning

from_position	*Meaning*
ios::beg	Beginning of the file
ios::cur	Current byte position of the pointer
ios::end	End of the file

Examples of the usage of fseekg() with various from_positions

`fin.seekg(0, ios::beg);`	moves the get pointer to the beginning of the file
`fin.seekg(10, ios::beg);`	moves the get pointer to the 10th byte from the beginning in the file
`fin.seekg(0, ios::end);`	moves the get pointer to the end of the file
`fin.seekg(-10, ios::end);`	moves the get pointer to the 10th byte from the end of the file
`fin.seekg(10, ios::cur);`	moves the get pointer to the 10th byte from the current position of the file
`fin.seekg(-10, ios::cur);`	moves the get pointer to the 10th byte backwards from the current position of the file

Note: Since the byte numbering starts from zero, **n**th byte actually refers to the byte number **n + 1**. In the examples, 10th byte refers to the byte number 11 in the file.

The tellg() and tellp() member functions: The `ifstream` class provides the member function by name `tellg()`. The purpose of the function is to return the current position of the get pointer in the file. The syntax of its usage is as follows:

```
int position;
position = fin.tellg();
```

and the member function `tellp()` of `ofstream` class is to return the current position of the put pointer in the file.

```
int position = fout.tellp();
```

Program 17.6 To Append Records to the Employee File

```
#include <fstream.h>
#include <iomanip.h>

class emp
{
   private:
      int empno;
      char name[20];
      float salary;
   public:
      void get()
      {
         cout << "Enter empno, name and salary \n";
         cin >> empno >> name >> salary;
      }

      void display()
      {
         cout << setw(6) << empno << setw(12) << name
              << setw(8) << salary << "\n";
      }

};
```

```
int main(void)
{
    fstream empfile("emp.dat", ios::in |ios::app | ios::binary);
    emp e;
    int n, i;

    cout << "Enter the number of employees to be appended\n";
    cin >> n;
    cout << "Enter" << n << "Employees details \n";
    for(i = 1; i <= n; i++)
    {
        e.get();
        empfile.write((char*) &e, sizeof(e));
    }
    empfile.seekg(0);

    cout << "Contents of empfile after appending \n";
    empfile.read((char*) &e, sizeof(e));
    while(!empfile.eof())
    {
        e.display();
        empfile.read((char*) &e, sizeof(e));
    }
    empfile.close();

    return 0;
}
```

Input-Output:

```
Enter the number of employees to be appended
1
Enter 1 Employees details

Enter empno, name and salary
124 Dev 4509

Contents of empfile after appending
121        Nishu          2300
122        Harsha         4500
124        Dev            4509
```

Explanation

The file **emp.dat** is opened with the statement `fstream empfile("emp.dat", ios::in|ios::app|ios::binary);`. Note that **empfile** is an object of type **fstream** and the file is opened in both input and append mode. The mode **ios::app** enables us to append new records to the file by positioning the put pointer of the stream at the end of the file. The number of employees to be appended is accepted into the variable *n*. The segment of code responsible for accepting *n* employees' details and writing them onto the file is:

```
    for(i = 1; i <= n; i++)
    {
        e.get();
        empfile.write((char*) &e, sizeof(e));
    }
```

Once the loop completes, *n* employee records are appended to the file **emp.dat**.

Now, to enable reading the records in the file from the beginning, the get pointer of the stream is positioned at the beginning of the file with the statement `empfile.seekg(0);`. Note that **fstream** objects are equipped with both put pointer and get pointer. The employees' details are then displayed with the following segment of code:

```
        empfile.read((char*) &e, sizeof(e));
        while(!empfile.eof())
        {
            e.display();
            empfile.read((char*) &e, sizeof(e));
        }
```

Once all the records are displayed, the file is closed with the statement `empfile.close();`.

Program 17.7 To Count the Number of Records in a File

```
#include <fstream.h>
#include <iomanip.h>

class emp
{
    private:
int empno;
        char name[20];
        float salary;
    public:
        void get()
        {
            cout << "Enter empno, name and salary \n";
            cin >> empno >> name >> salary;
        }

        void display()
        {
            cout << setw(6) << empno << setw(12) << name
                 << setw(8) << salary << "\n";
        }

};

int main(void)
{
    ifstream empfile("emp.dat");
    emp e;
```

```
    int position, nor;

    empfile.seekg(0, ios::end);
    position = empfile.tellg();
    nor = position / sizeof(e);
    cout << "The number of records = " << nor << "\n";

    return 0;
}
```

Input-Output:

```
The number of records = 3
```

Explanation

The file **emp.dat** is opened in input mode with the statement `ifstream empfile("emp.dat");`. In order to find the number of records in the file, the get pointer of the input stream associated with the file is moved to the end of the stream with the statement `empfile.seekg(0, ios::end);`. The current byte position of the get pointer is collected by the variable **position** after the statement `position = empfile.tellg();` is executed. The expression `position/sizeof(e)` gives the number of records in the file and it is displayed.

Program 17.8 Reading *n*th Record in empfile

```
#include <fstream.h>
#include <process.h>
#include <iomanip.h>

class emp
{
    private:
        int empno;
        char name[20];
        float salary;
    public:
        void get()
        {
            cout << "Enter empno, name and salary \n";
            cin >> empno >> name >> salary;
        }

        void display()
        {
            cout << setw(6) << empno << setw(12) << name
                 << setw(8) << salary << "\n";
        }

};

int no_of_recs(ifstream&);
```

```
int main(void)
{
    ifstream fin("emp.dat");
    emp e;
    int nor, rno, position;

    nor = no_of_recs(fin);
    cout << "The number of records = " << nor << "\n";

    cout << "Enter record number \n";
    cin >> rno;
    if (rno > nor)
    {
        cout << "The reocrd does not exist";
        exit(1);
    }

    cout << "The record at position" << rno << "\n";
    position = (rno - 1) * sizeof(e);
    fin.seekg(position);
    fin.read((char*)&e, sizeof(e));
    e.display();

    return 0;
}

int no_of_recs(ifstream& fin)
{
    int last_byte, nor;

    fin.seekg(0, ios::end);
    last_byte = fin.tellg();
    nor = last_byte / sizeof(emp);
    return nor;
}
```

Input-Output:

```
Number of Records = 5
Enter record number
2
The record at position 2
122     Harsha   4500
```

Explanation

The function `no_of_recs()` is defined with an argument **fin**, a reference to **ifstream** type and it is made to return a value of `int` type. The purpose of the function is to find the number of records in the employee file represented by the reference **fin** and return it to the calling program.

In the `main()`, the file **emp.dat** is opened in input mode with the statement `ifstream fin("emp.dat");`. The number of records in the file is assigned to the variable **nor** with the statement `nor = no_of_recs(fin);`. The record number of the record to be read is accepted into the variable **rno**.

The value of **rno** is checked against **nor**, the number of records in the file. If **rno** is greater than **nor**, the message "Record does not exist" is displayed and the program is exited. Otherwise, starting byte number of the record to be read is assigned to the variable **position** with the statement `position = (rno - 1) * sizeof(e);`. Then the statement `fin.seekg(position);` moves the get pointer to the required record and it is read with the statement `fin.read((char*)&e, sizeof(e));` and the read record is displayed with the statement `e.display();`.

Program 17.9 To Update *n*th Record in a File

```
#include <fstream.h>
#include <process.h>

class emp
{
    private:
        int empno;
        char name[20];
        float salary;

    public:
        void get();
        void display();

};

    void emp :: get()
    {
        cin >> empno >> name >> salary;
    }

    void emp :: display()
    {
        cout << empno << name << salary << "\n";
    }

void show_recs(fstream&);
int no_of_recs(fstream&);

int main(void)
{
    fstream fin("emp.dat", ios::out | ios::in);
    emp e;
    int position, nor, rno;

    cout << "Contents of emp.dat \n";
    show_recs(fin);

    nor = no_of_recs(fin);

    cout << "Enter record number \n";
```

```
    cin >> rno;
    if (rno > nor)
    {
        cout << "The record does not exist";
        exit(1);
    }
    fin.seekg(0, ios::beg);

    position = (rno - 1) * sizeof(e);
    fin.seekp(position);
    cout << "Enter new details \n";
    e.get();
    fin.write((char*)&e, sizeof(e));
    fin.seekg(0, ios::beg);
    show_recs(fin);

    return 0;
}

int no_of_recs(fstream& fin)
{
    int nor, last_byte;

    fin.seekg(0, ios::end);
    last_byte = fin.tellg();
    nor = last_byte / sizeof(emp);
    return nor;
}

void show_recs(fstream& fin)
{
    emp e;

    while(fin.read((char*)&e, sizeof(e)))
          e.display();
    fin.clear();
}
```

Input-Output:

```
Contents of emp.dat

121 Raghav 23000
122 Ravi   45000
123 Mahesh 46000

Enter record number
2
Enter new details
122 Ravikumar 36000

After updation
```

```
121 Raghav 23000
122 Ravikumar 36000
123 Mahesh 46000
```

Explanation

The function `show_recs()` is defined with an argument **fin**, a reference to **fstream** type and it does not return any value to the calling function. The purpose of the function is to display all the records in the employee file. The function `no_of_recs()` is to find the number of records in the employee file and return it to the calling program.

In the `main()`, the statement `fstream fin("emp.dat", ios::out | ios::in);` opens the file **emp.dat** in both input and output mode. The records in the file are displayed with the statement `show_recs(fin);` Note that the statement `fin.clear();` within the function `show_recs()` is to clear the **eof** flag for the file. The **eof** flag has to be cleared if we want to manipulate the get pointer and the put pointer of the file, and if we want to read the contents of the file. The number of records in the file is assigned to the variable **nor** with the statement `nor = no_of_recs(fin);`. The number of the record to be updated is accepted into the variable **rno**. After confirming the availability of the required record in the file, starting byte number of the record is obtained and assigned to the variable **position** with the statement `position = (rno - 1)*sizeof(e);`. The put pointer is then moved to the byte position with the statement `fin.seekp(position);`. New details for the record are accepted and they are written into the file at the record position. All the records are once again displayed with the statement `show_recs(fin);`.

Program 17.10 To Delete a Record in empfile

```
#include <fstream.h>
#include <iomanip.h>
#include <stdio.h>

class emp
{
    public:
        int empno;
        char name[20];
        float salary;
    public:
        void get()
        {
            cout << "Enter empno, name and salary \n";
            cin >> empno >> name >> salary;
        }

        void display()
        {
            cout << setw(6) << empno << setw(12) << name
                << setw(8) << salary << "\n";
        }
        int is_empno_equal(int eno)
        {
            return empno == eno;
```

```
    }

};

void show_recs(ifstream&);

int main(void)
{
    ifstream fin;
    ofstream fout;
    emp e;
    int eno;

    fin.open("emp.dat");
    fout.open("emp1.dat");

    show_recs(fin);
    cout << "Enter empno of the employee to be deleted \n";
    cin >> eno;

    fin.seekg(0);
    while (fin.read((char*)&e, sizeof(e)))
    {
        if (!(e.is_empno_equal(eno)))
            fout.write((char*)&e, sizeof(e));
    }

    fin.close();
    fout.close();
    remove("emp.dat");
    rename("emp1.dat", "emp.dat");

    cout << "Records after deletion \n";
    fin.open("emp.dat");
    show_recs(fin);

    return 0;
}

void show_recs(ifstream& fin)
{
    emp e;

    while(fin.read((char*)&e, sizeof(e)))
        e.display();
    fin.clear();
}
```

Input-Output:

```
Contents of emp.dat
121 Nishu 2500
```

```
122 Harshith 3400

Enter empno of the employee to be deleted
121

After deletion, the contents of emp.dat
122 Harshith 3400
```

Explanation

The function `show_recs()` is defined with an argument **fin**, a reference to **fstream** type and it does not return any value to the calling program. The purpose of the function is to display all the records in the file **emp.dat**.

In the `main()`, **fin** is declared to be an object of **ifstream** type and **fout** is declared to be an object of **ofstream** type. The file **emp.dat** is opened in input mode with the statement `fin.open("emp.dat");` and a new file **emp1.dat** is opened in output mode with the statement `fout.open("emp1.dat");`. The records in the file **emp.dat** are displayed with the use of the function call `show_recs(fin);`. The empno of the employee to be deleted is accepted into the variable **eno**. The statement `fin.seekg(0);` on its execution moves the get pointer of the file to the beginning of the file so that we can read from start of the file.

The following segment of code reads each record from the file **emp.dat** copies it to the file **emp1.dat** except the record to be deleted, i.e., the record with **empno** in **eno**.

```
while (fin.read((char*)&e, sizeof(e)))
{
    if (!(e.is_empno_equal(eno)))
            fout.write((char*)&e, sizeof(e));
}
```

Note that `is_empno_equal()` is a member function of the class `emp` and it compares empno of the object with which it is called with the integer value passed as the argument to it and returns one if they match, otherwise zero.

Once all the records but the record to be deleted are copied to the file **emp1.dat**, both the files are closed with the statements `fin.close();` and `fout.close();`. The file **emp.dat** is removed from the directory with the statement `remove("emp.dat");` and now the file **emp1.dat** is renamed as **emp.dat** with the statement `rename("emp1.dat", "emp.dat");`. The file **emp.dat** will now have all the records but the record with **empno** equal to **eno**. Note that both the files were closed before removing the original **emp.dat** and renaming **emp1.dat** as **emp.dat**. This is required for the functions `remove()` and `rename()` to work. Note also that `remove()` and `rename()` are the built-in functions supported by standard C library. Since they are declared in the header file **stdio.h**, the header file has been included as part of the program. The records in the file **emp.dat** are once again displayed with the statement `show_recs(fin);`.

We will now write a program to sort the records in the file **emp.dat** in the increasing order of salary. The task involves fetching all the records of the file into the memory, sorting the records and copying the sorted records to a new file.

Program 17.11 Sorting a List of Employees

```
#include <fstream.h>

class emp
{
   public:
      int empno;
      char name[20];
      float salary;

   public:
      void get();
      void display();

};

void emp :: get()
{
   cin >> empno >> name >> salary;
}

void emp :: display()
{
   cout << empno << name << salary << "\n";
}

void show_recs(ifstream&);
int no_of_recs(ifstream&);

int main(void)
{
   ifstream fin;
   ofstream fout;
   emp *ep, e, t;
   int position, i, j, nor;

   fin.open("emp.dat");
   cout << "\n Unsorted List of Employees \n";
   show_recs(fin);

   nor = no_of_recs(fin);
   ep = new emp[nor];

   i = 0;
   fin.seekg(0);        // Move the file pointer to the beginning
   while (fin.read((char*)&e, sizeof(e)))
   {
      ep[i] = e;
      i++;
   }
```

```
    fin.close();

    /* sorting begins */

    for(i = 0; i < nor; i++)
    for(j = i + 1; j < nor; j++)
        if (ep[i].salary > ep[j].salary)
        {
            t = ep[i];
            ep[i] = ep[j];
            ep[j] = t;
        }

    /* sorting ends */

    fout.open("emps.dat");
    for(i = 0; i < nor; i++)
        fout.write((char*)&ep[i], sizeof(ep[i]));

    fout.close();
    cout << "\n Sorted List of Employees in the increasing order of salary \n";


    fin.open("emps.dat");

    show_recs(fin);

    return 0;
}


int no_of_recs(ifstream& fin)
{
    int last_byte, nor;

    fin.seekg(0, ios::end);
    last_byte = fin.tellg();
    nor = last_byte / sizeof(emp);
    return nor;

}

void show_recs(ifstream& fin)
{
    emp e;

    while(fin.read((char*)&e, sizeof(e)))
        e.display();
    fin.clear();
}
```

Input-Output:

```
Unsorted List of Employees
121 Nishu 2900
122 Harsh 2500

Sorted List of Employees in the increasing order of salary
122 Harsh 2500
121 Nishu 2900
```

Explanation

The function `show_recs()` is defined with an argument **fin**, a reference to **fstream** type and it does not return any value to the calling program. The purpose of the function is to display all the records in the file **emp.dat.**

The function `no_of_recs()` is defined with an argument **fin**, a reference to **ifstream** type and it is made to return a value of `int` type. The purpose of the function is to find the number of records in the employee file represented by the reference **fin** and return it to the calling program.

In the `main()`, the file **emp.dat** is opened in input mode with the statement `fin.open("emp.dat");`. The records in the file are displayed with the statement `show_recs(fin);`. The number of records in the file is obtained and assigned to the variable **nor** with the statement `nor = no_of_recs(fin);`. The number of records is required to know the amount of memory space needed to store the records in the memory. The required amount of memory space is then allocated with the statement `ep = new emp[nor];`. The variable **ep**, pointer to **emp** type, collects the address of the first record. After moving the **get pointer** of the file to the beginning, all the records are read from the file and copied to the memory allocated with the following segment of code:

```
i = 0;
fin.seekg(0);          // Move the file pointer to the beginning
while (fin.read((char*)&e, sizeof(e)))
{
    ep[i] = e;
    i++;
}
```

Consider the statement `ep[i] = e;`. The array notation is used while assigning the records read from the file to dynamically allocated memory. It is perfectly valid since **ep** being a pointer to the first record in the memory, `ep[0]` denotes the first **emp** variable, `ep[1]` denotes the second **emp** variable and so on.

The records in the memory are sorted in the increasing order of salary with the segment:

```
for(i = 0; i < nor; i++)
for(j = i + 1; j < nor; j++)
    if (ep[i].salary > ep[j].salary)
    {
            t = ep[i];
            ep[i] = ep[j];
            ep[j] = t;
    }
```

Once the records are sorted, they are written onto a new file **emps.dat** with the following block of statements:

```
fout.open("emps.dat");
for(i = 0; i < nor; i++)
    fout.write((char*)&ep[i], sizeof(ep[i]));
```

The file **emps.dat** is closed and reopened in input mode with the statement `fin.open("emps dat");` and the sorted records are displayed with the statement `show_recs(fin);`.

17.8 SENDING DATA TO A PRINTER

Most of the operating systems use predefined file names for the printers. The predefined names are PRN or LPT1, LPT2 and LPT3 representing the first, second and the third parallel port respectively. We can use these names similar to the way we use any other user defined file name. For example, if we link an output file stream to the file name PRN, any subsequent write operation sends the data to the printer connected to the first parallel port. Programs 17.12 and 17.13 illustrate printing with the printer connected to the port PRN.

Program 17.12 To Illustrate Sending Output to Printer

```
#include <fstream.h>

int main(void)
{

    ifstream fin("text.dat");
    ofstream fout("PRN");
    char ch;

    while (!fin)
    {
        fin.get(ch);
        fout.put(ch);
    }

    fin.close();
    fout.close();

    return 0;
}
```

The contents of the file **text.dat** are sent to the printer.

Program 17.13 To Illustrate Sending Output to Printer

```
#include <fstream.h>
#include "emp.h"

int main(void)
{

    ifstream fin("emp.dat");
    ofstream fout("PRN");
    emp e;

    fout << "Employees' Details\n\n";
```

```
    fout << "=================================\n";
    fout << "Empno    Name        Salary\n";
    fout << "=================================\n";

    fin.read((char*)&e, sizeof(e));

    while(!fin.eof())
    {
        fout << setw(10) << setiosflags(ios::left) << e.empno
             << setw(10) << setiosflags(ios::left) << e.name
             << setw(10) << setiosflags(ios::right) << e.salary << "\n";
        fin.read((char*)&e, sizeof(e));

    }

    return 0;
}
```

The contents of the file **emp.dat** are sent to the printer.

Note: The header file **emp.h** is assumed to contain the `emp` class definition and the member data are assumed to be public.

17.9 ERROR HANDLING DURING FILE I/O OPERATIONS

The file I/O operations can not always be expected to be smooth sailing. During the course of I/O operations, some errors may be encountered. As a consequence of the error conditions, the underlying program may prematurely terminate or it may produce erroneous results. Let us now try to enumerate the situations which lead to the error conditions and then understand how they can be countered. Following are the circumstances under which the file I/O operations fail:

1. Trying to open a file, which does not exist, for reading purpose.
2. Trying to open a file for writing purpose when there is no disk space.
3. Trying to write to a read-only file.
4. Trying to perform an operation over a file when the file has been opened for some other purpose.
5. Trying to read a file beyond its end-of-file-mark.

Even the error-capturing feature is incorporated into the built-in classes. Associated with each file stream is a member data by name **stream-state** inherited from the class `ios`. The member **stream-state** is an integer member and its low order four bits store the status values of the file.

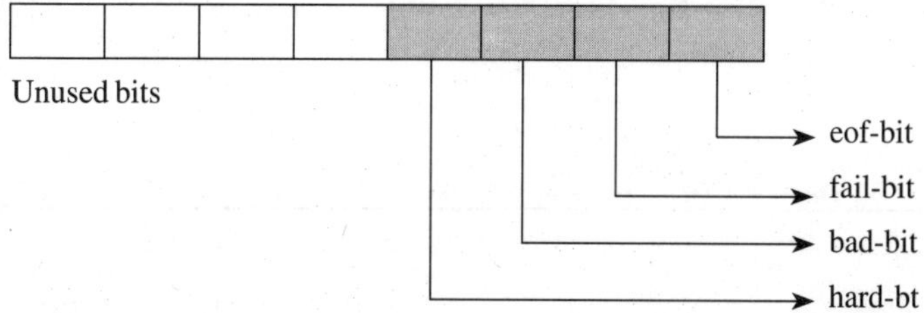

The names of the status bits and the circumstances when they are set to 1 are given in Table 17.4.

Table 17.4 Status bits

Status bits	*Circumstances when the corresponding bit is set to 1*
eof-bit	When the end of file is reached.
fail-bit	When an operation fails.
bad-bit	When an invalid operation is attempted.
hard-bit	When an unrecoverable error occurs.

C++ also provides member functions to read the values of status bits and helps the programmer take corrective steps. Table 17.5 depicts the functions and their purposes.

Table 17.5 Error handling functions

Function	*Purpose*
eof()	Checks whether the end of file is reached by reading the eof-bit. If the eof-bit is 1, the function returns a non-zero value (true). Otherwise it returns zero (false).
fail()	Reads the fail-bit, bad-bit and hard-bit. If any bit is 1, the function returns a non-zero value. Otherwise it returns zero.
bad()	Reads the bad-bit and hard-bit. If the bit is 1, the function returns a non-zero value. Otherwise it returns zero.
good()	Returns a non-zero value(true) when all the earlier functions return zero (false). Otherwise it returns zero.
rdstate()	Reads the stream state and returns the value.
clear(int = 0)	To set particular bit(s), clear() clears all the bits. clear(ios::fail-bit) clears only the fail-bit.

Program 17.14 To Illustrate Error Handling Functions during File I/O

```
#include <fstream.h>

int main(void)
{
   ifstream fin("students.dat");

   cout << "rdstate = " << fin.rdstate() << "\n";
   cout << "fail = " << fin.fail() << "\n";
   cout << "bad = " << fin.bad() << "\n";
   cout << "good = " << fin.good() << "\n";

   fin.close();

   return 0;
}
```

Input-Output:

```
rdstate = 4
```

```
fail = 4
bad = 4
good = 0
```

Explanation

Since an attempt is made to open the file **students.dat** in input mode, which does not exist, the operation of opening becomes an invalid one. As a result, the bad-bit in the **ios::state** variable is set to 1. The status is then displayed by calling the functions `rdstate()`, `fail()`, `bad()` and `good()` with the object **fin**. Since the positional weight of the bad-bit is four, four is returned by the functions `rdstate()`, `fail()` and the `bad()` member functions. Note that the member function `good()` returns zero as the file could not be opened.

Reading a file should proceed only when the file is opened successfully. The following conditional statement is recommended to be used for smooth going as far as the reading operation is concerned.

```
if (!fin.fail())            // No problem in reading the file
{
  statements for reading
}
```

When the test-expression `!fin.fail()` evaluates to true (non-zero value), then the statements for reading are executed.

Program 17.15 To Illustrate Error Handling Functions during File I/O

```
#include <fstream.h>
int main(void)
{
    ofstream fout("books.dat");

    cout << "rdstate = " << fout.rdstate() << "\n";
    cout << "fail = " << fout.fail() << "\n";
    cout << "bad = " << fout.bad() << "\n";
    cout << "good = " << fout.good() << "\n";

    fout.close();

    return 0;
}
```

Input-Output:

```
rdstate = 6
fail = 6
bad = 4
good = 0
```

Explanation

The file **books.dat** is a read-only file and an attempt is made to open it in output mode. The operation fails and both the fail-bit and the bad-bits are set to 1. As a result, the functions `rdstate()` and `fail()` return the value six. The `bad()` returns the value four. They are displayed.

```
if (!fout.fail())    // No problem in writing to the file
{
    statements for writing
}

    return 0;
}
```

17.10 COMMAND LINE ARGUMENTS

We know that the arguments play a vital role of establishing data communication between a calling function and a called function. It is through arguments, a calling function passes inputs to a called function, which in turn performs required manipulations over them. So far, we have discussed passing arguments to functions other than `main()`. It is important to note that we can even pass arguments to `main()` also. If the `main()` is to be defined to accept arguments, the actual arguments should be provided at the command prompt itself along with the name of the executable file. Hence these arguments are called **command line arguments**. For example, consider TYPE command of DOS, which displays the contents of a file. To display the contents of **emp.dat**, we use the following command:

```
C:\> type emp.dat
```

Here **type** is the program file name (Executable) and **emp.dat** is the input file, the contents of which are displayed.

To make `main()` of a program take command line arguments. The function header will have the following form:

```
void main(int argc, char *argv[])
```

Here, **argc** and **argv[]** are the formal arguments, which provide mechanism for collecting the arguments given at command line when the program is launched for execution. The **argc** is to collect the no. of arguments passed and the array of pointers to char type **argv** is to collect the arguments themselves. **argv[0]** will always represent the program file name (Executable) and **argv[1]**, **argv[2]**... represent arguments passed to the `main()`. In the case of the DOS command **type emp.dat**, the command **type** is denoted by **argv[0]** and the file **emp.dat** is denoted by **argv[1]**.

Program 17.16 To Illustrate Command Line Arguments—Copying One File to Another File

```
#include <fstream.h>
#include <process.h>

int main(int argc, char *argv[])
{
    ifstream fin;
    ofstream fout;
    char c;

    if (argc != 3)
    {
        cout << "Invalid number of arguments\n";
        exit(1);
```

```
    }
    fin.open(argv[1]);
    fout.open(argv[2]);
    while (!fin.eof())
    {
        fin.get(c);
        fout.put(c);
    }


    return 0;
}
```

Input-Output:

The program is executed as follows:

```
C:\>copy text.dat text1.dat
```

As a result, the contents of **text.dat** are copied to **text1.dat**. We have thus simulated DOS copy command.

Explanation

fin is declared to be an object of **ifstream** type and **fout** is declared to be an object of **ofstream** type. The purpose of the program being copying one text file to another, the number of arguments should be three. **argv[0]** representing the program name and **argv[1]** and **argv[2]** representing the source file and the target file respectively. If the number of arguments provided is not equal to three, the program gets terminated displaying the message "Invalid number of arguments". Once the correct number of arguments are provided, the source file represented by **argv[1]** is opened in input mode with the statement `fin.open(argv[1]);` and the target file represented by **argv[2]** is opened in output mode with the statement `fout.open(argv[2]);` All the characters in the source file are read and are written into the target file with the following segment of code:

```
while (!fin.eof())
{
    fin.get(c);
    fout.put(c)
}
```

After the execution of the program if we open the target file with any text editor, we will see that the target file is a duplicate of the source file.

Note: The source code of the program is entered into the file **copy.cpp**.

REVIEW QUESTIONS

17.1 Explain the need for files.

17.2 Explain various built-in classes supporting file management.

17.3 Distinguish between a text file and a binary file.

17.4 Explain opening a file and its implementation in C++.

17.5 What are the different modes of opening a file?

17.6 Explain closing a file and its implementation in C++.

17.7 How do we detect the end of a file with or without the member function eof().

17.8 Explain character I/O with respect to files.

17.9 Explain string I/O with respect to files.

17.10 Explain mixed types data I/O with respect to files.

17.11 Explain the binary I/O functions.

17.12 What is a get pointer? How do we manipulate it?

17.13 What is a put pointer? How do we manipulate it?

17.14 How do we know the current position of get pointer and put pointer of a stream?

17.15 Explain the procedure of finding the number of records in a file.

17.16 How do we update a given record in a file?

17.17 Why do we need error handling during file I/O?

17.18 Explain the member functions, which support error handling.

17.19 Explain the ios::state variable's significance.

True/False Questions

T17.1 A file stores data temporarily.

T17.2 Every file needs to be opened before performing any operation over it.

T17.3 Each file gets automatically closed on the exit of the program.

T17.4 The default mode of opening with an ifstream object is input.

T17.5 When a file is opened in output mode, it is erased if it had contents earlier.

T17.6 When we open a file with fstream object, we should specify the mode of opening explicitly.

T17.7 Only one mode of opening can be specified when we open a file.

T17.8 The statements `fin.seekg(0);` and `fin.seekg(0, ios::beg);` are same.

T17.9 There is no difference between ios::app and ios::ate, both move the file pointer to the end on opening.

T17.10 We can not prevent a file losing its data when we open it in output mode.

T17.11 To open a file in input mode, the file should exist.

T17.12 To update the required record in a file we should move the get pointer to that record.

PROGRAMMING EXERCISES

P17.1 Write a program to count the no. of characters in a text file.

P17.2 Write a program to copy the contents of one text file to another text file.

P17.3 Write a program to sort a file consisting of names of students and display them.

P17.4 Write a program to sort a file consisting of books' details in the alphabetical order of author names.

The details of books include book_id, author_name, price, no_of_pages, publisher, year_of_ publishing.

P17.5 Write a menu driven program to perform the following operations over a student file:

(a) Addition of records

(b) Deletion of records

(c) Updation of records

(d) Displaying the records interactively. The details of students include roll_no, name, marks in five subjects.

P17.6 Suppose there are two files **emp.dat** and **dept.dat** storing the details of employees and the departments respectively. The employee file has empno, name, salary and deptno as the fields with the empno being unique, and the dept file has the fields deptno, deptname with the deptno being unique. Write a program to display empno, name, deptname and salary of all the employees.

P17.7 In Program 17.9, the data file **emp.dat** is assumed to have some records. Modify the program to add records to the file if it is empty and then sort the records.

P17.8 Modify Program 17.4 so that the uniqueness of the empno values is maintained while accepting records.

P17.9 Write a program to insert a record into the sorted employee file (sorted on salary).

P17.10 Write a program to merge two files.

(***Note:*** The two files should have been sorted on the same field and the newly obtained file after merging should reflect the ordering on the same field).

P17.11 Suppose **emp1.dat** and **emp2.dat** are two files having employees' details. Write a program to create a new file **newemp.dat** with records, which are either in **emp1.dat** or in **emp2.dat** or in both.

Chapter 18

String Handling

18.1 INTRODUCTION

Earlier, we discussed C-strings at length. The C-style strings are character arrays terminated by a special character namely null character `'\0'`. Even though the C-style strings provide complete control with regard to operations over them, at times, they lead to runtime errors if the presence of the null character at the end of each string is not ensured. Standard C++ provides a built-in class by name **string**, the objects of which can be used to deal with strings. The standard C++ strings are regarded as a safe alternative to C-strings since there is no direct reliance on the string terminating character `'\0'`. To be able to use the C++ standard strings, the header file **`string.h`** should be included as part of the program.

The `string` class is provided with constructors, a number of member functions and overloaded operators, which help perform varieties of operations over strings.

The operations include the following:

- Creating string objects
- Accepting strings from the standard input device, keyboard
- Displaying strings on the standard output device, screen
- Comparison of two strings
- Concatenation of strings
- Finding one string in another
- Accessing individual characters in a string
- Retrieving the length of a string, etc.

18.2 STRING CLASS AND ITS CONSTRUCTORS

In order to create string objects, the string class provides three constructors. The prototypes of the constructors and their working are given as follows:

1. `string()`

Constructor without any arguments. It creates an empty string.

```
string s1;
```

Here, the object **s1** will have an empty string.

2. `string(const char*)`

Constructor with a null terminated string as the argument and it creates a string object with the string.

```
string s2("Ramanujam";);
```

Here, the object **s2** will have the string "Ramanujam".

3. `string(const string&)`

Copy constructor. It requires a reference to an existing string object.

```
string s3(s2);
```

Here, the object **s3** is constructed as a copy of **s2**.

18.3 THE ASSIGNMENT OPERATOR =

The assignment operator = is overloaded in the string class so that it can be used to assign one string object to another. We can even assign a string constant to a string object. The assignment operator is thus used to create a string object.

```
string s1;
string s2("Kiran");
s1 = s2;
```

Here, **s2** is assigned to **s1** and as a result, the object **s1** also will have the string "Kiran".

```
s1 = "Karan"
```

Here, the string constant "Karan" is assigned to the object **s1**.

18.4 THE EXTRACTION OPERATOR >> AND THE INSERTION OPERATOR <<

Both the >> and << operators are overloaded in the `string` class so that they can be used to accept and display string objects.

```
cin >> s;
```

accepts a string (single word) into the string object **s**.

```
cout << s;
```

displays the string (single word) in the object **s**.

Program 18.1 To Illustrate Constructors in String Class

```
#include <string.h>
#include <iostream.h>

int main(void)
{
    string s1;              //empty string
    string s2("Ramanujam";);    // string constant as the argument
    string s3(s2);            // copy constructor
    cout << "s1 = " << s1 << "\n";
    cout << "s2 = " << s2 << "\n";
    cout << "s3 = " << s3 << "\n";
    string s4;
    s4 = s3;                // Assignment of string objects
    cout << "s4 = " << s4 << "\n";
    string s5;

    s5 = "String Handling";     // Assignment of a string constant
    cout << "s5 = " << s5<< "\n";

    return 0;
}
```

Input-Output:

```
s1 =
s2 = Ramanujam
s3 = Ramanujam
s4 = Ramanujam
s5 = String Handling
```

Explanation

The default constructor gets called to initialize the object **s1** with an empty string. Since the object **s2** is declared with a string constant as its initial value, the constructor in the `string` class with one argument gets called to initialize the object **s2** with the string constant specified within the parentheses. For the object **s3**, copy constructor in the `string` class gets called to make a duplicate of **s2** in **s3**. The strings in all the three objects are displayed. The string object **s4** is assigned **s3** and the string constant "string handling" is assigned to the string object **s5** with the help of the overloaded assignment operator. Both **s4** and **s5** are displayed.

18.5 THE RELATIONAL OPERATORS (<, <=, >, >=, ==, ! =)

All the relational operators are overloaded to perform comparison of two string objects. If **s1** and **s2** are string objects, the expression `s1 < s2` is a valid conditional expression and it evaluates to 1 (true) if string in **s1** is lexicographically less than that in **s2**. Otherwise it evaluates to 0 (false). Similarly, the other operators can be used to compare two string objects.

Program 18.2 Relational Operators at Work

```
#include <iostream.h>
#include <string.h>

int main(void)
{
    string s1("Ramya"), s2("Rajini");

    cout << "s1 = " << s1 << "\n";
    cout << "s2 = " << s2 << "\n\n"

    cout << "s1 < s2 =" << (s1 < s2) << "\n";
    cout << "s1 <= s2 =" << (s1 <= s2) << "\n";
    cout << "s1 > s2 =" << (s1 > s2) << "\n";
    cout << "s1 >= s2 =" << (s1 >= s2) << "\n";
    cout << "s1 == s2 =" << (s1 == s2) << "\n";
    cout << "s1 != s2 =" << (s1 != s2) << "\n";

    return 0;
}
```

Input-Output:

```
s1 = Ramya
s2 = Rajini

s1 < s2  = 0
s1 <= s2 = 0
s1 > s2  = 1
s1 >= s2 = 1
s1 == s2 = 0
s1 != s2 = 1
```

18.6 CONCATENATION (+, +=)

Concatenation of two strings is nothing but appending one string to the end of another. Both + and += are overloaded to perform concatenation of two strings. Let us understand how they can be put to use by the following examples:

```
string s1("Greater");
string s2("Bangalore");
```

The operands to the + operator can be string objects or string constants.

```
s3 = s1 + s2;
```

s3 will have "Greater Bangalore".

```
s3 = "Greater" + s2;
```

Here also, **s3** will have "Greater Bangalore".

```
s3 = s1 + "Bangalore"
```

Again, **s3** will have “Greater Bangalore”.

```
s3 = "Greater" + "Bangalore";
```

Again, **s3** will have “Greater Bangalore”.

```
s1 += s2;
s1 += "Bangalore"
```

s1 will have “Greater Bangalore”.

Program 18.3 The Operators + and += at Work

```
#include <iostream.h>
#include <string.h>

int main(void)
{
   string s1("Greater");
   string s2(" Bangalore");

   s3 = s1 + s2;
   cout << "s3 =" << s3 << "\n";

   s3 = "Greater" + s2;
   cout << "s3 =" << s3 << "\n";

   s3 = s1 + " Bangalore"
   cout << "s3 =" << s3 << "\n";


   s3 = "Greater" + " Bangalore";
   cout << "s3 =" << s3 << "\n";

   s1 += s2;
   cout << "s1 =" << s1 << "\n";

   s1 += " Bangalore"
   cout << "s1 =" << s1 << "\n";

   return 0;
}
```

Input-Output:

```
s3 = Greater Bangalore
s3 = Greater Bangalore
s3 = Greater Bangalore
s3 = Greater Bangalore
s1 = Greater Bangalore
s1 = Greater Bangalore
```

18.7 MEMBER FUNCTIONS OF STRING CLASS

`String` class includes a number of member functions, which are of very much use to deal with strings. They are tabulated in Table 18.1.

Table 18.1 Member Functions in String Class

Function	*Purpose*
at()	Returns the character at a given position
begin()	Returns the reference to the start of a string
capacity()	Returns the total number of characters that can be stored
compare()	Compares the string object with another string (argument)
empty()	Returns true if the string is empty, otherwise returns false
end()	Returns the reference to the end of a string
erase()	Removes the specified characters
find()	Finds the position of occurrence of a string in the string object
insert()	Inserts one string into another
length()	Returns the number of characters in the string object
max_size()	Returns the maximum possible size of a string object in a given system
replace()	Replaces the specified part of the string object with a given string
resize()	Changes the size of the string as specified
size()	Returns the number of characters in the string object
swap()	Interchanges the string object and the string object passed as the argument

Retrieving attributes of strings: The `string` class provides member functions to retrieve the attributes of strings like size, length, capacity and maximum size. The member functions do not require any arguments. The attributes size and length both represent the number of characters stored in a string. The attribute capacity of a string represents the total number of characters that can be stored in it. The attribute maximum size gives the highest possible number of characters that the given system can support for a string object. The member functions for the purpose of retrieving the above mentioned attributes are `size()`, `length()`, `capacity()` and `max_size()` respectively.

Program 18.4 Retrieving Attributes of Strings

```
#include <iostream.h>
#include <string.h>

int main(void)
{
    string str("Standard C++ Strings");

    cout << "str = " << str << "\n";
    cout << "Size = " << str.size() << "\n";
    cout << "Length = " << str.length() << "\n";
    cout << "Capacity = " << str.capacity() << "\n";
```

```
    cout << "Maximum Size = " << str.max_size() << "\n";
    return 0;
}
```

Input-Output:

```
str = Standard C++ Strings
Size = 20
Length = 20
Capacity = 31
Maximum size = 4294967293
```

Accessing individual characters in strings: The `string` class provides a member function by name `at()` which enables us to access the individual characters in a **string** object. It takes an integer as the argument and it specifies the position of the character to be accessed. We can even use the `subscription operator []` to access the individual characters in the manner similar to that with normal arrays.

Program 18.5 Accessing Individual Characters in Strings

```
#include <iostream.h>
#include <string.h>

int main(void)
{
    string s1("Data Encapsulation");
    string s2("Polymorphism");
    int i;
    for(i = 0; i < s1.length(); i++)
        cout << s1[i];
    for(i = 0; i < s2.length(); i++)
        cout << s2.at(i);

    return 0;
}
```

Input-Output:

```
Data Encapsulation
Polymorphism
```

Explanation

The characters stored in the string objects **s1** and **s2** are retrieved and displayed with the array subscription operator as well as the `at()` member function of the string class. Note that a loop is set up with the control variable **i**, which takes the character position values ranging from 0 to the length – 1 of the corresponding string.

We can even provide a string to a string object on a character by character basis. The following segment is to accept a line of text into the object **s**:

```
string s;
char ch;
```

```
cin >> ch;
while (ch != '\n')
{
   s[i] = ch;
   cin >> ch;
}
```

The statement `cout << s;` displays the line of text.

Fiddling with strings: We can fiddle with the contents of strings like inserting one string into another, replacing a part one string with another string and erasing the specified number of characters and so on. The above mentioned operations are accomplished with the help of the member functions `insert()`, `replace()` and `erase()` respectively.

Program 18.6 Fiddling with Strings

```
#include <iostream.h>
#include <string.h>
int main(void)
{
   string s1("abc");
   string s2("pqr");
   string s3("xyz");

   cout << "s1 = " << s1 << "\n";
   cout << "s2 = " << s2 << "\n";
   cout << "s3 = " << s3 << "\n";

   // Inserting s2 into s1 at position 2
   s1.insert(2, s2);
   cout << "s1 after inserting s2 at position 2 = " << s1 << "\n";

   // Removing a part of s1
   s1.erase(2, 3);
   cout << "s1 after removing its three characters from position 2 =
      " << s1 << "\n";

   // Replacing a part of s2 with s3
   s2.replace(1, 2, s3);
   cout << "s2 After replacing its two characters from position 1 with s3=" <<
   s2 << "\n";

   // Removing a part of s1
   s2.erase(1, 3);
   cout << "s2 after removing its three characters from position 2 =
   "    << s1 << "\n";

   return 0;
}
```

Input-Output:

```
s1 = abc
s2 = xyz
s3 = pqr
s1 after inserting s2 at position 2 = abxyzc
s1 after removing its three characters from position 2 = abc
s2 After replacing its two characters from position 1 with s3= xpqr
s2 after removing its three characters from position 2 = x
```

Explanation

The constructor with one argument in the string class gets called to initialize the objects **s1**, **s2** and **s3** with the string constants provided with them. The strings in the objects are displayed.

The string **s2** is inserted into **s1** at position 2 with the statement `s1.insert(2, s2);`. As a result, the string in **s1** will now become **abxyzc**. The newly obtained string is displayed. Note that the character positions in a string start from 0.

Three characters of **s1** starting from position 2 are erased with the statement `s1.erase(2, 3);`. **s1** will now be left with the string **abc**, its original string, and it is displayed.

Two characters of **s2** from position 1 are replaced with the string in **s3** with the statement `s2.replace(1, 2, s3);`. The string object **s2**, which had **xyz** earlier, will now have **xpqr** and it is also displayed.

Three characters of **s2** from position 1 are erased with the statement `s2.erase(1, 3);`. As a result, the object **s2** will be left with the string consisting of the single character **x** and it is displayed.

Pattern matching: The `string` class provides the member function `find()` which can be used to find whether one string is found in another string or not. It takes a string object or string constant or a string variable (Name of a char array) as its argument. The other two member functions `find_first_of()` and `find_last_of()` return the position of the first and the last occurrence of the given character in a string. Program 18.7 illustrates these.

Program 18.7 To Illustrate Pattern Matching

```
#include <iostream.h>
#include <string.h>

int main(void)
{
    string str("Jacob Manohar Abraham");

    cout "<< str = " << str << "\n";
    int i = str.find("Manohar");
    cout << "Manohar is found at position = " << i << "\n";

    int j = str.find_first_of('a');
    cout << "First occurrence of 'a' is at position = " << j << "\n";

    int k = str.find_last_of('a');
    cout << "Last occurrence of 'a' is at position = " << k << "\n";

    return 0;
}
```

Input-Output:

```
str = Jacob Manohar Abraham
Manohar is found at position = 6
First occurrence of 'a' is at position = 1
Last occurrence of 'a' is at position = 19
```

Explanation

The string object **str** is initialized with the string constant "Jacob Manohar Abraham".

The statement `int i = str.find("Manohar");` on its execution finds the position of the occurrence of the string "Manohar" in the string **str** and assigns it to the variable **i**, which is then displayed.

The first occurrence of the character 'a' in the string **str** is found and assigned to the variable **j** with the statement `int j = str.find_first_of('a');`.

The last occurrence of the character 'a' in the string **str** is found and assigned to the variable **k** with the statement `int k = str.find_first_of('a');`.

The values collected by the variables **j** and **k** are displayed.

Sorting a list of strings: We know that sorting is nothing but arranging a list of elements in increasing or decreasing order. It involves two basic operations. They are comparison and interchanging of elements. The string class provides member functions namely `compare()` and `swap()` which perform the operations of comparison and interchanging of two strings respectively. Program 18.8 uses these to sort a list of strings.

Program 18.8 To Sort a List of Strings

```
#include <iostream.h>
#include <string.h>

int main(void)
{
    string names[5], tname;
    int i, j;

    cout << "Enter 5 Names \n";
    for(i = 0; i < 5; i++)
        cin >> names[i];

    cout << "Unsorted List of Names\n";
    for(i = 0; i < 5; i++)
        cout << names[i] << "\n";

// Sorting Begins

    for(i = 0; i < 4; i++)
    for(j = i + 1; j < 5; j++)
        if(names[i].compare(names[j]) > 0)
            swap(names[i], names[j]);
// Sorting ends

    cout << "Sorted List of Names\n";
```

```
    for(i = 0; i < 5; i++)
        cout << names[i] << "\n";

    return 0;
}
```

Input-Output:

```
Enter 5 Names
Ramu
Vishnu
Ganesh
Supriya
Sony

Unsorted List of Names

Ramu
Vishnu
Ganesh
Supriya
Sony

Sorted List of Names
Ganesh
Ramu
Sony
Supriya
Vishnu
```

REVIEW QUESTIONS

18.1 What is a string? Differentiate between a C-style string and standard C++ string.

18.2 Explain the constructors of the string class.

18.3 List all the operators overloaded in the string class and explain their usage.

18.4 What is concatenation? How is it accomplished with standard C++ strings.

18.5 Explain the member functions size(), capacity(), length(), max_size() of string class.

18.6 Explain insert(), erase() and replace() member functions.

True/False Questions

T18.1 We should ensure the presence of the null character at the end of each standard C++ string.

T18.2 Standard C++ strings are safer than C-style strings.

T18.3 String `s("anubhav");` is not a valid declaration.

T18.4 `s = "Prashanth"` is a valid assignment where **s** is a string object.

T18.5 Both length() and size() member functions return the number of characters in a string.

PROGRAMMING EXERCISES

P18.1 Write a program to accept a name and encrypt it and later decrypt it.
(**Example: ramesh** can be encrypted as **sbnfti**. Note that each letter is replaced by its next letter in the English alphabet. You can employ any encryption rule.

P18.2 Write a program to accept *n* names and search for a given name in the list.

P18.3 Accept a date in the format dd-mm-yyyy and find whether the given date is valid or not.

Chapter 19
Exception Handling

19.1 INTRODUCTION

In the programming world, it is every programmer's experience that writing programs and executing them without any errors for the first time is a difficult task. We come across different types of errors. The two most common errors are: (a) Syntactical errors and (b) Logical errors. The syntactical errors occur if the programs do not conform to the grammatical rules of the language being used. They are caught during compilation itself. We correct the syntactical errors and recompile the programs until the compiler is satisfied with the syntactical correctness of the programs and produces the equivalent object code. The second category of errors, i.e., logical errors occur if the solution procedure for the given problem itself is wrong. In this case the outputs produced by the programs would be incorrect. Correcting the solution procedure itself by better understanding of the problem eliminates these errors.

There is one more type of errors namely **runtime errors**. As the name itself indicates they occur during the course of execution of programs. Runtime errors occur due to both program internal factors and external factors. Examples of runtime errors due to internal factors include "Division by zero", "Array subscript out of bounds". Examples of runtime errors due to external factors include "Running out of memory", "Printer out of paper", etc. The term *exception* is used to represent a runtime error and *exception handling* is about anticipating exceptions, identifying them and taking corrective steps when they occur thereby avoiding abnormal termination of a program.

19.2 EXCEPTION HANDLING MECHANISM

A structured approach towards exception handling has been made a part of C++. At the outset, exception-handling code consists of two segments. The first segment is responsible for detecting the errors and informing them to the error-handling routine and the second one, the error handling routine, is for receiving the errors and initiate appropriate measures. Central to exception handling in C++ are three keywords: *try*, *throw* and *catch*.

A block of statements enclosed within braces, which may raise exceptions, follows the keyword *try*. The block is called the **try block**.

```
try
{
    .
    .             // Statements for detecting exception

    throw exception;
}
```

Within in the try block, if an exception is generated it is informed to the error handler routine with the help of *throw* keyword. If an exception is informed to the error handler routine by the throw statement, the exception is said to have been thrown to the error handler routine.

The syntax of using the throw statement is as follows:

```
throw (exception)
throw exception
```

The keyword *catch* with a pair of parentheses is also followed by a set of statements enclosed with braces and the block is called the **catch block**. The general form of the catch block is as follows:

```
    catch(type argument)
    {
        .  // Statements that handle
        .  //the exception thrown by the try
        .  //block.
    }
```

The catch block is responsible for receiving (catching) the exception thrown by the throw statement of the try block and handling it appropriately.

The general form of these blocks is as follows:

```
try
{
.
.
.      // Statements for detecting exception

throw exception;


}

catch(type argument)
{
    .  // Statements that handle
    .  //the exception thrown by the try
    .  //block.
}
```

A catch block that catches an exception must follow the try block that throws the exception.

Relationship between try block and catch block is shown in Figure 19.1.

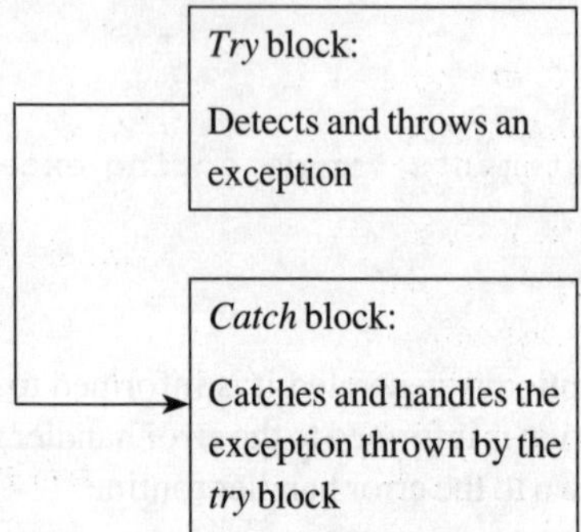

Fig. 19.1 A schematic representation of the relationship between the try and catch blocks.

An exception is basically an object, which is used to transmit the error situation to the catch block so that it can take corrective steps. The object can be a built-in type value like int, char, float, etc. or it can also be a user-defined type value like an object of a class.

Execution sequence of a program, which contains a try and a matching catch block, is as follows:

If the try block does not detect any exception then the matching catch block is simply skipped during execution.

If try block detects and throws an exception, the control is transferred from the try block and reaches the catch statement of the matching catch block (i.e., the catch block the argument type of which matches with that of the exception thrown by the try block). The catch block receives the exception and handles it. After the execution of the catch block, the control reaches the first statement after the closing brace of the catch block. Note that the control is not transferred back to the try block that threw the exception.

If the try block detects an exception and throws it and there is no matching catch block then the program is terminated.

If the try block does not detect any exception then the matching catch block is simply skipped during execution.

Program 19.1 To Illustrate Division by Zero Exception

```
#include <iostream.h>

int main(void)
{
    int a, b;

    cout << "Enter values of a and b \n";
    cin >> a >> b;

    try
    {
    if (b != 0)
        cout << "a/b = " << a/b;
    else
        throw b;
    }
```

```
    catch(int x)
    {
        cout << "Exception caught = " << x;
    }

    return 0;
}
```

Input-Output:

```
First-Run:
Enter values of a and b
4 2
a / b = 2

Second-Run:
Enter values of a and b
4 0
Exception caught = 0
```

Explanation

a and **b** are declared to be variables of `int` type. The values of both are accepted with the statement `cin >> a >> b;`. The purpose of the program is to display the value of the expression `a/b`. Here we foresee the possibility of **b**, the denominator, taking a value zero, which gives rise to an exception.

In the first run we accept 4 and 2 to the variables **a** and **b** respectively. In the try block the value of `4/2` is displayed and no exception is detected. As a result, the catch block is skipped.

In the second run we accept the values 4 and 0 to **a** and **b** respectively. Since **b** is zero, the exception "division by zero" is detected by the try block and throws **b**. The catch block receives the exception and displays the message "exception caught = 0". After the execution of the catch block, the control reaches the return 0 statement of the `main()`, which when executed causes the exit of the `main()`.

Program 19.2 To Illustrate Array out of Bounds Exception

```
#include <iostream.h>

int main(void)
{
    int a[5] = { 1, 3, 4, 5, 6}, i;

    try
    {
        i = 0;
        while(1)
        {
            cout << a[i] << "\n";
            i++;
            if (i == 5)
                throw (i);
        }
    }
```

```
    catch(int j)
    {
        cout << "Array out of bounds = "<< j;
    }

    return 0;
}
```

Input-Output:

```
1
3
4
5
6
Array out of bounds = 5
```

Explanation

The array **a** of `int` type and of size 5 is initialized with five values. We set up a loop in the try block to display the elements in the array and intentionally we try to display the elements beyond the array. The attempt to go beyond the array gives rise to an exception, which is thrown by the try block and the catch block catches it and displays the message `Array out of bounds = 5`. The control then reaches the end of the `main()`.

19.3 THROWING IN ONE FUNCTION AND CATCHING IN THE OTHER

Sometimes exceptions are thrown by functions that are invoked within try blocks and the exceptions are to be handled by the calling functions.

Suppose the function `f1()` throws an exception and the function is called in `f2()`. The statement which invokes the function `f1()` is placed within the try block of `f2()`, the guarded section. The catch block in `f2()` handles the exception. The general form of the functions is:

```
type f1(arguments)
{
    ..................
    throw exception;
    ..................
    ..................
}

 type f2(arguments)
{
    ........................
    ........................

    try
    {
        f1();
    }
```

```
    catch(type argument)
    {

    }
}
```

Here f1() throws an exception and f2() handles the exception.

Program 19.3 Throwing in One Function and Catching in the Other

```
#include <iostream.h>
void divide(int a, int b)
{

    if (b != 0)
        cout << "a/b =" << a / b;
    else
        throw b;

}

int main(void)
{
    try{
    divide(4,2);
    divide(4, 0);]
    catch(int x)
    {
        cout << "Exception caught =" << x;
    }

    return 0;
}
```

Input-Output:

```
a / b = 2
Exception caught = 0
```

Explanation

The function `divide()` is defined with two arguments **a** and **b** of `int` type. The purpose of the function is to display the value of `a/b`. The function displays the value of `a/b` if **b** is non-zero and throws an exception if **b** is zero (Division by zero).

In the `main()`, the function `divide()` is invoked twice. The call `divide(4, 2);` displays the value of `4/2`, which is `2`. But the second function call `divide(4, 0);` throws an exception since division by zero is not defined. The catch block which follows the function call receives the exception and displays the message "`exception caught = 0`".

Here the function `divide()` throws an exception and the exception is handled by `main()`.

19.4 SINGLE TRY BLOCK AND MULTIPLE CATCH BLOCKS

There may be situations wherein a program segment gives rise to more than one exception subject to different conditions, which are mutually exclusive. At any point of time only one condition will be true and the segment throws the corresponding exception. In this situation, the program segment is embedded within a single try block and multiple catch blocks, one for each exception, will follow the try block. The catch block, the argument of which matches with that of the exception thrown, will get executed.

```
try
{
    if (cond1)
        throw exception1;
    else if (cond2)
        throw exception2;
    else if (cond3)
        throw exception3;

    ......................

    ......................
    else
        throw exceptionn;
}

catch(type1 arg)
{
    statements
}

catch(type2 arg)
{
    statements
}

..........................
..........................
..........................

catch(typen arg)
{
    statements
}
```

After the catch block is executed, the control is transferred to the first statement after all the catch blocks. If the arguments of more than one catch block match with the type of the exception then the first catch block that matches will get executed. If there is no matching catch block then the program is abnormally terminated.

Program 19.4 To Illustrate Single Try Block and Multiple Catch Blocks

```
#include <iostream.h>

int main(void)
{
   int x;

   cout << "Enter a value for x \n";
   cin >> x;
   try
   {
      switch (x)
      {
         case 1:
            throw 'a';
            break;
         case 2:
            throw x;
            break;
         case 3:
            throw (float)x;
            break;
         case 4:
            throw "xyz";
            break;
      }
   }

catch(int i)
{
   cout << "Exception caught = " << i;
}

catch(float f)
{
   cout << "Exception caught = " << f;

}

catch(char c)
{
   cout << "Exception caught = " << c;

}

catch(char* cp)
{
   cout << "Exception caught = " << cp;
}
```

```
    return 0;
}
```

Input-Output:

```
First-Run:
Enter a value for x
1
Exception caught = a
Second Run:
Enter a value for x
2
Exception caught = 2
```

Explanation

Depending on the value of *x*, an exception is thrown by the program segment embodying the try block and the exception is received by the appropriate catch block and handled.

If the value of *x* is 1, the catch block that receives a character is executed; if the value of *x* is 2, the catch block that receives an integer is executed and so on.

19.5 CATCHING ALL THE EXCEPTIONS IN A SINGLE CATCH BLOCK

In many real-world programming situations, we may not be able to predict all the possible types of exceptions and as a consequence, we will not be able to design independent catch blocks to handle all the unforeseen exceptions. Fortunately, C++ provides a mechanism of handling this situation, wherein a single catch block would suffice to catch all the exceptions.

The syntax of the catch block is as follows:

```
catch (...)
{
    statements
}
```

Note the presence of three dots within the parentheses of the catch block.

Program 19.5 To Illustrate Catching All the Exceptions in a Single Catch Block

```
#include <iostream.h>

int main(void)
{
    int x;

    cout << "Enter a value for x \n";
    cin >> x;
    try
    {
        switch (x)
        {
            case 1:
                throw 'a';
```

```
            break;
        case 2:
            throw x;
            break;
        case 3:
            throw (float)x;
            break;
        case 4:
            throw "xyz";
            break;
      }
   }

   catch(...)
   {
      cout << "Exception caught ";
   }

   return 0;
}
```

Input-Output:

```
Enter a value for x
3
exception caught
```

Explanation

The try block can throw four types of exceptions and the single catch block catches each of them.

19.6 RE-THROWING AN EXCEPTION

If need be, a catch block can rethrow an exception that is caught by it. It is done with the use of the statement `throw`; without specifying any exception after the keyword throw. Program illustrates this.

Program 19.6 To Illustrate Rethrowing an Exception

```
#include <iostream.h>

void divide(int a, int b)
{
   try
   {
      if (b != 0)
         cout << "a / b =" << a/b << "\n";
      else
         throw b;

   }
```

```
catch(int x)
{
    cout << "Rethrown by the catch block in divide() \n";
    throw;
}
}

int main(void)
{
    try
    {
        divide(4, 0);
    }

    catch(int x)
    {
        cout << "Caught and handled in the catch block of main(); " << "\n";
    }

    return 0;
}
```

Input-Output:

```
Rethrown by the catch block in divide()

Caught and handled in the catch block of main();
```

Explanation

The `divide()` throws an exception and it is caught by the catch block in the same function. But instead of handling the exception, the catch block rethrows the exception. Then the exception is handled by the catch block in the `main()`.

19.7 SPECIFICATION OF EXCEPTIONS

We can restrict functions to throw some specified exceptions only with the use of `throw(exceptions-list)` in the header of the functions. The general form of a function, which is restricted to throwing specific exceptions, is as follows:

```
type function(arguments-list) throw(exceptions-list)
 {
    statements
    try
    {
        statements
    }

 }
```

Program 19.7 To Illustrate Specifications

```
#include <iostream.h>

void test(int x) throw(int, float, char)
{
    switch (x)
    {
        case 1:
            throw x;
            break;
        case 2:
            throw 'x';
            break;
        case 3:
            throw double (x);
            break;
        case 4:
            throw float (x);
            break;
    }
}

int main(void)
{
    try
    {
    test(1); //Also try test() with 2, 3 and 4 as actual arguments
    }

    catch(int i)
    {
        cout << "caught int type exception \n";
    }

    catch(float f)
    {
        cout << "caught float type exception \n";
    }

    catch(char c)
    {
        cout << "caught char type exception \n";
    }

    catch(double d)
    {
        cout << "caught double type exception \n";
```

```
    }
    return 0;
}
```

Input-Output:

```
caught int type exception
```

Explanation

The function `test()` is restricted to throw only three types of exceptions (`int, float, char`). In the program the function call `test(1);` throws `int` type exception and it is received by the catch block with `int` type as the argument. The function call `test(2);` throws `char` type exception and it is received by the catch block with `char` type as the argument. The third call to the function `test(3);` tries to throw an exception of type `double`, but the function can not throw `double` type exception, and this results in abnormal program termination. The function call tes(4) throws float type exception and it is caught by the catch block meant for it.

If we intend to prevent a function from throwing any type of exceptions, we can do so by not specifying anything in the throw list. The general form of the function appears as follows:

```
type function(args-list)  throw()
{
    statements
}
```

Here `function` is prevented from throwing any exception. In case it throws an exception, it results in abnormal termination of the program.

REVIEW QUESTIONS

19.1 What is an exception?

19.2 Explain the use of the keywords try, throw and catch.

19.3 Explain the syntax of the try and catch blocks.

19.4 Explain the exception handling mechanism.

19.5 Give an account of the execution sequence effected by try and catch blocks.

19.6 Explain how an exception thrown by one function is caught by another function.

19.7 Explain how a single try block can be associated with multiple catch blocks.

19.8 Explain how a single catch block can handle all exceptions.

19.9 Explain the concept of rethrowing an exception.

19.10 How can we restrict functions to throw only certain types of exceptions? Explain.

True/False Questions

T19.1 Exceptions are triggered during compile time.

T19.2 An exception unhandled causes the abnormal exit of a program.

T19.3 For every try block there should be a catch block.

T19.4 `throw(a, b);` is a valid statement.

T19.5 A function can be made to throw only certain exceptions.

T19.6 Control from catch block is transferred back to the try block that threw the exception.

PROGRAMMING EXERCISES

P19.1 Suppose M1 and M2 are two matrices, they are said to be compatible for addition if the number of rows in M1 is equal to that in M2 and the number of columns in M1 is equal to that in M2. Write a program to accept M1 and M2 and find the sum of them. There is a possibility of an exception if the compatibility is not ensured. Incorporate the try and the catch blocks as a part of the program to handle the exception.

P19.2 Suppose M1 and M2 are two matrices, they are said to be compatible for multiplication if the number of columns in M1 is equal to the number of rows in M2. Write a program to accept M1 and M2 and find the product of them. There is a possibility of an exception if the compatibility is not ensured. Incorporate the try and the catch blocks as a part of the program to handle the exception.

P19.3 Suppose a program tries to read a record in a file, if the record is not found, a runtime error is encountered. Handle this with the help of the exception handling mechanism.

P19.4 Think of your own programming situation wherein multiple catch blocks are required and implement it.

P19.5 Think of your own programming situation wherein `catch(...)` handler is useful and implement it.

P19.6 Think of your own programming situation wherein a function has to be restricted to throwing only certain exceptions and implement it.

Chapter 20 Templates

20.1 INTRODUCTION

Templates are an important and distinctive feature of C++ that sets the language apart from most other programming languages. The templates enable us to define generic classes and generic functions, which in turn help create families of classes and functions. They avoid duplication of code and thus play a vital role in substantial improvement of the programming efficiency. Programming with templates is often referred to as generic programming.

As has already been indicated, there are two categories of templates: (a) Class template, which is used to create a family of classes with the same member functions but with different types of data. (b) Function template, which is used to create a family of functions performing the same operation but over different types of data.

We will now get to know these in detail.

20.2 CLASS TEMPLATES

Consider the following two classes.

```
class integer
{
    int x;

    public:

        integer()

        {

            x = 0;

        }
```

```
class real
{
    float x;

    public:

        real()

        {

            x = 0;

        }
```

```
    integer(int y)
    {
        x = y;
    }
    int sum(integer b)
    {
        int t;
            t = x + b.x;
        return t;
    }
};
```

```
    real(float y)
    {
        x = y;
    }
    float sum(real b)
    {
        float t;
        t = x + b.x;
        return t;
    }
};
```

Have a closer look at the classes. They look exactly similar except the fact that in the class `integer`, the member data is of type **int** and in the class `real`, the member data is of type **float**. We may have some more similar classes with only type of the member data being different. If that is the case, for each data type, a new class has to be defined all over again, which results in duplication of code (which in turn consumes more memory space) and decline in programming efficiency. It would have been better if we could define a single class with the provision for specifying anonymous type for the member data as a parameter and providing the actual type of the member data while the objects are declared. This is where class templates come into play. A class template facilitates definition of a class with anonymous type for its member data. Since class templates enable us to specify anonymous type as a parameter, they are also called **parameterized classes**.

The general syntax of a class template is as follows:

```
template <class T>
class tagname
{
    //usage of anonymous type T
    //wherever required
};
```

The syntax of declaring an object is as follows:

```
Tagname<type> object_name;
```

Note that the actual type of the member data is specified within a pair of pointed brackets followed by the tagname while declaring objects.

If the class template is provided with constructors, we can initialize the objects while they are declared. The syntax of declaration would then be:

```
tagname<type> object_name(arguments);
```

Let us now write a class template for the above two classes.

```
template <class T>
class scalar
```

```
{
    T x;

    Public:
        scalar()
        {
            x = 0;
        }

        scalar(T y)
        {
            x = y;
        }

        T sum(scalar b)
        {
            T t;

            t = x + b.x;

            return t;
        }
};
```

Now, `scalar<int> a;` declares **a** to be an object of **scalar** type with **int** as the type of its member data. The object **a** is equivalent to an object of `integer` class type.

`scalar<float> r;` declares **r** to be an object of **scalar** type with **float** as the type of its member data. The object **r** is equivalent to an object of `real` class type.

Program 20.1 To Illustrate Class Template

```
#include <iostream.h>

template <class T>
class scalar
{
    T x;

    public:
        scalar()
        {
            x = 0;
        }

        scalar(T y)
        {
            x = y;
        }
```

```
        T sum(scalar b)
        {
            T t;

            t = x + b.x;

            return t;
        }
};

int main(void)
{
    scalar<int> a(6), b(7);
    scalar<float> r(5.6), s(7.5);


    cout << "Sum of integers = " << a.sum(b)<< "\n";
    cout << "Sum of reals   = " << r.sum(s)<< "\n";

    return 0;
}
```

Input-Output:

```
Sum of integers = 13
Sum of reals = 13.1
```

Explanation

a and **b** are declared to be the objects of type **scalar<int>** and also initialized with integer values. The member function `sum()` has been called to find the sum of the member data of the objects **a** and **b** in the statement `cout << "Sum of integers = " << a.sum(b)<< "\n";`, which displays the value returned by the `sum()`. Similarly, **r** and **s** are declared to be objects of type **scalar<float>** and also initialized with float values. The member function `sum()` has been called to find the sum of the member data of the objects and in the statement `cout << "Sum of reals = " << r.sum(s)<< "\n";`, which displays the value returned by the `sum()`.

Program 20.2 To Illustrate Class Template

```
#include <iostream.h>

template<class T>
class vector
{
    private:
        T a[5];
    public:
    vector()
    {
        for(int i = 0; i<5; i++)
            a[i] = 0;
    }
```

```
    vector(T b[])
    {
        for(int i = 0; i<5; i++)
            a[i] = b[i];
    }

    void display()
    {
        for(int i = 0; i<5; i++)
            cout << a[i] << "\n";
    }
};

int main(void)
{
    int b[] = {1,3,6,7,8};
    float c[] = {1,3.7,6.9,7,8};

    vector<int> v1(b);
    vector<float> v2(c);

    cout << "The elements of vector v1 \n";
    v1.display();
    cout << "The elements of vector v2 \n";
    v2.display();

    return 0;
}
```

Input-Output:

```
The elements of vector v1
1
3
6
7
8
The elements of vector v2
1
3.7
6.9
7
8
```

Explanation

b is declared to be an array of **int** type and it is initialized with integer five values with the statement `int b[] = {1,3,6,7,8};`. Similarly, **c** is declared to be an array of **float** type and it is initialized with five **float** values with the statement `float c[] = {1,3.7,6.9,7,8};`. These two arrays are used to initialize the objects of class template vector in the code to follow.

v1, declared to be an object of class template vector with **int** type as its parameter, is initialized with the array **b** with the statement `vector<int> v1(b);` . Similarly, **v2**, declared to be an object of class template vector with **float** type as its parameter, is initialized with the array **c**. Note that the initialization of both the vectors is accomplished with the execution of the constructor in the class template, which is defined to take an array as its argument. Both the vectors **v1** and **v2** are displayed with the statements `v1.display();` and `v2.display();`.

20.3 CLASS TEMPLATES WITH MULTIPLE PARAMETERS

A class template can have more than one anonymous type specifiers, which are separated by commas. The syntax of a class template with multiple anonymous type specifiers is as follows:

```
template<class T1, class T2, ….>
class tagname
{
    //Usage of T1 and T2 as type specifiers
    //wherever required
};
```

The syntax of declaring an object of the class type is as follows:

```
tagname<type, type> object_name;
```

If the class template is provided with constructors, we can initialize the objects while they are declared. The syntax of declaration would then be:

```
tagname<type, type> object_name(arguments);
```

Program 20.3 To Illustrate Class Templates with Multiple Parameters

```
#include<iostream.h>

template<class T1, class T2>
class temp
{
    private:
        T1 a;
        T2 b;

    public:
        temp(T1 c, T2 d)
        {
            a = c;
            b = d;
        }
        void display()
        {
            cout << a << "  " << b;
        }
};

int main(void)
{
```

```
    temp<int, float> t1(5, 6.25);
    temp<char, int> t2('a', 8);
    temp<char, float> t3('b', 7.45);

    cout << "Values of t1: ";
    t1.display();
    cout << "\n Values of t2: ";

    t2.display();
    cout << "\n Values of t3: ";

    t3.display();
    return 0;
}
```

Input-Output:

```
Values of t1: 5  6.25
Values of t2: a  8
Values of t3: b  7.45
```

Explanation

The class template **temp** is defined to take two types **T1** and **T2** as parameters. The member data **a** and **b** are declared to be of type **T1** and **T2** respectively. The class template includes a constructor with an argument of type **T1** and an argument of **T2** type, which are assigned to the member data of the class template. The member function `display()` is just to display the members of an object of the class template.

t1, declared to be an object of the class template **temp** with **int** type as its parameter and **float** as its second type parameter, is initialized with the values 5 and 6.25. **t2**, declared to be an object of the class template **temp** with **char** type as its parameter and **int** as its second type parameter, is initialized with the values 'a' and 8. **t3**, declared to be an object of the class template **temp** with **char** type as its parameter and **float** as its second type parameter, is initialized with the values 'b' and 7.45. The values of all the three objects are then displayed.

20.4 FUNCTION TEMPLATES

A function template is a generic function with generic types as arguments specified as its arguments while it is defined. It creates a family of functions with similar properties.
The general form of a function template is as follows:

```
template<class T>
type function_name(Arguments of type T)
{
    //Usage of type T wherever required

}
```

EXAMPLE

Consider the following code:

```
template<class T>
void max(T a, T b)
{
    if ( a> b)
    cout << "a is greater than b ";
    else
    cout << "a is not greater than b";
}
```

```
max(4,5);
```

is a valid function call and it works on values of `int` type.

```
max(4.5, 8.9);
```

is also a valid function call and it works on values of `float` type.

Having defined the function template we have avoided defining two separate functions.

Program 20.4 To Illustrate Function Template

```
#include <iostream.h>

template <class T>
void display(T x)
{
    cout << x << "\n";
}


int main(void)
{
    int a = 5;
    float f = 19.29;
    char c = 'x';

    cout << "a =" ;
    display(a);

    cout << "f = ";
    display(f);

    cout << "c = ";
    display( c );

    return 0;
}
```

Input-Output:

```
a = 5
f = 19.29
c = x
```

Explanation

The function template `display()` is defined with an argument of anonymous type **T**. The purpose of the function is to display the value passed to it. In the `main()`, three calls are made to the function to display an integer, a float value and a character. The statement `display(a);` displays the value of the variable **a**; `display(f);` displays the value of the variable **f** and the statement `display(c);` displays the character stored in the variable **c**.

Program 20.5 To Sort the Elements in a Vector Using Exchange Sort Method

```
#include <iostream.h>

template<class T>
int compare(T a, T b)
{
    if (a > b)
        return 1;
    else
        return 0;
}

template<class T>
void swap(T& x, T& y)
{
    T t;

    t = x;
    x = y;
    y = t;
}

template <class T>
void xchange_sort(T *a, int n)
{
    T t;
    for(int i = 0; i < n - 1; i++)
    for(int j = i + 1; j < n; j++)
        if(compare(a[i],a[j]))
            swap(a[i], a[j]);
}

template<class T>
void display(T *a, int n)
{
    for(int i = 0; i < n; i++)
        cout << a[i]<< "\n";
}

int main(void)
{
    int a[] = {5, 6, 4, 8, 2};
```

```
    float f[] = { 4.5, 7.8, 5, 9.2, 4};

    xchange_sort(a, 5);
    xchange_sort(f, 5);

    display(a, 5);
    display(f, 5);
    return 0;
}
```

Input-Output:

```
Sorted integer array
2
4
5
6
8

Sorted float array
4
4.5
5
7.8
9.2
```

Explanation

The function template `compare()` is defined with two arguments **a** and **b** of anonymous type **T** and it is made to return a value of **int** type. The purpose of the function template is to return 1 if a is greater than b, otherwise 0.

The function template `swap()` is defined with two arguments **x** and **y**, which are references to anonymous type **T** and its purpose is to interchange the values of the variables of the calling program referred to by **x** and **y**.

Another function template `xchange_sort()` is defined with two arguments **a** and **n**. **a** is a pointer to the anonymous type **T** and **n** is of **int** type. The purpose of the function template is to sort a list of values of **T** type. Within the function exchange sorting method is employed to sort the values. Since the method involves comparison and swapping of values, the function templates `compare()` and `swap()` are invoked within the function.

The function template `display()` is to display the values in an array of the anonymous type **T**.

In the `main()`, **a** and **f** are declared to be arrays of **int** and **float** type respectively. They are also initialized while they are declared. The function template `xchange_sort()` is invoked to sort the values in the array **a** of **int** type with the statement `xchange_sort(a, 5);` The function template `xchange_sort()` is invoked for the second time to sort the values in the array **f** of **float** type with the statement `xchange_sort(f, 5);`.

The sorted arrays are displayed with the statements `display(a, 5);` and `display(f, 5);`.

20.5 FUNCTION TEMPLATES WITH MULTIPLE PARAMETERS

Just like a class template, a function template also can have multiple anonymous type specifiers, which are separated by commas. The syntax of a function template with multiple type specifiers is:

```
template<class T1, class T2, ….>
type function_name (arguments of type T1, T2...)
{
    //Usage of type specifiers T1, T2
wherever required
}
```

EXAMPLE

```
template <class T1, class T2>
void display(T1 x, T2 y)
{
    cout << x << "  " << y << "\n";
}
```

The function template `display()` is defined with two arguments **x** and **y** of anonymous types **T1** and **T2** respectively. Its purpose is to display the values of both **x** and **y**.

```
display(10, 12.67);
```

displays the **int** value `10` and the **float** value `12.67`.

```
display(17.65, 'a');
```

displays the **float** value 17.65 and the character ‘a’.

```
display(48700, "xyz");
```

displays the **long int** value 48700 and the string “xyz”.

Consider Program 20.6:

Program 20.6 To Illustrate Function Template with Multiple Parameters

```
#include <iostream.h>

template <class T1, class T2>
void sum(T1 a, T2 b)
{
    cout.setf(ios::fixed);
    cout.precision(2);
    cout << a + b << "\n";
}

int main(void)
{
    int a = 5;
    float f = 19.29;
    long int l = 35768;

    cout << "sum of a and f =";
    sum(a, f);
    cout << "sum of f and l =";
    sum(f, l);
    cout << "sum of a and l =";
```

```
    sum(a, l);

    return 0;
}
```

Input-Output:

```
sum of a and f = 24.29
sum of f and l = 35787.29
sum of a and l = 35773
```

Explanation

The function template `sum()` is defined with two arguments **a** and **b** of anonymous types **T1** and **T2** respectively. The purpose of the function template is to find the sum of the two values passed to it and display it.

In the `main()`, the statement `sum(a, f);` displays the values of the **int** variable **a** and the **float** variable **f**; the statement `sum(f, l);` displays the values of **float** variable **f** and the **long int** variable **l**, and the statement `sum(a, l);` displays the values of the **int** variable **a** and the **long int** variable **l**.

20.6 MEMBER FUNCTION TEMPLATES

The member functions of a class if they are defined outside the class should be defined as function templates with the anonymous type specified for each member function. The general form of a member function template is as follows:

```
template<class T>
type classname <T> :: function_name(arguments)
{

    //statements
}
```

EXAMPLE

Consider the following class definition:

```
template<class T>
class temp
{
    private:
        T x;

    public:
        void get();
        void display();
};

template<class T>
void temp<T> :: get()
{
    cin >> x;
}
```

```
template<class T>
void temp<T> :: display()
{
    cout << x;
}
```

The class template **temp** is defined with a member data **x** of anonymous type **T** and it includes the member functions `get()` and `display()`. The member functions are declared within the class and they are defined outside the class function templates with the anonymous type **T** specified for both the member functions. Note also that the scope resolution operator **::** is preceded by `temp<T>` , the class name and the anonymous type **T**.

Let us rewrite the programs involving **scalar** class and **vector** class by making the member functions as function templates.

Program 20.7 To Illustrate Member Function Templates

```
#include <iostream.h>

template <class T>
class scalar
{
    T x;

    public:
        scalar();
        scalar(T);
        T sum(scalar<T>);
};

template<class T>
scalar <T> :: scalar()
{
    x = 0;
}

template<class T>
scalar <T> :: scalar(T y)
{
    x = y;
}

template<class T>
T scalar<T> :: sum(scalar<T> b)
{
    T t;

    t = x + b.x;

    return t;
}
```

```
int main(void)
{
    scalar<int> a(6), b(7);
    scalar<float> r(5.6), s(7.5);

    cout << "Sum of integers = " << a.sum(b)<< "\n";
    cout << "Sum of reals  = " << r.sum(s)<< "\n";

    return 0;
}
```

Input-Output:

```
Sum of integers = 13
Sum of float numbers = 13.1
```

Explanation

The class **scalar** includes the prototyes of the constructors and the member function `sum()` and they are defined outside the class as function templates. Note that each member function is defined as a normal function template with **scalar<T> ::** just before the function name in their header, which is to indicate that the functions belong to the class **scalar**.

Program 20.8 To Illustrate Member Function Templates

```
#include <iostream.h>

template<class T>
class vector
{
    private:
        T a[5];
    public:
        vector();
        vector(T b[]);
        void display();
};

    template<class T>

    vector <T> ::vector()
    {
        for(int i = 0; i<5; i++)
            a[i] = 0;
    }

    template<class T>
vector <T> ::vector(T b[])
{
        for(int i = 0; i<5; i++)
```

```
            a[i] = b[i];
    }

template<class T>
void vector <T> :: display()
{
        for(int i = 0; i<5; i++)
            cout << a[i] << "\n";
}

int main(void)
{
    int b[] = {1,3,6,7,8};
    float c[] = {1,3.7,6.9,7,8};

    vector<int> v1(b);
    vector<float> v2(c);

    cout << "Vector v1: \n";
    v1.display();
    cout << "Vector v2: \n";
    v2.display();

    return 0;
}
```

Input-Output:

```
Vector v1:
1 3 6 7 8

Vector v2:
1 3.7 6.9 7 8
```

Explanation

The class vector includes the prototyes of the constructors and the member function `display()` and they are defined outside the class as function templates. Note that each member function is defined as a normal function template with **vector<T> ::** just before the function name in their header, which is to indicate that the functions belong to the class **vector**.

20.7 OVERLOADING TEMPLATE FUNCTIONS

C++ permits us to use name of a template function for a normal function also. If a normal function has the same name as that of a template function, we say that the template function is overloaded. In this case, the function calls are resolved according to the following rules in sequence.

If the signature of the called function matches exactly with that of a normal function, then invoke the normal function.

Otherwise, invoke the template function, which could be created, with the exact match.

Otherwise, apply the predefined function overloading resolution rules (Automatic Conversions) to normal functions and invoke the one that matches.

If none of the above hold good, the compiler will generate an error. Note that automatic conversion rules are not applied to the arguments of the template function.

Program 20.9 To Illustrate Overloading of Function Templates

```
#include <iostream.h>

template<class T>
void display(T a)
{
    cout << "In template display() " << a << "\n";
}

void display(int a)
{
    cout << "In normal display() " << a << "\n";
}

int main(void)
{

    display(10);
    display(5.25);
    display('d');
    display("OOPS");

    return 0;
}
```

Input-Output:

```
In normal display()  10
In template display() 5.25
In template display() d
In template display() OOPS
```

Explanation

The function call `display(10);` finds an exact match with the normal function `display()`, which also takes an argument of **int** type and the normal function gets called. In all the other cases, the function template `display()` gets called to display the values, since each of these fails to match with the normal function and an exact match could be created with the function template. The last case of resolving the function calls based on the overloading resolution rules does not arise.

20.8 NON-TYPE TEMPLATE ARGUMENTS

We know that a class template may have multiple parameters. Some of the parameters can be of ordinary non-type. Examples of ordinary non-type include built-in types like int, float, etc. The values passed to non-type parameters must be constants.

Consider the following example:

```
template<class T, int  size>
class vector
{
    T a[size]:


};

vector<int, 5> v1;
```

v1 is created as a vector of **int** type and of size five.

```
vector<float, 4> v2;
```

v2 is created to be a vector of **float** type and of size 4.

Program 20.10 To Illustrate Non-type Template Arguments

```
#include <iostream.h>

template<class T, int  size>
class vector
{
    T a[size]:

    public:
        void get()
    {
        for(i = 0; i < size; i++)
            cin >> a[i];
    }

        void display()
        {
            for(int i = 0; i < size; i++)
                cout << a[i] << "  ";
        }
};

int main(void)
{
    vector<int, 5> v1;

    vector<float , 5> v2;

    cout << "enter the elements of integer vector\n";
    v1.get();
    cout << "Integer Vector: \n";
    v1.display();
```

```
    cout << "enter the elements of float vector\n";
    v2.get();
    cout << "Float Vector: \n";
    v2.display();

    return 0;
}
```

Input-Output:

```
Enter the elements of integer vector
2 4 5 6 7
integer vector:
2
4
5
6
7
Enter the elements of float vector
3.4  5.6  7  8.9  6.4

float Vector:
3.4  5.6  7  8.9  6.4
```

REVIEW QUESTIONS

20.1 What is generic programming?

20.2 What is a class template? Explain its syntax.

20.3 Explain class templates with multiple parameters.

20.4 What is a function template? Explain its syntax.

20.5 Explain function templates with multiple parameters.

20.6 How is a member function template defined? Explain.

20.7 Can you overload function templates? Explain.

20.8 Explain the concept of non-type template arguments and their use.

True/False Questions

T20.1 Templates avoid duplication of code.

T20.2 A class template is a parameterized class.

T20.3 Class templates can be designed even for user-defined types also.

T20.4 A class template can not have multiple arguments.

T20.5 Function templates can be nested.

T20.6 A function template can not have non-type arguments.

T20.7 When a function template is overloaded with normal functions, functions that can be created with exact match are given priority.

PROGRAMMING EXERCISES

P20.1 Write a class template by name vector and perform the following:

(a) Find the smallest of the elements in the vector.
(b) Search for an element in the vector.
(c) Find the average of the elements in the array.

P20.2 Write a class template by name matrix and perform the following:

(a) Find the sum of two matrices.
(b) Find the product of two matrices.
(c) Find the sum of each row of a matrix and display them.
(d) Find the sum of each column of a matrix and display them.

P20.3 Write a generic function for finding the largest of three numbers.

Chapter 21

New Features of C++

21.1 INTRODUCTION

The ANSI/ISO committee has added new features like new data types, new-style casts, new keywords, keywords for operators, the concept of namespaces, new header files as part of the specifications of C++. The features are intended mainly to improve the degree of readability of programs and the level of convenience offered to the programmers.

We will now get to know the significance of these in the following sections.

21.2 NEW DATA TYPES

The ANSI C++ standard now has added two more new data types namely **bool** and **wchar_t** to the already rich set of data types of C++.

The **bool** data type can store either **true** or **false** value. The numerical value of **true** is 1 and that of **false** is 0.

```
bool v1, v2, v3, v4;
```

v1, **v2**, **v3** and **v4** are declared to be variables of **bool** type.

```
v1 = true;
v2 = false;
```

are valid statements.

```
v3 = 3 > 5;
```

Here **v3** would get the value 0.

```
v4 = 5 > 4;
```

Here **v4** would get the value 1.
Note that **true** and **false** are now the keywords of C++.

The **wchar_t** data type has been included to store two-bytes wide characters. We know that a **char** variable is one-byte wide and can store 128 characters. There are a number of languages across the globe, the alphabet of which have more than 128 characters. In order to represent the characters in these languages, **wchar_t** data type becomes handy because it can represent 256 characters.

21.3 NEW-STYLE CASTS

We have learnt about typecasting or forcible conversion. We will be inclined to use typecasting when the automatic conversions do not work out in some situations.

Consider the following example:

```
float f;

f = 5/2;
```

Here **f** would collect the value 2.0 even though the exact result is 2.5.

```
f = (float)5/2;
```

In this case, **f** would collect 2.5. This is because we have used the casting operator (float) to forcibly convert 5 to float type. As a result, the expression is made to produce the exact result.

Even though C-style casts work well and do the intended job, as the program size grows, it becomes difficult to trace the casts if anything goes wrong. To remedy this problem, ANSI C++ provides four casting operators. They are **static_cast**, **dynamic_cast**, **reinterpret_cast** and **const_cast**. These provide safer notation, which reflects the design of the polymorphic class hierarchies and it enables easier finding of the operators in the source code with the help of text searching tools.
The syntax of their usage is as follows:

```
cast_operator <type> (object)
```

`cast_operator` is any of the four mentioned above, `object` is the operand to the operator and `type` is the target type which `object` gets converted to.

The static_cast operator: The `static_cast operator` is used to perform implicit conversions of standard data types, which are already defined. Type checking and validation of the conversion take place during compilation itself and hence the name `static_cast`.

EXAMPLE

```
int i = 35;

float f = static_cast<float>(i);
```

converts **i** to **float** type.

```
long l = 34987;

float f = static_cast<float>(l);
```

converts the value of **l** to **float** type.

The dynamic_cast operator: The `dynamic_cast operator` is used to convert a base class pointer or reference to a derived class pointer or reference and vice-versa. For this to happen, the base class should have at least one virtual function. The operator performs type checking during runtime of a program and hence the name dynamic_cast.

EXAMPLE

```
class A
{

};

class B : public A
{

};

A *ap;

B *bp;

ap = dynamic_cast<A*> (bp);
```

converts the derived class pointer **bp** to the base class pointer type.

```
bp = dynamic_cast<B*> (ap);
```

converts the base class pointer **ap** to the derived class pointer type.

In the event of the failure, the `dynamic_cast operator` returns 0 This fact can be used to determine the type during runtime.

The reinterpret_cast operator: The `reinterpret_cast operator` is used to convert one pointer type to another pointer type, numbers to pointers, and pointers to numbers.

```
char *cp;

cp = reinterpret_cast<char*> (allocate_mem());
```

where `allocate_mem()` is a user-defined function, which allocates a block of memory and return a **void** pointer, and the **void** pointer is converted to char type by the `reinterpret_cast operator`.

```
int *ip;
ip = reinterpret_cast<int*> (allocate_mem());
```

Here the function `allocate_mem()` allocates a block of memory and return a **void** pointer and the **void** pointer is converted to int type by the `reinterpret_cast operator`.

As already mentioned, we can convert numbers to pointer type and vice-versa.

Consider the following:

```
int a = 100, *ap, b;

ap = reinterpret_cast<int*> (a);
```

converts the integer value **a** to integer pointer, which is collected by **ap**.

```
b = reinterpret_cast<int> (ap);
```

converts the pointer value **ap** to integer value, which is collected by **b**.

The const_cast operator: The `const_cast operator` is used to convert a **const** object to its **non-const** equivalent. Consider the following example:

```
const int b = 10;
int *bp;

bp = const_cast<int*>(&b);
```

Here `&b`, a constant pointer to **int** type, is converted to non-const pointer, which is collected by the pointer variable **bp**.

When the `const_cast operator` is used, the target type should be same as that of the object being converted.

```
int a = 10;
long* lp = const_cast<long*> (&a);
```

The conversion is wrong since `&a` is **const** pointer to **int** type whereas **lp** is a pointer to **long** type. The compiler flags an error.

We know that member functions of a class declared as **const** can not change the member data of the class. The `const_cast operator` would be of use to change them even in the **const** member functions.

Consider the following code:

```
class temp
{
    private:
        int x;
    public:
        temp()
        {
            x = 10;
        }
        void change() const
        {
            (const_cast<temp*>(this))->x = 20;
        }

        void display()
        {
            cout << x << "\n";
        }
};

int main(void)
{
    temp t;
```

```
    t.display();
    t.change();
    t.display();
}
```

The object **t** of **temp** type is initialized with the value 10 on its creation. The first call to `display()` would display 10. The function `change()` is then invoked and it changes the value of **t** to 20 even though the function is declared as **const**. It is possible because of the statement:

```
(const_cast<temp*>(this))->x = 20;
```

Here **this**, the **const** pointer to **temp** type is converted to **non-const** pointer and then the location addressed by it is assigned 20. The second call to `display()` displays the value 20.

21.4 NEW-STYLE HEADERS

So far, all the header files were ending with the extension **.h**. ANSI C++ now permits us to skip the extension for the header files, i.e., the header file **iostream.h** can be written as just **iostream**. As a result,

```
#include <iostream.h>
```

can now be written as #include <iostream>.

```
#include <iomanip.h>
```

can now be written as #include <iomanip> etc.

However, the header files with extension **.h** are also allowed.

21.5 NEW KEYWORDS FOR OPERATORS

ANSI C++ has provided keywords for some of the operators. The keywords can be used in place of the operators. They increase the readability of the programs. Table 21.1 lists the operators and their keywords equivalents.

Table 21.1 Operators and Their Keywords Equivalents

<table>
<tr><th>Operator</th><th>Keyword</th></tr>
<tr><td>!=</td><td>not_eq</td></tr>
<tr><td>&&</td><td>and</td></tr>
<tr><td>||</td><td>or</td></tr>
<tr><td>!</td><td>not</td></tr>
<tr><td>&</td><td>bitand</td></tr>
<tr><td>|</td><td>bitor</td></tr>
<tr><td>^</td><td>xor</td></tr>
<tr><td>~</td><td>compl</td></tr>
<tr><td>&=</td><td>and_eq</td></tr>
<tr><td>|=</td><td>or_eq</td></tr>
<tr><td>^=</td><td>xor_eq</td></tr>
</table>

Now the expressions:

`(a != b)` can be written as `(a not_eq b)`

`(a > b) && (a > c)` can be written as `(a> b) and (a > c)` and so on.

21.6 THE explicit KEYWORD

We know that constructors in a class are used to initialize the objects of the class while they are declared. A constructor with one argument can also be used to convert from the argument's type to the class type, of which the constructor is a member.

Consider the following class definition:

```
class integer
{
    private:
        int x;
    public:
        integer(int y)
        {
            x = y;
        }
};
```

Because of the availability of the constructor, we can use the statements:

```
integer a(4);
```

The object **a** is created with the value **4** for its member data.

```
integer b = 5;
```

Here the value of **int** type 5 is converted into the class **integer** type. Here the constructor acts as a converter from **int** type **integer** type.

The *explicit* keyword when used with the constructor of this kind restricts the constructor only to create an object with the statement `integer a(6);` and denies the power of conversion. The statement `integer a = 5;` will no longer be valid.

```
#include <iostream.h>

class measure
{
    private:
        int feet;
        float inches;

    public:

    explicit measure(float meters)
        {
            float f1;
```

```
            f1 = 3.28 * meters;
            feet = f1;
            inches = (f1 - feet);
        }

    void display()
    {
        cout << feet << "-" << inches << "\n";
    }
    measure operator +(measure m)
    {
        measure s;

        s.feet = feet + m.feet;
        s.inches = inches + m.inches;
        if ( s.inches >= 12)
        {
            s.feet++;
            s.inches -= 12;
        }

        return s;
    }
};

int main(void)
{
    measure m1(3.4);

    m1.display();

    measure s = m1 + 7.4; //error

    measure m2 = 5.6;  // error

    return 0;
}
```

Because of the fact that the constructor with one argument is made an explicit constructor, the statement `measure m2 = 5.6;` will be invalid and even the statement `s = m1 + 7.4;` will result in error since 7.4 can not be converted into an object of **measure** type, which is the requirement by the + operator overloading function.

21.7 THE MUTABLE KEYWORD

The mutable keyword is used to change the values of member data of a class even within a member function declared as const. Earlier we implemented this with the help of the new-style casting operator `const_cast`. It can be achieved in much simpler way with the help of the keyword *mutable*. The following program illustrates it:

```
#include <iostream.h>

class integer_pair
{
   private:
      int x;
   mutable int y;

   public:
      void get()
      {
         cin >> x >> y;
      }

      void display() const
      {
         cout << " x = " x << "\n";
         cout << "y = " << y << "\n";
      }
      void show() const
      {
         cout << " x = " x << "\n";
         y += 5;
         cout << "y = " << y << "\n";
      }
}

int main(void)
{
   integer_pair a;

   a.get();
   a.display();

   a.show();

   return 0;
}
```

The member data **y** is made as mutable and hence it can be changed in const the member function `show()`. Whereas the value of the member **x** can not be altered.

21.8 NAMESPACES

We know that identifiers are used to designate different program elements like variables, arrays, functions, structures, unions and classes, etc. The C++ language enforces a couple of rules to be followed while constructing them, which we are bound to adhere to. We, the programmers are given liberty to construct our own identifiers by following the rules to represent our program elements. We normally use this liberty to construct meaningful names reflective of the purpose of using them so that the readability of the programs is increased. One important thing to be kept in mind while naming the program elements is that the names chosen for the program elements in a single scope like function scope (The area within the opening and the closing brace of a function), class scope (The area between the opening brace and the closing brace of a class), block scope (The area between a pair of braces in a function) should be unique so that it is identifiable. We have been following the uniqueness of the names in all our programs that were written so far. Even if we are compelled to use the same name for two program elements, we can use if they belong to two different scopes. They are still treated as unique because they differ by their scope. So, the different scopes mentioned earlier help us in avoiding the clashing of names, if any.

If a software project is divided among a number of programmers, there is always a possibility that there may be conflicts with the names used by different programmers. In order to resolve this problem, ANSI C++ has proposed the concept of **namespaces**. Wherein, a programmer can create his own namespace for his program elements and each program element accessible uniquely with the namespace as the additional qualifier to the program element.

```
namespace namespace1
{
    int a;
    void display();

    class temp
    {
    };
}

namespace namespace2
{
    int a;
    void display();

    class temp
    {
    };
}
```

Note that the syntax of defining a namespace is similar to that of a class with no semicolon as the terminator.

Now, even though the program elements in both the namespaces have the same names, they are uniquely distinguishable with the namespace qualifier and the scope resolution operator as follows:

```
namespace1 ::  a
namespace1 :: display()
namespace1 :: temp

namespace2 :: a
namespace2 :: display();
namespace2 :: temp
```

There is another keyword namely **using**, which can be used to refer to the program elements of a namespace, where the usage of **namespace ::** for each program element can be avoided.

```
using namespace1
{
    a
    display()
    temp
}
```

C++ provides global level namespace with the name **std**. All the namespaces that we create come under the global namespace.

To explicitly use the global namespace in our programs, we should include the following statement:

```
using namespace std;
```

21.9 RUN TIME TYPE INFORMATION (RTTI)

Suppose **A** is the base class for the classes **B**, **C** and **D**. We know that a pointer to the base type **A** can be made to point to an object of its any derived classes. Not only that, we can implement runtime polymorphism or late binding through the base pointer. Many a time, we may not be knowing the derived type which the base pointer points to and we may require to know it to execute some derived classes specific code during runtime. ANSI C++ has now included a new feature for the purpose called **Run Time Type Information (RTTI)** which enables us to know the type information of objects during runtime. It has provided a new operator namely **typeid** to implement this feature.

The syntax of its usage to retrieve the type of the object pointed to by the base pointer is as follows:

```
typeid(*bp).name()
```

returns the type name (class name) of the object pointed to by **bp** where **bp** is the base pointer. * **bp** refers to the object pointed to by it.

The following program throws more light on the usage of the operator:

```
#include <iostream.h>
class account
{
    protected:
        int accno;
        char name[20];
    public:
        virtual void get() = 0;
        virtual void display() = 0;

};


class sb_acc : public account
{
    private:
        float roi;
    public:
        void get()
```

```
{
    cout << "Enter accno, name and roi \n";
    cin >> accno >> name >> roi;
}

void display()
{
    cout << "Account Number = " << accno << "\n";
    cout << "name = " << name << "\n";
    cout << "Rate of Interest = " << roi << "\n";
}

};

class cur_acc : public account
{
    private:
        float odlimit;
    public:
        void get()
{
    cout << "Enter accno, name and odlimit \n";
    cin >> accno >> name >> odlimit;
}

void display()
{
    cout << "Account Number = " << accno << "\n";
    cout << "name = " << name << "\n";
    cout << "OD Limit = " << odlimit << "\n";
}

};
int main(void)
{
    account *ap;

    sb_account sb;
    cur_account ca;

    ap = &sb;

    cout << "type of object pointed to by ap = " << typeid(*ap).name()

    ap = &ca;

    cout << "type of object pointed to by ap = " << typeid(*ap).name()

    return 0;
}
```

During runtime we can execute blocks of statements specific to a particular account type, if any, by enclosing them within opening and the closing braces of the following if statements as:

```
if (typeid(*ap).name == "sb_account")
{

}



if (typeid(*ap).name == "cur_account")
{

}
```

21.10 SMART POINTERS

Consider the following class definition:

```
class integer
{
    private:
        int x;

    public:

        integer(int y =0)
        {
            x = y;
        }

        void display()
        {
            cout << x << "\n";
        }

};

integer a;

integer *ap;

ap -> display();
```

may result in crash since **ap** has some garbage value.

```
ap = & a;
ap->display();
```

displays the value of **a** since it is now pointing to it.

To ensure that a pointer always points to some object we can use the concept of smart pointers. A smart pointer is one, which always points to some object. Consider further the following class definition. The class `integer_ptr` has a pointer to **integer** type as its member and, a constructor and the member function, which overloads the pointer to member operator **->,** are wrapped around it.

```
class integer_ptr
{
    integer *p;

    public:
        integer_ptr(integer* a = 0)
        {
            p = a;
        }

        integer* operator -> ()
        {
            static integer nullint(0);
            if (p == 0)
                reurn &nullint;

            return p;
        }
};

int main(void)
{
    integer_ptr ap;

    ap -> display();  // now a valid call since ap is assigned the
                      //address of nullint object

    integer a(10);
    ap = &a;

    ap ->display(); //ap being a pointer to a displays its value.

    return 0;

}
```

The constructor with default argument is used to create an object of **integer_ptr** type. The pointer to member operator **->** is overloaded to return an address. It can be the address of the object nullint or the address of any other valid object.

The first call `ap->display();` even though **ap** is not assigned the address of any object is valid. The second call `ap->display();` displays the value of **a**.

21.11 POINTERS TO MEMBER FUNCTIONS

We know that we can have pointers to normal functions and the functions can be called through pointers indirectly. The syntax of declaring a pointer to a function is as follows:

```
type (*ptr)(arguments);
```

ptr is declared to be a pointer to a function which takes the arguments **arguments** and returns a value of type **type**.

EXAMPLE

```
int (*p)(int, int);
```

Here **p** is declared to be a pointer to a function, which takes two arguments of **int** type and returns a value of **int** type.

```
int sum(int, int);

p = sum;
```

The function name gives its address and it is assigned to **p**.

```
s = (*p)(4, 5);
```

The function `sum()` is called through the pointer **p**.

On the lines of having pointers to normal functions, we can think of pointers to member functions of classes as well. The syntax of declaring a pointer to a member function is as follows:

```
type (classname::*ptr)(arguments);
```

The only extra thing in the declaration is **classname** followed by the scope resolution operator **::**. This is required to indicate to the compiler that **ptr** is a pointer to a member function of the class.
The syntax of calling a member function through its pointer is as follows:

```
(classname::*ptr)(arguments);        // if the return type is void.

variable =(classname::*ptrname)(arguments); //if the function returns a value

#include <iostream.h>

class temp
{
    private:
        int a;

    public:
        temp(int b = 0)
        {
            a = b;
        }

        void display()
        {
            cout << a;
        }

        int sum(temp t)
```

```
        {
            int s;

            s = a + t.a;
            return s;
        }

};

int main(void)
{
    temp t1(10), t2(20);
    void (temp::*td) ();

    td = &temp::display;

    cout << t1 = " ;
    (t1.*td) ();
    cout << "t2 = " ;
    (t2.*td) ();

    int (temp::*ts) (temp);
    ts = &temp::sum;
    int s = (t1.*ts) (t2);

    cout << "sum = " << s << "\n";
    return 0;
}
```

t1 and **t2** are declared to be objects of **temp** type, and are initialized with the values 10 and 20 respectively. **td** is declared to be a pointer to a member function of `temp` class with the return type **void** and which does not take any argument. It is to point to the member function `display()`. The statement `td = &temp::display;` assigns the address of the member function `display()` to the pointer **td**. The statement `(t1.*td) ();` displays the value of **t1**. The statement `(t2.*td) ();` displays the value of **t2**. **ts** is declared to be a pointer to a member function of the `temp` class with **temp** as its argument type and which returns a value of **int** type. It is to point to the member function `sum()` of the class. The statement `ts = &temp::sum;` assigns the address of the `sum()` to **ts** and the statement `s = (t1.*ts) (t2);` finds the sum of **t1** and **t2** and assign it to the variable **s**, which is then displayed.

REVIEW QUESTIONS

21.1 What are the new data types supported by ANSI C++?

21.2 What is the difference between the c-style casting and the ANSI C++ new-style casting?

21.3 When do we use static_cast operator? Give an example.

21.4 When do we use dynamic_cast operator? Give an example.

21.5 When do we use const_cast operator? Give an example.

21.6 When do we use reinterpret_cast operator? Give an example.

21.7 List the operators, which are provided with keywords equivalents.

21.8 What is the significance of explicit keyword?

21.9 What is the significance of mutable keyword?

21.10 What is the need for namespaces? Explain.

21.11 Explain the need for smart pointers.

21.12 Explain the concept of pointers to member functions of a class.

Appendix A
Prototypes of Functions

MATHEMATICAL FUNCTIONS (Header file: math.h)

Since the prototypes of the mathematical functions are made available in the header file **math.h**, the header file **math.h** has to be included as part of the source programs, which use these functions. The preproccssor directive `#include <math.h>` is used for this purpose.

Function prototype	*Purpose*
`double cos(double x);`	Takes an angle **x** (in radians) as the argument and returns the cosine value for the angle (in the range –1 to 1).
`double sin(double x);`	Takes an angle **x** (in radians) as the argument and returns the sine value for the angle (in the range –1 to 1).
`double tan(double x);`	Takes an angle **x** (in radians) as the argument and returns the tangent value for the angle.
`double cosh(double x);`	Takes an angle **x** (in radians) as the argument and returns the hyperbolic cosine value for the angle.
`double sinh(double x);`	Takes an angle **x** (in radians) as the argument and returns the hyperbolic sine value for the angle.
`double tanh(double x);`	Takes an angle **x** (in radians) as the argument and returns the hyperbolic tangent value for the angle.
`double exp(double x);`	Takes a value **x** of type double as its argument and returns its exponential function value e^x.
`double log(double x);`	Takes a value **x** of type double as its argument and returns the natural logarithmic of the value.
`double log10(double x);`	Takes a value **x** of type double as its argument and returns the base 10 logarithm of the value.
`double pow(double x,double y);`	Takes two values **x** and **y** of type double as its arguments and returns the value of *x* raised to the power of y.

`double sqrt(double x);`	Takes a value **x** of type double as its argument and returns the square root of the value.
`double ceil(double x);`	Takes a value **x** of type double as its argument and returns the smallest integral value not less than **x**.
`double floor(double x);`	Takes a value **x** of type double as its argument and returns the largest integral value not greater than **x**.
`double fabs(double x);`	Takes a value **x** of type double as its argument and returns the absolute value of **x**.
`double acos(double x);`	Takes a cosine value **x** of type double as its argument and returns equivalent angle (in radians in the range 0 to π).
`double asin(double x);`	Takes a sine value **x** of type double as its argument and returns equivalent angle (in radians in the range $-\pi/2$ to $\pi/2$).
`double atan(double x);`	Takes a tangent value **x** of type double as its argument and returns equivalent angle (in radians in the range $-\pi/2$ to $\pi/2$).
`double fabs(double x);`	Takes a value **x** of type double as its argument and returns the absolute value of **x**.

CHARACTER TEST FUNCTIONS (Header file: ctype.h)

Since the prototypes of the character test functions are made available in the header file `ctype.h`, The header file `ctype.h` has to be included as part of the source programs, which use these functions. The preprocessor directive `#include <ctype.h>` is used for this purpose.

Function prototype	*Purpose*
`int isalpha(int c)`	Takes a character as its argument and returns true if the character is an alphabetic letter (*A* to *Z* or *a* to *z*). Otherwise, false
`int isalnum(int c)`	Takes a character as its argument and returns true if the character is an alphabetic letter or a digit (*A* to *Z*, a to *z*, 0 to 9). Otherwise, false.
`int isdigit(int c)`	Takes a character as its argument and returns true if the character is a digit. (0 to 9). Otherwise, false.
`int isxdigit(int c)`	Takes a character as its argument and returns true if the character is an hexadecimal digit (0 to 9, *A* to *F*). Otherwise, false.
`int islower(int c)`	Takes a character as its argument and returns true if the character is a lower case letter (*a* to *z*). Otherwise, false.
`int isupper(int c)`	Takes a character as its argument and returns true if the character is an upper case letter (*A* to *Z*). Otherwise, false.
`int isspace(int c)`	Takes a character as its argument and returns true if the character is a space, form feed, newline, horizontal tab or vertical tab. Otherwise, false.
`int ispunct(int c)`	Takes a character as its argument and returns true if the character is any punctuation character like comma, etc. Otherwise, false.
`int isctrl(int c)`	Takes a character as its argument and returns true if the character is a control character. Otherwise, false.

`int isprint(int c)`	Takes a character as its argument and returns true if the character is a printable character including space. Otherwise, false.
`int isgraph(int c)`	Takes a character as its argument and returns true if the character is a printable character excluding space. Otherwise, false.
`int toupper(int c)`	Takes a character as its argument and converts it to upper case if it was a lower case letter and returns the uppercase letter. If the character was not a lower case letter, the character is returned unchanged.
`int tolower(int c)`	Takes a character as its argument and converts it to lower case if it was an upper case letter and returns the lower case letter. If the character was not an upper case letter, the character is returned unchanged.

STRING MANIPULATION FUNCTIONS (Header file: string.h)

Since the prototypes of the string manipulation functions are made available in the header file **`string.h`**, the header file **`string.h`** has to be included as part of the source programs, which use these functions. The preprocessor directive `#include <string.h>` is used for this purpose.

Function prototype	*Purpose*
`int strlen(char* s);`	Takes a string **`s`** as an argument and returns its length.
`char* strcpy(char* trg, char* src);`	Takes two strings **`trg`** and **`src`** as its arguments, copies **`src`** to **trg** and returns **`trg`**. The size of **`trg`** is expected to be large enough to collect the string in **`src`**.
`char* strcat(char* trg, char* src);`	Takes two strings **`trg`** and **`src`** as its arguments, adds **`src`** to the end of **trg** and returns **`trg`**. The size of **`trg`** is expected to be large enough to collect the string in **`src`** in addition to its own.
`int strcmp(char* s1, char* s2);`	Takes two strings **`s1`** and **`s2`** as its arguments, compares them and returns the numerical value of the difference between the ASCII values of the first non-matching pair of characters of the two strings. The value returned is +ve if **`s1`** is lexicographically greater than **`s2`**. It is –ve if **`s1`** is lexicographically less than **`s2`**. And the value returned is zero if **`s1`** and **`s2`** are same.
`char* strncpy(char* trg, char* src, int n);`	Takes two strings **`trg`** and **`src`**, and an integer *n* as its arguments, copies **n** characters of **`src`** to **trg** and returns **`trg`**. The size of **`trg`** is expected to be large enough to collect **n** characters in **`src`**.
`char* strncat(char* trg, char* src, int n);`	Takes two strings **`trg`** and **`src`**, and an integer *n* as its arguments, adds **`n`** characters of **`src`** to the end of **trg** and returns **`trg`**. The size of **`trg`** is expected to be large enough to collect **`n`** characters in **`src`** in addition to its own contents.
`int strcmpi(char* s1, char* s2);`	Similar to `strcmp()`. But ignores case while comparing **`s1`** and **`s2`**. That is, the strings "ABC" and "abc" are treated as same.

`int strchr(char*s1, char c);`	Takes a string **s1** and a character **c** as its arguments, returns the pointer position of the first occurrence of **c** in the string **s1**. If the character is not found, the function returns NULL value.
`char* strstr(char* s1, char* s2);`	Takes two strings **s1** and **s2**, and returns the pointer position of the first occurrence of the entire string **s2** in **s1**. If **s2** is not found in **s1**, it returns NULL.

UTILITY FUNCTIONS (Header File :stdlib.h)

Since the prototypes of the utility functions are made available in the header file **stdlib.h**, the header file **stdlib**.h has to be included as part of the source programs, which use these functions. The preprocessor directive `#include <stdlib.h>` is used for this purpose.

Function prototype	*Purpose*
`void abort();`	Terminates a process abnormally.
`int abs(int x);`	Takes an integer value *x* and return its absolute value.
`long labs(long x);`	Takes a long value *x* and returns its absolute value.
`double atof(char *s);`	Takes a string **s** as its argument and returns its double equivalent. If the conversion is not possible, it returns 0.
`int atoi(char *s);`	Takes a string **s** as its argument and returns its integer equivalent. If the conversion is not possible, it returns 0.
`long atol(char *s);`	Takes a string **s** as its argument and returns its long integer equivalent. If the conversion is not possible, it returns 0.
`char* itoa(int i, char* s, int radix);`	Takes an integer **i**, a string **s** and an integer **radix** as its arguments; converts the integer **i** into a string collected by **s**. **radix** specifies the base being used while converting.
`void *calloc(unsigned no_of_items, unsigned size);`	Allocates **size * no_of_items** bytes in the memory heap and returns a pointer to the block of memory.
`void *malloc(unsigned size);`	Allocates **size** bytes in the memory heap and returns a pointer to the block of memory.
`void* realloc(void *ptr, unsigned size);`	Adjusts the previously allocated block pointed to by **ptr** to size bytes and moves the data to new location, if necessary.
`void free(void *ptr);`	Takes a pointer to a block of memory as its argument and releases the memory block.

Appendix B

Standard C++ Operators

The C++ operators, their meaning, priority (precedence levels), associativity, arity, i.e., over how many operands they are defined, whether they overloadable or not and example of the usage of each of them are depicted in the following table:

Operator	*Name*	*Priority*	*Associativity.*	*Arity*	*Overloadable*	*Example*
::	Global scope resolution	1	R to L	Unary	No	::a
::	Class scope resolution	1	L to R	Binary	No	A::a
.	Member operator	2	L to R	Binary	No	a.x
->	Indirect member operator	2	L to R	Binary	Yes	p->x
[ ]	Subscript	2	L to R	Binary	Yes	a[I]
()	Function call	2	L to R	n/a	Yes	sum()
()	Type construction	2	L to R	n/a	Yes	float (x)
++	Post-increment	2	R to L	Unary	Yes	n++
- -	Post-decrement	2	R to L	Unary	Yes	n--
sizeof	Size of data type	3	R to L	Unary	No	sizeof(a)
++	Pre-increment	3	R to L	Unary	Yes	++n
- -	Pre-decrement	3	R to L	Unary	Yes	--n
~	Bitwise complement	3	R to L	Unary	Yes	~j
!	Logical not	3	R to L	Unary	Yes	!a
+	Unary plus	3	R to L	Unary	Yes	+i
-	Unary minus	3	R to L	Unary	Yes	-i
*	Dereference	3	R to L	Unary	Yes	*p
&	Address of	3	R to L	Unary	Yes	&a

<table>
<tr><td>new</td><td>Memory allocation</td><td>3</td><td>R to L</td><td>Unary</td><td>Yes</td><td>new A</td></tr>
<tr><td>delete</td><td>Memory deallocation</td><td>3</td><td>R to L</td><td>Unary</td><td>Yes</td><td>delete p</td></tr>
<tr><td>( )</td><td>Type conversion</td><td>3</td><td>R to L</td><td>Binary</td><td>Yes</td><td>int(ch)</td></tr>
<tr><td>.*</td><td>Direct member selection</td><td>4</td><td>L to R</td><td>Binary</td><td>No</td><td>a.*x</td></tr>
<tr><td>. >*</td><td>Indirect member selection</td><td>4</td><td>L to R</td><td>Binary</td><td>Yes</td><td>p ->x</td></tr>
<tr><td>*</td><td>Multiplication</td><td>5</td><td>L to R</td><td>Binary</td><td>Yes</td><td>a * b</td></tr>
<tr><td>/</td><td>Division</td><td>5</td><td>L to R</td><td>Binary</td><td>Yes</td><td>a / b</td></tr>
<tr><td>%</td><td>Remainder</td><td>5</td><td>L to R</td><td>Binary</td><td>Yes</td><td>a % b</td></tr>
<tr><td>+</td><td>Addition</td><td>6</td><td>L to R</td><td>Binary</td><td>Yes</td><td>a + b</td></tr>
<tr><td>-</td><td>Subtraction</td><td>6</td><td>L to R</td><td>Binary</td><td>Yes</td><td>a – b</td></tr>
<tr><td><<</td><td>Shift left</td><td>7</td><td>L to R</td><td>Binary</td><td>Yes</td><td>a << n</td></tr>
<tr><td>>></td><td>Shift right</td><td>7</td><td>L to R</td><td>Binary</td><td>Yes</td><td>a >> n</td></tr>
<tr><td><</td><td>Less than</td><td>8</td><td>L to R</td><td>Binary</td><td>Yes</td><td>a < b</td></tr>
<tr><td><=</td><td>Less than or equal to</td><td>8</td><td>L to R</td><td>Binary</td><td>Yes</td><td>a <= b</td></tr>
<tr><td>></td><td>Greater than</td><td>8</td><td>L to R</td><td>Binary</td><td>Yes</td><td>a > b</td></tr>
<tr><td>>=</td><td>Greater than or equal to</td><td>8</td><td>L to R</td><td>Binary</td><td>Yes</td><td>a >= b</td></tr>
<tr><td>==</td><td>Equal to</td><td>9</td><td>L to R</td><td>Binary</td><td>Yes</td><td>a == b</td></tr>
<tr><td>!=</td><td>Not equal to</td><td>9</td><td>L to R</td><td>Binary</td><td>Yes</td><td>a != b</td></tr>
<tr><td>&</td><td>Bitwise AND</td><td>10</td><td>L to R</td><td>Binary</td><td>Yes</td><td>a & b</td></tr>
<tr><td>^</td><td>Bitwise XOR</td><td>11</td><td>L to R</td><td>Binary</td><td>Yes</td><td>a ^ b</td></tr>
<tr><td>|</td><td>Bitwise OR</td><td>12</td><td>L to R</td><td>Binary</td><td>Yes</td><td>a | b</td></tr>
<tr><td>&&</td><td>Logical and</td><td>13</td><td>L to R</td><td>Binary</td><td>Yes</td><td>c && d</td></tr>
<tr><td>| |</td><td>Logical or</td><td>14</td><td>L to R</td><td>Binary</td><td>Yes</td><td>c || d</td></tr>
<tr><td>?:</td><td>Conditional operator</td><td>15</td><td>L to R</td><td>Ternary</td><td>No</td><td>c ? a : b</td></tr>
<tr><td>=</td><td>Assignment</td><td>16</td><td>R to L</td><td>Binary</td><td>Yes</td><td>a = 12</td></tr>
<tr><td>+=</td><td>Addition assignment</td><td>16</td><td>R to L</td><td>Binary</td><td>Yes</td><td>a += 20</td></tr>
<tr><td>-=</td><td>Subtraction assignment</td><td>16</td><td>R to L</td><td>Binary</td><td>Yes</td><td>a -=20</td></tr>
<tr><td>*=</td><td>Multiplication assignment</td><td>16</td><td>R to L</td><td>Binary</td><td>Yes</td><td>a *= 20</td></tr>
<tr><td>/=</td><td>Division assignment</td><td>16</td><td>R to L</td><td>Binary</td><td>Yes</td><td>a /= 20</td></tr>
<tr><td>%=</td><td>Remainder assignment</td><td>16</td><td>R to L</td><td>Binary</td><td>Yes</td><td>a %= 5</td></tr>
<tr><td>&=</td><td>Bitwise AND assignment</td><td>16</td><td>R to L</td><td>Binary</td><td>Yes</td><td>a &= 2</td></tr>
<tr><td>^=</td><td>Bitwise XOR assignment</td><td>16</td><td>R to L</td><td>Binary</td><td>Yes</td><td>a ^= 2</td></tr>
<tr><td>|=</td><td>Bitwise OR assignment</td><td>16</td><td>R to L</td><td>Binary</td><td>Yes</td><td>a |= 2</td></tr>
<tr><td><<=</td><td>Shift left assignment</td><td>16</td><td>R to L</td><td>Binary</td><td>Yes</td><td>a <<= 2</td></tr>
<tr><td>>>=</td><td>Shift right assignment</td><td>16</td><td>R to L</td><td>Binary</td><td>Yes</td><td>a >>= 2</td></tr>
<tr><td>.</td><td>Comma</td><td>17</td><td>L to R</td><td>Binary</td><td>Yes</td><td>a=2, b=a</td></tr>
</table>

Bibliography

AI Stevens, *C++ Programming Bible*, IDG Books, New Delhi, 2000.

Ali Bahrami, *Object Oriented Systems Development*, McGraw-Hill, 1999.

B. Jarne Stroutrup, *The C++ Programming Language*, Addison-Wesley, 1997.

Barkakati Nabajyoti, *Object-Oriented Programming in C++*, SAMS Publishing, 1991.

Dietel and Deitel, *C++ How to Program*, Prentice Hall, Englewood Cliffs, New Jersy, 1998.

E. Balagurusamy, *Object Oriented Programming with C++*, Tata McGraw-Hill, New Delhi, 2005.

Herbert Schildt, *The C++ Complete Reference*, Tata McGraw-Hill, New Delhi, 2003.

John Hubbard, *Programming with C++* (Indian Adapted Edition), Tata McGraw-Hill, New Delhi, 2006.

K.R. Venugopal, *Mastering C++*, Tata McGraw-Hill, New Delhi, 2005.

M.T. Somashekara, *Programming in C*, Prentice-Hall of India, New Delhi, 2005.

Robert Lafore, *Object-Oriented Programming in TURBO C++*, Waite Group, New Delhi, 1994.

Stanley B. Lippman, *The C++ Primer*, Pearson Education (Singapore) Pte. Ltd., Delhi, 2003.

Stephen Prata, *C++ Primer Plus*, Pearson Education (Singapore) Pte. Ltd., Delhi, 2002.

Ted Faison, Borland, *C++ Object Oriented Programming*, SAMS Publishing, Indiana, USA, 1994.

Yashavanth P. Kanetkar, *Let us C++*, BPB Publications, New Delhi, 1999.

Index